Relational Databases and Knowledge Bases

Georges Gardarin
INSTITUT NATIONAL DE RECHERCHE EN INFORMATIQUE ET EN
AUTOMATIQUE (INRIA)
UNIVERSITY OF PARIS, VI (MASI)

Patrick Valduriez
MICROELECTRONIC AND COMPUTER TECHNOLOGY CORPORATION (MCC)

 ADDISON-WESLEY PUBLISHING COMPANY
Reading, Massachusetts • Menlo Park, California • New York
Don Mills, Ontario • Wokingham, England • Amsterdam • Bonn
Sydney • Singapore • Tokyo • Madrid • San Juan

Library of Congress Cataloging-in-Publication Data

Gardarin, G. (Georges)
    Relational databases and knowledge bases.

    Bibliography: p.
    Includes index.
    1. Data base management.   2. Relational data bases.
I. Valduriez, Patrick.   II. Title.
QA76.9.D3G375 1989   005.75′6   88–6295
ISBN 0–201–09955–1

CDEFGHIJ–DO–89

PREFACE

A database management system (DBMS), or simply database system, is characterized by the data model it supports. The first DBMSs, designed in the 1960s, were based on hierarchical or network models and have been viewed as extensions of file systems in which interfile links are provided through pointers. The data manipulation languages of these systems are low level and require users to optimize the access to the data by carefully navigating in hierarchies or networks.

Since its inception in 1970, the relational data model has continued to gain wide acceptance among database researchers and practitioners. Unlike the hierarchical and network models, the relational model has a solid theoretical basis and provides simple and uniform representation for all data independent of any physical implementation. These advantages enabled the development of high-level data manipulation languages, freeing the user from data access optimization, and provided a solid basis for automating the database design process.

In the early 1980s, the first relational database systems appeared on the market, bringing definite advantages in terms of usability and end user productivity. Since then, their functional capabilities and performance have been significantly improved. Most relational DBMSs today support an integrated set of fourth-generation programming language tools to increase end user productivity. Most also provide extensive support for distributed database management. The development of fourth-generation tools and distributed database management capabilities has been facilitated by the relational model.

Current relational DBMSs are targeted to traditional data processing (business) applications. More recently, important application domains, such as expert systems and computer-aided design, have shown the need to manage large amounts of data. Many believe the relational model will be used in future database systems that will support these new applications.

This book gives a comprehensive presentation of the relational model and the state-of-the-art principles and algorithms that guide the design of relational DBMSs. In addition, it shows how these systems can be extended to support new database application domains that typically require deductive capabilities and the support of complex objects. Such extensions are the basis of relational knowledge base systems (KBMSs) as developed in several research centers. Finally, the book introduces the use of technology to manage distributed databases. This book will enable readers to appreciate the practical superiority of the relational model for intensive database management. The application of the principles and algorithms presented in this book is illustrated in our recent book *Analysis and Comparison of Relational Database Systems,* (Addison-Wesley), which examines the best relational database systems and main relational database machines.

The current book is based on material used in undergraduate and graduate courses taught at the University of Paris 6 and other French schools. It follows a natural progression from introductory matter, such as file systems, to advanced topics, such as deductive databases. Knowledge of the basic principles of database systems will facilitate reading of this book but is not necessary. The book can be used by teachers to extend a traditional introduction to database technology and by professionals to extend their understanding of relational databases and knowledge bases. The main concepts are clearly exhibited by informal definitions.

The book contains twelve chapters. **Chapter 1** gives an introduction to first-order logic and operating systems, important topics since relational DBMSs and KBMSs are mainly implementations of logic-based languages on operating systems. Chapters 2 and 3 provide an introduction to database technology. **Chapter 2** deals with file management, more in the perspective of data access methods used by relational DBMSs. **Chapter 3** introduces the objectives and architectures of DBMSs, emphasizing standardization and relational DBMS architectures.

Chapters 4 and 5 present the relational data model and associated database design technology. **Chapter 4** gives a comprehensive presentation of the relational model including the model data structures and associated query languages based on relational algebra and relational calculus. In particular, the high-level, and now standard, Structured Query Language (SQL) is introduced. **Chapter 5** deals with database design in a relational framework. It demonstrates the value of the relational model and the associated normalization theory in helping the database designer's task.

Chapters 6 to 9 treat problems peculiar to the implementation of a relational DBMS. **Chapter 6** looks at semantic data control: views, security, and semantic integrity. Chapters 7 and 8 deal with transaction management in DBMSs in general. **Chapter 7** is devoted to concurrency control. **Chapter 8** is devoted to reliability; it examines the solutions that maintain data consistency despite system and media failures. **Chapter 9** deals with query processing and query optimization.

Chapters 10 to 12 deal with the extension of relational database systems to support knowledge based applications and distributed environments. **Chapter 10** is devoted to the addition of deductive capabilities in relational database systems. These capabilities are of major importance for knowledge-based applications. **Chapter 11** deals with the incorporation of some key aspects of object orientation in relational database systems. These aspects are the support of potentially large objects of rich type and complex structures. These capabilities are required by applications such as office automation and computer-aided design. **Chapter 12** is an introduction to distributed databases whose management, although difficult, is simplified by the relational model.

We have been helped by many colleagues that we would like to thank: S. Abiteboul, B. Boettcher, H. Boral, C. Delobel, M. Franklin, G. Kiernan, R. Krishnamurthy, G. Lohman, R. Michel, C. Mohan, P. Neches, F. Pasquer, M. Scholl, E. Simon, M. Smith, Y. Viemont, and J. Zeleznikow. We are also grateful to the following reviewers for their comments and suggestions: Daniel Rosenkrantz, State University of New York at Albany and Dennis Shasha, Courant Institute of Mathematics. Furthermore, we would like to thank all our colleagues of the Advanced Computer Architecture program at MCC, Austin, and the SABRE project at INRIA, Paris, and the University of Paris, VI, for their support.

CONTENTS

1

PRELIMINARIES

1.1 Introduction

Database management systems (DBMSs) are software products managing large sets of data stored in computers that can be queried and updated by end users. The design and implementation of DBMSs require practical and theoretical knowledge. In this chapter, operating system concepts and logic concepts relevant to the study of DBMSs are presented.

1.2 Disk Operating Systems

Operating systems are the basic data management tool offered by general-purpose modern computers. A relational database management system is built on top of a disk operating system (DOS). It stores structured data on a magnetic disk and retrieves structured data from a magnetic disk. The disk and the computer are managed by the operating system. Thus a DBMS is a layer of software components between the user and the DOS. It strongly interacts with the operating system. Clearly it is important to understand the functions and services offered by an operating system before studying database systems.

1

1.2.1 Computer Architecture

For a discussion on disk operating systems, it is useful to review computer architecture (see, for example [Baer80], for a detailed analysis). A simple computer architecture is shown in Fig. 1.1. At the heart of the computer is the *instruction* processor (CPU). It decodes and processes instructions that it obtains from main memory through the bus, the information highway on which all units talk and listen. Specialized sets of instructions can be executed by special-purpose processors in an enhanced computer architecture. Such a processor would be the input/output (I/O) processor, which, operating in parallel with other processors, transfers data from main memory to secondary peripheral devices (output) or from these devices to main memory (input).

A computer architecture like the one in Fig. 1.1 supports a basic software program that is the DOS. The DOS is a set of software layers built around a hardware machine to take charge of the user commands. These commands execute user programs submitted by multiple users in parallel. Thus the DOS supports the simultaneous execution of user programs that reside in main memory. One of the main functions of a DOS is to manage these simultaneous executions.

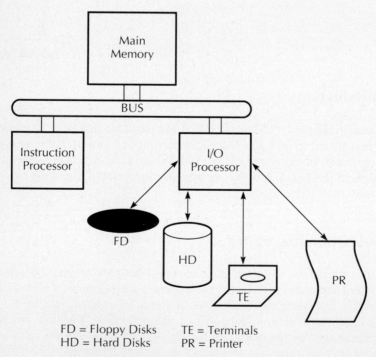

FD = Floppy Disks   TE = Terminals
HD = Hard Disks   PR = Printer

FIGURE 1.1 A typical computer architecture

To run several user programs simultaneously, a DOS must share the computer resources between them. Resources are the CPU, main memory, external devices, and mass memory.

1.2.2 CPU Management

Resource sharing and simultaneous execution of user programs require the management of parallel processes. In general, a process is created by a master process using a special command. The process dedicated to receiving and analyzing user commands is responsible for creating first-level user processes. When a process has been created, it can execute a program by overlaying itself with the program machine code. It can also create new processes. Processes are deleted either by themselves or by other processes. In general, creating and deleting processes is the role of the *process manager*.

Processes must be synchronized as they compete for the machine resources. The main resource is the CPU. It is shared among the processes by time-sharing techniques. The system is organized around a *scheduler*, which allocates the CPU to the processes for a given period of time (perhaps a few milliseconds). Because certain resources cannot be simultaneously shared (such as I/O devices), a process may be waiting either for the completion of an external task (for example, an I/O on a disk) or for the exclusive use of a resource (for example, an I/O channel or a shared portion of main memory). In that case, it is in a dormant state, meaning that it is not candidate for the CPU. Each time the scheduler is invoked, it must select one process among the ready list of processes (those that are ready to use the CPU). Then it gives the CPU to the elected ready process, which becomes active. Up to the completion of either the task it wants to perform or its period of time, the active process code is executed by the CPU. The active process can also try to use a resource that is not free (because it is used in parallel by another process). The scheduler makes it wait and then reallocates the CPU to another ready process, if any, or waits for a ready process. A process waiting for a resource is awakened (put in ready state) by a *signal handler*, which receives and processes external events (interruptions).

In summary, the first layer of a DOS is the CPU manager, which may be divided in three modules (Fig. 1.2).

1.2.3 Memory Management

The next layer of a DOS is the *memory manager*. Memory management shares the main memory among the concurrent processes. A process may need memory space to store program code and data. It then demands allocation of memory

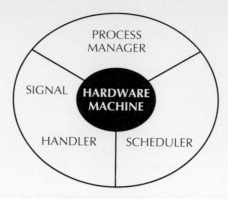

FIGURE 1.2 CPU manager

pages (that is, blocks of continuous memory space, such as 4K bytes) to that part of the memory manager called the *memory allocator.* If pages are available, they are allocated to the process. When no page is available, a page replacement strategy is applied to bring out a page content and reallocate it to the demanding process. Such strategies may consist of writing on disk the content of the least recently used page (LRU) or the least frequently used one (LFU) or be more sophisticated. When a process no longer needs a memory page, it must release it, using a page release command of the memory allocator.

As pages are allocated and deallocated dynamically to processes, there is no reason for the memory space of a process to be continuous. Thus the memory manager must perform the mapping of continuous virtual addresses to the discontinuous physical space. This can be done by keeping pages allocated to processes continuous (one solution is to move process code and data in main memory when necessary) or by using a virtual memory management unit. Virtual memory management organizes pages in segments. A virtual address is composed of a segment number (S#), a page number in the segment (P#), and an offset in the page (D#). A hardware device called the *memory management unit* (MMU) maps virtual addresses <S#,P#,D#> to physical addresses. The role of the memory manager is to maintain the necessary tables for the MMU. This includes segment tables and page tables for each process. The memory manager must also ensure that processes correctly access to memory, particularly that a process does not read or write the memory allocated to another process (except if both processes agree to share memory). Such violations are generally detected by the machine hardware, which then invokes the memory manager.

In summary, the memory manager may be seen as composed of three parts, the first one allocating/deallocating pages (the page allocator), the second one controlling accesses to pages, and the third one swapping in/out pages from memory to disk (Fig. 1.3).

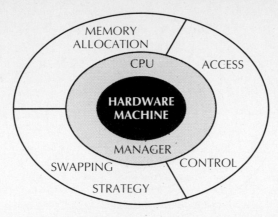

FIGURE 1.3 Memory management functions in the DOS architecture

1.2.4 I/O Management

The DOS must also be able to communicate with the external world. This is the role of the I/O control layer. I/O management performs data transfer between the external devices (such as the magnetic disk and the user terminal) and a buffer pool maintained in main memory. A *buffer* is a data space in main memory composed of continuous pages in which data enter and go out at different speeds, generally in blocks of different sizes. A buffer pool is composed of several buffers, which are often shared between user processes and system I/O processes to avoid data moves.

Specific modules called *device handlers* read and write buffer contents (blocks of data) on devices. In general, there is one handler per class of device. A handler may manage a queue of I/O requests. When a data unit is to be read from a device by a process, the system checks to see if it is in the buffer pool. If it is, the system does not have to access the device, avoiding an I/O. If it is not, then a full block is read from the device in a buffer. When a data unit is to be written, it is put in a buffer, and control is often returned to the calling process before the actual I/O is performed on the device.

The effectiveness of the I/O manager is measured as a ratio between the number of I/O requests it saves (because data units are found or stored in buffers) and the number of requests it receives. To improve effectiveness, I/O managers use sophisticated strategies, such as read ahead and deferred write. Also the strategy for replacing buffers in the pool when none is free is an important parameter.

In summary, the I/O manager has two parts: the buffer pool manager and the I/O device handler (Fig. 1.4).

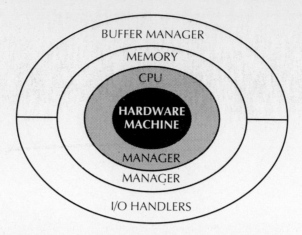

FIGURE 1.4 I/O management in the DOS architecture

1.2.5 File and Basic Communication Management

With the next layer of the system, a user process can communicate with external memories, with other processes, and with terminals. Messages or records may be sent to or received from ideal external memories identified by a name (a file), other processes, or terminals. The exchange of messages requires that a communication path be opened between the sender and the receiver using a specific open command. Then reading and/or writing of messages can be done using the name of the logical path. At communication end, the communication path must be closed.

File management systems will be examined in Chapter 2. Communication management is a complex process; only a basic part is included in the DOS kernel presented here. This part corresponds to the basic functions of communication access methods, such as exchanging blocks of data between processes with possible synchronization of the processes and communicating with terminals. Fig. 1.5 depicts the system architecture as it appears now.

1.2.6 Program Management and Utilities

The interface between the end user and the system implies a *command language*. Thus the last layer of the DOS supplies a language to enter or leave the system, to control files, and to manage programs. Program management includes the necessary tools to execute a program. We briefly summarize the execution cycle of a program.

Application programs are translated from high-level source program code to executable machine instructions. Fig. 1.6 illustrates the steps performed to

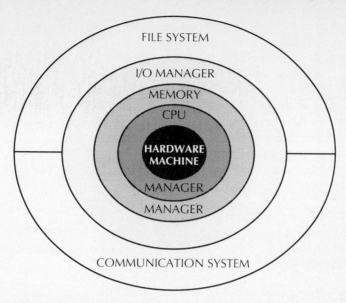

FIGURE 1.5 File and basic communication in the DOS architecture

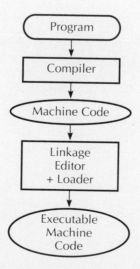

FIGURE 1.6 Source program translation

obtain the desired machine code. High-level source code is translated into object code by the programming language compiler. The object code produced by the compiler contains the system calls to the required services. The linkage editor produces a program from resolving the addressing of the different object programs that comprise the application program. The loader loads the resulting program into main memory. Once it is in main memory, the individual machine instructions can be accessed and executed by the instruction processor. During execution, system calls are processed by the internal layers.

Fig. 1.7 gives an overview of the model of a DOS architecture. In fact, it is our own simplified model; different approaches are possible. For further reading on operating systems, consult [Deitel83], [Davis87], or [Peterson85].

1.3 First-Order Logic

1.3.1 Motivations

First-order logic (FOL) (for more detail, see [Kowalski79], [Manna74], [Nilsson82]), also called *predicate calculus,* is a formal language used to represent relations between objects and to infer new relations between objects from existing ones. It may be viewed as a formal language used to translate English sentences

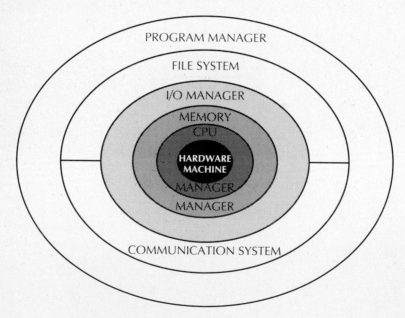

FIGURE 1.7 Disk operating system architecture model

and to derive new sentences from known ones. For instance, the following sentences will translate into the given formal expressions:

1. Volnay is a French wine:
    FRENCH_WINE(Volnay)
2. Mary is a female who drinks Volnay:
    FEMALE(Mary)∧DRINK(Mary,Volnay)
3. John loves any female who drinks French wine:
    ∀x((Female(x)∧∃y(DRINK(x,y)∧FRENCH_WINE(y)))→LOVE(John,x))

We would like to deduce from the above sentences that John loves Mary, which may be formally written as: LOVE(John,Mary).

We now examine the FOL up to the resolution method, a set of algorithms to perform such deductions automatically.

1.3.2 Syntax

The alphabet of FOL languages uses the following kinds of symbols:

1. *Variables* such as $x, y, z, \ldots$
2. *Constants* such as $a, b, c, \ldots$
3. *Predicates* such as $P, Q, R, \ldots$
4. *Logical connectors* ∧, ∨, ¬, →.
5. *Functions* such as $f, g, h, \ldots$
6. *Quantifiers* ∀, ∃.

Symbols such as $\{x,y,x, \ldots, a,b,c, \ldots, P,Q,R, \ldots, f,g,h, \ldots\}$ constitute a formal FOL alphabet. Other possible alphabets may be chosen, such as the informal one $\{x,y,z, \ldots,$ John, Mary, Julie, Peter, $\ldots,$ LIKE, LOVE, FEMALE, MALE, $\ldots,$ Father,Mother, $\ldots \}$. The important point is to have constants, variables, predicates, and logical connectors. Functions are additional; we do not often consider them in databases. The names given to variables, constants, predicates, and symbols are a matter of convention. The logical connectors are always *and* (∧), *or* (∨), *not* (¬) and *implies* (→).

Syntactical rules govern the construction of the sentences of the corresponding FOL language. A *term* is defined recursively as being a variable or a constant or the result of the application of a function to a term. For example, $a, x, f(x)$ and $f(f(x))$ are terms. The sentences of a first-order language are *well-formed formulas* (or simply formulas) defined as follows:

1. If P is an *n*-ary predicate (a predicate with *n* parameters) and $t1, \ldots, tn$ are terms, then $P(t1,t2, \ldots, tn)$ is an *atomic formula*.
2. An atomic formula is a well-formed formula.

3. If $F1$ and $F2$ are well-formed formulas, so are $F1 \land F2$, $F1 \lor F2$, $F1 \rightarrow F2$, and $\neg F1$.
4. If F is a formula and x a not quantified variable in F, then $\forall x(F)$ and $\exists x(F)$ are also well-formed formulas.

To avoid parentheses when possible, we shall assume a priority among logical connectors in the descending order $\neg$, $\lor$, $\land$, and $\rightarrow$ ($\neg$ is applied the most internally, then $\lor$, then $\land$, and finally $\rightarrow$). We call *literal* an atomic formula ($P(t1, t2, \ldots, tn)$) or the negation of an atomic formula ($\neg P(t1, t2, \ldots, tn)$).

With the formal alphabet, examples of well-formed formulas are:

$P(a,x) \land Q(x,y)$,
$\neg Q(x,y)$,
$\forall x \exists y(Q(x,y) \land P(a,x))$
$\forall x(R(x) \land Q(x,a) \rightarrow P(b,f(x)))$.

With the informal alphabet, examples are:

FRENCH_WINE(Volnay) $\land$ FEMALE(Mary)
DRINK(Mary,Volnay)
$\forall x(\neg$LOVE(John,x) $\lor$ FEMALE(x) $\land$ LOVE(John,Brother(John))
$\forall x$(FEMALE(x) $\land$ $\exists$y(DRINK(x,y) $\land$ FRENCH_WINE(y)) $\rightarrow$
    LOVE(John, x)).

1.3.3 Semantics

A formula can be interpreted as a sentence on a set of objects, called the *domain of discourse*. More formally, an interpretation of a formula over a domain of discourse D is defined by mapping each constant to a specific object of D, each predicate to a specific relation between objects of D, and each function with n arguments to a specific function of D^n in D. These mappings define the semantics of the FOL language. For example, the formula $\forall x(\neg$LOVE(John,x) $\lor$ FEMALE(x)) $\land$ LOVE(John,Brother(John)) can be interpreted on a domain of discourse composed of persons {John, Peter, Marie, . . . }. LOVE can be interpreted as the binary relation "x love y" where x is the first argument and y the second of the LOVE predicate; FEMALE can be interpreted as the unary relation "is a female." Brother is a function from D to D (for example, Peter is the brother of John).

As another example, the formula $\forall x(x < \text{SUCC}(x))$ can be interpreted on the set of positive integers {1,2,3, . . . } where $<$ is the less-than relation and SUCC is the successor function. Note that $<$ is a binary predicate whose first argument is written before and second after. Note also that the domain of discourse is infinite.

Given an interpretation for a formula F, it is possible to compute a truth value for this formula. To avoid ambiguity, we consider only formulas in which all variables are quantified. A formula in which all variables are quantified is said to be *closed*. For instance, the formula $\forall x \, \exists y \, \text{LOVE}(x,y)$ is closed; the formula $\exists y \, \text{LOVE}(x,y)$ is not (because x is not quantified). A closed formula F has a unique truth value $V(F)$, which may be computed by applying the following rules ($F_{x=a}$ means F in which x has been replaced by a):

$V(F1 \vee F2) := V(F1) \vee V(F2)$

$V(F1 \wedge F2) := V(F1) \wedge V(F2)$

$V(\neg F) := \neg V(F)$

$V(\forall x F) := V(F_{x=a}) \wedge V(F_{x=b}) \wedge \ldots$ where $a, b, \ldots$ are the constants of D.

$V(\exists x F) := V(F_{x=a}) \vee V(F_{x=b}) \vee \ldots$ where $a, b, \ldots$ are the constants of D.

$V(P(a,b, \ldots)) :=$ true if $<a,b, \ldots >$ satisfies the relation P and false otherwise.

Given an interpretation, a nonclosed formula (one with no quantified variable, called an *open formula*) is ambiguous. There exists one truth value for each possible assignment of a constant to the free variables (the nonquantified variable).

For instance, let us assume the domain $D = \{$John, Peter, Mary$\}$. Suppose that only John loves Mary. The truth values of some formulas are computed below:

$V(\forall x \text{LOVE}(\text{John},x)) :=$
$V(\text{LOVE}(\text{John},\text{John})) \wedge V(\text{LOVE}(\text{John},\text{Peter})) \wedge V(\text{LOVE}(\text{John},\text{Mary})) = \text{false}$
$V(\exists x \text{LOVE}(\text{John},x)) :=$
$V(\text{LOVE}(\text{John},\text{John})) \vee V(\text{LOVE}(\text{John},\text{Peter})) \vee V(\text{LOVE}(\text{John},\text{Mary})) = \text{true}$

LOVE(John, x) has three possible truth values: false for x assigned to John, false for x assigned to Peter, and true for x assigned to Mary.

A *model* of a formula F is an interpretation that gives value true to F. For example, $D = \{$John, Peter, Mary$\}$ as defined above is a model for the formula $\exists x \text{LOVE}(\text{John}, x)$. Also the set of positive integers is a model for the formula $\forall x(x < \text{SUCC}(x))$. However, note that computing the truth value of this formula leads to an infinite expression that is true. Certain formulas do not have any model; these formulas are unsatisfiable. They correspond to contradictions, such as $P(x) \wedge \neg P(x)$. Others are true for any intrepetation. They are valid formulas (or tautologies), such as $P(x) \vee \neg P(x)$.

1.3.4 Clause Form

A convenient form has been proposed for closed formulas, called *clause form*. The idea is to eliminate quantifiers by introducing either parameters (Skolem constants or functions) or implicit quantifiers. Also implication signs are eliminated, and the formula is written as a conjunction (and) or disjunction (or) of predicates or negation of predicates. This last transformation is possible because there are several equivalent ways to write formulas.

Writing a formula in clause form requires successive transformations as described briefly below. We illustrate the transformations with the formula:

$$\forall x \ (\text{LOVE}(\text{John}, x) \ \rightarrow \ \text{FEMALE}(x))$$
$$\wedge \ \exists x \ (\neg(\text{LOVE}(x, \ \text{Brother}(x)) \vee \text{FEMALE}(x))).$$

1. *Eliminate implication signs.* This is done by replacing $A \rightarrow B$ by $\neg A \vee B$, which is an equivalent formula (one having the same truth value for all interpretations). The example formula becomes:

    $$\forall x \ (\neg \text{LOVE}(\text{John}, x) \vee \text{FEMALE} \ (x))$$
    $$\wedge \ \exists x \ (\neg(\text{LOVE}(x, \ \text{Brother}(x)) \wedge \text{FEMALE}(x)))$$

2. *Reduce the scope of negation signs.* The purpose of this step is to make negation signs apply to atomic predicates. By repeated use of the simple transformations:

    $$\neg(A \vee B) \text{ gives } \neg A \wedge \neg B$$
    $$\neg(A \wedge B) \text{ gives } \neg A \vee \neg B$$
    $$\neg(\forall x A) \text{ gives } \exists x \neg A$$
    $$\neg(\exists x A) \text{ gives } \forall x \neg A$$
    $$\neg \neg A \text{ gives } A$$

    it is possible to obtain formulas with only negation of the form $\neg P$ where P is a predicate. This transformation applied to the given example yields:

    $$\forall x \ (\neg \text{LOVE}(\text{John}, x) \vee \text{FEMALE}(x))$$
    $$\wedge \ \exists x \ (\neg \text{LOVE}(x, \ \text{Brother}(x)) \vee \neg \text{FEMALE}(x))$$

3. *Rename variables.* Within the scope of a quantifier, the name of a variable can be changed to a nonexisting name without changing the formula truth value. Because the purpose is to eliminate quantifiers, it is important to avoid confusion among variables quantified by different occurrences of quantifiers. Thus it is necessary to name variables quantified by different quantifiers with different names. This transformation applied to the example yields:

    $$\forall x \ (\neg \text{LOVE}(\text{John}, x) \vee \text{FEMALE}(x))$$
    $$\wedge \ \exists y \ (\neg \text{LOVE}(y, \ \text{Brother}(y)) \vee \neg \text{FEMALE}(y))$$

4. *Move quantifiers in front of formulas.* This step consists of pushing quantifiers with associated variables (such as ∀x and ∃y) in front of the formula in the order they appear. It is possible because quantified variables have different names. This transformation applied to the example yields:

$$\forall x \exists y \ (\neg \text{LOVE}(\text{John}, x) \vee \text{FEMALE}(x) \wedge$$
$$\neg \text{LOVE}(y, \text{Brother}(y)) \vee \neg \text{FEMALE}(y))$$

5. *Eliminate quantifiers.* Variables that are existentially quantified may be replaced by a parameter constant representing the object that must exist for the formula to be true. Such a constant is called a *Skolem constant.* Where the existentially quantified variable is preceded by a universally quantified one, the Skolem constant is in fact a function of the universally quantified variable. In this case, an existentially quantified variable is replaced by a Skolem function whose arguments are the preceding universally quantified variable. Thus existential quantifiers are eliminated, and the only remaining variables are universally quantified. Therefore the universal quantifiers may be removed and considered implicit. This transformation applied to the example requires introducing a Skolem function $s(x)$. It yields:

$$\neg \text{LOVE}(\text{John}, x) \vee \text{FEMALE}(x) \wedge$$
$$\neg \text{LOVE}(s(x), \text{Brother}(s(x))) \vee \neg \text{FEMALE}(s(x))$$

6. *Put in conjunctive normal form.* The remaining formula is a combination of ∧ and ∨ of positive or negative literals (of predicates with arguments). It can be written as a conjunction of a set of disjunctions (a ∧ of ∨) by distributing ∨ with regards to ∧ with the rule $A \vee (B \wedge C)$ gives $(A \vee B) \wedge (A \vee C)$. The example is already in conjunctive normal form.

7. *Write one clause per line.* Finally, it is possible to eliminate the ∧ sign by writing each disjunction on a separate line. The resulting form is called *clause form.* The general form of a formula in clause form is:

$$\neg P11 \vee \neg P12 \ldots \vee \neg P1n_1 \vee Q11 \vee Q12 \vee \ldots$$
$$\neg P21 \vee \neg P22 \ldots \vee \neg P2n_2 \vee Q21 \vee Q22 \vee \ldots$$
$$\ldots$$
$$\neg Pq1 \vee \neg Pq2 \ldots \vee \neg Pqn_q \vee Qq1 \vee Qq2 \vee \ldots$$

which may be written using implication signs:

$$P11 \wedge P12 \ldots \wedge P1n_1 \rightarrow Q11 \vee Q12 \vee \ldots$$
$$P21 \wedge P22 \ldots \wedge P2n_2 \rightarrow Q21 \vee Q22 \vee \ldots$$
$$\ldots$$
$$Pq1 \wedge Pq2 \ldots \wedge Pqn_q \rightarrow Qq1 \vee Qq2 \vee \ldots$$

Thus each clause (a line) states that if a premise $Pi1 \wedge Pi2 \ldots \wedge Pin_i$ is true, then a conclusion $Qi1 \vee Qi2 \vee \ldots$ is true. Finally, a clause appears as a simple if-then statement. With the example, we obtain:

$$\neg \text{LOVE}(\text{John}, x) \vee \text{FEMALE}(x)$$
$$\neg \text{LOVE}(s(x), \text{Brother}(s(x))) \vee \neg \text{FEMALE}(s(x))$$

which can also be written:

$$\text{LOVE}(\text{John},x) \rightarrow \text{FEMALE}(x)$$
$$\text{LOVE}(s(x), \text{Brother}(s(x))) \wedge \text{FEMALE}(s(x)) \rightarrow \wedge$$

The meaning of the formula appears to be "If John loves x, then x is a female" and "If $s(x)$ loves his brother and $s(x)$ is a female, then there is an impossibility."

1.3.5 Principles of a Deduction Algorithm

A *deduction algorithm* is a procedure to prove a formula T from a given set of formulas $\{A1, A2, \ldots, An\}$ known as true. T is a theorem to demonstrate. $A1$, $A2, \ldots, An$ are axioms. The existence of a proof of T from $A1, A2, \ldots, An$ is formally denoted $\{A1, A2, \ldots, An\} \models T$. For example, from the axioms:

FRENCH_WINE(Volnay)
FEMALE(Mary) ∧ DRINK(Mary,Volnay)
∀x(FEMALE(x) ∧ ∃y (DRINK(x,y) ∧ FRENCH_WINE(y)) → LOVE(John,x))

we would like to deduce the theorem:

LOVE(John,Mary).

A deduction algorithm has several interests, among them checking the validity of human reasoning, proving properties of computer programs, and developing programming languages and inference engines.

To prove a theorem, a deduction algorithm generally derives from the axioms a sequence of formulas using *inference rules*. An inference rule is a rule to generate a new formula from two or more formulas. A correct inference rule derives a valid formula from two valid ones. An inference rule is often written on two lines separated by an underline, the first line giving the source formula and the second line giving the generated formula. Two well-known inference rules are the following:

Modus ponens rule. It generates a formula P from two formulas F and $F \rightarrow P$. It is formally denoted:

$$\frac{F \qquad F \rightarrow P}{P}$$

Informally the rule means that if F and $F \rightarrow P$ are proved, then P is proved.

Specialization rule. It generates a simple formula $F(a)$ from a universally quantified formula $\forall x F(x))$. It is formally denoted:

$$\frac{\forall x (F(x))}{F(a)}$$

Informally the rule means that if F is proved for all value of x, it is proved for any particular value a.

There is a general inference rule that generates by recursive application all formulas that may be proved from two given axioms in clause form. This is the *Robinson inference rule* [Robinson65]. Before presenting this rule, we must present an algorithm to compare two formulas known as the *unification algorithm*.

1.3.6 Unification Algorithm

The ability to decide whether two atomic formulas can be identified by assigning values to certain variables is central to most deduction methods. Given two literals $L1(t1,t2, \ldots tn)$ and $L2(s1,s2, \ldots , sn)$ where ti and si are terms with possible functions and variables, a *unification algorithm* decides if the two formulas can be identified by valid substitution of variables (renaming or assignment of values). The algorithm returns:

- FAIL if it is impossible to replace certain variables involved by other terms in such a way that the two formulas become identical.
- SUCCESS and an assignment of certain variables to certain terms under which the two formulas become identical if identification is possible.

Let us illustrate the unification with simple examples. An assignment of variables $x, y, \ldots ,$ to the terms $t1, t2, \ldots ,$ respectively, is denoted $[x/t1, y/t2, \ldots]$. Thus unification of LOVE(John,x) and LOVE(John,y) yields SUCCESS $[y/x]$. Unification of LOVE(x, Father(x)) and LOVE(Marie,y) yields SUCCESS $[x/$Marie, $y/$Father(Marie)]. Unification of $P(x,h(g(y),f(x)))$ and $P(f(z),h(g(g(g(a))), f(g(a))))$ fails. The program corresponding to a typical unification algorithm is given in Fig. 1.8.

1.3.7 Resolution Method

This method is the basis of many theorem provers. To prove a theorem T from a set of axioms $\{A1,A2, \ldots , An\}$, the method refutes the negation of the theorem $(\neg T)$ by showing a contradiction between the axioms and the theorem. The method has two steps. First, all axioms and the negation of the theorem are put

Procedure UNIFY($L1,L2,S$);
Begin
  $S := \phi$;
  While "$L1$ and $L2$ contain a next symbol" **do**
    SYMB1 = NEXT_SYMBOL($L1$);
    SYMB2 = NEXT_SYMBOL($L2$);
    If (SYMB1 ≠ SYMB2) **then**
      Begin Case of
      (SYMB1 **or** SYMB2 = ¬) : UNIFY := FAIL;
      (SYMB1 **or** SYMB2 = PREDICATE) : UNIFY := FAIL;
      SYMB1 **or** SYMB2 = FUNCTION) : UNIFY := FAIL;
      (SYMB1 = VARIABLE **and** SYMB2 = TERM):
        If "VARIABLE ∈ TERM" **then** UNIFY := FAIL
        else
          begin
            $S = S$ ∪ [VARIABLE/TERM];
            $L1 = (L1)$ [VARIABLE/TERM];
          end;
      (SYMB1 = TERM **and** SYMB2 = VARIABLE):
        as previous case but apply S to $L2$;
      End case of;
    End while;
  if "$L1$ or $L2$ contains a next symbol" **then** UNIFY := FAIL
    else UNIFY := SUCCESS;
End.

FIGURE 1.8 A unification algorithm

in clause form. Thus the formula $A1 \wedge A2 \wedge \ldots \wedge An \wedge \neg T$ is transformed in clauses. Second, new clauses are generated from two existing ones using the Robinson inference rule, presented below. If the empty clause is generated by repeated application of the Robinson inference rule, there exists a contradiction between the original clauses. Thus if the set of axioms is valid (there is no contradiction among the axioms), inferring the empty clause means that $\neg T$ contradicts the axioms. Therefore the theorem T is proved when the empty clause is generated.

We now present the Robinson inference rule. Let $C1$ and $C2$ be two clauses such that:

$C1 = F1 \vee L1$
$C2 = F2 \vee \neg L2$
$L1$ and $L2$ can be unified with a substitution s.

Then $F1_{[s]} \vee F2_{[s]}$ is generated as a new clause by the Robinson inference rule. It is called a *resolvent* of $C1$ and $C2$. More formally, the rule can be written:

$$\frac{F1 \lor L1 \qquad F2 \lor \neg L2 \qquad L1_{[s]} = L2_{[s]}}{F1_{[s]} \lor F2_{[s]}}$$

Note that, after detecting a possible identification of two opposed literals in the formulas ($L1$ and $\neg L2$), the rule consists of adding (using or) the two initial formulas ($F1 \lor L1$, $F2 \lor \neg L2$) and then performing the unification substitution and suppressing the two literals, which nullify each other.

In summary, the resolution method works as follows:

1. Put the axioms and the negation of the theorem $\neg T$ in clause form.
2. Add resolvents to the set of clauses up to generating the empty clause. Resolvents are obtained by repeated selections of two clauses (including previously inferred resolvents), which can be combined by the Robinson inference rule.

It can be demonstrated that if a proof of T exists, the resolution method will terminate and find it. If no proof exists, the method can loop forever (generate more and more new clauses). Predicate calculus is semidecidable [Manna74].

In our example, the axioms are:

FRENCH_WINE(Volnay)
FEMALE(Mary) $\land$ DRINK(Mary,Volnay)
$\forall x$ (FEMALE(x) $\land$ $\exists y$ (DRINK(x,y) $\land$ FRENCH_WINE(y))
$\quad \rightarrow$ LOVE(John, x)).

The negation of the theorem to demonstrate is:

$\neg$LOVE(John,Mary).

To put

$\forall x$ (FEMALE(x) $\land$ $\exists y$ (DRINK(x,y) $\land$ FRENCH_WINE(y)) $\rightarrow$ LOVE (John,x))

in clause form, we must first eliminate the $\rightarrow$ sign, which yields:

$\forall x$ ($\neg$(FEMALE(x) $\land$ $\exists y$ (DRINK(x,y) $\land$ FRENCH_WINE(y))) $\lor$ LOVE(John, x)).

Then, reducing the scope of negation, we obtain:

$\forall x$ ($\neg$FEMALE(x) $\lor$ $\forall y$ ($\neg$DRINK(x,y)
$\lor$ $\neg$FRENCH_WINE(y)) $\lor$ LOVE(John,x)).

Therefore, eliminating quantifiers, the clause form turns out to be:

$\neg$FEMALE(x) $\lor$ $\neg$DRINK(x,y) $\lor$ $\neg$FRENCH_WINE(y) $\lor$ LOVE(John,x).

Finally, putting every formula in clause form, we obtain the clauses:

1. FRENCH_WINE(Volnay)
2. FEMALE(Mary)
3. DRINK(Mary,Volnay)

4. ¬FEMALE(x) ∨ ¬DRINK(x,y) ∨ ¬FRENCH_WINE(y)
    ∨ LOVE(John,x))
5. ¬LOVE(John,Mary).

Combining these clauses two by two using the Robinson rule, we infer the empty resolvent (denoted ϕ) as shown in Fig. 1.9. Thus, Fig. 1.9 gives a proof by resolution that John loves Mary.

Resolution is a flexible method in the sense that various strategies are possible when selecting two clauses to infer a resolvent. A popular strategy is known as *SLD resolution* (selection linear for definite clause resolution). This strategy is linear in the sense that each resolvent has at least one parent belonging to the initial clauses (one derived from the axioms or the theorem negation). It uses a selection function to select the clauses to combine at each step [Kowalski71]. Strategies going from the theorem to the axioms are usually called *backward*. Conversely a *forward* strategy goes from the axioms to the theorem.

An interesting case is that of *Horn clauses*. A Horn clause has at most one positive literal. Thus a Horn clause may generally be written as:

$$A \lor \neg B1 \lor \neg B2 \lor \ldots \lor \neg Bn$$

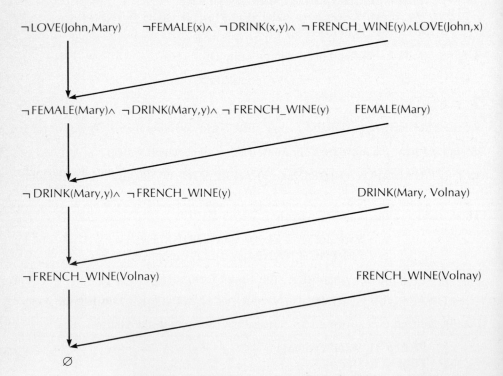

FIGURE 1.9 Resolution tree for the example

and with the implication sign (written in reverse direction for clarity):

$$A \leftarrow B1 \wedge B2 \wedge \ldots \wedge Bn$$

where A and Bi's are positive literals.

In the case of Horn clauses, resolution can be given a procedural interpretation. Briefly, a clause $A \leftarrow B1 \wedge B2 \wedge \ldots \wedge Bn$ is regarded as a program definition. Computing a resolvent from two clauses may then be regarded as performing a subprogram call. For example, assuming possible unification with substitution s between the two occurrences of $B1$:

$$A \leftarrow B1 \wedge B2 \wedge \ldots \wedge Bn$$
$$B1 \leftarrow C1 \wedge C2 \wedge \ldots \wedge Ck$$

yields a resolvent of the form:

$$(A \leftarrow C1 \wedge C2 \wedge \ldots \wedge Ck \wedge B2 \wedge \ldots \wedge Bn)_{[s]}.$$

Clearly the substitution of variables during unification corresponds to parameter passing. The computation terminates when the empty goal is produced (no more subprograms can be called). These considerations have been the basis for developing logic programming [Lloyd84], more precisely PROLOG, a Horn clause – based programming language. From a theoretical point of view, most PROLOG interpreters demonstrate a theorem using SLD resolution with backward selection. From a practical point of view, they perform successive expansion of a subprogram by calling the component subprograms as defined with the Horn clauses. A study of PROLOG is beyond the scope of this book (see, for example, [Clocksin81]).

1.4 Conclusion

We have surveyed the main aspects of operating systems and logic. It could seem strange to start databases from two very different points of view: the system one and the logic one. We do it on purpose. Relational database systems are particular system implementations of the logic paradigm. The ultimate goal of a relational DBMS is to demonstrate efficiently and in parallel theorems with a huge number of axioms stored on magnetic disks. The theorems are the user queries. The axioms are the database records. They are in general axioms without variables (ground axioms), but we shall see that axioms with variables are supported with extended relational technology (deductive databases or knowledge bases). Moreover, as data are updated, the axioms change frequently, posing difficult problems.

The logical view of relational database technology may be considered a philosophical point of view. We take in general a system approach and present the main practical objectives and problems a relational DBMS must address and solve. We also study the most important techniques that have been implemented and used in database systems or applications. It is only at the end of Chapter 4 and in Chapter 10 that we consider further the logical point of view in the relational approach. Logic is a sophisticated tool for understanding and improving relational database functionalities.

1.5 References and Bibliography

[Baer80] Baer J. L., *Computer Systems Architecture,* Computer Science Press, 1980.

[Clocksin81] Clocksin W. F., Mellish C. S., *Programming in Prolog,* Springer-Verlag, 1981.

[Davis87] Davis S. W., *Operating Systems, A Systematic View,* Addison-Wesley, 1987.

[Deitel83] Deitel H. M., *An Introduction to Operating Systems,* Addison-Wesley, 1983.

[Kowalski71] Kowalski R. A., Kuehner D., "Linear Resolution with Selection Function," Artificial Intelligence, V2, 1971, pp. 227 – 60.

[Kowalski79] Kowalski R., *Logic for Problem Solving,* Artificial Intelligence Series, North-Holland, 1981.

[Lloyd84] Lloyd J. W., *Foundations of Logic Programming,* Springer-Verlag, 1984.

[Manna74] Manna L., *Mathematical Theory of Computation,* Computer Sciences Series, McGraw-Hill, 1974.

[Nilsson82] Nilsson J. N., *Principles of Artificial Intelligence,* Springer-Verlag, 1982.

[Peterson85] Peterson J., Silberschatz A., *Operating Systems Concepts,* Addison-Wesley, 1985.

[Robinson65] Robinson J. A., "A Machine-Oriented Logic Based on the Resolution Principle," Journal of the ACM, JACM, V12, N1, 1965, pp. 23 – 41.

2
FILE MANAGEMENT

2.1 Introduction

A file is a data recipient identified by a name. The management of these recipients is a basic function of all systems. By using files, it is possible to process and store large quantities of data and to share these data among programs. A file management system should be able to resolve certain storage and processing problems of enterprises. Program data and enterprise data are stored in computer external memories. The processing of these data can be in batch (month-end or day-end processing), or it can be complex transactional processing (unit processing at each occurrence of a particular event in the real world). For example, a file management system can handle the accounting application of a delivery firm. This application (Fig. 2.1) manages customer accounts and billings that correspond to deliveries. To compute the debit and credit of customer accounts, a price catalog is maintained. Batch processing of deliveries can be done at month end. In this case, information for the month gathered from delivery slips is recorded in one file and processed. Or transactional processing of deliveries can be handled from a data entry terminal, and associated tasks can be immediately run.

In this chapter, the objectives of file management are first introduced. The core functions of a file management subsystem (FMS) — the basic file management operations, relative addressing inside a file, space allocation on secondary memory, file classification, and control — are then presented. Next, space alloca-

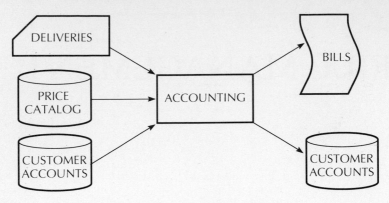

FIGURE 2.1 An example application

tion strategies on disks are reviewed. Finally, we concentrate on file organization and file access methods.

2.2 File Management Objectives and Basic Notions

2.2.1 Memory Hierarchy

Companies need to store and have access to large quantities of data — as much as millions of bytes of data and sometimes billions of bytes of data. Main memory is not large and reliable enough to store such amounts of data. Therefore data need to be recorded on *secondary storage.*

Definition 2.1 Secondary storage (external storage)
Storage space that is not directly addressable by processor instructions but by specialized I/O instructions with access times far above those obtained in main memory.

There are numerous specialized I/O devices for secondary storage. Magnetic recording, the standard I/O technique, is used on various supports. Magnetic tape offers high density, low cost, and portability. The tape is stored in reel forms and mounted on a tape unit for reading and writing. Because they are accessible only in sequential, tapes are mainly used to save data in case of system crash. They may also be used for data entry, although a cassette is a simple and cheaper form of magnetic tape for data entry. Magnetic disk is the standard form of secondary storage to store data and retrieve them using direct access. There are three basic types of direct access disk storage systems: moving-head disks, fixed-head disks, and floppy disks. The most complex and most used disk form is the moving-head disk. Table 2.1 shows the main characteristics of most secondary storage devices.

TABLE 2.1 Characteristics of secondary storage devices

SUPPORT	TYPE	SIZE	CAPACITY (IN MEGA-BYTES)	ACCESS TIME (AVERAGE)
Magnetic disk	Fixed head	3½–5¼ in.	0.5–2	5–10 ms
Magnetic disk	Floppy		0.5–3	40–100 ms
Magnetic disk	Moving head	Less than 4 in.	10–40	40–100 ms
Magnetic disk	Moving head	5¼ in.	20–100	20–50 ms
Magnetic disk	Moving head	8–14 in.	50–800	20–50 ms
Magnetic tape	Cartridge	½ in.	10–100	
Magnetic tape	Cassette	¼ in.	1–80	
Magentic tape	Tape	½ in.	20–800	
Optical disk	CD-ROM		500–1000	50–150 ms

It is also desirable to understand the way data migrate from the user program to secondary storage, and vice-versa. The data processed by a user program are stored in main memory in a private space allocated to the program. To improve secondary storage performances, the file system and often the operating system manage buffers in main memory. User data are grouped in buffers that are written in one I/O instruction on secondary storage. In the reverse direction, a full buffer is read in one I/O while small pieces are delivered to the user for processing. Thus buffers help to avoid costly I/Os. However, in certain systems, the data are moved along as illustrated in Fig. 2.2. In several systems, the interaction between operating systems and file systems has deserved more attention. Thus the file system buffers and the I/O buffers are often identical to avoid moving data in main memory, always a costly operation.

2.2.2 Magnetic Disks

There are several models of magnetic disk. The storage capacity of these disks has increased since 1955 to attain several billion bytes today. Access time is on average 15 to 25 ms, about 30,000 times slower than the average access times found in main memory.

For processing large applications, it is necessary to dispose of infinite secondary storage space. For this purpose, removable disk packs are used.

Definition 2.2 Disk pack
Removable secondary storage unit composed of piles of magnetic disks.

A disk pack is mounted on a disk driver. A disk controller usually handles many disk drivers. Disk packs are mounted and unmounted by the computer operators,

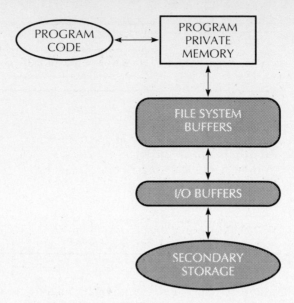

FIGURE 2.2 Displacement of data from user programs to secondary storage

usually from requests issued by the system. Magnetic tapes are also secondary storage devices.

A disk pack, along with the reading/writing devices included in the disk driver, are represented in Fig. 2.3. A disk pack is composed of p disks (for example, 9), of which $2p - 2$ surfaces are usable. The two outer surfaces are not usable. The disk drivers have one read/write head per usable surface. Each head is fixed on a movable arm that displaces the head horizontally on the entire surface of a disk. A disk pack is divided into concentric *tracks* numbered from 0 to N (for example, $N = 512$). All arms are fixed on a vertical holder, which moves the heads simultaneously. The rotation speed of the disk pack is continuous at approximately 10 to 20 rotations per second. The tracks on equal positions on all the surfaces comprise a *cylinder*. Some disk drives have fixed heads, one per track.

Each track of a disk pack supports many physical records called *sectors*. These sectors are of constant or variable size, depending on the type of disk used. Sector access time is an essential characteristic of disk packs. This access time is composed of the following activities:

● The *head displacement time* is needed to move the read/write heads above the required cylinder. This time can range from a few milliseconds to about 10 milliseconds depending on the disk type and the displacement distance.

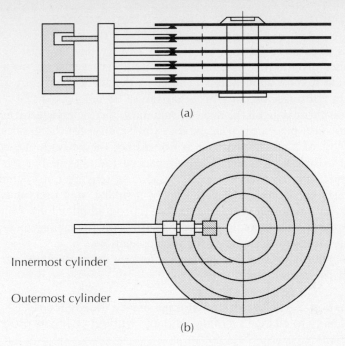

(a)

Innermost cylinder

Outermost cylinder

(b)

FIGURE 2.3 Removable disk pack with movable heads (a) side view and (b) top view

- The *latency time* is the disk rotation time needed for the physical record to pass under the read/write heads. This delay can be a few milliseconds depending on the position of the record relative to the read/write heads and the rotation speed of the disk.
- The *transfer time* is the time required to transfer a sector from disk to main memory when selected on disk.

If i is the distance from the searched record track and the current head position, a good approximation of the time required to seek the record is:

$$T(i) = to + ki.$$

With current technology typical values of the constants are $to = 5$ ms and $k = 0.5$ ms.

Thus, in essence, disk access time is variable according to the distance between the desired record and the read/write head position. The trend is to reduce this delay with constant acceleration motors and more densely packed cylinders. Then, the seek time for a record may be approximated by a nonlinear function

$$T(i) = to + k \sqrt{i}.$$

2.2.3 Program and Storage Device Independence

Disk packs and, more generally, secondary storage devices must be usable by different user programs. Consequently secondary storage space must be shared by data from diverse applications. Therefore the file system must manage this space. Data addresses used by programs must be independent of the physical placement of those data on the disk. In summary, the file management subsystem must ensure data placement transparency (invisibility) for the applications.

The cost of secondary storage is decreasing; the performance-cost ratio is increasing. Information is more densely packed (number of bits per inch) and doubles approximately every two years. A good system must be upgradable without too much difficulty. New disks can be installed, and users may use them without having to modify programs. Indeed reprogramming must be avoided because it is expensive in human resources. In brief, the file management subsystem must ensure storage transparency for the applications.

Data placement and storage transparencies help guarantee *program and storage device independence.*

Definition 2.3 Program and storage device independence
The ability to change secondary storage without changing programs.

To achieve this independence, an intermediary object, a *file,* is introduced between program and storage.

Definition 2.4 File
Ideal secondary storage information recipient referenced by a name to permit the writing of secondary storage independent application programs.

Thus application programs need only to be aware of the names of files used on secondary storage devices. An application program does not manipulate a file globally but reads/writes successive portions of files that correspond to real-world objects, such as customers, accounts, and bills. Such a portion is called a *record.*

Definition 2.5 Record
Element of a file that is the processed unit of information by application programs.

Records are collected together to form a file. The structure of the links between records of a same file constitutes the *file organization.*

Definition 2.6 File organization
The arrangement of records in a file.

Application programs can access records sequentially from the first record to the last or by using an individual record identifier and using a specific *access method*.

Definition 2.7 Access method
The selection method of records in a file by application programs.

2.2.4 Host Programming Languages

The file management system must be accessible from within the high-level programming language (COBOL, PL/1, Pascal and so on). Such programs result in compiled object code, which includes FMS calls. File manipulation from within the language must be as close as possible to other language facilities to remain coherent with the language's programming structure. A *host programming language* integrates file manipulation verbs.

Definition 2.8 Host programming language
Programming language including data type definition and data manipulation verbs.

To illustrate a host language and the kind of integration that may exist between a programming language and file system commands, Fig. 2.4 provides

```
MODWINE : PROC OPTIONS(MAIN) ;
     DCL   WINE FILE RECORD KEYED ENV(REGIONAL(1)) ;
     DCL  1 ENREG,
            2 W# PIC '999',
            2 VINEYAR CHAR(15),
            2 VINTAGE PICTURE '9999',
            2 PERCENT FIXED(4,1) ;
OPEN FILE (WINE) SEQUENTIAL UPDATE ;
DO WHILE NOT ENDFILE(WINE) ;
     READ FILE(WINE) INTO(ENREG) ;
     IF VINTAGE < 1980 THEN
          DO
               PERCENT = PERCENT - 1 ;
               REWRITE FILE(WINE) FROM(ENREG) ;
          END ;
     END ;
END MODWINE ;
```

FIGURE 2.4 Example of a PL1 program manipulating a file

an example of a simple PL1 program. All commands in **boldface** type are either file declarations or manipulations. This program modifies a file describing French wines by decrementing the percentage of alcohol by 1 if the vintage is earlier than 1980. The program sequentially scans the file and rewrites qualifying records.

2.2.5 Sequential and Random Access Methods

Two measures are introduced to evaluate program behavior. The consultation ratio (CR) is the ratio of the number of records read over the total number of records in the file. The update factor (UF) is the ratio of the number of records modified by a program over the total number of records in the file. We look at two types of access method.

> **Definition 2.9 Sequential access method**
> An access method whereby each record is accessed one by one, from the first to the last.

The sequential access method is efficient for a program when CR or CR + UF equals 1. In general, the sequential access method is efficient in batch processing where CR is close to 1.

> **Definition 2.10 Key access methods**
> A set of access methods whereby an individual record can be read or written in only a few disk accesses (fewer than five and ideally one), for very large files.

Such methods are applicable when CF or CF + UF for a program are low. Key access methods are generally efficient for transactional processing.

A file management system must support both sequential and key access methods to facilitate, respectively, batch and transactional processing. In order to use key access methods, individual records must have unique identification. Key access methods must determine the location (starting address) of a record from the record's identifier and reach the record in fewer than five I/Os. The record's identifier is called the *key* (more specifically, the primary key).

> **Definition 2.11 Record key**
> Identifier by which a unique record can be selected in a file.

The record key can also be considered a data item whose information value identifies the record. It is generally stored in the record. Let us consider a file containing student records. The format of each record is defined by the following structure:

STUDENT(N#, Family_name, First_name, City, Enrollment_date, Results)

Each record contains the data specified above in parentheses. The key is N#; it is a data item in the record. Using this key, the student number, a key access method can determine the record's address in the file.

There are many different key access methods (with associated file organizations). These organizations can be of two types: *hashing access methods,* which compute the record's address using the key data value, and *indexed access methods,* which use tables generally stored on disk to memorize the key address association.

2.2.6 Multiple Users

In upgraded computers, the central processor can run while awaiting the result of an I/O instruction. To make full use of this feature, the system runs many user programs simultaneously, thus achieving *interuser parallelism.*

Definition 2.12 Interuser parallelism
Type of parallelism whereby one program is run by the central processor while the other is waiting for an I/O response.

A file management system shares files among applications without user intervention. Sharing can be simultaneous or successive.

2.2.7 File Protection and Security

File security requirements are for unauthorized or unlawful access. The problem stems from the need to share files among users. The owner needs to control access to his or her file by determining who can and cannot access the file. The file management system should offer the necessary tools to protect files. A file protection technique is to use passwords, names or encoded keys that the user must supply to access the file or the record.

The file management system must also provide data security in the case of a system crash. If this happens, the system should restart with coherent files. Two types of crashes can be isolated: a standard crash, where only the main memory is lost, and a severe crash, where secondary storage is affected. It is thus necessary to incorporate crash recovery procedures in the file management system.

2.3 File Management System Architecture and Functions

2.3.1 System Architecture

A file management system is built around a nucleus of basic operations: the creation and destruction of a file, secondary storage space allocation, the lookup of files on a disk pack, and the management of buffers (intermediate memory). The access methods are specific modules built over the core operations. Fig. 2.5 shows the different modules comprising a typical file management system.

 The core of the file management system accesses secondary storage through the I/O manager. The I/O manager is an independent process that manages physical I/O, reading and writing physical blocks on secondary storage devices. It manages the devices and the I/O queues. Each access method module is responsible for file organization and record retrieval from a known key value. A good file management system should offer a wide variety of access methods.

2.3.2 File Management Core Operations

File Manipulation
Using a set of file manipulation instructions, the assembly language programmer and the access method modules access the core of the file management system. Two instructions allow external levels to create or destroy a file. Two others read and write data contained in a file, which must be initially identified. The open primitive establishes a link between the program reading or writing and the secondary storage. The close primitive removes this data link.

Relative Addressing
Because files grow and retract, they are generally stored in noncontiguous space on secondary storage. It is therefore useful to be able to address continuous space from 0 to *N,* called *relative space.* Relative space permits data addressing using an offset in the file; it is independent of the physical location of the file on secondary storage. When a duplicate file is made, relative addressing from within each file is identical. It is also easy to ensure that file access does not surpass the file limit by controlling whether the relative address is not greater than the file size. Thus *relative addressing* within a file is a useful concept for secondary storage independence and access control.

> **Definition 2.13 Relative addressing**
> Offset from the beginning of the file in units of addressing within the file.

 To achieve relative addressing, the file is generally divided into *pages* (or blocks, groups, paquets, intervals, or buckets, depending on the vendor). A byte

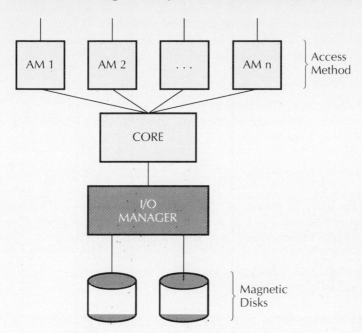

FIGURE 2.5 Typical architecture of a file system

relative address is composed of a page number and a byte number relative to the beginning of the page. To avoid too many I/Os, a page generally contains entire records (records are not split into several pages), and page buffers are used. Page size can be system determined or set at file creation and is most often around a few K bytes (2K or 4K). Page size can vary according to file organization.

Thus the first layer of a file management system generally offers primitives to access one or more pages of given relative addresses. This level of the file management system is essentially composed of secondary storage space allocation algorithms and conversion algorithms from page relative address to physical record address, and vice-versa. In general, this piece of software standardizes secondary storage with a few restrictions due to different device characteristics. For example, it is only possible to have sequential access to magnetic tape or it is only possible to read on a numerical optical disk already written.

Records are thus placed on secondary storage according to the chosen access method. If more than one record is placed on a page, the records are said to be blocked by a blocking factor of N records per page. If records are placed one behind the other, they are said to be packed. In that case, no storage space is lost but some records may be split between pages.

Space Allocation on Secondary Storage
File size may be static or fixed at file creation, or it may be dynamic, with its size varying with the storage requirements for that file. Intermediate storage solutions

use an initial storage size with a fixed-size allocation of space that can be extended. In all cases, it is necessary to reserve zones of continuous secondary storage space, which are allocated to files when necessary. These zones are called *allocation regions.*

> **Definition 2.14 Allocation region**
> Set of adjacent secondary memory zones (such as tracks) allocated
> together to a file.

Because of file modifications, allocated regions are not generally contiguous on secondary storage. The file management system must be able to reconstruct the file from the regions composing it. To do this, the FMS can either keep the regions composing a file in a table or link regions together. The size of a region can vary. The minimum region is an *allocation granule.*

> **Definition 2.15 Allocation granule**
> Secondary storage file allocation unit.

When a file is destroyed or it shrinks, the storage space allotted to it is collected.

File Lookup on Disk Space
When a disk pack is not mounted on a disk drive, it is stored in a disk library. Operator intervention is required to mount and unmount the disk packs on disk drives. Therefore each disk pack must be identified by a name or number. This *label* is found on a tag on the disk and also written on the disk pack to be machine readable and thus avoid operator error.

> **Definition 2.16 Label**
> A disk pack identifier in the form of a unique name or number.

After finding the disk pack on which a file resides, the operator must locate the requested file. For this purpose, each disk pack contains, for each local file, a file *directory entry,* which holds the name, address, and other information for each file.

> **Definition 2.17 Directory entry**
> Set of information comprising the characteristics of a file, including
> the file name, the file size, and the location on the disk.

The file descriptors on a disk pack must describe all its files. Therefore each disk pack is self-documented and portable. File descriptors for each disk pack are grouped on a table called a *directory.*

Definition 2.18 Directory
Table contained in a file on each disk pack with the descriptors of all
files on that disk pack.

The directory is either located at a specific place on the disk pack (for example,
starting at sector one) or written in a file with a reserved name in which the
descriptor for this file is contained in the label of the disk pack. Fig. 2.6 illustrates
the organization of information on a disk pack.

Hierarchical Classification of Files
When the number of files at an installation becomes important, they may be
grouped into subdirectories. Files may be grouped in different directories per
user. More generally directory entries can be separated according to application
types. Directory descriptors are thus permitted as entries in directories. The resulting *hierarchical directory* may be found in numerous systems [Daley65].

Definition 2.19 Hierarchical directory
Directory organized as a hierarchy of files, each file containing directories of immediately inferior files.

In a system where hierarchical directories are available, the upper levels are
generally specialized, and the lowest are not. For example, level 1 contains a
directory descriptor per user. For each user, level 2 can contain directory descriptors per application. For each couple <user-application>, level 3 can contain
directory descriptors grouped as desired by the user (for example, by type of file:

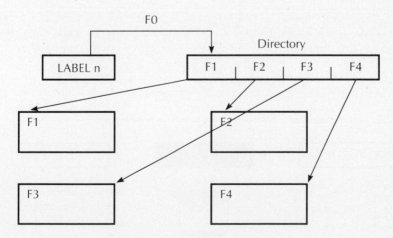

FIGURE 2.6 Disk pack organization

source code, object code, data file, and so on). At level 0, the unique directory descriptor is called the root.

The use of hierarchical directories implies specifying the path to reach a desired file. Using the example in Fig. 2.7, different levels can be attained with the following specifications:

> > PIERRE
> > PIERRE > DATABASE
> > PIERRE > DATABASE > MODELS

It is also possible to create more than one logical link to the same file so that different users can use the same copy of a file. For example, the file descriptor > LIONEL > DATABASE > LANGUAGES can be a *link* indicating that the descriptor name is a synonym of the file name > PIERRE > DATABASE > LANGUAGES.

To facilitate file access, systems that use hierarchical directories usually have a *home directory* associated with a specific account name or number that identifies the user and is supplied by him or her at log-in time. The user can navigate within the hierarchy starting at the home directory. For example,

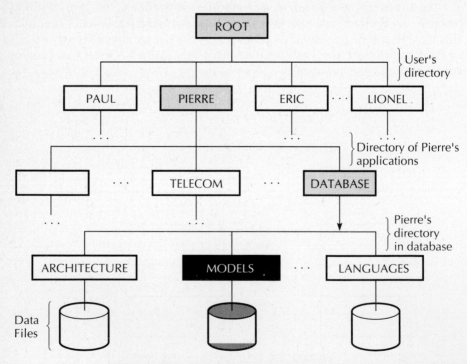

FIGURE 2.7 Example of a hierarchical directory

PIERRE could reach the DATABASE directory by supplying the following entry when at home directory:

> DATABASE

Once entered and accepted by the system, this would become the current or *working directory*. To access the file called MODELS, the following entry would be given:

> MODELS

To move up the hierarchy back to PIERRE, the command < < would be used. Directory names are uniquely determined when going up in a hierarchy.

File Control
The core of a file management system also contains functions and modules to perform file sharing and crash recovery and to control data security and privacy. These are operations of special interest in DBMSs and will therefore be covered in more detail in Chapters 7 and 8.

2.3.3 Secondary Storage Allocation Strategies

Strategy Objectives
There are different secondary storage allocation strategies for files. A good strategy should attempt to:

1. Minimize the number of different regions allocated to a file in order to reduce the number of head displacements when reading a sequential file and reduce the number of region descriptors associated with a file.
2. Minimize the physical distance between regions comprising one file in order to reduce the amplitude of head displacements.

The strategy can vary according to its complexity. The simplest class of these strategies allocates fixed-size portions of secondary storage equal to a granule. More complex strategies allocate regions of variable size composed of successive granules. In all methods, a table recording the free granules is managed on secondary storage. The table itself can be organized according to:

- An ordered or nonordered free granule or region list. Region allocation consists of removing the corresponding entry in the free list and adding the entry to the file list.
- A bit map in which each bit corresponds to a granule. The allocation of a granule entails finding a 0-valued bit, updating it to 1, and adding the corresponding granule's address to the file descriptor.

Fixed-Size Region Strategies

These simple strategies do not differentiate granule and region and are generally found on small systems. They allocate one granule at a time to a file. The *first-found strategy* allocates the granule at the head of the free list or the first zero bit in the free table. The *best-choice strategy* allocates the closest granule (in terms of head displacement) to the last allocated granule among the possible free candidate granules.

Variable-Size Region Strategies

These strategies allocate regions composed of consecutive granules according to the required space. The file management core receives requests for secondary storage space allocation and deallocation. Requested sizes are variable. If contiguous space is not available, the storage requirements can be met by several regions.

In the *closest-choice strategy,* two consecutive free regions are appended. When a request for space arrives, the free list is traversed for free regions of the required length. If no such region exists, the first region of superior size is split into two regions: one of the required size and the other added to the free region list.

The *buddy strategy* offers the possibility of allocating regions of 1, 2, 4, 8, ... , 2^k granules. Separate lists are kept for regions of size $2^0, 2^1, \ldots, 2^k$ granules. When a request for space of size 2^i arrives, it can be satisfied either with a free region taken from the 2^i list or with a free region of size 2^{i+1}, which is divided in two buddies of size 2^i. When space is freed, two consecutive regions (buddies) of size 2^i are merged to create a free region of size 2^{i+1}. The free region lookup algorithm of size 2^i consists of looking for regions of this size. If none exists, a free region of size 2^{i+1} is searched. If one is found, it is divided in two, one allocated to satisfy the request, the other chained to the 2^i free region list. If none is found, then the next level, 2^{i+2}, is searched; thus the search process is recursive up to level k. It is only when lists 2^i to 2^k are empty that the storage request cannot be satisfied by contiguous space. This algorithm, borrowed from the principle of segment allocation mechanisms in paging systems, is the most efficient. It is also well adapted to certain access methods.

In brief, variable region strategies are more efficient with respect to head displacement and file region table size. When too much splitting has occurred and no region exists whose size is superior to a granule, secondary storage space must be reorganized (garbage collection). This is the reason that granule strategies are the strategies most often used.

2.4 Hashing Access Methods and Organizations

Hashing access methods and organizations apply a transformation operation to the record key value to determine the relative address of a zone, called a *bucket,* in which to place the record. We will look at static hashing methods and dynamic hashing methods.

2.4.1 Static Hashing Organization

This is the older and simpler method. The file is fixed at a constant size at creation. It is divided into p buckets of size L. The record key is used to determine a bucket number N whose relative address can be obtained from the following formula $RA = N * L$. The concept of *static hashed file* organization can be defined.

> **Definition 2.20 Static hashed file**
> Fixed-size file in which records are placed in buckets whose addresses can be obtained by applying a hashing function to the record key value.

Within a bucket, records are placed in order of arrival. A record is retrieved with its key value. Fig. 2.8 illustrates an example of the internal structure of a bucket. When a new record arrives, it is placed at the end of data in the bucket. If there is no more place, there is said to be *overflow*. It is important to control

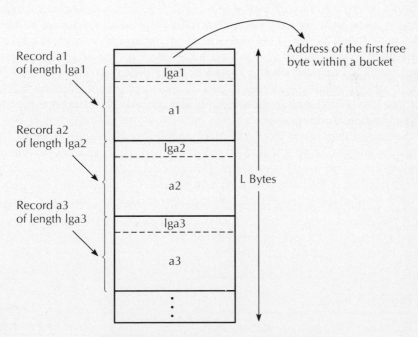

FIGURE 2.8 Internal structure of a bucket

the uniqueness of key value when inserting records so that no duplicate keys can arise. Within a bucket, a record is searched for sequentially. More sophisticated bucket structures enable direct access to a record by key value from within a bucket.

The bucket number of a record is calculated from a hashing function applied to the record key value (Fig. 2.9). A good hashing function should evenly distribute records among buckets. One technique is *folding,* or selecting and combining the bits forming the key value. *Conversion* is a key transformation into a real or an integer using the mantis to determine a bucket number. With *modulo,* the most widely used technique, the derived bucket number is the remainder of the integer division of the key value by the total number of buckets. These can also be combined for a more sophisticated hashing function.

For example, let us assume a file with 47 buckets with records holding numerical keys. Modulo 47 will thus be chosen for the hashing function. The record with key value 100 will be placed in bucket 6, the record with key value 47 will be placed in bucket 0, the record with key value 123 will be placed in bucket 29, and so on.

An overflow problem occurs when a bucket is full. One solution is to return the message "saturated file" to the user, who should reorganize the file by extending it or changing the hashing function, or both. But this is a poor solution because records may not be evenly distributed throughout the file. The following solutions are better [Knuth73]. *Open addressing* consists of placing the record that could not go into the full bucket into the first neighboring bucket with room. It implies that all the buckets in which a full bucket has leaked must be memorized for that full bucket. *Linking* consists of constituting a logical bucket by linking an overflow bucket to a full bucket. *Rehashing* consists of reapplying a second hashing function when a record is to be placed in a full bucket. This second hashing function is generally used to place records in overflow buckets. In all cases, overflow management complicates hashed file management and degrades overall performance.

Static hashing access methods offer numerous advantages. In particular, they can be adapted to files with any type of key and offer excellent performance as long as there is no overflow to manage. Record retrieval can be achieved within one I/O (reading a bucket); record writing generally requires two I/Os (reading and then writing a bucket). Overflows quickly degrade performance. Further-

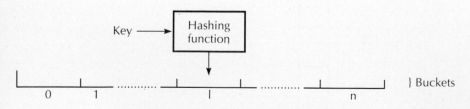

FIGURE 2.9 Illustration of a static hashed file

more the ratio of occupied space to file size can be far from 1. If the storage requirements surpass file size, the entire file must be reorganized.

2.4.2 Dynamic Hashing Organization

Dynamic Hashing Principles
The first dynamic hashing organization was proposed for tables represented in main memory [Knott71]. Different techniques, based on the same principle, were proposed to extend hashing techniques to dynamic files [Fagin79, Larson78, Litwin78, Larson80, Litwin80]. The basic principle of these resides in the progressive digitalization of the hashing function. The bit sequence resulting from the application of the hashing function is used progressively, one bit at a time as needed following file extension.

Dynamic methods use a key hashing function $h(K)$ generating a chain of N bits from the key K, where N is large (for example, 32). A function is chosen according to the probability of any bit value being equal. At file creation, only the M first bits of $h(K)$ (M being smaller than N) are used to place the record in a bucket. When the file is saturated, part of the file (for example, the saturated bucket) is doubled. A new region is allocated for this part, and the old records are redistributed among the old and the new buckets using the $(M+1)$th bit of the hashing function. This process is applied in a recursive fashion each time the file is saturated. Thus bits $(M+1)$, $(M+2)$, $(M+3)$, ... of the hashing function are successively used, and the file can grow to 2^N buckets, a size sufficient for the largest files required in management applications.

Dynamic hashing methods differ according to the way they respond to the following questions:

1. Which criterion is used to decide whether a hash file is saturated?
2. Which part of the hashed file is doubled when the file is saturated?
3. How can one find the parts of the file that have been doubled and the number of times they have been doubled?
4. Must an overflow method be chosen? If so, which method is chosen?

We will look at two hashing methods: the extendible hashing method [Fagin79] and the linear hashing method [Litwin80]. More elaborate methods are examined in [Larson80], [Lomet83] and evaluated in [Scholl81] and [Larson82].

Extendible Hashing
Extendible hashing [Fagin79] brings forth the following answers to the previous questions:

1. The file is extended as soon as a bucket is full, in which case a new bucket is added at file end.

2. Only the saturated bucket is doubled (i.e., split) when the file is extended.

3. The hashing function addresses a directory of bucket addresses. The directory's size is 2^{M+P}, where P is the depth of the bucket that was doubled the greatest number of times. Each directory entry supplies a bucket address. The 2^{P-Q} addresses corresponding to a bucket doubled Q times are identical and point to this bucket. Thus applying an indirection on the directory entry, the system finds requested buckets. The header of each bucket contains the number of bits to use for this bucket, which may be used for splitting or grouping buckets.

4. Overflow management is not necessary.

In brief, *extendible hashing* is specified in def. 2.21. As stated above, in this definition M is the number of bits of $h(K)$ used at file creation, and P is the greatest number of times a bucket is split in two.

> **Definition 2.21 Extendible hashing**
> A dynamic hashing method consisting of doubling a full bucket and memorizing bucket addresses in a directory addressed directly by using the lowest $(M+P)$ bits of the hashing function result.

An extendible hashed file has two structures: a directory and a bucket structure. The directory has a header that indicates the value of $M+P$, which is the number of bits used from the hashing function for the bucket of greatest depth (the file depth). After the header follow the bucket pointers. The first pointer corresponds to the value 0 of the first $(M+P)$ bits of the hash function. The last pointer corresponds to the value $2^{(M+P)}-1$, that is, all first $(M+P)$ bits set to 1. Each bucket contains a header that specifies the value $(M+Q)$, where Q is the depth of doubling of the bucket. Each bucket is associated to $2^{(P-Q)}$ twin pointers in the directory, which indicate its address. This organization is illustrated in Fig. 2.10 [Fagin79].

Record insertions in an extendible hashed file require an initial directory access. For this access, the lowest $(M+P)$ bits of the hashed key are used. The address of the bucket in which the record is to be placed is read in the corresponding entry in the directory. If the bucket is full, it must be doubled and its depth Q increased by 1; a twin bucket at the same depth must be created. The records are then split in the two buckets according to the value of bit $(M+Q+1)$ of the hashing function. If the depth P of the directory is greater than Q, the directory is simply updated; $2^{(P-Q+1)}$ pointers address the new bucket. If P is equal to Q, the directory must be doubled.

Record suppression in a bucket must theoretically lead to directory reorganization. In fact, if the concerned bucket and its twin bucket are the only buckets at that depth and the suppression of a record leaves enough room to merge the two buckets, the merge can be undertaken. The depth of the directory can be

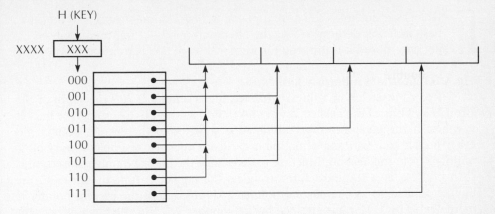

FIGURE 2.10 Directory and buckets of an extendible hashed file

reduced by 1 if the merge is performed; the directory size is then divided by 2 by merging twin blocks.

Linear Hashing

Linear hashing [Litwin80] brings forth the following solutions to the problems presented by dynamic hashing:

1. The file is lengthened as soon as a bucket is full; a new bucket is added to the file at each extension.
2. The doubled bucket is not the saturated one but the one pointed to by a current pointer, initialized to the first bucket and incremented by a factor of 1 each time a bucket is doubled (thus, at saturation). When this pointer reaches the end of the file, it is repositioned at the beginning of the file.
3. The depth F of a file (initialized to 0 and incremented when the current pointer reaches the beginning of the file) is recorded in the file descriptor. For a bucket located before the current pointer, $(M+F+1)$ bits of the hashing function must be used. Only $(M+F)$ bits need to be used for a bucket address located after the current pointer and before bucket $2^{(M+F)}$.
4. Overflow management is necessary because full buckets are not generally doubled; a bucket will be doubled only when the current pointer passes its address, at which point any overflow method can be used.

Definition 2.22 Linear hashing
Dynamic hashing methods necessitating overflow management and consisting of doubling a bucket pointed to by the current pointer

when one bucket is full and applying at first a number of bits of the hash function determined by the file depth minus 1, and then applying one more bit if the result is located before the current pointer.

Fig. 2.11 illustrates a linearly hashed file.

Record insertion in a linearly hashed file is simple. If F is the depth of the file, $(M+F)$ bits of the hashed key are taken into account to determine the bucket number. If the bucket number obtained is superior to the current pointer, no other bucket address transformation is needed. Otherwise a supplementary bit is required from the hashing function to determine the bucket number. Insertion is then possible in a standard fashion unless the bucket is full. In this case, the bucket pointed to by the current pointer is doubled, and the current pointer is incremented by 1. If it has attained bucket number $2^{(M+F)}$ of the file, it is brought to point to the beginning, and the depth of the file is increased by 1.

In a way similar to that of extendible hashing, record suppression in a bucket can produce the merge of two buckets and decrement the current pointer by 1. It is important to note that the merged buckets in general do not include the bucket that contained the suppressed record. The merger can bring forth overflow record distribution.

A variant of this method, proposed in [Larson80], is to change the condition that triggers the doubling of buckets. The new proposed condition is the occupation ratio of the file, that is the space occupied by data over the total space occupied by the file.

To recapitulate, dynamic hashing methods are well adapted for small, evolving files—that is, files of variable length but not too big to avoid too many bucket saturations or too large an increase in the size of the directory. The problem with extendible hashing is that the directory may increase exponentially. The problem of linear hashing is overflow management. The limits of both methods are still not well known. The extendible hashing method seems better equipped to deal with uneven key distributions. Directory management is more troublesome than current pointer management. The basic problems with hashing methods remain sorted accesses and range queries.

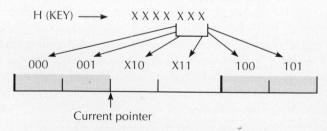

FIGURE 2.11 Linearly hashed file

2.5 Indexed Access Methods and Organizations

2.5.1 Informal Principles

The Index

The basic principle of indexed organization and access method is to associate to a file a table of contents having for each entry the key value of the record and its relative address in the file.

> **Definition 2.23 Index**
> Table(s) associating the key values of records to corresponding relative addresses in the file.

Fig. 2.12 illustrates the principle of indexed organizations. The index of a file can be stored in the file itself or in another special index file.

The following steps are performed to access a record in an indexed file:

1. Accessing the index.
2. Key lookup to obtain the record or bucket relative address.
3. Relative address conversion to absolute address.
4. Disk access to the record or bucket.
5. Data transfer from the disk to main program memory.

Variations

A file's index can be sorted. The fact that an index is sorted authorizes the binary searching of the index. Thus an index with N keys divided in b blocks (of one sector) will need an average of $N/2b$ accesses to find the key if not sorted. If the index is sorted, the number of accesses needed will be reduced to LOG_2N/b. For example, $N=10^6$, $b=100$ keys, 10 accesses will be the average when sorted as opposed to 5000 when not sorted. An index can contain entries for all or some records. In order to differentiate between methods, the concept of *index density* may be used.

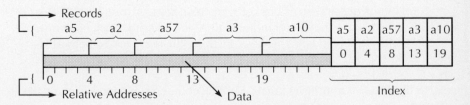

FIGURE 2.12 Example of an indexed file

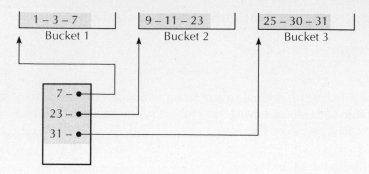

FIGURE 2.13 Example of a nondense index

> **Definition 2.24 Index density**
> Ratio of the number of keys in the index to the total number of records in the file.

Two variants are distinguished. If density equals 1, the index is dense. If density is less than 1, the index is nondense. In the case of a nondense index, the records in the file and the keys in the index must be sorted. The file is divided in fixed-size buckets, and each bucket has an entry in the index. This entry is the pair <greatest key value in the bucket, relative address of the bucket>. Fig. 2.13 illustrates a nondense index with corresponding file.

Variations are theoretically possible with regard to sorted or nonsorted file or a dense or nondense index that is sorted or not sorted. Fig. 2.14 illustrates the practical possibilities.

Multilevel indexes
An index can be viewed as a file of keys. If the index is large (for example, more than one page), it is necessary to create an index for the index (that is, create levels of indexing), called a *multilevel index.*

> **Definition 2.25 Multilevel index**
> A two-level multilevel index is a one-level sorted index contained in buckets and having its own sorted index, the keys in this second-level index being the first-level bucket's greatest keys. A multilevel index with N levels is a multilevel index with $N-1$ levels, having itself one additional sorted index, the keys in this Nth level index being the $(N-1)$th bucket's greatest keys.

Fig. 2.15 illustrates a multilevel index. Multilevel indexes can have as many levels as needed.

			File	
			Sorted	Nonsorted
I N D E X	Dense	Sorted	Possible	PISM
		Nonsorted		Possible
	Nondense	Sorted	ISAM VSAM UFAS	
		Nonsorted		

PISM = Pure indexed sequential
ISAM = IBM indexed sequential
VSAM = Regular indexed sequential (IBM)
UFAS = Regular indexed sequential (Honeywell-BULL)

FIGURE 2.14 Variants of index access methods

2.5.2 Formal Principles

B-trees
B-trees [Bayer72, Comer79] were introduced to implement multilevel tree structures as implementation-independent multilevel indexes of variable depth.

Definition 2.26 B-tree
A B-tree of order *m* is a graph tree such that all the leaves are at the
same level, and all nonleaf nodes have *ND* descendants such that

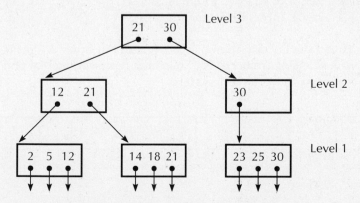

FIGURE 2.15 Example of a multilevel index

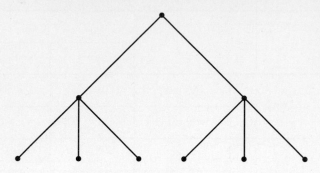

FIGURE 2.16 B-tree of order 2

$m + 1 \leq ND \leq 2m + 1$, except for the root, which has NDR descendants such that $0 \leq NDR \leq 2m + 1$.

Fig. 2.16 represents a B-tree of depth 2.

A B-tree can be used to constitute a multilevel index of a file. In that case, the nodes represent the pages of the index. The pages contain the keys sorted by ascending order of values and two types of pointers. The *internal pointers* designate descendants and define the tree's structure; the *external pointers* designate data pages (relative address in general). Fig. 2.17 gives the structure of a node.

With B-trees, the set of keys needs to be sorted in postfix order to have the number of accesses required in a search equal to the depth of the B-tree. More precisely, by designating $K(Pi)$ the set of keys figuring in the subtree pointed to by Pi, the following conditions must be true:

1. $(X_1, X_2, \ldots X_k)$ is a sequence of keys in ascending order.
2. Each key Y of $K(P0)$ is inferior to X_1.
3. Each key Y of $K(Pi)$ is within X_i and X_{i+1}.
4. Each key Y of $K(Pk)$ is superior to X_k.

Fig. 2.18 is an example illustration of a B-tree index of order 2. This B-tree contains key values ranging from 1 to 25. Solid lines represent internal pointers, and nonsolid lines represent external pointers.

P0	x1 a1 P1	x2 a2 P2	. . .	xi ai Pi	. . .	xk ak Pk

Pi = internal pointer representing the tree; the leaves do not contain such pointers;

ai = external data page pointer;

xi = key value.

FIGURE 2.17 B-tree node structure

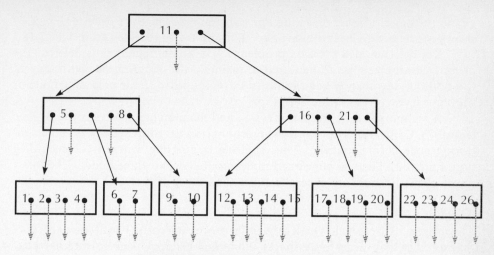

FIGURE 2.18 Example of a B-tree index

A B-tree key search starts at the root of the B-tree. In general, values are partitioned into intervals, the number of intervals being equal to the number of branches. The first branch is visited by the search algorithm if the search value is less than the key value. If the search value is within the first key value and the second key value, then the second branch is visited, and so on. If the search value is not found in a terminal node, the value does not exist.

The number of levels in a B-tree is determined by its degree and the number of keys it contains. Thus in the worst case, if the tree is full, it has the following elements: a root key, two branches leaving the root with m keys, and $(m+1)$ branches leaving each internal node with m keys. For a depth h tree, the number of keys is then:

$$1 + 2m[1 + (m+1) + (m+1)^2 + \ldots + (m+1)^{h-2}]$$
$$= 1 + 2[(m+1)^{h-1} - 1]$$

from which can be deduced the number of levels needed to store N keys:

$$h = 1 + \text{LOG}_{m+1} \frac{N+1}{2} \text{ levels.}$$

For example, to store 1,999,999 keys with a B-tree of 99 degrees, $h = 1 + \text{LOG}_{100}10^6 = 4$. A maximum of four levels is needed. Thus, a record in a file containing 2 million records with a hierarchical index organized as a B-tree could be found in four I/Os.

Key insertion in a B-tree is a complex operation. First, search for the terminal node, which should contain the key, and insert the key there. If the number of keys in the node after the insertion is greater than $2m$, then migrate the median key to the superior level, repeating the insertion procedure at this level. Fig. 2.19 shows the steps required to insert key 25 in the B-tree represented in Fig. 2.18.

Key deletion also presents problems. If a nonterminal key is deleted, the order following key has to be raised to maintain the organization. Furthermore if a node has less than *m* keys, it has to be regrouped with the preceding node of the same level to respect the definition.

A variant of the B-tree for creating and maintaining indexes is the B*-tree [Knuth73, Comer79]. The insertion algorithm tries to redistribute keys in a neighboring node before splitting. Thus splitting occurs only when two consecutive nodes are full. The two concerned nodes are burst into three nodes. The index pages of the B*-trees are generally fuller than those of B-trees.

B+-trees

The usage of B-trees incurs high sequential processing costs. File access according to ascending key order necessitates numerous external page to internal page passes. To avoid this inconvenience, keys occurring in internal nodes may be repeated in external nodes, and leaf pages may be linked together. The resulting tree is a B+-tree. Fig. 2.20 presents a B+-tree corresponding to the B-tree of Fig. 2.18. External pointers are found only at the leaf level.

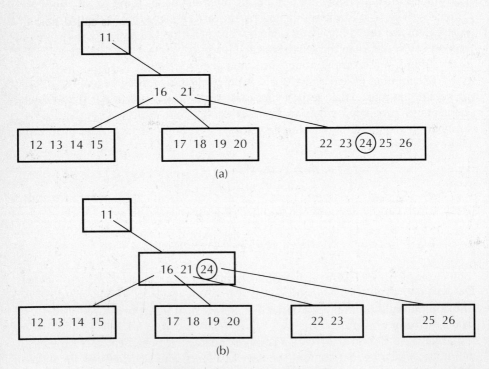

(a)

(b)

FIGURE 2.19 Insertion of key 25

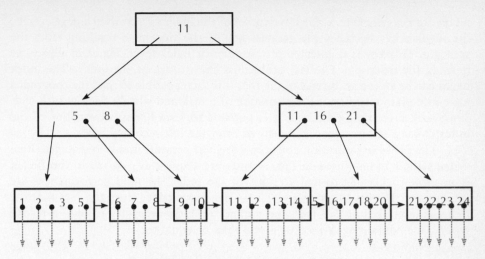

FIGURE 2.20 Example of a B⁺-tree index

B⁺-trees can be used to create multilevel indexed files in at least the two following ways. First, the B⁺-tree can be for index use only. The records are stored in a standard sequential file, and the B⁺-tree contains all the keys and corresponding record relative addresses. Such an organization is called here *indexed sequential* (IS). Second, the B⁺-tree can be used to manage both index and file. To do so, the external pointers are replaced by the record contents. The records are thus sorted. Only the record keys are displaced at a higher index level to constitute a nonselective index. This method corresponds to the regular IBM indexed organization known as VSAM and also to the Honeywell Bull indexed sequential organization known as UFAS.

2.5.3 Pure Indexed Sequential Method (PISM)

With this organization, records are sequentially stored in a file where the index is dense and organized as a B⁺-tree.

> **Definition 2.27 Pure indexed sequential file**
> Nonsorted file with sorted dense B⁺-tree index.

Definition 2.27 raises many problems. First, the order of the B⁺-tree that constitutes the index must be defined. The solution is to divide the index in pages (one page = 1 to p sectors). The pages are not completely filled when first written onto the file. If a page is full, it is split into two half-filled pages. Then the median key is raised to the superior index level. A second problem consists of keeping the index dense. In fact, it is a multilevel index dense at the lowest level. That is, all record keys are kept at the lowest level of the index. Thus when a page is split, the median key becomes the greatest key of the first page resulting from the splitting. This key is duplicated at the superior index level. Fig. 2.21 illustrates indexed file insertion. The last problem is the storage of the index. The index pages can be stored at the end of the file. It is then possible to read the root index page into main memory at the beginning of a task and write it back at task end. With such a recording method, it is possible to keep historical versions of the index as long as new records are stored after the last recorded index.

The PISM organization and access method presents many advantages. Record insertion is simplified in that records are sequentially stored in the file; it is possible to keep historical versions of the index. Method performances are satisfactory. If m is the number of keys per index page, from the fact that the index is organized as a B-tree, the number of I/Os necessary to read a record from a file containing N records is less than or equal to:

$$2 + LOG_{m/2} \frac{N + 1}{2}$$

Record writing generally requires two disk accesses except where index pages are doubled, requiring one read and two writes per splitting level in general. For example, a file containing fewer than 10^6 records will not need more than three I/Os when reading.

This method presents three serious inconveniences. Because records and in-

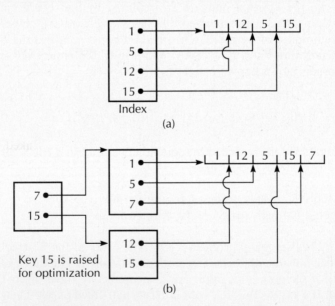

FIGURE 2.21 Pure indexed sequential file insertion. (a) Before insertion of (7) and (b) after insertion of (7).

dex are separated, disk arm movements are generally important. Sequential access by ascending key order must be done by index consultation and is thus very expensive. And being dense, the index becomes very large if no compacting technique is used.

2.5.4 Indexed Sequential Access Method (ISAM)

The Method
ISAM (indexed sequential access method) [IBM78] is an organization used in the DOS, OS/VS IBM systems.

> **Definition 2.28 ISAM file**
> File with sorted records and a nondense sorted index composed of a primary area and an overflow area in which a saturated track overflows into a logical extension constituted by a list of records in overflow.

An ISAM file has three areas: a primary area where records are written at file creation; an overflow area where records are transferred when records are inserted; and an index area where the index is written.

Primary Area
The primary area is composed of contiguous cylinders on which certain tracks are reserved for the index and overflow areas. In primary areas, records are stored in ascending key order. They can be blocked or not. At file creation, the records must be delivered to the file system in ascending key order. Fig. 2.22 illustrates an ISAM file after the initial writing. This file is composed of two cylinders.

Overflow Area
There are two types of overflow areas: the *cylinder overflow area,* composed of a few tracks per cylinder, and the *independent overflow area,* composed of the last cylinders of a file (Fig. 2.23).

In the overflow area, records are not blocked. They are linked together in

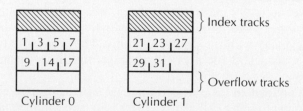

FIGURE 2.22 ISAM file after the initial loading of records 1,3,5,7,9,14,17,21,23,27,29,31 (in that order)

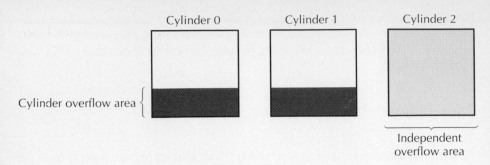

FIGURE 2.23 ISAM file overflow areas

order to rebuild the track that overflowed. When a record is inserted, its position is searched in the logical track. If it is in the primary area, the records that follow are displaced, and the last ones are moved in the overflow area. The links are updated. If the record is to be placed in the overflow area, it is inserted in the right place in the link of records in the overflow area.

The cylinder's overflow area is used first. When it is saturated, the independent overflow area is used. Because the links are made by ascending key order, it is possible for the chain of records to go from the cylinder overflow area to the independent overflow area and back to the cylinder overflow area, and so on. For this reason, this method becomes inefficient when searching for a record in the overflow area due to disk arm displacement.

Index Area

There are two necessary index levels and optionally three index levels: track indexes, cylinder indexes, and master index(es).

The first necessary index level is the *track index*. There is one track index per cylinder (usually located on the first track of the cylinder). Each entry in the track index corresponds to a track on the cylinder and stores the greatest key value of the logical track, including the address of the first record in the overflow area should there be one. Fig. 2.24 illustrates this format.

The second necessary index level is the *cylinder index*. A cylinder index per file exists. This index contains one entry per cylinder. Each entry stores the greatest key of the cylinder with the cylinder address. The cylinder index is generally memorized in a particular file area (for example, in the independent overflow area).

The third optional index level is the *master index*. It is used when the cylinder index is too big to index efficiently. There is an entry in the master index for each track of the cylinder index. This entry contains the address of the track and the value of the greatest key of the track.

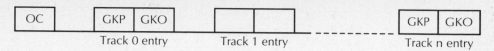

Track 0 entry   Track 1 entry   Track n entry

OC = Overflow control including the address of the record in the overflow area

GKP = Greastest key value in the primary area, including the address of the track

GKO = Greastest key value in the overflow area, including the address of the first
       record in the overflow area

FIGURE 2.24 Track index format

Overall View

Fig. 2.25 gives an overall view of an ISAM file after record insertions, with a two-level index. The advantages of this method are the fact that the file is sorted, which facilitates sorted sequential access and random access time as long as the file has not overflowed (three I/Os to read a record). The main inconveniences are that overflows are complex to manage and degrade performance to the point where it is necessary to reorganize files that have overflowed, and that the access method is related to the characteristics of the physical device. Performance depends on overflows. If a track has d records in overflow, reading a record will require approximately $3 + [d/2]$ I/Os, and writing a record will require $2 + [d/2] + 4$ I/Os to locate the record's position, write it, and update links. This can become very expensive.

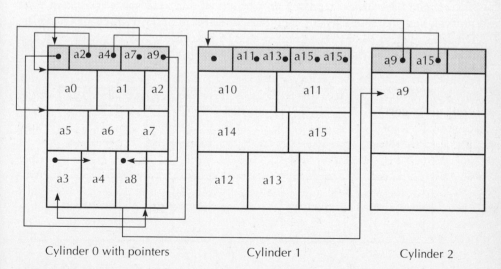

Cylinder 0 with pointers   Cylinder 1   Cylinder 2

FIGURE 2.25 Overall view of an ISAM file. (Pointers issuing from cylinder 1 are not represented)

2.5.5 Virtual Sequential Access Method (VSAM)

General Presentation
The main IBM file organization used under IBM OS/VS is called VSAM [IBM78].

> **Definition 2.29 Virtual sequential file**
> Sorted file with a nondense sorted index distributed in the file, organized as a B$^+$-tree.

The file is divided into *regions*. A region is a set of tracks on a cylinder or on contiguous cylinders. Each region is divided into *intervals*. An interval consists of either part of a track or several contiguous tracks read in one I/O access. When an interval is saturated, it is split into two intervals. When a region is saturated, it is split into two regions. Thus the file reorganizes itself incrementally.

This file organization resulted from a critical analysis of ISAM. In VSAM, the file is more independent from the physical structure of the secondary storage. The track is replaced by the interval that can be a fraction of a track or several tracks; the cylinder is replaced by the region. Overflows are no longer a problem in that the overflow mechanism is that of the B-tree — that is, a saturated interval or region is split in two.

Analysis of the Data Regions
The area that contains the records is divided into intervals and regions (Fig. 2.26). At file creation, as for ISAM files, the records must be sent to the access method in ascending key order. Updates are accounted for, free space is kept in each interval, and free intervals are kept in each region in order to insert new records. The file in Fig. 2.26 has been created with 25 percent free bytes per interval and 25 percent free intervals per region. At file creation, the program creating the file

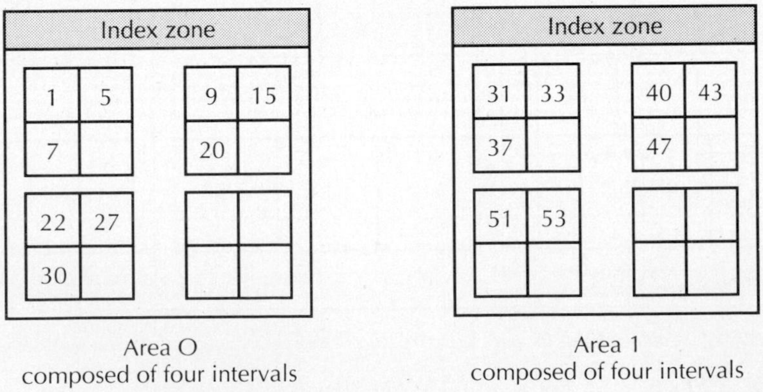

Area O
composed of four intervals

Area 1
composed of four intervals

FIGURE 2.26 VSAM file after creation

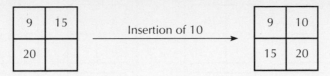

FIGURE 2.27 Inserting the record with key 10 in the file represented in Fig. 2.26

delivered to the file system the following records in the given increasing order: 1,5,7,9,15,20,22,27,30,33,37,40,43,47,51,53.

The insertion algorithm determines where the record will be placed with the help of the interval index. Two possible cases follow. If the interval has free space, the record is placed in that interval in the right place respecting lexicographical order. For example, inserting a record with key 10 will produce the substitution of the interval represented in Fig. 2.27. If the interval is full, it is split into two half-full intervals. Two subcases are possible. First, if there is a free interval in the region, it is used to store one of the two intervals resulting from the split. For example, inserting the record with key 13 in the file resulting after the insertion of the record with key 10 (Fig. 2.27) will produce the file represented in Fig. 2.28. Second, if there is no free interval in the region, a free region is allocated to the file, and the full region is split into two half-full ones. When splitting, half of the intervals containing the greatest keys are recopied in the new region. For example, insertion of records with keys 11 and 12 in the file is represented in Fig. 2.29. The resulting index is portrayed in Fig. 2.30.

Overall View

Fig. 2.31 gives an overall view of another VSAM file composed of two regions, with only two index levels. The advantage of the method is that the file is sorted, which facilitates sequential sorted access and record access delays (reading a record occurs within three I/Os). However, writing a record can be costly when intervals or, worse, areas need to be split.

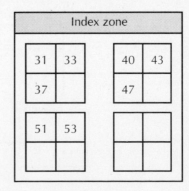

FIGURE 2.28 File after inserting records 10 and 13

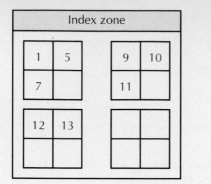

FIGURE 2.29 File after insertion of records with keys 10 and 12

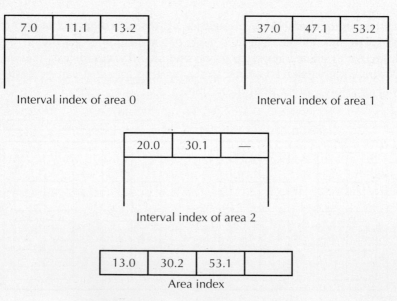

Interval index of area 0

Interval index of area 1

Interval index of area 2

13.0	30.2	53.1	

Area index

FIGURE 2.30 Index of the Fig. 2.29 file

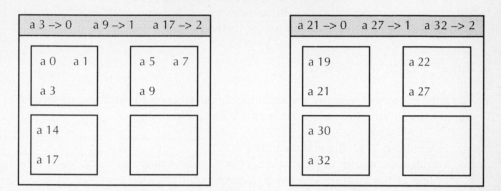

FIGURE 2.31 Overall view of a VSAM file

2.6 Multiattribute Access Methods

2.6.1 Motivations and Objectives

The access methods we have examined can determine the address of a record in a file being given a unique key value — that is, the value of a specific determinant field (also called attribute) in the file. In indexed methods, an index associates key values with page addresses or record addresses. Indexes implemented as B-trees or variations of B-trees permit the positioning of keys according to their sorted order. Such methods easily support range queries, those that specify an interval of values for a given record field (a record attribute). Also they adapt gracefully to variations of the file content and hence provide constant access time for match queries. In hashed methods, keys undergo a computational transformation (hashing) and generally lose their natural lexical order property. Hence hashed methods do not easily support range queries. However, they generally provide random accessing with better performance than indexed methods.

Although indexed and hashed methods are efficient methods to support dynamic files, they require selecting a unique field in the records of a file, which is the key. Accessing through the record key is generally efficient while accessing through other data is a priori performed using a sequential scan. Thus to allow users to access a file on various record fields, systems designers have generalized indexing or hashing methods to *multidimensional access methods*.

> **Definition 2.30 Multidimensional access methods**
> Access methods whereby an individual record (or a set of records) can be accessed in a few disk I/Os from the value of any attribute chosen among N access attributes, with $N > 1$.

Multidimensional access methods are important for database management systems because they avoid sequential scan of files by supplying direct access paths to records on various attributes. Both indexing schemes and hashing schemes can be extended to multidimensional access methods.

2.6.2 Secondary Indexes

The simplest way to support a multidimensional access is the addition of *secondary indexes* to an indexed file, such as a VSAM file.

> **Definition 2.31 Secondary index**
> Index on a record attribute that is not discriminating, giving for each value of the attribute the list of records having this value.

A secondary index is often organized as a B-tree, although other organizations are possible. A file with secondary indexes may be indexed or hashed on a discriminating record attribute, called the *primary key*. In contrast, the attribute on which the secondary index is built is called a *secondary key*.

There are several ways to refer to file records in a secondary index entry. For a given value of the secondary key, one may store a list of record relative addresses (offsets) in the file. One may store only page addresses; in that case, a search in the page will be necessary to determine the exact records matching the secondary key value. One may also store primary keys; the search of records then is done through the primary index. Indeed the choice is difficult and depends on several parameters. While record relative addresses allow the system to go directly to the record or at least the record page when searching, modifying the secondary index is necessary each time the record moves in the file (for example, with a VSAM file organization, each time a page splits). Primary key values require several additional I/Os to look up a record given its key value.

With secondary indexes, the search of records in a file is generally performed from a key value. According to the known key, an index is selected, and records are looked up in the file. When several key values are known, the index selection may be difficult. The most discriminating index is generally chosen; records are then accessed successively through that index, and other key values are compared to each accessed record. If there is a match for all known keys, the record is selected and delivered to the user. Another approach is to access all index entries corresponding to the known keys and then to perform an intersection of the list of record addresses (or primary keys) in main memory. Only the resulting addresses will generate access to records in the file.

2.6.3 Multiattribute Hashing

With hashing, it is possible to develop a multidimensional access method by applying hash functions to several attributes and then compacting the hash functions result to get a bucket number. The method is the basis for what is known as *multiattribute clustering*.

Definition 2.32 Multiattribute clustering
Multidimensional access method whereby a bucket address is determined by applying hash functions to different record fields.

With *static multiattribute clustering,* the multiattribute hashing is performed in a fixed, perdefined way. In that case, if $A1, A2, \ldots, An$ are the clustering attributes, each is mapped to a fixed number of b_i bits of the bucket address, which is composed of B bits, with $B = b_1 + b_2 + \ldots + b_i + \ldots b_n$. Thus attribute Ai is hashed using a hash function h_i mapping its value to $[0, 2^b i]$. A record is placed in the bucket of address $< h_1(A1) | h_2(A2) | \ldots h_n(An >$ where | means the chains of bits concatenation. To retrieve a record, if a given attribute, say Ai, is known, the system will only access buckets of address $< \ldots | h_i(Ai) | \ldots >$, where $\ldots$ means any sequence of bits of length $b_1 + b_2 + \ldots + b_{i-1} + b_{i+1} + \ldots b_n = B - b_i$. Thus the number of buckets to scan will be reduced from 2^B to $2^{B-b}i$. According to the probabilities of knowing the value of each attribute in a query, it is possible to determine the values of b_i's that minimize the expected number of bucket searches [Ullman80].

With the advent of dynamic hashing, *dynamic multidimensional clustering* schemes have been proposed. The best-known scheme is the *grid file* [Nievergelt84]. The method may be seen as an extension of extendible hashing. One hashing function is associated with each clustering attribute in such a way that the hashed address is composed of a sufficiently large number of bits. An extendible hashing is applied using a multidimensional hashed address. To clarify the grid file presentation, one may represent tuples as a point in an n-dimensional hyperspace, the dimensions of which are the domains of the clustering attributes. For simplicity, let us assume two clustering attributes, A1 and A2, and a file with a unique bucket (Fig. 2.32a). When the file grows, the bucket saturates. It is split in two according to dimension A1, using the first bit of the hashing function applied to A1 (see Fig. 2.32b). When one of the buckets, say B0, is full, it is again split in two buckets, B00 and B01, but according to the other dimension, A2, using the first bit of the hashing function applied to A2 (Fig. 2.32c). Bucket B1 is split in two only in the sense that two pointers referring to B1 will appear in the directory. B1 will be physically split only when it saturates. If bucket B01 becomes full, it will again be split in two buckets, B010 and B011, according to dimension A1 (using the second bit of the hashing function applied to A1). The process will continue by successive splitting according to one or the other dimension.

To retrieve a bucket, there is a multidimensional directory associated to a grid file. Each entry in the directory corresponds to a logical grid region. The directory is stored on a contiguous sequence of disk pages but is logically organized as a multidimensional array. For example, with a two-dimensional clustering, the address of the bucket for region i, j will be determined by a classical

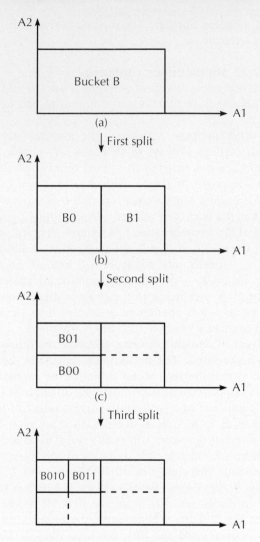

FIGURE 2.32 Bucket splitting in a grid file

mapping from a two-dimensional array to the one-dimensional directory (the entry in the directory is the $(N \cdot i + j)$th, where N is the number of intervals in dimension A1). Thus when a new logical split is performed, the directory must be expanded by doubling one dimension; its size increases exponentially in function of the data size.

To improve directory management and make it grow linearly in relation to the number of data buckets, several schemes have been proposed. One of the most efficient is that developed with the predicate tree structure [Gardarin83], which is implemented in the SABRINA DBMS. Here the set of hashing functions is defined as an ordered set $\{h0(A_{k0}), h1(A_{k1}), \ldots, hn(A_{kn})\}$ (note that *ki* may be equal to *kj*), each corresponding to a level in a balanced tree called the *predicate tree*. The branches in the tree starting from any node at level *i* are identical. Each corresponds to a value of $hi(A_{ki})$ from 0 to N_i. N_i must generally be small to guarantee a quick traversal of level *i* when the file grows. When the file grows, buckets are split following the predicate tree structure. Thus each bucket is characterized by a binary address in the tree, from the root to the node representing it in the tree. This hierarchical binary address, called a *bucket signature,* is stored in the directory with the physical address of the bucket on disks. A predicate tree with the associated buckets and directory is represented in Fig. 2.33.

The directory itself is organized as a clustered file, clustering being defined by a specific predicate tree according to the digits of the signature. When a record is searched, a signature or part of a signature (called a *signature profile*) is elaborated; it is used to access the directory and retrieve the relevant bucket(s) address(es). With this complex scheme, the number of entries in the directory is equal to the number of buckets in the file.

Other structures, such as the interpolation-based grid file [Burkhard83, Ozkarahan85], also maintain one directory entry per data bucket. Here the idea

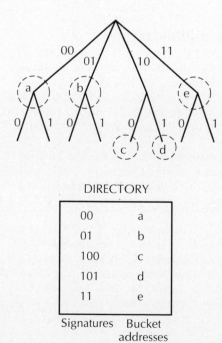

DIRECTORY

Signatures	Bucket addresses
00	a
01	b
100	c
101	d
11	e

FIGURE 2.33 Predicate tree – based file with the associated directory

is to address a bucket by a level v and a region number r while the domain of each region is simply divided into two equal intervals when splitting. Recently a new multiattribute clustering organization, the BANG file [Freeston87], has been introduced with similar properties, in which the directory is organized as a tree.

2.7 Conclusion

The essential functions and basic techniques of file management systems have been reviewed. More information can be found in [Widerhold83, Koshafian85]. A file management system is the basic building block of a database system. For database systems, new and higher-level software is created to manage access paths from file to file, centralized data description, and various data management interfaces including query languages, fourth-generation languages, and so on.

To support database systems, the file management tools need to be elaborated. It is possible to find extended file systems that perform both multiattribute clustering and secondary index management on different keys for one file. Database systems need to use different paths to access records based on different criteria in data consultation. Choosing a path is the role of the database query optimizer. These problems will be studied in Chapter 9.

2.8 References and Bibliography

[Bayer72] Bayer R., McCreight C., "Organization and Maintenance of Large Ordered Indexes," Acta Informatica, V1, N3, 1972, pp. 173 – 89.

[Burkhard83] Burkhard W. A., "Interpolation Based Index Maintenance," Proc. PODS Second ACM SIGMOD-SIGACT Symposium, March 1983, ACM Ed.

[Comer79] Comer D., "The Ubiquitous B-Tree," Computing Surveys, V11, N2, June 1979.

[Daley65] Daley R. C., Neuman P. G., "A General Purpose File System for Secondary Storage," Fall Joint Computer Conference, 1965, pp. 213 – 29.

[Fagin79] Fagin R., Nivergelt J., Pippengar N., Strong H. R., "Extendible Hashing — A Fast Access Method for Dynamic Files," ACM TODS, V4, N3, September 1979, pp. 315 – 44.

[Freeston87] Freeston M., "The BANG File: A New Kind of Grid File," ACM SIGMOD, May 1987, San Francisco, ACM ed., pp. 260 – 69.

[Gardarin83] Gardarin G., Faudemay P., Michel R., Valduriez P., Viemont Y., "An Integrated Approach to Multi Dimensional Searching Using Predicate Trees and Filtering," INRIA Research Report, No. 203, April 1983.

[IBM78] IBM Corporation, "Introduction to IBM Direct-Access Storage Devices and Organization Methods," student text, Manual Form GC20-1649-10.

[Knott71] Knott G. D., "Expandable Open Addressing Hash Table Storage and Retrieval," Proc. ACM SIGFIDET Workshop on Data Description, Access, and Control, 1971, pp. 186 – 206.

[Knuth73] Knuth D. E., *The Art of Computer Programming,* Addison-Wesley, 1973.

[Koshafian85] Koshafian S., Banerjee J., Copeland G., Valduriez P., "A Performance Directed Taxonomy for Simple Key and Multiple Key File Structure," MCC Database Program Report, April 1985.

[Larson78] Larson P., "Dynamic Hashing," BIT 18, 1978, pp. 184–201.

[Larson80] Larson P., "Linear Hashing with Partial Expansions," Sixth Int. Conf. on Very Large Data Bases, Montreal, October 1980, ACM ed., pp. 224–32.

[Larson82] Larson P., "Performance Analysis of Linear Hashing with Partial Expansions," ACM TODS, V7, N4, December 1982, pp. 566–87.

[Litwin78] Litwin W., "Virtual Hashing: A Dynamically Changing Hashing," Fourth Int. Conf. on Very Large Data Bases, Berlin, 1978, pp. 517–23.

[Litwin80] Litwin W., "Linear Hashing — A New Tool for File and Table Addressing," Sixth Int. Conf. on Very Large Data Bases, Montreal, 1980, pp. 212–23.

[Litwin81] Litwin W., "Trie Hashing," ACM SIGMOD Int. Conf., Ann Arbor, Mich., 1981.

[Lomet83] Lomet D., "A High Performance, Universal Key Associative Access Method," ACM SIGMOD, San Jose, Calif., 1983.

[Nievergelt84] Nievergelt J., Hinterberger H., Sevcik K., "The Grid File: An Adaptable Symmetric Multi-key File Structure," ACM TODS, V9, N1, March 1983.

[Ozkarahan85] Ozkarahan E. A., Ouksel M., "Dynamic and Order Preserving Data Partitioning for Database Machines," Eleventh Int. Conf. on Very Large Data Bases, Stockholm, August 1985.

[Scholl81] Scholl M., "New File Organizations Based on Dynamic Hashing," ACM TODS, V6, N1, March 1981, pp. 194–211.

[Ullman80] Ullman J. D., *Principles of Database Systems,* Computer Science Press, 1980.

[Wiederhold83] Widerhold G., *Database Design,* McGraw-Hill, 1983.

3
DBMS OBJECTIVES
AND ARCHITECTURES

3.1 Introduction

The concept of database may be viewed in different ways. From a system point of view, a database is a collection of related files. From a management point of view, a database is a collection of data that model an enterprise activity. Although these are two different points of view, they support commonalties: functions to describe, query, and update the database; high-level interfaces that are easy to use and offer machine-independent features; and a better understanding of the static and dynamic properties of the data. A database management system (DBMS), the software subsystem managing databases, must offer data description and manipulation facilities (query and update facilities), high-level interfaces to data independent of the machine data structures, and a set of design tools that provides a good understanding of the modeled enterprise (the real-world computerized application of interest).

In this chapter, we clarify the main objectives of a DBMS, some of them already achieved by current market products. (In research prototypes, new objectives, not described in this chapter, have been added.) This chapter also presents the main concepts underlying the database approach. Then the ANSI/X3/SPARC reference model for the architecture of a DBMS is introduced. It was an important step for DBMS technology development, which clarified the data mappings and functions that may be included in a DBMS. We conclude with a brief overview of relational system architectures. Since there is no standardized

65

relational architecture, we propose a classification of relational DBMSs in two categories.

3.2 Objectives of a DBMS

The main objectives of DBMSs may be summarized as follows:

- Separation of data description and data manipulation.
- Logical data independence.
- Physical data independence.
- Procedural and nonprocedural interfaces.
- Efficient processing of database operations.
- Easy data administration and control.
- Minimal redundancy and minimal storage space.
- Data integrity.
- Data sharing.
- Data security.

Detailed descriptions of similar objectives may be found in [Cardenas79, Date81].

3.2.1 Separation of Data Description and Data Manipulation

The central idea behind databases is probably the separation between data description and manipulation. Assuming a set of objects, two points of view can typically be considered:

1. The set may be represented by its extension. It is seen as elements that may be deleted, inserted, or modified. Thus set elements may be manipulated using operations.
2. The set may be represented by its intention. It is seen as a whole that characterizes a given collection of objects. Thus an object may be described in terms of object type. A type is characterized by the common properties shared by the objects in the corresponding set. Those properties may include operations applicable to the set elements.

Considering object descriptions and object manipulations separately provides a better understanding of objects and more flexibility to query and update them. A DBMS usually offers two different sets of commands: one to describe objects, another to manipulate objects.

A simple example of these approaches to describing objects may be given using a set of integers $\{0, 1, \ldots, N, \ldots\}$. A given integer object I is described using a type INTEGER and is manipulated using specific operations such as INCREASE, DECREASE. The abstraction that maps an object to the corresponding type is called a *classification*. Thus, a set of integers $I_1, I_2, \ldots, I_n$ may be classified as a collection corresponding to the type of integer. The classification process is illustrated by a graph in Fig. 3.1, where an arc, *c*, represents a classification.

To facilitate data classification, the database approach distinguishes clearly between data description and data manipulation. Thus all objects must be precisely described before being inserted, modified, and finally deleted from the database. The advantages of separating description and manipulation are:

1. Controlling object types and structures when operations are performed.
2. Retrieving from the database object type and structure information.
3. Dealing with sets of objects in a similar way, particularly for query and update requirements.

In addition, such a separation enables the system to achieve a high degree of data independence.

3.2.2 Logical Data Independence

Data items describe atomic events in the real world. For example, the data item $10,000 may correspond to a salary or a price. John DOE is a name. Makes is an action. In the real world, data items are aggregated together to describe events, objects, or facts. The abstraction that concatenates data items (and more generally objects) together is called an *aggregation*. The fact that John DOE makes $10,000 may be illustrated by the aggregation graph of Fig. 3.2, where *a* designates an aggregation arc. Facts and objects resulting from the aggregation of real data items are meaningful independently of the existence of any computer.

Often data item groups may be distinguished in two types: entities and relationships. Intuitively, an *entity* corresponds to a noun or a noun group. A *relationship* represents a verb or a verbal group. For example, in the sentence "John DOE makes $10,000," we can see the two entities, "John DOE" and "salary,"

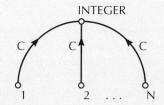

FIGURE 3.1 Classification graph

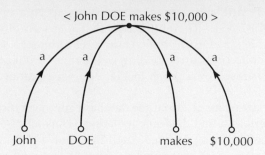

FIGURE 3.2 Aggregation graph

and one relationship, "make." Different people may see different entities and relationships; however, an entity always represents a real-world object, event, or person, and a relationship indicates an association between two or more entities [Chen76]. Both entities and relationships are described by specific data items corresponding to adjectives or complements in natural language sentences. Such properties of entities and relationships are called *attributes*.

The set of sentences

Drinkers drink wines in certain quantities at given dates.
A drinker has a name, an address, and a type.
A wine is characterized by a vineyard, a vintage, and a percentage of alcohol.

may be seen as defining different sets of entities, relationships, and attributes. It is convenient to assume that a common agreement among all participants is possible to define and represent entities and relationships (this may imply certain drinking habits). This agreement is in some sense a canonical view of the situation at the logical level. For the example, a canonical view could be defined as follows:

Entity set = {DRINKER, WINE}.
Relationship set = {DRINK}.
Attribute set = {NAME, ADDRESS, TYPE, VINEYARD, VINTAGE, PERCENT, DATE, QUANTITY}.

To display entities, relationships, and attributes, an appropriate graphical representation has been introduced [Chen76]. A rectangle depicts an entity; a diamond depicts a relationship; and a circle depicts an attribute. Relationships are connected to the participating entities. Attributes are linked to the entities and relationships they characterize. Fig. 3.3 shows the entity-relationship diagram corresponding to the canonical view derived from the sentences.

If we admit the existence of a canonical view derived from a set of sentences, generally each specific group of users handles only part of the situation

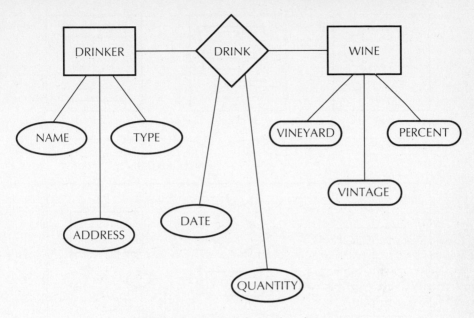

FIGURE 3.3 Entity-relationship diagram

and therefore has its own specific view. The canonical view may be seen as the integration and the synthesis of several particular views (Fig. 3.4). Consequently each user group that implements an application on a database may be able to see a subset of the database and to arrange the data as desired — for example, to describe entities and relationships of particular interest for the group. Each end user may be able to concentrate on the relevant objects and events while not being distracted by other considerations.

To illustrate the objective with file records, let us consider a set of records formated as follows:

    DRINKER (D#, NAME, ADDRESS, TYPE)
    WINE (W#, VINEYARD, VINTAGE, PERCENT)
    DRINK (W#, D#, DATE, QUANTITY)

It is indeed the record type representation of the canonical view derived from the given set of sentences. An end user interested only in drinker excesses would like to see only the record type:

    DRINKER_ EXCESS (D#, NAME, ADDRESS, QUANTITY, DATE)

while another would like to see only wines

    WINE (VINTAGE, VINEYARD, PERCENT).

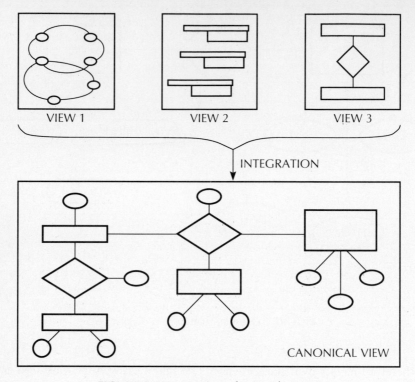

FIGURE 3.4 Integration of particular views

Consequently it appears to be desirable for the DBMS to support a high degree of independence between the canonical view description of the database and the particular descriptions corresponding to the user views. The advantages of this type of independence, often called *logical independence,* are that the end user groups will be able to see the data they want to see, in the desired formats, and an end user database view will be able to evolve without changing the canonical view and the other end user database views, at least to a certain extent. The addition of new attributes, entities, and relationships to the database canonical view or to specific end user views is possible without having to modify the application programs that manipulate the database.

3.2.3 Physical Data Independence

Databases are stored on external storage media, in general magnetic disks. Because of the relative slowness of disk I/Os, DBMSs are I/O bounded. Thus the physical data organization on disks must be driven by the goal of I/O efficiency. Due to the large volume of CPU and memory operations needed to retrieve data,

DBMSs are also CPU bounded. Thus physical data organizations must also be driven by the goal of CPU efficiency. It follows that the choices at the physical organization level are internal to the computer world and must achieve both I/O and CPU efficiency. To achieve this objective, the physical structure must be independent of the logical organizations of data seen in the previous section. A physical data structure is defined by aggregations of data items arranged in records stored in files, with specific access paths (such as indexing and hashing methods to access the files) and specific data format (such as fields with length or records with arrays of pointers to fields). One important objective of a DBMS is to realize the independence between physical and logical data structures [Date71, Stonebraker74].

The advantages of this type of independence can be seen by considering the drawbacks of no independence, implying that the physical data structure must be the direct image of the canonical view. Therefore performance improvements would imply changing the canonical view — that is, the end user's common view of the data. This is not desirable for several reasons, among them avoiding conflicts between end users and computer specialists, saving reprograming, and avoiding problems of DBMS optimization. We must be able to change the physical data organization without changing the logical one, and vice-versa.

3.2.4 Procedural and Nonprocedural Interfaces

In general, two kinds of users manipulate the database: the interactive end users and the programmers. The interactive end user must be able to query and update the database. These users are not database professionals and require languages easy to learn. Such data manipulation languages may be formal (such as first-order logic-based languages) or informal (such as menu-driven languages). In either case, they should allow the user to specify the set of data he or she wants to retrieve or update in a declarative way without specifying the procedures to access the data. Such languages are called *nonprocedural*. A large set of nonprocedural languages must be offered by a DBMS, including menu-driven, two-dimensional, and graphics languages. The upper limit for such languages is natural language.

The programmers writing programs using classical languages or more recent ones must also be able to access databases. Special commands must be included in the program to get data from the database or to put data into it. Such commands may be nonprocedural or procedural, but they should deliver one record at a time for processing by sequential program. Thus it is important that the DBMS supplies appropriate programming facilities to retrieve and update data. If the programmer needs to specify the order of the procedures used to access the database inside a command, the interface is said to be procedural. Whether procedural interfaces are desirable is a subject of controversy.

3.2.5 Efficient Processing of Database Operations

Computer performance is a key issue in data processing. High-level nonprocedural languages imply significant savings in terms of system development time and cost, at the expense of higher processing overhead. This overhead has two origins. I/O overhead is a fundamental factor. Systems remain limited by their disk I/O bandwidth [Dewitt86]. Therefore a DBMS must optimize the disk accesses carefully. The way current DBMSs actually solve that problem is often by using large cache memories ("buying" the I/O bottleneck) and decreasing the multiprogramming level so that most data accesses are done in main memory. On the other hand, modern DBMSs offer large facilities to process data (e.g., sorting). Thus DBMSs appear to be CPU bounded. It is therefore necessary to optimize the CPU activity for processing database operations in main memory.

3.2.6 Easy Data Administration

A DBMS must supply powerful tools for data description. These tools must provide good control over the various data descriptions, including the logical and physical descriptions. In the late 1960s, it was thought that data description should be done in a centralized way by a unique group of people in order to guarantee the consistency of the database descriptions. Now database design facilities are supplied so that anyone with appropriate rights may use them to describe data. The main concern becomes the consistency of the various data descriptions. Also to guarantee application evolution, data descriptions must be easy to change and easy to retrieve. A new trend is to include facilities to describe not only the static aspects but also the dynamic aspects of objects [Bancilhon88]. Easier data administration requires user-friendly tools to help in the definition of the data structures and the operation of these structures.

3.2.7 Minimal Redundancy and Minimal Storage Space

In classical file-based applications, each user owns his or her specific files. This leads to a large amount of data redundancy and wasted storage space. The main problem of data redundancy is the additional cost of maintaining the duplicates. For example, data entry must be performed several times. Also duplicates may diverge if different processes update them concurrently. Thus blind copy processing is wasteful. This observation led to the introduction of centralized database administration in order to avoid data redundancy.

In the late 1970s, distributed database technology [Ceri84] demonstrated that multiple copies of data may be useful for both efficiency and reliability. However, it is desirable for the end users that data redundancy be known and automatically controlled by the DBMS to avoid giving several identical update commands, one for each copy. Now redundancy is widely accepted but under the assumption that the DBMS maintains this redundancy. Redundancy is a matter of optimization. In general, the number of copies must remain at a minimum for storage and update costs; however, several copies are desirable to increase query processing performance in a multiprocessor or distributed system.

3.2.8 Data Integrity

Even when data redundancy is avoided, the database must satisfy specific semantics assertions, called *integrity constraints,* either at the data item level (for example, a salary must be an integer between 100 and 10,000) or at any data set level (for example, the drinker number in the DRINK file must appear in the DRINKER table). To avoid introducing incorrect data, the DBMS must be able to control data correctness when data are inserted or updated. Among the rules that may be used are data types, logical links between data, and known redundancy. Controlling such rules is neither obvious nor efficient. It is important to avoid database alteration in the presence of erroneous updates. Such updates should be rejected to guarantee database semantics consistency.

3.2.9 Data Sharing

A database is a common set of data shared by different and concurrent users. Each user must be given the illusion that he or she is working alone with the database. In other words, no interference between concurrent programs should arise. The DBMS must prevent or correct such interferences. For example, in an airline reservation system, an airplane seat must be assigned to one and only one passenger, even if two clerks are trying to get it concurrently. The order in which the passengers are served is not important because concurrency means that they try to get their boarding passes at the same time. Thus a DBMS must guarantee that whenever two updating programs run concurrently, the result is the same as the one obtained by running in a sequential manner.

3.2.10 Data Security

This objective is twofold. First, the physical integrity of the database must be guaranteed in case of system failure, where only the main memory content is lost, and media failure, where part of the database on disks is lost. A good DBMS must be able to recover after both cases of failure, with a consistent and up-to-date database. Second, the database must be protected against unauthorized and even malicious updates. Appropriate techniques must be supplied to grant and deny access rights and to control them.

3.3 Basic Concepts and Methods

3.3.1 Data Description

Basic Concepts
A data description consists of formally representing sets of objects, with their common properties, which may include operations on these objects. Therefore a data description is a collection of program-independent formal definitions of object structures and properties — that is, a collection of *object type* specifications.

> **Definition 3.1 Object type**
> Set of objects having similar properties and behaviors, described in an intentional way.

For example, the object type POSITIVE INTEGER can be defined as a sequence of objects denoted $\{0,1,2, \ldots, N, \ldots, +\infty\}$ with the operations SUCC(x), PLUS(x,y), MULT(x,y), MINUS(x,y), . . . The object type WINE can be defined as an aggregation of atomic object types W#, VINEYARD, VINTAGE, PERCENT_OF_ALCOHOL with the generic operations CREATE, DESTROY, MODIFY, and RETRIEVE.

An object type is a set of objects, some of which may exist at a given time in the database. A specific object is called an *instance* (or *occurrence*) of an object.

> **Definition 3.2 Object instance**
> Specific element of an object type.

For example, integer 10 and wine $<100,\text{Volnay},1978,11.1>$ are object instances.

Data description is therefore expressed at the type level. One way to describe a data type is to use mathematical definitions, as for the real numbers. Abstract data-type specifications is another way. *Data models* are used as structural forms of specifications by database specialists; from these models are derived the tools used to implement the objects in an actual system.

> **Definition 3.3 Data model**
> Set of concepts with associated composition rules used to specify the structure of a database.

While theorists often use logic to understand a data model, most practitioners use a graphical representation that allows the user to visualize the object types and the links between these types. Because a data model is a set of concepts, it is necessary to design a language to support these concepts. Such a language is understood by the DBMS. It is called a *data description language*.

Definition 3.4 Data description language
Specification language allowing the user to describe a database using
a specific data model in a way understandable by the DBMS.

Using a data description language to describe a given set of data — for example, to model an enterprise — leads to a complete specification of the enterprise's data types in the given language. Such a specification is called a *schema*.

Definition 3.5 Schema
Description of a specific set of data corresponding to a model of an
enterprise (or part of it) obtained by using a particular data description
language.

The schema defined in the data description language is generally called the *source
schema*. A source schema is given to the DBMS, which compiles it into an internal form called a *compiled schema*. A compiled schema is directly used by the
DBMS to retrieve and verify the properties of object instances when they are
inserted in or extracted from the database.

Levels of Data Description
To ensure a high degree of logical and physical data independence, the ANSI/
X3/SPARC study group on DBMSs [ANSI78] proposed to distinguish three levels of data description. Although, for performance reasons, the three levels are
not implemented in most current relational DBMSs, the distinction among these
levels is important to understand the DBMS functionalities.

The central level is the *conceptual schema*.

Definition 3.6 Conceptual schema
A representation-independent description of the database corresponding to a global canonical view of the modeled enterprise.

The conceptual schema describes the syntax and semantics of the data types that
exist in the enterprise. It is a canonical integration of the particular views of each
working group. In a sense, it may be considered the universal view of the world.
A possible data model for describing a conceptual schema may be the entity-
relationship model [Chen76]. A conceptual schema in this model consists of specifying (1) a set of real-world entities, (2) the set of relationships between these
real-world entities, (3) the set of attributes belonging to these entities and relationships, and (4) specific properties of entities, relationships, and attributes, such
as the minimum and maximum number of entity instances participating in one
relationship (cardinalities).

A conceptual schema should satisfy a given set of desirable properties such
as the molecularity of entities (an entity should represent a minimum object of the

real world), the molecularity of relationships (a relationship should correspond to a unique association between two or more entities), and the absence of redundancy among the various elements. Such properties guarantee that the conceptual schema is a stable platform corresponding to a global and largely accepted description of the enterprise. To illustrate a conceptual schema, let us assume a database modeling a wine production cooperative. The conceptual entities are DRINKER, WINE, and PRODUCER. DRINK and HARVEST are the relationships. Fig. 3.5 depicts the conceptual schema corresponding to this enterprise. (It should be clear that the entity-relationship model is used only for illustrative purposes. We do not claim that the entity-relationship data model is the best conceptual model; however, it is a possible choice.)

Going to the end user level, the program's own perspective may require combining data from several parts of the conceptual schema. Also each programming language or style may require a specific data model. Moreover, to ensure logical data independence, any change in the conceptual schema must not imply changes in the program view, and vice-versa. Thus another level of schema is

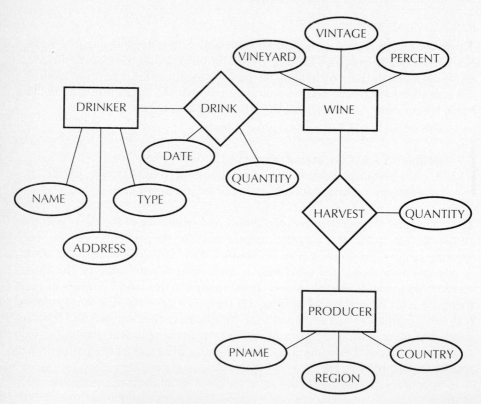

FIGURE 3.5 Example of a conceptual schema

needed to describe data in the way that applications and users see it. This is the role of the *external schema*.

> **Definition 3.7 External schema**
> A description of a part of the database corresponding to a program or a user view of the modeled enterprise.

An external schema is often a particular view of a set of objects pertinent to a given user or group of users; consequently it is also called a *user view* or simply a view. The external model is often dependent on the programming language used to develop database applications. Fig. 3.6 portrays two external schemas for the database whose conceptual schema was given in Fig. 3.5. One schema is specified using a tabular model; the other is given using Pascal-like records. It is interesting to notice that the notion of external schema provides a partial solution to the objective of data security; more precisely, it provides a tool to control access to the database. A user may access only the part of the database described in its external schema. Thus the complement of the external schema (the data not described in it) is protected against unauthorized access from the users referencing the database through this external schema.

At the physical layer, a database must be stored on disks. This requires a description of the storage structures, including the files (if files are used), the record formats, the field definitions, the indexes and hashing schemes, and any other physical characteristics of the database's physical implementation. This implementation-oriented description composes the *internal schema*.

> **Definition 3.8 Internal schema**
> A representation-dependent description of the database corresponding to a precise specification of the storage structures and access methods used to store data in secondary memory.

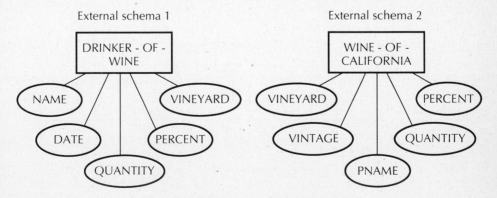

FIGURE 3.6 Two external schemas

Thus, for a given database, there exists a unique internal schema. The internal model used to define this schema is DBMS dependent. An illustration of such a model for the COOPERATIVE database is given in Fig. 3.7. Arrows represent pointers or indices.

3.3.2 Data Mapping

Because three levels of schema may exist to describe a specific database, a DBMS must theoretically support the three levels and any correspondence between those three levels. For example, a DBMS must be able to implement an external data type in terms of internal types. The procedures that translate data types from one level to another are called *data mappings*.

> **Definition 3.9 Data mapping**
> Function that transforms a set of data instances corresponding to a given schema in a set of instances corresponding to another schema.

In a DBMS with three levels of schemas, it is possible to concentrate on two levels of data mapping. First, the internal-to-conceptual mapping transforms objects (often records) stored in the actual database into logical objects corresponding to the conceptual view of the enterprise; the conceptual-to-internal mapping performs the reverse transformation. Second, the conceptual-to-external mapping transforms objects in conceptual format into user objects required by and designed for a specific application. The reverse mapping translates a user object into a conceptual one. An illustration is given in Fig. 3.8.

To map data from one form to another, a DBMS requires the specification of both schemas and also the specification of the correspondence between the two schemas. A data mapping can be seen as a function going from one data type to another. The full specification of this function requires the definition of *mapping rules*.

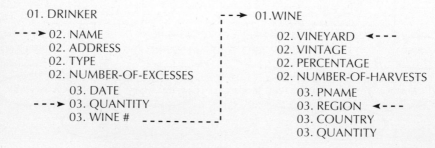

FIGURE 3.7 Illustration of an internal schema

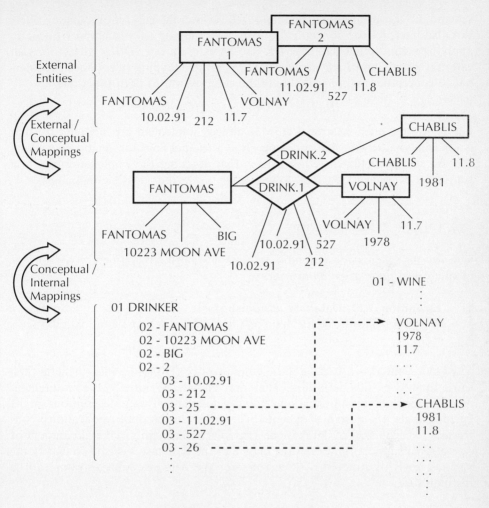

FIGURE 3.8 Examples of mapping

Definition 3.10 Mapping rules
Set of declarations that specifies a data mapping from one schema to another.

In a system implementing the three levels of schemas, we could find a set of rules specifying the internal-conceptual data mapping and, for each external schema, a set of rules specifying the conceptual-external mapping. Most relational DBMSs perform directly the internal to external mapping. Formally we may interpret the internal to conceptual mapping as a function $IC_{IS,CS,IRU}$ applying an internal database DB_{IS} to a conceptual one DB_{CS}, where IS is an internal schema, *CS* a conceptual schema, and *IRU* an internal level set of mapping rules. We also interpret the conceptual-to-external mapping as a function $CE_{CS,ES,ERU}$ applying a conceptual database DB_{CS} to an external one, DB_{ES}, where *ES* is an external schema and *ERU* an external level set of mapping rules. Then the internal to conceptual mapping is simply the composition of both functions:

$$IE_{IS,ES,RU} = CE_{CS,ES,ERU} (IC_{IS,CS,IRU})$$

For efficiency, most relational DBMSs directly implement the mapping *IE*, that is, the internal-to-external mapping. It is then possible to see the conceptual schema as a particular external schema that describes the whole enterprise in a somewhat canonical view. Fig. 3.9 portrays the various possible mappings.

3.3.3 Data Administration

The various schemas describing a database are normally defined by a group of people called *database administrators*.

> **Definition 3.11 Database administrator**
> A person responsible for defining the database schema and mapping rules.

In practice, the tasks of a database administrator (DBA) are more general than those implied by this definition. They may include [Weldon79] the requirement analysis for database applications, the development of data descriptions at the various levels, the design of specific procedures for database applications, controlling the evolution of database descriptions and contents, a certain amount of operational support, and even the choice of the database system. To clarify the various levels of functions, three roles for the database administrator can be distinguished:

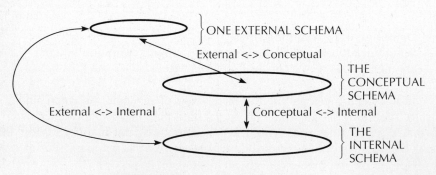

FIGURE 3.9 Possible data mappings

As *system administrator,* responsible for the machine-oriented functions.

As *enterprise administrator,* responsible for defining the enterprise data organization and the view of the data required for its operations.

As *application administrator,* in charge of the support of user views of data and related tools.

These three roles are often performed by the same group of persons. A key role is that of the enterprise administrator; he or she defines the global semantics contents of the database. Such a person is assisted by formal methodologies and tools.

The different schemas and mapping rules are useful for the DBMS to perform data mapping and for the users to get acquainted with the data descriptions. Thus they are stored in the *data dictionary* and generally explained there.

Definition 3.12 Data dictionary
Database containing the set of schemas and mapping rules corresponding to a database, with human-readable explanations.

The data dictionary is generally a database that may be queried and updated by the DBMS. It is often called a *metabase*, although this term is usually restricted to the database's formal descriptions (the various schemas and data mapping functions). A metabase is a database containing the description of the user's database.

3.4 ANSI/X3/SPARC Three-Schema Architecture

In the late 1970s, the ANSI/X3/SPARC study group on databases proposed a general architecture for database management systems [ANSI78]. Although this architecture was not standardized, it is a model that provides a basis for understanding DBMS functionalities. The keystone of this architecture is the conceptual schema, an explicit description of the enterprise information modeled in the database. It portrays the entities, relationships, and properties of interest to the enterprise and constitutes a stable platform to map the external schemas, which describe the data as seen by the programmers, onto the internal one, which describes the data as seen by the system. Consequently the ANSI/X3/SPARC study group proposed a three-level organization of three levels of data administration tasks and three levels of data manipulation functions. The architecture is divided in two parts and organized around the data dictionary: the data description part and the data manipulation part. Each part is composed of three essential modules, called *processors* in the ANSI terminology. Only functions are specified, not their implementation. Thus the ANSI architecture is functional. It is globally represented in Fig. 3.10.

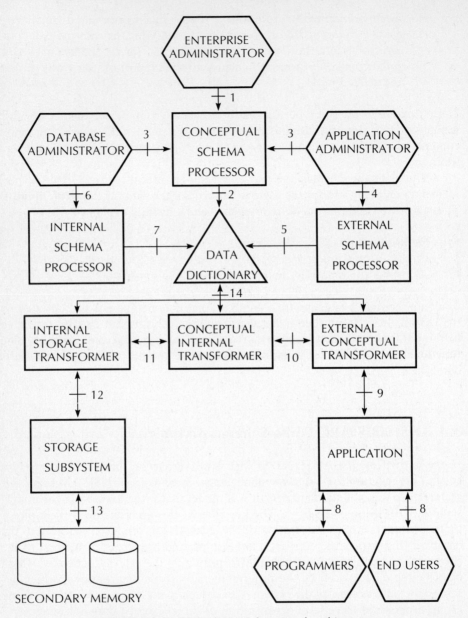

FIGURE 3.10 ANSI/X3/SPARC functional architecture

Let us first introduce the data description part. A hexagon represents a DBA's role, and a box represents a processor. The *enterprise administrator's* role is to define the conceptual schema using interface 1. The conceptual schema is then compiled by the conceptual schema processor. If it is correct, it is stored in the data dictionary, which contains all schemas and mapping rules. The *application administrators* are in charge of defining the external schemas. They use specific external schema description languages (interface 2), according to the user's needs and the system capabilities. To specify the mapping rules between an external schema and the conceptual schema, the *application administrators* may consult the conceptual schema using interface 3. When an external schema with the associated mapping rules is correctly defined, it is compiled by the external schema processor and stored in the data dictionary. Finally, the *system administrators* complete a database description by defining the database's internal schema and the rules mapping it to the conceptual schema. They use an internal description language (interface 6) to give the internal schema and mapping rules for compilation by the internal schema processor. System administrators may ask the DBMS for an edited version of the conceptual schema using interface 3. The correctly compiled internal schema is stored in the data dictionary using interface 7.

The various interfaces corresponding to the data description that appear in Fig. 3.10 are mostly data description languages (DDL) of various levels, in various formats. More precisely, they are the following:

- The *conceptual data description language source format* is used to define the conceptual schema by the enterprise administrator.
- The *conceptual data description language compiled format* is the internal form of the previous DDL. It allows the conceptual schema processor to store the internal form of the conceptual schema in the data dictionary.
- The *conceptual data description languages report format* enables database administrators to consult the conceptual schema.
- The *external data description languages source formats* are used by the application administrators to define the external schemas and the external-conceptual mapping rules. One such DDL exists for each external model supported by the DBMS.
- The *external data description languages compiled formats* are the compiled forms of the previous ones, used by the external schema processor to store internal forms of external schemas in the data dictionary.
- The *internal description language source format* allows the system DBA to describe the internal schema and the associated mapping rules.
- The *internal data description language compiled format* is the compiled form of the previous one, used by the internal schema processor to store the internal form of the internal schema in the data dictionary.

Let us now move on to the data manipulation part. User requests to the DBMS are either embedded in application programs or directly introduced at a keyboard by an end user. After correct parsing, they are received by an *external-conceptual transformer* (interface 9). There may be several such processors, at most one for each external data model. They perform the external-to-conceptual data mapping. Consequently such a processor transforms an external request referencing an external schema into a conceptual one. In the reverse direction, it transforms conceptual records into external ones. To perform this mapping, the external-conceptual transformer gets the conceptual and external schemas (including the mapping rules) in the data dictionary (interface 14). The next processor is the *conceptual-internal transformer,* which receives conceptual requests from the previous processors. The conceptual-external transformer maps conceptual requests into internal ones. It also transforms internal records into conceptual ones. It gets the necessary schemas (the internal and conceptual schemas) and the mapping rules in the data dictionary (interface 14). At the bottom, the *internal-storage transformer* receives internal requests and performs them using the storage subsystem. It also puts/gets internal records into/from physical pages. This processor is often implemented using the highest modules of the file system. Any mapping can be performed at compile time. Indeed for predefined queries used repeatedly, the external-conceptual-internal mappings are generally performed once; the internal compiled query is saved for subsequent use to avoid repeating work.

The various interfaces corresponding to data manipulations that appear in Fig. 3.10 are mostly data manipulation languages (DML) of various levels, in various formats. More precisely, the following interfaces are given:

● The *external data manipulation languages source formats* allow the application programmers or the end users to interact with the database in procedural and nonprocedural languages.
● The *external data manipulation languages compiled formats* are the internal versions of the previous ones.
● The *conceptual data manipulation language compiled format* is a unique language produced by the external-conceptual transformers to update and retrieve conceptual objects.
● The *internal data manipulation language compiled formats* is used to manipulate internal objects.
● The *storage subsystem language compiled format* is the set of primitives used to store objects in pages and to retrieve them.
● The *secondary storage interface* allows the system to read and write pages on disks.
● The *data dictionary access interface* allows the various processors to retrieve schemas or part of them from the data dictionary.

The ANSI/X3/SPARC framework presents, at least in theory, several advantages. It allows a global and complete description of the database semantics at the conceptual level. It permits full control over storage, record placement, and use of indexes and access paths at the internal level. External schemas are user oriented and facilitate the development of applications. Moreover, the ANSI/X3/SPARC architecture achieves the physical and logical data independence objectives. However, not many relational DBMSs follow this framework. The main reason is probably performance. It is more efficient to map data and commands directly from the internal to the external levels, and vice-versa, than to go through the conceptual level. Also the ANSI/X3/SPARC architecture clearly separates data description and manipulation, thus leading to a certain lack of flexibility, which may be a disadvantage for certain evolving applications. Finally, the three-level schema architecture is useful for database design and thus used in most design methodologies.

3.5 Relational DBMS Architectures

3.5.1 Distinctive Features of Relational Architectures

Relational DBMSs support more or less the relational model. Apparently there is no reason for them to follow special architectural requirements. In 1979, an ANSI/X3/SPARC group, RDBTG (Relational Data Base Task Group), began its effort to standardize relational databases. Its final report [ANSI81] emphasized the need for standards in concepts and interfaces but deemphasized the architectural issues. Thus today the relational language SQL is standardized, but each relational system has its own architecture.

In the realm of relational system architectures, two types of architectures may be clearly separated [Schmidt83]. Both classes are built around a relational kernel that manages the internal level of the DBMS. This internal level generally stores relations as flat files and offers various file organizations, such as B-trees and hashing. There is no agreement on which interface better supports the relational model at the internal level. Both a network interface such as NDL [ANSI84] and SQL [ANSI85] could be considered as possible candidates, although SQL seems more natural. Other types of interfaces might be more suitable for efficiency and generality purposes.

3.5.2 The Separate Architecture

This class of system separates the data description and data manipulation interfaces (Fig. 3.11). Systems of this class are NOMAD and SUPRA. They offer a set of utilities to manage the data dictionary and to define the schemas. Query and update languages are separated from these sets of utilities. Such systems often support an architecture with three levels of schemas, close to the ANSI/X3/SPARC architecture. They also include facilities to integrate existing files

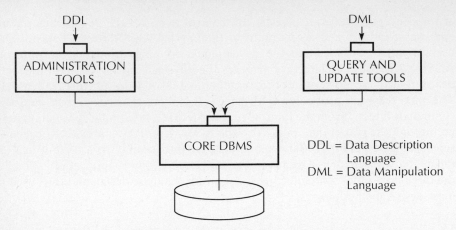

FIGURE 3.11 The separate architecture

into the database. These mapping tools allow the system to transform existing files in conceptual tables. A drawback of these systems is probably a lack of flexibility for the end users who serve also as database administrators as they have two languages to learn and to move explicitly from one to the other.

3.5.3 The Uniform Architecture

This class of system integrates the data description and data manipulation interfaces (Fig. 3.12). Example systems are DB2, INGRES, and SABRINA. They offer a uniform set of commands to manage the data dictionary, to define the schemas, and to query and update the databases. These systems often support

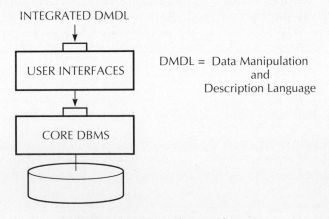

FIGURE 3.12 The uniform architecture

an architecture with two levels of schemas, performing direct mapping from the external level to the internal one. The conceptual schema may always be implemented at the external level as a global external view, but this is not required. A drawback of these systems is that they lack facilities to integrate heterogeneous files. They are more homogeneous and generally more relational than the separate architecture systems.

3.5.4 Steps toward DBMS Architecture Normalization

A report of the ANSI/X3/SPARC Database Architecture Framework Task Group (DAFTG) [ANSI-DAFTG85] proposes a reference model for relational and nonrelational DBMSs. The proposed architecture encompasses the old ANSI/SPARC DBMS framework presented above and includes a core DBMS (the Data Mapping Control System, DMCS) around which various data management tools are offered. This architecture is a generalization of the uniform architecture introduced above to nonrelational systems. It identifies clearly two interfaces: the DL and the i-DL (Fig. 3.13).

The data language interface is the integrated data description and manipulation language for the DMCS data model. All data definitions, retrievals, and manipulations are provided by the DL interface. The i-DL is the interface with the operating system (OS). Data management tools are software components that communicate with the DMCS through the DL interface. These tools provide data

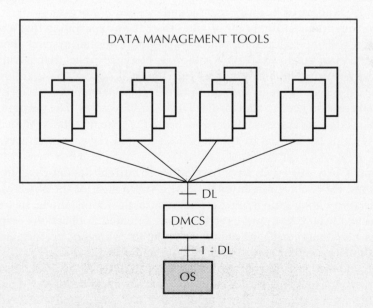

FIGURE 3.13 The core DBMS and its environment

interfaces oriented toward more specific applications than the DL interface. Examples include high-level query languages, graphics systems, report writers, database design tools, application generators, and integrated data dictionary management help facilities.

The main functions of the core DBMS are:

- Creating, referencing, and deleting an object.
- Transforming objects between external, conceptual, and internal forms.
- DL processing.
- Integrity, authorization, and concurrency control.
- Physical access and performance optimization.

Thus the DMCS supports all essential DBMS functions.

3.6 Conclusion

In this chapter, we have studied the objectives and examined the different architectures of DBMSs. We also introduced the main concepts of the database approach. The objectives have not yet been achieved; however, the recent development of relational DBMS products has greatly improved the situation. There are great expectations that database technology will keep its promises. The contributions of the relational model, compared to traditional DBMSs, are mainly a higher degree of data independence, better nonprocedural interfaces, easier data administration, and better understanding of integrity and redundancy requirements.

From an architectural point of view, there is no expectation that a standard architecture will be developed for relational (or nonrelational) systems. The ANSI/X3/SPARC three-level architecture is more a reference model than a truly operational architecture. Not many successful relational systems have followed this guideline. Also some systems support both the relational and the network models. Actually there is no need to standardize DBMS architectures. The purpose of standardization is to guarantee user independence to the system vendors. With database technology, this is achieved by the standardization of the user interfaces, such as SQL.

Finally, new objectives have been added to current database technology for two reasons. First, current relational DBMSs fulfill most of the objectives. Thus researchers are willing to do more. Second, nonclassical applications, such as office automation, CAD/CAM, and expert system – oriented applications, express the need for better data sharing, modeling, and usability with good performance. Thus future DBMSs should be able to support more complex data types, such as graphs, long text, and pictures. They should also support inference facilities, allowing the user to query not only the database but also data instances deduced from the database using inference rules. They could also have an extensible architecture [Carey85].

3.7 References and Bibliography

[ANSI78] ANSI/X3/SPARC Study Group, Data Management Systems, *Framework Report on Database Management Systems,* AFIPS Press, 1978. Also in Information Systems, V3, N3, 1978.

[ANSI81] ANSI/X3/SPARC DBS-SG, "Final Report of the Relational Database Task Group," ACM SIGMOD Record, V12, N4, 1982, pp. 1 – 62.

[ANSI84] ANSI X3H2 (Database), Database Language NDL, ANSI dpANS X3.133-198x, ISO DP 8907, August 1984, ANS Institute, New York.

[ANSI85] ANSI X3H2 (Database), Database Language SQL, ANSI dpANS X3.xxx-198x, March 1985, ANS Institute, New York.

[ANSI-DAFTG85] ANSI/X3/SPARC Database System Study Group, Database Architecture Framework Task Group (DAFTG), "Reference Model for DBMS Standardization," ACM SIGMOD Record, V15, N1, March 1986, pp. 19 – 58.

[Bancilhon88] Bancilhon F., "Object-Oriented Database Systems," ACM Symposium on Principles of Database Systems, Austin, Texas, 1988.

[Cardenas79] Cardenas A. F., *Data Base Management Systems,* Allyn and Bacon, 1979.

[Carey85] Carey M. J., DeWitt D. J., "Extensible Database Systems," Islamorada Workshop, 1985, in *On Knowledge Base Management Systems,* Springer-Verlag ed., 1986.

[Ceri84] Ceri S., Pelagatti G., *Distributed Databases: Principles and Systems,* McGraw-Hill, 1984.

[Chen76] Chen P. P., "The Entity-Relationship Model — Toward a Unified View of Data," Transactions on Database Systems, V1, N1, March 1976, pp. 9 – 36.

[Date71] Date C. J., Hopewell P., "File Definition and Logical Data Independence," ACM SIGFIDET Workshop on Data Description, Access and Control, 1971.

[Date81] Date C. J., *An Introduction to Database Systems,* 3rd ed., Addison-Wesley, 1981.

[DeWitt86] DeWitt D., Gerber R., "GAMMA: A High Performance Dataflow Database Machine," VLDB Conference, Tokyo, August 1986.

[Schmidt83] Schmidt J. W., Brodie M. L., eds., *Relational Database Systems: Analysis and Comparison,* Springer-Verlag, 1983.

[Stonebraker74] Stonebraker M. R., "A Functional View of Data Independence," ACM SIGMOD Workshop on Data Description, Access and Control, May 1974.

[Weldon79] Weldon J. L., "The Practice of Data Base Administration," National Computer Conference, AFIPS Proc., V48, 1979, pp. 709 – 12.

4

THE RELATIONAL MODEL

4.1 Introduction: Objectives of the Model

The relational model was introduced by E. F. Codd [Codd70], although a design of a set-oriented model had already been propounded [Childs68]. Codd's model is used by many DBMSs. Even nonrelational systems are often described, for commercial purposes, as supporting relational features. Thus the relational model has overreached its objectives.

The model's first objectives were specified [Codd70] as follows:

- To allow a high degree of data independence. The application programs must not be affected by modifications to the internal data representation, particularly by the changes of file organizations, record orderings, and access paths.
- To provide substantial grounds for dealing with data semantics, consistency, and redundancy problems.

These two objectives were not achieved by the network and hierarchical models; they have been by the relational model, mainly because of the simplicity of the relational views presenting the data in two-dimensional tables and the application of the normalization theory to database design. In addition to these two objectives, the relational model has achieved a third aim:

- To enable the expansion of set-oriented data manipulation languages.

This has been achieved by the use of relational algebra, which manipulates tables simply and formally in the same way as arithmetical operators manipulate integers, and by nonprocedural languages based on logical queries specifying the data one wishes to obtain without having to explain how to obtain them.

Finally, the relational model will probably attain a fourth objective, which had not been initially anticipated: to become an extensible model that can describe and manipulate simple and complex data. This objective is the essence of current developments concerning extended relational models [Codd79, Stonebraker84, Zaniolo83] and of some work on deductive databases and on object orientation in relational databases (see Chapters 10 and 11).

In this chapter, we first present the basic structural concepts of the relational model for modeling data in two-dimensional tables. Then we introduce integrity rules. We provide a detailed description of relational algebra, an indispensable tool for manipulating relations. A large range of extensions to this algebra is also set out. Next we give a summary of the principles of a nonprocedural language, illustrating it essentially by SQL, which is currently being normalized [ISO86]. Finally we develop a logical model for relational languages and databases to demonstrate that the essence of relational databases is indeed logic. To conclude, we introduce the wide range of ways to enrich the relational model.

4.2 Data Structures of the Model

4.2.1 Domain, Attribute, and Relation

The relational model is based on three fundamental concepts derived from set theory. The first helps to define the original sets of data values used to model data. These sets are called *domains*.

Definition 4.1 Domain
Set of values specified by a name.

Like sets, domains can be defined extensionally by enumerating the constituent values, or intensionally by defining a distinctive property of the domain's values. As an example, the wine color domain could be defined extensionally as WINE-COLOR = {ROSE, WHITE, RED}. It is possible to define intensionally the well-known domains INTEGER, REAL, and BOOLEAN.

The Cartesian product of a set of domains $D1,D2, \ldots ,Dn$ is the set of tuples $[V1,V2, \ldots ,Vn]$, $V1$ being a value of $D1,V2$ a value of $D2, \ldots ,Vn$ a value of Dn. For example, the Cartesian product of the domains WINE-COLOR = {ROSE, WHITE, RED} and VINEYARD = {VOLNAY, SANCERRE, TOKAY} is composed of nine tuples, as shown in Fig. 4.1.

Let us now introduce the principal definition in the relational model, that of *relation*.

COLOR-WINE	VINEYARD
ROSE	VOLNAY
ROSE	SANCERRE
ROSE	TOKAY
WHITE	VOLNAY
WHITE	SANCERRE
WHITE	TOKAY
RED	VOLNAY
RED	SANCERRE
RED	TOKAY

FIGURE 4.1 Example of Cartesian product

Definition 4.2 Relation
Subset of the Cartesian product of a list of domains characterized by a name.

Being a subset of a Cartesian product, a relation is composed of tuples. The convenient display for a relation is a two-dimensional table. Each line corresponds to a tuple and each column to a domain of the Cartesian product being considered. The same domain can appear several times. For example, from the WINE-COLOR and VINEYARD domains, it is possible to establish the COLOR-VINE-YARD relation (Fig. 4.2).

In order to distinguish between the columns and to disregard their classification order while enabling the existence of several columns for a domain, a name must be associated with each column. This refers to the *attribute* concept.

Definition 4.3 Attribute
Column of a relation designated by a name.

The name associated with an attribute is meaningful. It often differs from that of the domain, which may be seen as the attribute medium. Therefore in the example we are using, the first column of the COLOR-VINEYARD relation could be called COLOR and the second VINEYARD.

COLOR-VINEYARD	COLOR-WINE	VINEYARD
	RED	VOLNAY
	ROSE	SANCERRE
	WHITE	SANCERRE
	WHITE	TOKAY

FIGURE 4.2 A first relation example

The relation concept is well known in mathematics. An *n*-ary relation is a set of tuples. A particular case often used is the binary relation, which is a set of ordered pairs. An *n*-ary relation is frequently displayed by an *n*-dimensional diagram in which the coordinates correspond to the participating domains. Fig. 4.3 is an illustration of a statistical relation of attributes AGE and SALARY; this relation gives mean salary by age. In mathematics, a relation is often portrayed by a graph, as also illustrated in Fig. 4.3.

Another mathematical interpretation of a relation consists of defining each tuple as a function: $t:Ai \rightarrow Di$ for $i \in \{1,2, \ldots ,n\}$. This function applies the attributes to the domains. Therefore a relation can be considered as a finite set of functions. This set varies with time.

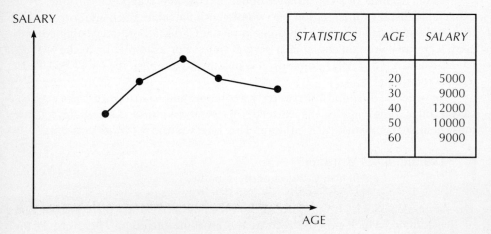

STATISTICS	AGE	SALARY
	20	5000
	30	9000
	40	12000
	50	10000
	60	9000

FIGURE 4.3 Possible representations of a relation

4.2.2 Extension and Intension of a Relation

The relational model enables one to manipulate data values that change over time. Relations change with time because tuples are added, modified, or deleted during the database lifetime. Nevertheless the structure of a relation described in terms of relation name, domains, and attributes is invariant for a given relation. This invariant structure is defined in the *relation schema*.

> **Definition 4.4 Relation schema**
> Name of the relation followed by the list of its attributes with their associated domains.

A relation schema is generally written as R ($A1:D1,A2:D2, \ldots , Ai:Di, \ldots , An:Dn$), where R is the name of the relation, Ai the attribute names, and Di the associated domain names. As examples, two relation schemas are given in Fig. 4.4: the COLOR-VINEYARD relation and the WINE relation in which the wines are characterized by number, vineyard, vintage, and percentage (of alcohol). The domains used are integers, reals, and character strings of variable length. Generally when the relation schema is defined, the domains are implicit and derive from the attribute's name; they are therefore not specified. They can be specified later as integrity constraints giving the domain intensions.

The schema of a relation represents its *intension,* that is, the properties (or at least some of them) the tuples have in common and those that are invariant over time. A table represents the *extension* of a relation (as shown in Fig. 4.2), that is, the display of the tuples it contains at a given moment.

COLOR-VINEYARD	COLOR-WINE: CHAR	VINEYARD: CHAR

WINE	W# : INTEGER	VINEYARD: CHAR	VINTAGE: INTEGER	PERCENT: REAL

FIGURE 4.4 COLOR-VINEYARD and WINE relations

4.3 Minimum Integrity Rules

Integrity rules are assertions that the data contained in the database must satisfy. It is possible to distinguish between structural rules, which are inherent in the data model, and the behavioral rules proper to a particular application. The relational model enforces a structural rule that is the uniqueness of key. It is convenient and usual to add two other types of structural rules: the referential and entity constraints. These three types of integrity constraints (key, referential, and entity) constitute the minimum integrity rules that should be supported by any relational DBMS.

4.3.1 Uniqueness of Key

A relation is by definition a set of tuples. Because a set has no duplicate elements, the same tuple cannot exist twice in a relation. To identify the relation's tuples without giving all the attribute values and efficiently check the absence of duplicate tuples in a relation, the concept of *key* is used.

> **Definition 4.5 Key**
> Minimal set of attributes whose values identify a unique tuple in a relation.

More formally, a key of a relation R is a set of attributes K such that:

- For any tuple $t1$ and $t2$ of any instance of R, $t1 (K) \neq t2 (K)$.
- There does not exist any proper subset of K having the previous property.

For convenience, a set of attributes containing a key is called a *superkey* [Ullman82].

Each relation has at least one key. The knowledge of all the attribute values composing this key identifies a unique tuple in the relation. When several keys exist, they are called *candidate keys*. One is generally chosen arbitrarily and called the *primary key*; the others are called *alternative keys*. For example, W# could be the primary key of the WINE relation, {VINEYARD, VINTAGE} being an alternative key.

The concept of key characterizes a relation's intension, that is, all possible extensions. Two tuples having the same key value cannot exist in any relation's extension. The choice of a key must result from a semantic study of the relation, that is, of all possible extensions and not only of a particular one.

4.3.2 Referential Constraints

The relational model is often used to represent real-life entities that are objects with their own existence and relationships existing between these objects

[Chen76]. Entities often correspond to nouns, and relationships model verbs. There are different ways of representing entities and relationships as relations. In a simple representation, an entity occurrence corresponds to a tuple in a relation; such a tuple is composed of a key that is the entity key; the entity properties are expressed as tuple attributes. A relationship type is generally modeled by a relation whose attributes represent the keys of the participating entities, as well as the relationship's own properties. For example, let us consider the entities DRINKER and WINE. The key of the DRINKER entity type is the drinker identifier D#; that of the WINE entity type is the wine number W#. Two entity occurrences, DRINKER and WINE, can then be associated through a relationship representing a wine drinker's consumption at a given date, in a given quantity. Consumptions would be modeled by the DRINK relation whose attributes would be the keys of the participating entities D# and W#, as well as the attributes characterizing this relationship — for example, the consumption DATE and the QUANTITY drunk. To identify a unique tuple in the DRINK relation, one needs the attributes D#, W#, and DATE because we assume that a drinker can drink the same wine at different dates; thus {D#,W#,DATE} is the key of the DRINK relation. In general, the key of a relation representing a relationship includes the keys of the participating entities. Modeling this situation leads to the construction of a relational database schema as shown in Fig. 4.5.

The structural integrity rule called *referential constraint* [Date81] is justified by the use of the relational model for representing entities and relationships.

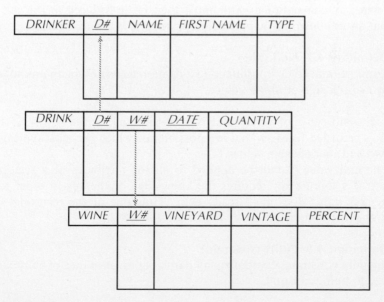

FIGURE 4.5 Example of a database representing entities and relationships

> **Definition 4.6 Referential constraint**
> Integrity constraint applied to a relation $R1$ asserting that the value of
> a set of attributes in $R1$ must be equal to a key value in a relation $R2$.

The set of attributes in $R1$ is called a *foreign key*. Such an integrity constraint is generally applied to relationships. A relationship can exist only if the participating entity instances are already recorded in the corresponding relations. Note that in the definition, $R1$ and $R2$ are not necessarily distinct; the constraint can be applied to two tuples of the same relation. Except when the relationship is functional, a foreign key in a relation $R1$ is a part of $R1$'s key because relationship keys include the keys of the participating entities.

Referential constraints can be defined by specifying the foreign keys. For example, because a foreign key in a relation is a set of attributes appearing as a key in another (or the same) relation, the relation DRINK(D#,W#,DATE,QUANTITY) may have D# and W# for foreign keys, respectively, to DRINKER and WINE. Note that the relation's key is (D#,W#,DATE); thus, foreign keys are part of the key in this example.

4.3.3 Null Values

When inserting tuples in a relation, frequently an attribute is unknown or inapplicable. For example, the quantity of wine absorbed by a drinker at a certain date can be unknown. If a wine has no vintage, the vintage attribute cannot be applied to the wine. A conventional value must then be introduced in the relation to represent an unknown or inapplicable attribute; it is the *null value*.

> **Definition 4.7 Null value**
> Conventional value introduced in a relation to represent an unknown
> or inapplicable attribute value.

The exact significance of a null value is often ambiguous; the ANSI/X3/SPARC group has recorded fourteen that are possible, of which the most typical are the unknown and inapplicable values.

The null value cannot be applied to all the attributes of a relation. The existence of a unique key requires the knowledge of the key in order to verify that this key value does not already exist. Thus one of the relational model's structural constraints is the *entity constraint* [Date85].

> **Definition 4.8 Entity constraint**
> Integrity constraint compelling all participating attributes of a primary
> key to being not null.

If it is not specified otherwise by a domain definition constraint, the relational model does not compel foreign keys not belonging to a primary key to be not null. This can enable some flexibility in the model (for example the recording of employees who are not attached to any department) [Date81].

4.3.4 Summary of Descriptive Concepts

In summary, the relational model supports the following data description concepts:

- Domains, often defined in intension as specific integrity rules.
- Relations, created by end users or database administrators.
- Attributes, names given to relation column.
- Relation schemas, which encompass the relation, attribute, and domain in a unique definition.
- Relation keys, which determine tuple user visible identifiers.
- Referential integrity constraints, which link relations together to model entities and relationships.
- Null values and entity constraints, which allow end users to record limited amounts of unknown information.

This is a simple set of concepts that is easy to use for describing the data of large applications. This set may be extended with more general integrity constraints, called nonprocedural integrity constraints, expressed as assertions of logic.

4.4 Relational Algebra and Its Extensions

Relational algebra was invented by E. F. Codd [Codd72] as a collection of formal operations acting on relations and producing relations as results. This algebra, which is the elementary manipulating component associated with the relational model, is one of the main strengths of the model. Codd initially introduced eight operations, some of which can be built from the others. First, we shall introduce six operations called basic operations. We then present a few more operations useful in particular cases. Other authors have introduced different operations that can be derived from the presented ones [Delobel83, Maier83].

4.4.1 Basic Operations

Basic operations can be classified in two groups: the traditional set operations (a relation is a set and can be manipulated like one) and the relation-oriented operations. The set operations are binary operations; from two relations, they build a third relation. These operations are the union, the difference, and the Cartesian product. The relational operations are the project and restrict unary operations and the join binary operation.

Union

The *union* is the classical operation of set theory adapted to relations having the same attributes, that is, relations that are union compatible.

> **Definition 4.9 Union**
> Operation building, from two relations RELATION1(A1,A2, . . . ,An) and RELATION2(A1,A2, . . . ,An), a third relation RELATION3 (A1,A2, . . . ,An) such that a tuple *t* ε RELATION3 if *t* ε RELATION1 or *t* ε RELATION2.

Several notations have been introduced by different authors for this operation:

RELATION1 ∪ RELATION2
UNION (RELATION1,RELATION2)
OR (RELATION1,RELATION2)
APPEND (RELATION1,RELATION2)

The graphical notation (Fig. 4.6) is also used.
The union of the relations WINE1 and WINE2 is represented in Fig. 4.7.

Difference

The *difference* is also a classical operation of the set theory adapted to relations that are union compatible, that is, having identical attributes.

> **Definition 4.10 Difference**
> Operation building, a relation RELATION3(A1,A2 . . . ,An) from two relations RELATION1(A1,A2, . . . ,An) and RELATION2(A1,A2, . . . , An), such that a tuple *t* ε RELATION3 if *t* ε RELATION1 and *t* ∉ RELATION2.

The difference is a noncommutative operator; the operant relation order is important. Several notations have been introduced for the difference:

RELATION1 − RELATION2
DIFFERENCE (RELATION1,RELATION2)

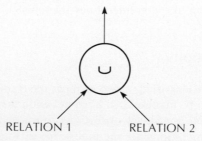

RELATION 1   RELATION 2

FIGURE 4.6 Graphical representation of a union

WINE 1	W #	VINEYARD	VINTAGE	PERCENT
	100	VOLNAY	1978	12.5
	110	CHABLIS	1979	12.0
	120	SANCERRE	1980	12.5
	130	TOKAY	1980	12.5

WINE 2	W #	VINEYARD	VINTAGE	PERCENT
	130	TOKAY	1980	12.5
	140	CHENAS	1981	12.7
	150	VOLNAY	1978	12.5

WINE	W #	VINEYARD	VINTAGE	PERCENT
	100	VOLNAY	1978	12.5
	110	CHABLIS	1979	12.0
	120	SANCERRE	1980	12.5
	130	TOKAY	1980	12.5
	140	CHENAS	1981	12.7
	150	VOLNAY	1978	12.5

FIGURE 4.7 A union example

REMOVE (RELATION1,RELATION2)
MINUS (RELATION1,RELATION2)

The graphical notation (Fig. 4.8) is also used. The difference of the relation WINE1 − WINE2 is represented in Fig. 4.9.

Cartesian Product

The *Cartesian product* is the previously described set operation (see Section 4.2.1) adapted to relations. For this operation, the involved relations may have different schemas.

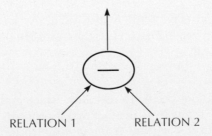

RELATION 1   RELATION 2

FIGURE 4.8 Graphical representation of a difference

WINE 1	W #	VINEYARD	VINTAGE	PERCENT
	100	VOLNAY	1978	12.5
	110	CHABLIS	1979	12.0
	120	SANCERRE	1980	12.5
	130	TOKAY	1980	12.5

—

WINE 2	W #	VINEYARD	VINTAGE	PERCENT
	130	TOKAY	1980	12.5
	140	CHENAS	1981	12.7
	150	VOLNAY	1978	12.5

↓

WINE	W #	VINEYARD	VINTAGE	PERCENT
	100	VOLNAY	1978	12.5
	110	CHABLIS	1979	12.0
	120	SANCERRE	1980	12.5

FIGURE 4.9 Example of a difference

Definition 4.11 Cartesian product
Operation building a relation RELATION3($A1,A2, \ldots An,B1,B2, \ldots,$ Bm) from two relations RELATION1($A1,A2, \ldots ,An$) and RELATION2($B1,B2, \ldots , Bm$) such that RELATION3 tuples are all the possible combinations of tuples of the two operant relations in the given order (if $t \in$ RELATION1 and $t2 \in$ RELATION2 then $t = t1,t2$ $\in$ RELATION3).

Possible notations for this operation are:

RELATION1 × RELATION2
PRODUCT (RELATION1,RELATION2)
TIMES (RELATION1,RELATION2)

The graphical notation (Fig. 4.10) is also used. As an example, the relation VINEYARD-YEAR, given in Fig. 4.11, is the Cartesian product of two relations, VINEYARD and YEAR.

Projection
Projection is an operation specific to relations, which erases certain attributes in the relation. Its name results from the fact that it proceeds from an n-ary relation to a p-ary relation with $p < n$, thus from an n-dimensional space to a restricted p-dimensional space.

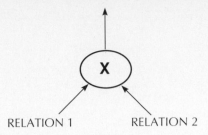

FIGURE 4.10 Graphical representation of Cartesian product

Definition 4.12 Projection
Operation building, from a relation RELATION1 a second relation RELATION2 by removing from RELATION1 all attributes (column) that are not mentioned (as projection parameters) and by keeping only one occurrence of tuples appearing several times.

Duplicate tuples are eliminated by projections for the result to be relation, that is, a set without duplicate elements. The following notations are used for this operation, where Attribute i, Attribute j, . . . , Attribute m designate the projection's attributes:

$\pi_{\text{Attribute } i, \text{ Attribute } j, \ldots, \text{ Attribute } m}$ (RELATION1)
RELATION1[Attribute i, Attribute j, . . . , Attribute m]
PROJECT (RELATION1, Attribute i, Attribute j, . . . , Attribute m)

VINEYARD	VINEYARD	AREA	COUNTRY
	Chenas	Beaujolais	France
	Volnay	Bourgogne	France
	Chanturgues	Auvergne	France

X

YEAR	VINTAGE	QUALITYY
	1979	Good
	1980	Average

VINEYARD YEAR	VINEYARD	AREA	COUNTRY	VINTAGE	QUALITY
	Chenas	Beaujolais	France	1979	Good
	Chenas	Beaujolais	France	1980	Average
	Volnay	Bourgogne	France	1979	Good
	Volnay	Bourgogne	France	1980	Average
	Chanturgues	Auvergne	France	1979	Good
	Chanturgues	Auvergne	France	1980	Average

FIGURE 4.11 Example of a Cartesian product

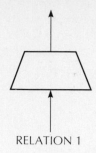

RELATION 1

FIGURE 4.12 Graphical representation of a projection

The graphical notation (Fig. 4.12) is also used. Fig. 4.13 gives an example of a projection of the WINE relation on attributes VINTAGE and QUALITY.

Restriction

The *restriction* is another specific unary operation, creating a new relation by removing tuples from the operant relation. It corresponds to the classical operation of selecting records in a file. It is often called selection, although we shall reserve this term for a combination of projection and restriction. The definition of the restriction requires the expression of conditions, which we shall see later.

> **Definition 4.13 Restriction**
> Operation building from a relation RELATION1(A1,A2, . . . , An) a second relation RELATION2(A1,A2, . . . , An) such that a tuple t ε RELATION2 if t ε RELATION1 and t satisfies a condition (condition(t) = true) given as an operation parameter.

Conditions are expressed in the form < Attribute> < Operator> < Value>, where the operator is a comparison operator chosen within the set

WINE	W #	VINEYARD	VINTAGE	PERCENT	QUALITY
	100	VOLNAY	1979	12.7	GOOD
	110	CHABLIS	1980	11.8	AVERAGE
	120	TOKAY	1981	12.1	EXCELLENT
	130	CHENAS	1979	12.0	GOOD
	140	VOLNAY	1980	11.9	AVERAGE

YEAR	VINTAGE	QUALITY
	1979	GOOD
	1980	AVERAGE
	1981	EXCELLENT

FIGURE 4.13 Example of a projection

$\{=,<,<=,>=,>,\neq\}$. Such conditions are called *elementary conditions*. It is possible to include Boolean expression (AND,OR,NOT) of elementary conditions. We shall not insist on such complex conditions in the context of relational algebra, as they can be obtained with union and intersection operations. For example, VINEYARD = "Chablis" is a condition; PERCENT = "12" is another condition.

The following notations are used for the restriction:

$\sigma_{\text{Condition}}$(RELATION1)
RELATION1 [Condition]
RESTRICT (RELATION1, Condition)

as well as the graphical notation shown in Fig. 4.14. Fig. 4.15 represents the restriction of a relation WINE by the QUALITY = "GOOD" condition.

Join
The *join* operation is one of the essential operations of relational algebra. It is a binary operation that allows the user to compose two relations in a generalized way. The join is one of the most difficult operations to implement efficiently in relational DBMS.

> **Definition 4.14 Natural join**
> Operation consisting of combining the tuples of two relations RELATION1($A1, \ldots, An,X$) and RELATION2($X,B1, \ldots, Bm$) having a common set of attributes X so as to build a third relation RELATION3($A1, \ldots An,X,B1, \ldots ,Bm$) such that any tuple resulting from the composition of a tuple of RELATION1 and a tuple of RELATION2 on equal values of the X attributes belongs to RELATION3 (if $t1 \in$ RELATION1 and $t2 \in$ RELATION2 and $t1.X = t2.X$,then $t = t1.A1, \ldots ,t1.An,t1.X,t2.B1, \ldots ,t2.Bm \in$ RELATION3).

Thus, the natural join of two relations builds a third relation containing all the compositions of tuples of the initial relations satisfying the equality condition on

RELATION 1

FIGURE 4.14 Graphical representation of the restriction

WINE	W #	VINEYARD	VINTAGE	PERCENT	QUALITY
	100	VOLNAY	1979	12.7	GOOD
	110	CHABLIS	1982	11.8	AVERAGE
	120	TOKAY	1982	12.1	EXCELLENT
	130	CHENAS	1979	12.0	GOOD
	140	VOLNAY	1980	11.9	AVERAGE

↓ QUALITY = "GOOD"

GOOD WINE	W #	VINEYARD	VINTAGE	PERCENT	QUALITY
	100	VOLNAY	1979	12.7	GOOD
	130	CHENAS	1979	12.0	GOOD

FIGURE 4.15 Example of a restriction

attributes of same names. The natural join may be generalized to the theta join, where a more general condition, of the form <Attribute 1> <Operator> <Attribute 2> is specified, where Attribute 1 comes from RELATION1 and Attribute 2 from RELATION2. In the case of theta join, all attributes of both relations are kept in the result relation, while only one occurrence of attributes of same names is kept in the case of natural join.

According to the type of operator, a difference can be made between the *equi-join,* when the operator is =, and the *inequi-join,* when the operator is chosen among $\{<, <=, >=, >, \neq\}$. It is possible to define the theta-join as a restriction of the Cartesian product of two relations with a special condition of the form <Attribute 1> <Operator> <Attribute 2>.

Definition 4.15 Theta join
Restriction of the Cartesian product of two relations RELATION1 X RELATION2 by a condition of the form <Attribute 1> <Operator> <Attribute 2>, where <Attribute 1> belongs to RELATION1 and <Attribute 2> to RELATION2.

The join operation is written as follows, the condition being simply omitted when it is a natural join (it is then the equality of attributes of the same name):

RELATION1 ⋈ RELATION2
Condition
JOIN (RELATION1,RELATION2, Condition)

Fig. 4.16 gives the graphical representation of the join operation. Fig. 4.17 is an illustration of this operation by executing the natural join of two relations WINE and LOCALIZATION, as well as the theta join of these two relations according to the condition QUALITY > AVERAGE-QUALITY (assuming a natural order among the qualities, we obtain the relation QUALSUP).

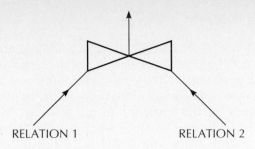

RELATION 1   RELATION 2

FIGURE 4.16 Graphical representation of the join

Wine	W #	Vineyard	Vintage	Quality
	100	Chenas	1977	Good
	200	Chenas	1980	Excellent
	300	Chablis	1977	Good
	400	Chablis	1978	Bad
	500	Volnay	1980	Average

⋈

Localization	Vineyard	Region	Average Quality
	Chenas	Beaujolais	Good
	Chablis	Bourgogne	Average
	Chablis	Californie	Bad

Wine ⋈ Localization	W #	Vineyard	Vintage	Quality	Region	Average Quality
	100	Chenas	1977	Good	Beaujolais	Good
	200	Chenas	1980	Excellent	Beaujolais	Good
	300	Chablis	1977	Good	Bourgogne	Average
	300	Chablis	1977	Good	Californie	Bad
	400	Chablis	1978	Bad	Bourgogne	Average
	400	Chablis	1978	Bad	Californie	Bad

Qualsup	W #	Vineyard	Vintage	Quality	Vineyard	Region	Average Quality
	100	Chenas	1977	Good	Chablis	Bourgogne	Average
	100	Chenas	1977	Good	Chablis	Californie	Bad
	200	Chenas	1980	Excellent	Chenas	Beaujolais	Good
	200	Chenas	1980	Excellent	Chablis	Bourgogne	Average
	200	Chenas	1980	Excellent	Chablis	Californie	Bad
	300	Chablis	1977	Good	Chablis	Bourgogne	Average
	300	Chablis	1977	Good	Chablis	Californie	Bad
	500	Volnay	1980	Average	Chablis	Californie	Bad

FIGURE 4.17 Join examples

The join may not be considered a basic operation of relational algebra. As stated in the above definition, by extending the definition of the restriction so that multiattribute conditions of the type <Attribute 1> <Operator> <Attribute 2> may be taken into consideration, the join may be obtained by the Cartesian product followed by the restriction of the described result: JOIN (RELATION1, RELATION2, Cond.) = RESTRICT (RELATION1 × RELATION2, Cond.). The importance of the join makes preferable to consider it as a basic operation.

4.4.2 Additional Operations

The operations described in this section are occasionally used to manipulate relations. They are not basic to the relational algebra operations because they can be derived from the combination of the preceding operations. Their expression in terms of basic operations may require the manipulation of constant relations whose tuples are built with given constants. Examples of constant relations are the Cartesian product of a given list of domains and the relation containing a unique null tuple (with null for all attribute values).

Intersection

The *intersection* is the classical operation of set theory adapted to relations having the same set of attributes. Thus intersection is possible only with union-compatible relations.

> **Definition 4.16 Intersection**
> Operation building a relation RELATION3($A1,A2, \ldots, An$) from two relations RELATION1($A1,A2, \ldots, An$) and RELATION2($A1,A2, \ldots, An$) such that a tuple $t \in$ RELATION3 if $t \in$ RELATION1 and $t \in$ RELATION2.

Several notations are used by different authors for this operation:

RELATION1 ∩ RELATION2
INTERSECT (RELATION1,RELATION2)
AND (RELATION1,RELATION2)

The graphical notation (Fig. 4.18) is also used.

Given the basic operations, the intersection is a redundant operation since it is possible to establish the intersection by using the difference according to the formulas:

RELATION1 ∩ RELATION2 = RELATION1 − (RELATION1 − RELATION2)

RELATION1 ∩ RELATION2 = RELATION2 − (RELATION2 − RELATION1)

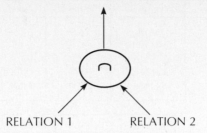

FIGURE 4.18 Graphical representation of the intersection

Division

The *division* enables one to identify, in a relation D, the subtuples that are completed by all the tuples of another relation d. This offers in a simple way the answers to questions such as "find y such that, whatever be $x \epsilon d$, $<y,x> \epsilon D$."

> **Definition 4.17 Division**
> Operation that builds the quotient of relation $D(A1,A2, \ldots , Ap,Ap+1, \ldots , An)$ by relation $d(Ap+1, \ldots , An)$ as the relation $Q(A1,A2, \ldots , Ap)$ such that every tuple of Q concatenated with every tuple of d gives a tuple of $D(t_Q \epsilon Q$ if for every $t_d \epsilon d$ there is a tuple $t_D \epsilon D$ with $t_Q,t_d = t_D)$.

Let us denote ai a value of the attribute Ai; a tuple is a sequence of values $<a1,a2,a3, \ldots >$. The quotient of D by d may be defined by:

$$Q = \{<a1,a2, \ldots , ap > \mid \text{for each} <ap+1, \ldots , an > \epsilon d \text{ there is} \\ <al,a2, \ldots , ap, ap+1, \ldots ,an > \epsilon D\}.$$

The notations used for the division are: $D \div d$ and DIVISION (D,d), as well as the graphical representation (Fig. 4.19). An example of a division is shown in Fig. 4.20.

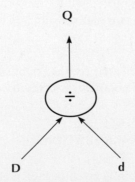

FIGURE 4.19 Graphical representation of the division

WINE	VINEYARD	VINTAGE	QUALITY
	CHABLIS	1977	GOOD
	CHABLIS	1978	BAD
	VOLNAY	1977	GOOD
	VOLNAY	1978	GOOD
	SAUMUR	1978	GOOD

÷

GOOD	VINTAGE	QUALITY
	1977	GOOD
	1978	GOOD

VINEYARD	VINEYARD
	VOLNAY

FIGURE 4.20 Example of a division

The division can be obtained from the difference, the Cartesian product and the projection, as follows: $D \div d = R1 - R2$, where $R1 = \pi_{A1,A2,\ldots,Ap}^{(D)}$ and $R2 = \pi_{A1,A2,\ldots,Ap}((R 1 \times d) - D)$.

External Join
The joins described above lose the tuples of at least one relation when the joined relations do not have identical projections on the join attributes. To retain all the information of both relations, it is desirable to define an extended join, which keeps the tuples having no corresponding values in both relations [Codd79] associated with null values. This is the *external join*.

Definition 4.18 External join
Operation that generates a relation RELATION3 from two relations, RELATION1 and RELATION2, as the join of these two relations, augmented with the tuples of RELATION1 and RELATION2 that are not contained in the join, completed with null values for the missing attributes.

This operation is useful in particular for the establishment of external views without loss of information. The notation generally used is:

RELATION 1 ⋈ RELATION2
EXT-JOIN (RELATION1,RELATION2)

An example of an external join is given in Fig. 4.21.

STOCK	VINEYARD	VINTAGE	AREA
	VOLNAY	1979	BOURGOGNE
	VOLNAY	1980	BOURGOGNE
	MEDOC	1980	BORDEAUX
	TOAKY	1981	ALSACE
	CHANTURGUES	1980	AUVERGNE

⋈

ESTIMATION	AREA	APPRECIATION
	BOURGOGNE	GOOD
	BORDEAUX	GOOD
	BEAUJOLAIS	AVERAGE

↓

EXT-JOIN	VINEYARD	VINTAGE	AREA	APPRECIATION
	VOLNAY	1979	BOURGOGNE	GOOD
	VOLNAY	1980	BOURGOGNE	GOOD
	MEDOC	1980	BORDEAUX	GOOD
	TOKAY	1981	ALSACE	--
	CHANTURGUES	1980	AUVERGNE	--
	--	--	BEAUJOLAIS	AVERAGE

FIGURE 4.21 Example of an external join

Semijoin

In some cases when a join is executed, it is not suitable to keep in the result all the attributes of the resulting relations; only the attributes of one of the two relations may be maintained. A specific operation, *semijoin,* is useful for query optimization [Bernstein81].

> **Definition 4.19 Semijoin**
> Operation building from two relations, RELATION1 and RELATION2, a relation RELATION3 having same attributes as RELATION1 and containing the tuples of RELATION1 joining with at least one tuple of RELATION2.

Possible notations for the semijoin of the relation RELATION1 by the relation RELATION2 are:

RELATION1 ⋉ RELATION2
SEMI-JOIN (RELATION 1,RELATION 2)

This is equivalent to the join of the relations RELATION1 and RELATION2 followed by the projection of the result on the attributes of the relation RELA-

TION1: RELATION 1 $\bowtie$ RELATION 2 $=$ $\pi_{\text{RELATION 1}}$(RELATION 1 $\bowtie$ RELATION 2). It can also be described as a restriction of the relation RELA-TION1 by the values of the joining attributes of the RELATION2. Fig. 4.22 illustrates the semijoin operation.

4.4.3 Nonalgebraic Operations

Other operations have been proposed to manipulate relations. The following ones do not belong to relational algebra, although they may be useful to express certain types of queries. These operations are not essential to the relational model, although aggregate operations are possible with most relational systems.

Complement
The *complement* finds the tuples that do not belong to a relation. If certain domains are infinite, the complement generates infinite relations. To avoid any problems, we assume in this chapter that the domains are finite.

Definition 4.20 Complement
Relation containing all tuples that belong to the Cartesian product of the attribute domains of a relation and that do not belong to this relation.

STOCK	VINEYARD	VINTAGE	AREA
	VOLNAY	1979	BOURGOGNE
	VOLNAY	1980	BOURGOGNE
	MEDOC	1980	BORDEAUX
	TOKAY	1981	ALSACE
	CHANTURGUES	1980	AUVERGNE

$\bowtie$

ESTIMATION	AREA	APPRECIATION
	BOURGOGNE	GOOD
	BORDEAUX	GOOD
	BEAUJOLAIS	AVERAGE

SEMI-JOIN	VINEYARD	VINTAGE	AREA
	VOLNAY	1979	BOURGOGNE
	VOLNAY	1980	BOURGOGNE
	MEDOC	1980	BORDEAUX

FIGURE 4.22 Example of a semijoin

The complement of a relation RELATION1 may be denoted as follows:

RELATION1
NOT (RELATION1)
COMP (RELATION1)

This operation is not often used because it generates tuples that are not in the base and that are generally large in number. If the notation $X \{Di \in R\}$ is adopted for the Cartesian product of the domains of R, the complement of a relation, RELATION1, is obtained by using the difference as follows: NOT (RELATION1) = $X \{Di \in$ RELATION1$\}$ — RELATION1. Fig. 4.23 illustrates the application of this operation in a simple case.

Split

The *split* [Fagin80] is an operation that does not really belong to relational algebra because it gives, from a relation, two relations as a result; however, it may be useful for extracting tuples from a relation.

> **Definition 4.21 Split**
> Operation that builds, from a relation RELATION1 and a condition, two relations, one containing the tuples of RELATION1 that satisfy the condition and the other those that do not.

Applied to the relation RELATION1, this operator generates two relations, $R1$ and $R2$, which would be obtained by restriction, as follows:

$R1$ = RESTRICT (RELATION1, Condition)
$R2$ = RESTRICT (RELATION1, NOT Condition)

Aggregate Functions

Aggregate operations are set-oriented operations that first partition a relation into subsets according to an attribute (or a group of attributes) value, then perform a function computation on each subset, and finally build a result relation composed of one tuple for each subset. Each result tuple contains the partition attribute value(s) with the computed function value. Thus an aggregate computation requires a function that applies to a set of values. Such functions are the average (AVG), maximum (MAX), minimum (MIN), count (COUNT), and sum (SUM) functions (among others). Let *AGG* be a generic function.

> **Definition 4.22 Aggregate**
> Function $AGG(R;X;B)$ where AGG is a set function symbol, R a relation, X a set of attributes of relation R and B an attribute of relation R, whose result is a relation $S(X, AGG\_B)$ composed of one tuple t for each distinct value v of X in R such that $t = \; <v, AGG \{x \mid R(A=v, B=x)\}>$.

VINEYARD = {CHABLIS, VOLNAY, MEDOC}
COLOR = {RED, ROSE, WHITE}

COLVINEYARD	VINEYARD	COLOR
	CHABLIS	ROSE
	CHABLIS	WHITE
	VOLNAY	RED
	MEDOC	WHITE

NOT (COLVINEYARD)	VINEYARD	COLOR
	CHABLIS	RED
	VOLNAY	ROSE
	VOLNAY	WHITE
	MEDOC	RED
	MEDOC	ROSE

FIGURE 4.23 Example of a complement

Less formally, t gives, for each value of A, the result of applying the aggregate function to the set of B corresponding values. The most used aggregate functions are:

COUNT, to count the number of elements of a set.
SUM, to sum up a set of values.
MIN, to get the minimal value of a set.
MAX, to get the maximum value of a set.
AVG, to compute the average value of a set.

Fig. 4.24 gives examples of aggregate function computations.
Aggregates may be generalized in several ways:

1. The attribute B to which the function is applied may be replaced by an arithmetic expression of the relation attributes. For example, SUM (DRINKER ⋈ DRINK; D#; QUANTITY * PERCENT /100) gives the quantity of alcohol drunk by each drinker.
2. A condition C on the attributes of R may be evaluated before the aggregate computation. The aggregate form would then be $AGG(R; A; B; C)$. For example, SUM (DRINKER ⋈ DRINK; D#; QUANTITY * PERCENT /100; DATE > '01-01-1986') gives the quantity of alcohol drunk by each drinker from 1986.
3. Aggregate functions can be applied after eliminating duplicates in the subsets but also without eliminating duplicates. In this case, a key word such as ALL must be included as an aggregate parameter.
4. Other set-oriented functions can be used.

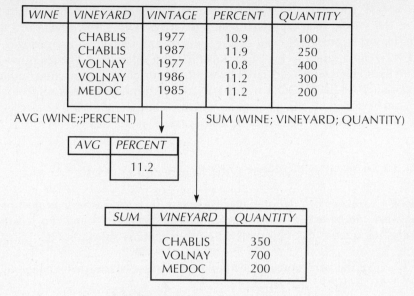

WINE	VINEYARD	VINTAGE	PERCENT	QUANTITY
	CHABLIS	1977	10.9	100
	CHABLIS	1987	11.9	250
	VOLNAY	1977	10.8	400
	VOLNAY	1986	11.2	300
	MEDOC	1985	11.2	200

AVG (WINE;;PERCENT)   SUM (WINE; VINEYARD; QUANTITY)

AVG	PERCENT
	11.2

SUM	VINEYARD	QUANTITY
	CHABLIS	350
	VOLNAY	700
	MEDOC	200

FIGURE 4.24 Examples of aggregates

Aggregates are considered important and useful operations in relational DBMSs.

Transitive Closure

The transitive closure is a special operation that enables one to derive new tuples from a relation and to add them to the relation. It does not belong to relational algebra but to its natural extensions [Merrett84]. It is impossible to perform this operation with a fixed number of relational algebra operations. It can be done by a loop of join/projection/union; the number of operations required depends on the content of the relation. The fact that one cannot define a transitive closure by an expression of constant elementary operations is considered a weakness of relational algebra.

Definition 4.23 Transitive closure
Operation on a relation R having two attributes ($A1$, $A2$) on the same domain that consists of adding to R all the tuples successively deduced by transitivity (if tuples a,b and b,c already exist then a,c is added).

Possible notations for this operation are:

$\tau (R)$
R^+
CLOSE (R)

It allows one, for example, to calculate from a relation PARENTHOOD (PARENT, CHILD) the relation ANCESTRY (ANCESTOR, DESCENDANT), thus establishing the ascendants and descendants of any individual appearing in the PARENTHOOD relation. Fig. 4.25 illustrates this operation. The transitive closure PARENTHOOD is calculated by a succession of join/projection/union of the relation PARENTHOOD with itself until saturation (that is until no new tuples can be added by join/projection/union). This operation will be used extensively in the context of deductive databases (see Chapter 10).

4.4.4 Queries and Updates with Relational Algebra

By using a sequence of relational algebra operations, the answers to most of the queries that can be addressed to a relational database are found. For example, the following queries can be expressed on the database shown in Fig. 4.5.

1. Give the percentage of alcohol of the wines of the 1978 vintage of the MORGON Vineyard:
    $R1$ = RESTRICT (WINE, VINEYARD = "MORGON")
    $R2$ = RESTRICT (WINE, VINTAGE = "1978")
    $R3$ = INTERSECT ($R1$, $R2$)
    RESULT = PROJECT ($R3$, PERCENT)
2. Give the name and first name of **MORGON** or **CHENAS** drinkers:

PARENTHOOD	PARENT	CHILD
	ERIC	LIONEL
	ERIC	FABRICE
	FABRICE	DOMINIQUE
	FABRICE	YVES
	LIONEL	BRIGITTE

ANCESTRY	ASCENDANT	DESCENDANT
	ERIC	LIONEL
	ERIC	FABRICE
	FABRICE	DOMINIQUE
	FABRICE	YVES
	LIONEL	BRIGITTE
	ERIC	DOMINIQUE
	ERIC	YVES
	ERIC	BRIGITTE

FIGURE 4.25 Example of transitive closure

$R1$ = RESTRICT (WINE, VINEYARD = "MORGON")
$R2$ = RESTRICT (WINE, VINEYARD = "CHENAS")
$R3$ = UNION ($R1$, $R2$)
$R4$ = JOIN ($R3$, DRINK)
$R5$ = JOIN ($R4$, DRINKER)
RESULT = PROJECT ($R5$, NAME, FIRSTNAME)

3. Give the name and first name of drinkers having absorbed one day more than 10 glasses of 1976 CHABLIS, as well as the percentage of alcohol of the wine:
$R1$ = RESTRICT (DRINK, QUANTITY > "10")
$R2$ = RESTRICT (WINE, VINEYARD = "CHABLIS")
$R3$ = RESTRICT (WINE, VINTAGE = "1976")
$R4$ = INTERSECT ($R2$, $R3$)
$R5$ = JOIN ($R1$, $R4$)
$R6$ = PROJECT ($R5$, D#, PERCENT)
$R7$ = JOIN ($R6$, DRINKER)
RESULT = PROJECT ($R7$, NAME, FIRSTNAME, PERCENT)

Provided constant relations are accepted, relational algebra allows updating. For example, the wine < 100,TOKAY,1978,13 > is inserted as follows:

R1 = CONSTANT (WINE, < 100,TOKAY,1978,13 >)
WINE = UNION (WINE,R1)

where CONSTANT allows one to define a relation of the same schema as the relation WINE containing the single tuple indicated as argument.

A large range of relational systems offers conversational languages based on relational algebra. These languages are generally extended by procedural possibilities (loop, test, switch, etc.) and by report generation facilities. They are sometimes marketed under the name of fourth-generation languages.

A query expressed in the form of relational algebra operations program can be represented by an algebraic expression, obtained from a sequence of relational operations by eliminating intermediate relations. For example, for the three previous queries, one obtains:

1. Give the percentage of alcohol of the wines of the 1978 vintage of the **MORGON VINEYARD**:
RESULT = PROJECT (INTERSECT (RESTRICT (WINE, VINEYARD = "MORGON"), RESTRICT (WINE, VINTAGE = "1978")),PERCENT)
more formally:
RESULT = π_{PERCENT} ($\sigma_{\text{VINEYARD}="\text{MORGON}"}$(WINE)$_\cap$ $\bowtie$ $_{\text{VINTAGE}="1978"}$(WINE))
2. Give the name and first name of **MORGON** or **CHENAS** drinkers:
RESULT = PROJECT (JOIN (JOIN

(UNION (RESTRICT (WINE, VINEYARD = "MORGON"),
RESTRICT (WINE, VINEYARD = "CHENAS")),
DRINK), DRINKER), NAME, FIRSTNAME)

more formally:

RESULT $= \pi_{NAME,FIRSTNAME}((\sigma_{VINEYARD = "MORGON"}$ (WINE) $\cup$
$\sigma_{VINEYARD = "CHENAS"}$(WINE)) $\bowtie$ DRINK $\bowtie$ DRINKER)

3. Give the name and first name of drinkers having absorbed more than
    10 glasses of 1976 CHABLIS, as well as the percentage of alcohol of
    the wine:

    RESULT = PROJECT (JOIN (PROJECT (JOIN
    (RESTRICT (DRINK, QUANTITY > "10"),
    INTERSECT (RESTRICT (WINE, VINEYARD = "CHABLIS"),
           RESTRICT (WINE, VINTAGE = "1976"))),
    D#, PERCENT), DRINKER), NAME, FIRSTNAME, PERCENT)

    more formally:

    RESULT $= \pi_{NAME,FIRSTNAME,PERCENT}$
    $(\pi_{D\#, PERCENT} (\sigma_{QUANTITY = "10"})$ (DRINK) $\bowtie$
    $(\sigma_{VINEYARD = "CHABLIS"}$ (WINE) $\cap$ $\sigma_{VINTAGE = "1976"}$ (WINE)))
    $\bowtie$ DRINKER)

It is not necessary to wait for the result of an operation before starting the
next operation. To visualize the inherent parallelism of relational algebra expressions, a tree is used. The nodes in the tree are the graphical representations of
the operations described above. The question, "Give the name and first name of
drinkers having absorbed more than 10 glasses of 1976 CHABLIS as well as the
percentage of the wine," may be expressed by the tree shown in Fig. 4.26.

4.5 Nonprocedural Languages

4.5.1 Overview of Relational Languages

The operations that can be expressed directly by end users are generally those of
nonprocedural languages. Several nonprocedural languages, such as SQL
[Chamberlin76, ISO86], QUEL [Stonebraker76, Stonebraker84], and QBE
[Zloof77, Zloof82], allow the manipulation of relational databases. These languages may be seen either as paraphrasing relational algebra or as paraphrasing
well-formed formulas of first-order logic. All use the query search conditions
(generalized conditions) built from first-order predicate logic. The most representative of these languages is SQL, which is currently being normalized. In this
chapter, we give an overview of SQL, the standardized language for relational
databases.

All nonprocedural languages have four basic operations:

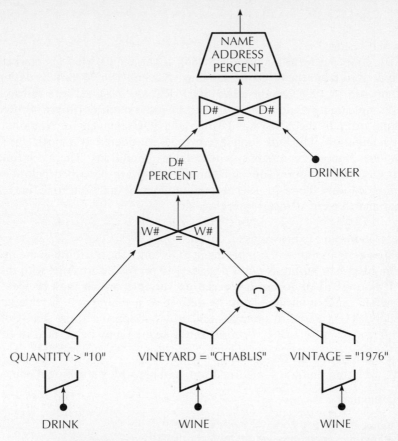

FIGURE 4.26 Example of tree representing a query

1. The *search* (RETRIEVE or SELECT or GET) retrieves tuples or parts of tuples that satisfy a given search condition.
2. The *insertion* (INSERT or APPEND or STORE) adds tuples to a relation; the tuples may be introduced by the user or built up from relations existing in the database.
3. The *suppression* (DELETE or SUPPRESS or ERASE) suppresses the tuples of a relation that satisfy a given search condition.
4. The *modification* (UPDATE or REPLACE or MODIFY) updates the tuples satisfying a given search condition with new attribute values or with the results of arithmetical operations performed on the existing values.

In addition to these basic operations, relation control operations such as schema definitions and modifications, integrity constraint and view definitions, and authorization control are also supported.

4.5.2 SQL ISO

Origin and history
The SQL nonprocedural language [ISO86], a variant of which is marketed by
IBM, is derived from the SEQUEL language [Chamberlin76] initially designed at
IBM San Jose. A first version called SQUARE was designed as a research language to implement relational algebra with English sentences [Boyce74]. Recently
a working group of the ANSI standardized the SQL language for relational database manipulation. The SQL language may be considered as a particular syntax
of relational algebra expressions, with complex conditions. The basic functions
(search, insertion, suppression, and modification) are described below, with a
few simplifications. The SQL ISO also admits control functions to define relation
schemas and to express integrity constraints.

Attribute and Value Expressions
To reference an attribute in a table using SQL, only the attribute name needs to
be given. In case of ambiguity, it is necessary to prefix the attribute with the table
name it belongs to or to use a correlation variable, which may be seen as an
abbreviation. Such a variable must be defined as a synonym of a table name in
the query (FROM part). In summary and at a first approach, the syntax of attribute reference (simply called *attribute* in the sequel) may be defined in BNF:

> <attribute reference> ::=
> [{<relation name> | <correlation variable>}.]<attribute name>

Examples:

WINE.PERCENT
W.PERCENT
PERCENT

SQL allows the use of value expressions, which may be:

1. An attribute reference.
2. A constant of the type character string, fixed or floating point real,
   long or short integer, and so on.
   Examples:
   > 1978
   > 'VOLNAY'
   > 11.7
   > 1.7E+03
3. One of the following aggregate functions: count (COUNT), average
   (AVG), maximum (MAX), minimum (MIN), or summation of values
   (SUM). The function must be applied to sets. The function may be
   applied either to all the values, whether or not they are distinct, or only
   to distinct values.

Syntax:
< aggregate function > ::=
COUNT(*) | {AVG|MAX|MIN|SUM}({DISTINCT|[ALL]} < attribute >)
Examples:
       COUNT(*)
       AVG (DISTINCT VINTAGE)
       MAX (PERCENT)

4. All arithmetical expression built from the preceding elements with the operators $+,-,/,*$
   Examples:
   PERCENT − AVG(PERCENT)
   (DRINK.QUANTITY * PERCENT) / 100

Predicates

In SQL ISO, a predicate specifies a condition that can be evaluated to give the truth value of "true," "false," or "unknown." There are several types of predicates. The simplest is the comparison predicate, defined as follows (in BNF):

    < comparison predicate > ::=
    < value expression > < comp operator > { < value expression > |
    < subquery >}

where a value expression is an arithmetic expression of attributes, values, or aggregate functions. The comparison operator (comp operator) must be chosen among $\{=,<>,<,>,>=,>=\}$. A subquery may be assimilated to a query. The result of the evaluation of a comparison predicate is:

● Unknown, if at least one of the value expression is null or the subquery answer is empty.
● True, if the left and right expressions satisfy the relation given by the comparison operator.
● False in all other cases.

Examples of simple comparison predicates are:

W# = 100
VINEYARD = 'VOLNAY'
WINE.W# = DRINK.W#
PERCENT > 10.7
PERCENT < (SELECT MAX(PERCENT)
        FROM WINE
        WHERE VINEYARD = 'VOLNAY')

A large diversity of other predicates exists in SQL. We briefly explain them and give an overview of the syntax with simple examples. For more details, the reader should consult [ISO86].

1. A predicate of interval BETWEEN determines whether a value expression is included between the values of two other value expressions.
   Syntax:
   <between predicate> ::=
   <value expression>
   [NOT] BETWEEN <value expression> AND <value expression>
   Examples:
   PERCENT BETWEEN 10.2 AND 12.7

2. A predicate of list membership IN checks if a value expression belongs to a subquery result or to a list of value expressions.
   Syntax:
   <in predicate> ::=
   <value expression> [NOT] IN { <subquery> | <value list> }
   Examples:
   VINTAGE NOT IN (1983,1984,1985)
   W# IN SELECT W# FROM WINE

3. A predicate of text comparison LIKE checks whether a value expression of the type character string contains one or more substrings (% means any substring, _ means any character).
   Syntax:
   <like predicate> ::=
   <attribute> [NOT] LIKE <pattern> [<escape character>]
   Examples:
   DATE LIKE '_____87'
   ADDRESS LIKE '%PARIS%'

4. A predicate of nullity test IS NULL checks whether a value expression is the null value.
   Syntax:
   <null predicate> ::=
   <attribute> IS [NOT] NULL
   Examples:
   PERCENT IS NOT NULL
   QUANTITY IS NULL

5. A predicate with quantifier ALL, SOME, or ANY preceding a subquery; ALL means that the comparison predicate must be true for all values of the subquery result; SOME or ANY means that it has to be true for at least one value of the subquery result.
   Syntax:
   <quantified predicate> ::=
   <value expression>
   <comp operator> <quantifier> <subquery>
   Examples:
   W# IN ALL SELECT W# FROM WINE
   D# IN SOME SELECT D# FROM DRINK

6. The existence predicate (EXISTS) tests whether the answer to a question is empty.
    Syntax:
    < exists predicate > ::=
    EXISTS < subquery >
    Examples:
    EXISTS SELECT D# FROM DRINK WHERE QUANTITY > 1000

Search Condition
A search condition specifies a condition that is true, false, or unknown depending on the result of applying Boolean operators to specified conditions. Indeed it is a Boolean expression of predicates. The general syntax definition of a search expression is:

< search condition > ::=
        < Boolean term >|< search conditon > OR < Boolean term >
< Boolean term > ::=
        [NOT] { < predicate >|< search condition} | < Boolean term >
AND < Boolean term >

Examples are:

DRINKER.D# = DRINK.D# AND DRINK.W# = WINE.W#

(((VINTAGE BETWEEN 1978 AND 1987) AND PERCENT IS NOT NULL)
    OR QUANTITY IS NULL) AND
    (EXISTS SELECT D# FROM DRINK WHERE QUANTITY > 1000)

The SELECT Statement
The search is carried out by the SELECT statement. This statement allows one to build a relation from those in the database using any kind of relational algebra operation. Aggregate functions are also supported. The general syntax of the select statement is:

        SELECT [DISTINCT | ALL]
            { *| < value expression >] [, < value expression >] . . . }
        FROM relation [(correlation variable)]
        [WHERE < search condition >]
        [GROUP BY < attribute > [, < attribute >] . . .]
        [HAVING < search condition >]
        [ORDER BY < attribute >[.{ASC|DESC}]
            [, < attribute >[.{ASC|DESC}]] . . .]

The name of a relation can always be replaced by any identifier (which therefore represents a variable in tuple relational calculus) by using the specific command of synomyms definition.

The *SELECT clause* is used to specify the required result. A list of value expressions is the general form of a result specification. To simplify the enumeration of value expressions, the notation *, relation .* and variable .* are allowed. Their respective meaning is list of all attributes issued from the FROM clause, list of all the attributes of a given relation or of that represented by the variable. The key words DISTINCT and ALL specify whether duplicate tuples must be (DISTINCT) or must not be (ALL) eliminated.

The *FROM clause* specifies the relations involved in the query. The declaration of a variable in the FROM clause defines a synonym for a relation's name. This synonym remains internal to the query and may be used in all parts of the query. The virtual relation from which a query extracts its result may be perceived as the Cartesian product of the named relations (the only named relation if a unique name is given). The result of the request will be built from this relation by application of the operations specified by the WHERE, GROUP BY, HAVING clauses (in that order), then by the selection of the value expressions stated in the SELECT clause, and last by presentation of the result in the order specified by the ORDER clause.

The *WHERE clause* specifies the search condition applied to all the tuples of the virtual relation specified with the FROM clause. The result of the WHERE clause is therefore a relation containing the tuples of the Cartesian product issued from the FROM that satisfy the condition (those for which the argument of the WHERE is true).

The *GROUP BY* clause performs the fragmenting of the relation issued from WHERE in tuple sets of same values for the columns specified in the group by arguments. Thus the result relation is horizontally divided in subrelations. The aggregate functions of the SELECT clause will then be applied to all the subrelations. Average, minimum, maximum, sum, and count are performed for each subrelation, after having applied the HAVING clause. This clause specifies an additional search condition applied to all the subrelations issued from the GROUP BY. Only the tuples that satisfy the search condition are kept, and the empty subrelations are erased.

The *ORDER* clause is used to specify the result sorting order. The sorting attributes, whose order may be ascendant (ASC) or descendant (DESC), must belong to the relation issued from the FROM clause.

Some examples of basic queries on a database whose schema is defined in Fig. 4.5 are given below.

Q1: Give the VINEYARD appearing in the WINE relation without duplicate.
SELECT DISTINCT VINEYARD
FROM WINE

Q2: Give the names of Beaujolais 1982 or 1983 drinkers.
SELECT DISTINCT NAME
FROM DRINKER (D), WINE (W), DRINK

```
WHERE (D.D# = DRINK.D#)
AND (DRINK.W# = W.W#)
AND (VINEYARD LIKE '%BEAUJOLAIS%')
AND (VINTAGE IN (1982, 1983))
```

Q3: Give the drinkers of wine from vineyard starting with "B," of un-known percentage of alcohol or between 11 and 13.
```
SELECT DRINKER.*
FROM DRINKER, WINE, DRINK
WHERE (DRINKER.D# = DRINK.D#)
AND (DRINK.W# = WINE.W#)
AND VINEYARD LIKE "B%"
AND ((PERCENT BETWEEN 11 AND 13) OR (PERCENT IS NULL))
```

Q4: Give the names of vineyards whose wines are drunk by at least one drinker.
```
SELECT DISTINCT VINEYARD
FROM WINE (W)
WHERE
EXISTS ( SELECT D.*
         FROM DRINKER (D), DRINK (A)
         WHERE (D.D# = A.D.#)
         AND (A.W# = W.W.#))
```

Q5: Calculate the average percentage for each vineyard.
```
SELECT VINEYARD, AVG (PERCENT)
FROM WINE
GROUP BY VINEYARD
```

Q6: Calculate the average percentage of all the vineyards whose minimum percentage is greater than 12.
```
SELECT VINEYARD, AVG (PERCENT)
FROM WINE
HAVING MIN (PERCENT) > 12
```

Q7: Give the names of drinkers having drunk more than 10 glasses of alcohol in 1986.
```
SELECT NAME
FROM DRINKER
WHERE D# IN
        SELECT D#
        FROM DRINK, WINE
        WHERE DATE LIKE '_____86'
        GROUP BY D#
        HAVING SUM (QUANTITY * PERCENT/100) > 10
```

The Insert Statement

The insertion adds new tuples to a relation. It can be made by providing directly the tuples to be inserted or by selecting the tuples to be inserted from a query.

The first alternative is direct insertion, the second the insertion via query. The syntax of the insertion statement of SQL is:

INSERT INTO < relation name > [(attribute [,attribute] . . .)]
{VALUES < value spec. > [, < value spec. >] . . . | < query specification > }

When the list of attributes is not specified, all the relation's attributes must be given in the creation order. If only some are specified, the others are filled up with null values.

To illustrate this statement, the insertion of a JULIENAS of unknown vintage and percentage of alcohol under the wine number 112 will be made by the command:

INSERT INTO WINE (W#, VINEYARD, VINTAGE)
VALUES 112, JULIENAS, NULL

Assuming a relation PRODUCER (P#,NAME,SURNAME,ADDRESS), it is possible to insert all producers whose address contains DIJON as drinkers of unknown type using the data-dependent INSERT command:

INSERT INTO DRINKER (D#,NAME,FIRSTNAME)
SELECT P#,NAME,SURNAME
FROM PRODUCER
WHERE ADDRESS LIKE '%DIJON%'

Update Statement
The update statement changes attribute values in existing tuples. The updating of a relation may be executed by directly providing the values to be modified or by building these values from an expression. The only updated tuples are those satisfying an optional search condition given as argument for a WHERE clause.

The syntax of the SQL update command is (in a simplified form):

UPDATE < relation name >
SET < attribute > = {value expression | NULL} [, < attribute > = {value
     expression | NULL}] . . .
[WHERE < search condition >]

As an example, the update of percentage for all 1983 Julienas by the value 13 is performed by the request:

UPDATE WINE
SET PERCENT = 13
WHERE (VINEYARD = 'JULIENAS') AND (VINTAGE = 1983)

The 10 percent increment of the quantity of 1983 Volnay drunk by any drinker is performed by the command:

```
UPDATE DRINK
SET QUANTITY = QUANTITY * 1.1
WHERE (DRINK.W# = WINE.W#)
AND (VINEYARD = 'VOLNAY')
AND (VINTAGE = 1983)
```

Delete Statement

The delete statement suppresses qualified tuples from a relation. The tuples are specified by a search condition unless the deletion of all the tuples in a relation is required. The syntax of the delete statement is:

DELETE FROM <relation name>
[WHERE <search condition>]

For example, the deletion of all the consumption of wines of unknown percentage is solved by the command:

```
DELETE FROM DRINK
WHERE W# IN SELECT W#
              FROM WINE
              WHERE PERCENT IS NULL
```

Table Creation and Integrity Constraints

SQL allows end users to express most of the integrity constraints at relation creation. Thus the syntax of the creation command is defined as follows:

CREATE TABLE <relation name>
(<attribute definition> [,<attribute definition>] . . .)

where:

  <attribute definition> : =
  <attribute name> <data type> [NOT NULL[UNIQUE]]
| CONSTRAINTS UNIQUE (<attribute name> [,<attribute name>] . . .)

A data type is either a character string (CHARACTER), a fixed (DECIMAL) or floating point (FLOAT or REAL or DOUBLE PRECISION) real, or an integer (INTEGER, SMALLINT). The UNIQUE constraint describes keys; NOT NULL option forbids null values. For example, the DRINK relation can be created using the following command:

```
CREATE TABLE DRINK
        (D# FIXED 15 NOT NULL, W# FIXED 15 NOT NULL,
        QUANTITY FIXED 15, DATE CHARACTER 8,
        CONSTRAINTS UNIQUE (D#, W#))
```

This command specifies that the attributes D# and W# must not be null and that they are the relation's key.

Finally, it is important to note that SQL does not allow the declaration of referential integrity constraints in its current form. In general, it does not support integrity constraints (for example, range-restricted domains are not possible) except keys.

4.6 A Logical Interpretation of Relational Databases

4.6.1 Introduction and Motivations

In the previous sections, we presented a relational database as a set of relations with operations on the relations. Another possible view is to see a relational database as a set of predicate extensions, each predicate being a relation. Thus a relational database may be seen as an implementation of a first-order logic language, the so-called *predicate calculus*. Predicate calculus (see Chapter 1 on background) is a formal language that may be used to represent relations and queries. The specific application of predicate calculus to relational database is known as *relational calculus*. The relational calculus we present here is a slight extension of the first-order language defined in [Reiter84]. It is general enough to encompass both the tuple calculus and the domain calculus [Ullman82], slight syntactic variations of the first-order language applied to databases.

The first reason to reconstruct databases with logic is to give a more formal view of relational databases. One advantage is that a formal tool is useful to prove the correctness of certain algorithms. The second reason is that logic is more powerful than relational databases; thus the reconstruction of databases with logic will lead to better DBMSs with deductive capabilities, as we will see in Chapter 10.

4.6.2 Relational Calculus

The formulas of the calculus are those of first-order logic (FOL) as defined in Chapter 1, although we do not use functions. Variables are called *domain variables* as they range on domains of the relational model in the interpretation of the FOL. To simplify the notations, we may rename a sequence of variables in a predicate with a unique *tuple variable*. A component of such a tuple may be denoted using the tuple variable followed by the rank of the variable in the predicate, or followed by a "." and the position name (the attribute name). Tuple variables are denoted with capital letters and domain variables with small letters. For instance, the formula:

$$\forall x\ \exists y\ (Q(x,y) \wedge P(a,x))$$

may be rewritten as:

$$\forall X1 \ \exists X2 \ (Q(X) \land P(a,X1))$$

or, if we call $A1$ the first position in Q and $A2$ the second:

$$\forall X.A1 \ \exists X.A2 \ (Q(X) \land P(a,X.A1)).$$

Like [Reiter84], we use a suitable subset of FOL languages called relational languages. In relational language, there is only a finite set of constants and predicates, and among the predicates, there is a distinguished subset of unary predicates, which represent the domains or simple types of the language [Reiter84]. Types are extended using union, intersection, and negation of simple types. We shall also use, if convenient, appropriate abbreviations for certain formulas, as follows:

$\forall x \epsilon \ R \ (F)$ abbreviates $\forall x \ (R(x) = \rangle F)$.
$\exists x \epsilon \ R \ (F)$ abbreviates $\exists x \ (R(x) = \rangle F)$.

Quantifiers in subformulas $\forall X \epsilon \ \tau$ and $\exists X \epsilon \ \tau$ are called *type-restricted quantifiers* [Reiter84].

The semantics of a first-order language is defined as follows. An interpretation I for the first-order language is composed of:

1. A domain of discourse D over which the variables of the language are meant to range.
2. A mapping K from the constants of the language onto D.
3. A mapping E from the predicates of the language into sets of tuples of elements of D. $E(P)$ is called the extension of predicate P in the interpretation I.

An interpretation I is a relational interpretation of a relational language if each constant of the relational language corresponds to a distinct constant in D (K is a bijection) and also if there exists a special predicate denoted $=$ such that $E(=)$ $= \{(d,d) \mid d \ \epsilon \ D\}$ (we may also introduce the special comparison predicates $>$ and $<$).

4.6.3 Logical Relational Databases

A *logical relational database* [Reiter84] is a simple model in logic of a relational database.

> **Definition 4.24 Logical relational database**
> A logical relational database is a triple (L,I,C) where L is a relational language, I a relational interpretation for L, and C a set of well-formed formulas called integrity constraints.

Among the integrity constraints, it is required that for each relation predicate (a predicate different from $=$, $<$, $>$ and simple types), there exist domain constraints of the form:

$$\forall x1 \forall x2 \ldots \forall xn(P(x1,x2, \ldots ,xn) \Rightarrow D1(x1) \wedge D2(x2) \ldots \wedge Dn(xn)),$$

where $D1$, $D2$, . . . ,Dn are simple types.

4.6.4 Queries

A query over a logical relational database is a formula of the form $\{x1/D1,x2/D2, \ldots , xn/Dn \mid W(x1,x2, \ldots , xn)\}$ where W is a well-formed formula, the only free variables in W are $x1$, $X2$, . . . , $xn,$ and all quantifiers in W are type-restricted quantifiers. In cases where a variable xi appears in a relation argument in $W,$ the type of xi can be determined using the domain integrity constraints. Thus we shall in general simplify query formulation as follows, with tuple variables: $\{X \mid W(X)\}$.

The semantic of a query is simply to find all X that satisfy the formula W. Formally, a tuple $T = <t1,t2, \ldots , tn>$ of constants ti of the relational language alphabet is an answer to a query Q with respect to the database if:

1. $Di(ti)$ is true in the relational interpretation I for $i = 1, 2, \ldots n$.
2. $W(T)$ is true in I.

Let us express query Q1 and Q2, given above in SQL, with the relational calculus:

Q1: Give the VINEYARD appearing in the WINE relation without duplicate.
{X.VINEYARD | WINE(X)}

Q2: Give the names of Beaujolais 1982 or 1983 drinkers.
{D.NAME | ∃W ∈ WINE ∃E ∈ DRINK (DRINKER (D)∧ (D.D# = E.D#)
∧ (E.W# = W.W#) ∧ (W.VINEYARD = '%BEAUJOLAIS%')
∧ ((W.VINTAGE = 1982)∨ (W.VINTAGE = 1983)))}

Other formulations are possible using domain variables or mixing domain and tuple variables.

A problem that appears when modeling databases with logic is the *problem of possibly infinite answers*. To avoid the problem in this chapter, we assume in the model that all domains are finite, as in [Reiter84]. For example, integer should be limited to a maximum value ω whose meaning is overflow. Accepting infinite domains brings difficulties because some queries can have infinite answers. (This problem, known as the *safety problem,* will be considered in Chapter 10.)

To express queries with arithmetic computations, it is necessary to introduce functions in the language, such as $+$, $-$, $*$, $/$. We can introduce finite functions; we assume then that all functions may be instantiated using finite tables, which is true with current computer data types (they are finite because of overflows). However, this is not sufficient to model aggregates, which necessitate the introduction of sets. We shall come to sets later in this book.

4.7 Conclusion: An Extensible Data Model

The basic concepts of the relational model, the relational algebra and its extensions, as well as the SQL nonprocedural language, have been described in this chapter. It has been shown that relational databases can be modeled with logic. At this stage two questions arise:

1. Can the relational model, whose concepts are very simple, be extended to support complex objects and deductive facilities without being reconsidered?
2. Do the basic operators of relational algebra form a set of independent and complete operators that have all the necessary properties to generate powerful and diversified languages?

These questions have been studied by researchers. As a data modeling tool, the relational model may be extended in many directions without having to reconsider the basic notions. A first direction is to model more accurately the data semantic using general integrity constraints expressed as logic formulas, which are always true. Another possible extension, which defines more precisely the semantic of the modeled data, is the classification of the relations in several types, such as entity, relationship [Chen76], and a large range of others [Codd79].

Another direction of extension is the capacity to support more complex data than those generally processed in management (integer, real, and character strings). One approach to that problem is defining more diversified domains than those generally admitted. The extensions of the concept of domain have not yet been completely explored and seem promising. We shall study some of them in the chapter devoted to complex object management (Chapter 11).

Another promising direction is the support of rules. Such an extension consists of adding general logic formulas to the database. These formulas allow the system to build derived predicates and to infer new facts from the known ones. We shall study this kind of generalization in Chapter 10, devoted to deductive databases.

4.8 References and Bibliography

[Bernstein81] Bernstein P. A., Chiu D. M., "Using Semi-joins to Solve Relational Queries," JACM, V28, N1, January 1981, pp. 25 – 40.

[Boyce74] Boyce R. F., Chamberlin D. D., "SEQUEL: A Structured English Query Language," ACM SIGMOD 1974, Workshop on Data Description, Access and Control, May 1974.

[Chamberlin76] Chamberlin D. D. et al. "SEQUEL 2—A Unified Approach to Data Definition, Manipulation and Control," IBM Journal of Research & Development, V20, N6, November 1976.

[Chen76] Chen P. P., "The Entity Relationship Model—Toward a Unified View of Data," ACM TODS, V1, N1, March 1976, pp. 9 – 36.

[Childs68] Childs D. L., "Feasibility of a Set-Theoretic Data Structure—A General Structure Based on a Reconstituted Definition of a Relation," IFIP Congress, Geneva, 1968, pp. 162 – 72.

[Codd70] Codd E. F., "A Relational Model of Data for Large Shared Data Banks," CACM, V13, N6, June 1970, pp. 377 – 87.

[Codd72] Codd E. F., "Further Normalization of the Database Relational Model," in *Data Base Systems,* Rustin ed., Prentice-Hall, 1972, pp. 65 – 98.

[Codd79] Codd E. F., "Extending the Relational Model to Capture More Meaning," ACM TODS, V4, N4, December 1979, pp. 397 – 433.

[Date81] Date C. J., "Referential Integrity," 7th Very Large Data Bases Conf., Cannes, France, September 1981, IEEE ed.

[Date85] Date C. J., *An Introduction to Database Systems,* 4th ed., Systems Programming Series, Addison-Wesley, 1985.

[Delobel83] Delobel C., Adiba M., *Bases de données et systèmes relationnels,* Dunod Informatique, 1983.

[Fagin80] Fagin R., "A Normal Form for Relational Databases That Is Based on Domains and Keys," ACM TODS, V6, N3, September 1981, pp. 387 – 415.

[ISO86] ISO/TC 97, "Information Processing Systems—Database Language SQL," ISO/DIS 9075, ANSI Secretariat, Draft International Standard.

[Maier83] Maier D., *The Theory of Relational Databases,* Computer Science Press, 1983.

[Merrett84] Merrett T. H., *Relational Information Systems,* Reston Pub. Co., 1984.

[Reiter84] Reiter R., "Towards a Logical Reconstruction of Relational Database Theory," in *On Conceptual Modelling,* Springer-Verlag Pub., Brodie and Schmidt eds., 1984, pp. 191 – 223.

[Stonebraker76] Stonebraker M., Wong E., Kreps P., Held G., "The Design and Implementation of Ingres," ACM TODS, V1, N3, September 1976, pp. 189 – 222.

[Stonebraker84] Stonebraker M., Anderson E., Hanson E., Rubinstein B., "QUEL as a Data Type," ACM SIGMOD 84 Proc., Boston, June 1984, pp. 208 – 14.

[Ullman82] Ullman J. D., *Principles of Database Systems,* 2d ed., Computer Science Press, 1982.

[Zaniolo83] Zaniolo C., "The Database Language GEM," ACM SIGMOD Conf., May 1983, San Jose, Calif., ACM Proc.

[Zloof77] Zloof M. M., "Query by Example: A Data Base Language," IBM Systems Journal, V16, N4, 1977, pp. 324 – 43.

[Zloof82] Zloof M. M., "Office-by-Example: A Business Language That Unifies Data and Word Processing and Electronic Mail," IBM Systems Journal, V21, N3, Fall 1982.

5
RELATIONAL
DATABASE DESIGN

5.1 Introduction

One of the most important tasks a relational DBMS user or administrator has to perform is database design, the activity of structuring the enterprise information in well-specified relational schemas that may be implemented in relational systems. Historically researchers and designers have separated the static and the dynamic aspects of database design. Static aspects are the design of data structures (relations and views) and time-independent integrity constraints (domain, keys, referential constraints). Dynamic aspects describe the actions operating on these data structures and the sequence of transactions modifying the database from one consistent state to another [Bouzeghoub86]. In this chapter, we shall concentrate on static aspects, although we encompass the whole database design process and consider dynamic aspects when necessary. Relational (or nonrelational) database design is so important because a good design is necessary for a good usage of the database, from a semantics point of view and for performance.

To capture the various requirements of the design process, different phases of design have been suggested. *User requirement analysis and specification* consists of collecting user needs in terms of data description, operations, events, and related constraints [DeAntonellis83]. *Conceptual design* is the phase that leads to the elaboration of the global conceptual schema. In our approach, conceptual design includes the integration of various views of a database from specific contexts and the normalization phase, which formally generates molecular relations without redundancy, free of update anomalies. The next phase, *logical design,* is based on an analysis of logical record accesses from a first definition of the transactions. This analysis allows the database designer to translate the conceptual schema into target logical structures. With relational DBMSs, logical relations result from natural joins of normalized conceptual relations. If needed, a rapid prototyping of the database is possible using the schema. *Physical design* concerns the internal schema, which specifies the internal data structures and access paths of the physical database. All details of access paths (i.e., relation clustering, indexes, hashing schemes, etc.) must be given. Transaction definitions must be refined.

In this chapter, we present an overview of relational database design practice and theory. First, we propose a division of the relational design process in clear and well-understood phases. We then analyze the basic principles used to carry out all the identified phases. A large part of the chapter is devoted to the normalization theory, which is the well formalized phase of relational database design. It is indeed the fundamental part of this chapter.

5.2 Design Process Analysis

A design methodology is generally based on a top-down approach going from the end users to machine implementation [Reiner86]. We present here the basic phases of a typical methodology:

- Capture and abstraction of user requirements.
- Integration of external views.
- Normalization of conceptual relations.
- Optimization of the internal schema.

The design process is sketched in Fig. 5.1. Most relational systems allow the database administrator to add or remove views, relations, attributes, integrity constraints, and indexes during the database life cycle. Thus iterative design must be supported, and backtracking must be possible with a relational database design methodology.

5.2.1 Capture and Abstraction of User Requirements

A top-down design of a relational database starts with user interviews and observations. By looking at existing forms, by questioning end users, and by analyzing the enterprise organization and the information flows, it is possible to capture user requirements and to divide them in more or less independent contexts. Abstracting from these limited portions of the information system leads to a formal representation of the objects, their properties and interrelationships, and the activities involving those objects [Sevcik81]. Thus a representation of each portion

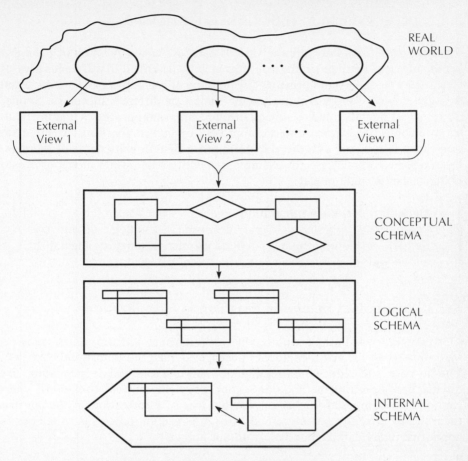

FIGURE 5.1 Sketch of the design process

of the modeled enterprise may be done, bringing out an external schema with static and dynamic aspects in a chosen formalism (e.g., entity-relationship diagrams). The appropriate selection of details of the enterprise to model depends on the transactions the user has in mind and, more generally, on the database purpose. It is not an easy task, many iterations are generally necessary. As output, the first phase of the database design, which is probably the most informal one, must deliver a set of external views for the static characteristics (the data descriptions) and the main dynamic aspects (a first specification of the typical transactions).

Definition 5.1 User requirement abstraction
Phase of the design process that consists of determining and formalizing external views, using a specific external data model.

5.2.2 Integration and Synthesis of External Views

The next phase is to integrate the various database views. A union of the views is not sufficient because similar concepts may be described in different views. It is necessary to understand precisely the meaning of each object and attribute and to isolate objects and attributes having similar or different meanings. Similar objects must be integrated. Knowing the most important processes that intend to act upon objects facilitates object comprehension and comparisons. The integration phase terminates with the elaboration of a first global schema of the database in some formalism — for example, the entity-relationship model or even a richer semantics data model.

> **Definition 5.2 View integration**
> Phase of the design process that consists of elaborating a unique, coherent, and nonredundant global conceptual schema by integrating all the various external views.

5.2.3 Conceptual Relation Design and Normalization

This phase starts with the previous conceptual schema, performs a first transformation in relations, and then applies dependency theory to improve the schema. The purpose is to reduce data redundancy and to avoid update anomalies. The nonloss decomposition method (see Section 5.5) yields molecular relations, which cannot be decomposed further on without loss of information. Although it is theoretically a well-founded method, the normalization process is so tedious to apply that many database designers do not bother.

> **Definition 5.3. Schema normalization**
> Phase of the design process that aims at obtaining molecular relations representing, without loss of information, unique facts, concepts, or events in order to avoid data redundancy and update anomalies.

5.2.4 Optimization and Internal Schema Design

The last phase is to specify the physical representation of the database. The basis for optimization is the knowledge of the most frequent transactions. This knowledge derives from the dynamic aspect modeling. The logical and physical design are generally based on cost models that are system dependent. Because joins are generally costly operations, they are avoided by implementing natural joins of relations with associated integrity constraints; this process is known as *denormalization*.

Definition 5.4 Schema denormalization
Optimization process that aims to determine the most suitable joins
of normalized relations to implement in the internal schema.

Denormalization is necessary to avoid costly join; however, too much denormalization leads to data redundancy. Relations become large, and selections are then costly. To avoid too many joins and too long selections, a compromise must be elaborated at the level of the internal schema. Also integrity constraints on the internal schema relations must be generated during the denormalization process to control data redundancy. A good system should enforce these integrity constraints, thus avoiding update anomalies.

Finally, file organizations and access paths such as relation clustering, hashing methods, and indexes must be chosen. This is part of the *physical design*.

Definition 5.5 Physical design
Optimization process that aims at choosing file organizations, access
methods, indexed attributes, and record clusterings for the implemented relations.

Physical design is, at least in theory, the only subphase that is system dependent.

5.3 User Requirement Analysis

To obtain from the information system participants a global strategic planning and detailed descriptions of the various external behaviors is the main goal of the user requirement analysis and specification phase. This includes the capture and the formalizing of the user data requirements and the acquisition of additional information, especially corporate constraints and typical processing requirements. It leads to the elaboration of a set of external views composed of nonmolecular relations with associated typical processing scenarios. The user requirement analysis phase may be decomposed in two steps.

The first step is the *isolation of the information system actors and main functions*. The actors include management people and users. Top management provides corporate goals and objectives; a view of the important functions and a link to the future are generally obtained from top management interviews. Middle management provides more detailed information about the goals and objectives and the identification of the operational users who will use the database. Information system planning must be done with the collaboration of management; it should include studies of the system feasibility and sound cost-benefit analysis.

The second step is the capture of the operational users' requirements and their formal definition. It corresponds to a *functional analysis of each user point of view.* Forms, charts, and functional description tools as PSL/PSA [Teichroew77] are useful. Various approaches may also be used in this process, such as analysis of the actual computer usage, an examination of written documentation, and interviews [Lum79]. Ideally this second step should lead to a functional model of the operational user requirements from a static and dynamic point of view. This model must include a first definition of the most typical screen forms and dialogs, a precise definition of the database user views, and a description of the most important transactions.

The choice of an external model is methodology dependent. However, several approaches are based on the entity-relationship (E/R) model with associated E/R diagrams. (See Chapter 3, Section 3.2.2). Using such a model, the following procedure has been suggested for designing external schemas [Chen76]:

1. *Identify entity sets of interest to the user group.* An entity is a thing that can be distinctly identified. Entities are classified into different entity types. In the E/R diagram, an entity type is portrayed by a rectangle.
2. *Identify the relationship sets of interest to the user group.* Entities are related to each other using relationships. Different types of relationships may exist between different types of entities. In the E/R diagram, a relationship type is represented by a diamond. There are many types of relationships. Simple relationships are binary; they link two entity types. A few may be ternary or more (link three or more entity types.) Useful characteristics of a binary relationship are its minimum and maximum *cardinalities* in each direction.

Definition 5.6 Relationship cardinalities
The cardinalities of a binary relationship linking two entities $E1$ and $E2$ are: (1) the minimum and maximum number of occurrences of $E2$, which may correspond to an occurrence of $E1$, and (2) the minimum and maximum number of occurrences of $E1$, which may correspond to an occurrence of $E2$.

Cardinalities of relationships are often illustrated in the E/R diagram as intervals written on the arcs linking entities to a relationship (Fig. 5.2). For example, the cardinalities on the arc going to the entity SUPPLIER must be understood as the minimum and maximum numbers of suppliers that supply a given part.

3. *Identify relevant properties of entities and relationships.* Entities and relationships have attributes that take values in certain domains (value set). The domains are portrayed in the E/R diagram as circles and the attributes as arrows going from the entity or relationship characterized by the attribute to the associated domain. Often E/R diagrams are sim-

plified by mixing the notions of attribute and domain; an attribute name is then simply written within the circle.

An E/R diagram is represented in Fig. 5.2 for a user view composed of two entities, PART and SUPPLIERS, a relationship, SUPPLY, and a few properties.

It is more difficult to model dynamic aspects. Certain methodologies recommend modeling user transactions with extended Petri net models [Tardieu83]. Others prefer dynamic logic. Logic programming could be a better support to express dynamic rules (see Chapter 10). A short natural language description of each transaction is probably the simplest way to describe the dynamic aspects. But no matter which model is chosen, user views must be elaborated with specific descriptions of user relations (or entities and relationships) and attributes and a clear understanding of the processing requirements. The design may then proceed to the next phase, the integration and synthesis of the external views.

5.4 View Integration Phase

Having precisely specified external views — for example, with the E/R model and natural language descriptions of transactions — the problem is to integrate all views in a unique global conceptual schema. This process can be done directly from E/R views or from relational external schemas resulting from a direct transformation of E/R diagrams. A direct mapping is possible from E/R views to relations. First, each entity is replaced by a unique relation whose keys and attributes are the entity keys and attributes. Then each relationship is replaced by a relation whose attributes are the relationship attributes and which has one key for each participating entity; the relation key is composed of the keys of the

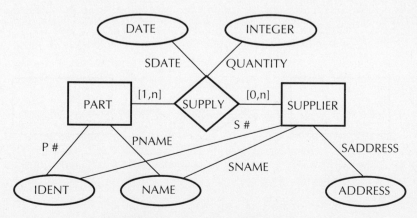

FIGURE 5.2 Entity-relationship user view

participating entities. This mapping may be improved in certain cases (Fig. 5.3). Starting from E/R diagrams or relations, the view integration phase requires knowledge of the keys. We shall see in the next section that formal methods exist to determine keys. For the time being, we assume that keys are intuitively defined.

   The first problem is the unique naming problem: two similar concepts may have a different name (synonym), and the same name may designate different concepts in different views (homonym). A useful tool to solve this problem is the data dictionary. Each object (domain, attribute, relation, entity, relationship) can be described in the dictionary by a sentence and a few key words. A computer program able to compare names and, within certain limits, definitions could ask the database designer whether two concepts are identical. Such tools to avoid naming ambiguities are described in [Batini84], [Dayal84], and [Tardieu83].

   The second problem is the detection of nondisjoint concepts. The problem appears at the domain, attribute, entity, and relationship levels. The unique name determination is generally sufficient to remove ambiguities among domains and attributes. Thus most methodologies consider only relations (or entities and relationships) at this step. Two relations having the same set of key attributes are generally not disjoint classes. Three cases must be isolated for relations of same keys:

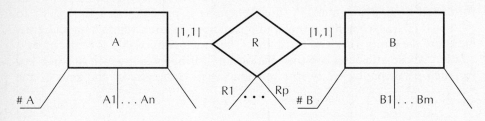

GIVES: R (# A, A1, . . . An, R1, . . . Rp, # B, B1, . . . Bm)
A and # B are candidate keys (we can choose one)

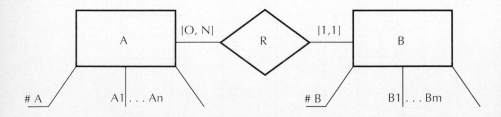

GIVES: A (# A, A1, . . . An, # B)
B (# B, B1, . . . Bm)

FIGURE 5.3 Simplification rules for mapping E/R diagrams to relations

1. If $R1$ is identical to $R2$ (same attributes and instances), they are candidates for merging.
2. If $R1$ is included in $R2$ (same attributes and inclusion of $R1$ instances into $R2$ instances), $R1$ is discarded and replaced by an attribute added to $R2$ to distinguish instances of $R1$.
3. If $R1$ and $R2$ have a nonempty intersection but do not satisfy $R1$ included in $R2$ or $R2$ included in $R1$, it may be desirable to integrate $R1$ and $R2$ in a unique relation R.

A more detailed discussion of these rules may be found in [Navathe84].

A third problem is the *detection of inconsistencies* among the different views. Inconsistencies mainly appear between integrity constraints of the various views. Two views may specify different keys for the same relation. The cardinalities of a relationship may be defined differently. Several approaches are possible, such as keeping only the less restrictive constraint, ordering the constraints and keeping the most important one, giving case-by-case solutions [El-Masri79], or going back to the end users in case of conflict.

When these problems have been solved, a first conceptual schema may be proposed. By successive iteration with the end users, it can be improved. It is then possible to move to the next phase, normalization.

5.5 Normalization Theory

5.5.1 Update Anomalies

The combination of attributes to build relations may lead to data replication and update anomalies. Consider a relation DRINKER-OF-WINE, which contains all attributes describing an entity DRINKER, an entity WINE, and a certain relationship between them. The relationship describes the fact that drinkers drank wines in certain amounts at given dates. Such a relation may have the following schema:

DRINKER-OF-WINE (W#, VINEYARD, VINTAGE, QUALITY, REGION, COUNTRY, D#, NAME, DATE, QTY)

The semantics of this relations schema is straightforward for wine specialists. W# is a wine number unique for a given bottle of wine. VINEYARD is the name of the district where the wine comes from. VINTAGE is the year in which a particular wine was bottled. QUALITY is an appreciation of the wine quality given by a taster institute to a vineyard for each vintage; there is a unique quality for each vineyard and vintage. REGION designates the geographical area that produces the wine. In general, a vineyard belongs to a unique region; however, there exist a few exceptions because some grapevines have been transplanted from

DRINKER-OF-WINE

W#	VINEYARD	VINTAGE	QUALITY	REGION	COUNTRY	D#	NAME	DATE	QTY
100	Chablis	1978	Good	Bourgogne	FRANCE	10	Dupont	10.02.87	53
100	Chablis	1978	Good	Bourgogne	FRANCE	20	Martin	10.02.87	37
200	Chablis	1985	Poor	California	U.S.A.	30	Doe	10.02.87	24
200	Chablis	1985	Poor	California	U.S.A.	40	Mickey	10.02.87	77
300	Julienas	1987	Average	Beaujolais	FRANCE	20	Martin	20.05.87	35

FIGURE 5.4 An instance of the DRINKER-OF-WINE relation

one region to another. (Chablis is a vineyard in Burgundy in France that has been transplanted in California). COUNTRY is the name of the country of the region; note that a region belongs to a unique country. D# is a drinker social security number. NAME is a drinker name. DATE is the date when the drinker drank the wine, and QTY is the quantity drunk that day; we assume that a drinker may drink the same wine several times, but only once a day. Fig. 5.4 gives a possible instance of the DRINKER-OF-WINE relation. For readers who do not like wine and have problems understanding their descriptions we present another example in Fig. 5.5. This relation describes the supplies of parts to clients. It has the following schema:

SUPPLY-OF-PART (C#, CNAME, P#, PNAME, TYPE, COLOR, S#, SNAME, DATE, QTY)

The attributes C# and CNAME give code numbers and names of clients. The attributes P#, PNAME, TYPE, and COLOR denote, respectively, the code numbers of parts, the part names, a classification of parts into types, and a standard set of colors. A given part name may correspond to several part numbers but all of same type. S# is a supplier number, which corresponds to a unique supplier name given by the attribute SNAME. DATE and QTY, respectively, represent the date of supply and the quantity supplied at that date for part P# by supplier S# to client C#.

The previous relations are two examples of poor design. Indeed, at first, the DRINKER-OF-WINE relation appears to be an aggregation of the entities DRINKER and WINE with the relationship DRINK. Even worse, the SUPPLY-OF-PART relation is an aggregation of three entities, CLIENT, SUPPLIER, and PART, with a relationship among them. Managing such poorly designed relations is bound to lead to inconsistency problems.

SUPPLY-OF-PART

C#	CNAME	P#	PNAME	TYPE	COLOR	S#	SNAME	DATE	QTY
100	Dupont	10	Wheel	A32	Black	30	Doe	10.02.87	25
100	Dupont	20	Tire	B12	Black	30	Doe	10.02.87	30
200	Martin	50	Door	X21	White	10	Mickey	20.05.87	50
200	Martin	20	Tire	B12	Black	10	Mickey	20.05.87	50
300	Dupont	70	Bumper	A10	Grey	30	Doe	20.05.87	20

FIGURE 5.5 An instance of the relation SUPPLY-OF-PART

First, an elementary fact may be recorded several times in a poorly designed relation. For example, the region of a vineyard appears several times in the DRINKER-OF-WINE relation. Also the name of a drinker is recorded as many times as he or she drank. In the SUPPLY-OF-PART relation, the name of a part is recorded as many times as the part has been supplied. Such redundancies of data are potentially dangerous. All tuples recording the same fact must be updated together if the fact changes. For example, if a part name changes, it must be changed for all its supplies. Thus recording the same fact several times may lead to inconsistencies. It is also wasteful of time and space.

Second, elementary facts cannot be inserted independently in a poorly designed relation. For example, the name of a drinker who has not yet drunk any wine cannot be recorded in the DRINKER-OF-WINE relation. If we want to record < 100-John DOE > as a drinker, null values must be entered in all columns except D# and NAME. The same phenomenon appears if we want to insert < 100-John DOE > as a client who has not been supplied yet in the SUPPLY-OF-PART relation. Null values are somewhat cumbersome when queries or updates are performed. It is not clear that John DOE must be selected if we ask for drinkers or clients having drunk or received parts in quantity less than 100. Also the null value should probably be removed when John DOE drinks or receives parts. All these problems are known as *insertion anomalies* [Codd72].

Another class of problems is known as *deletion anomalies*. For example, if we delete all information about drinkers of a given wine in the DRINKER-OF-WINE relation, we unintentionally delete the wine from the relation. The same problem appears with the client if we delete all supplies done to a client.

A simple analysis of these problems could lead to the conclusion that the poorly designed relations include too many attributes. A simple way to avoid the problems might be to use only binary or unary relations representing atoms of information. Examples of binary relations derived from the previous relations by projection are given in Figs. 5.6 and 5.7. The reader can verify that the join of

WINE	W #	VINEYARD	VINTAGE
	100	Volnay	1977
	200	Chablis	1978
	300	Chablis	1979
	400	Volnay	1982

WINE 1	W #	VINEYARD
	100	Volnay
	200	Chablis
	300	Chablis
	400	Volnay

WINE 2	VINEYARD	VINTAGE
	Volnay	1977
	Chablis	1978
	Chablis	1979
	Volnay	1982

FIGURE 5.6 Binary decomposition of WINE

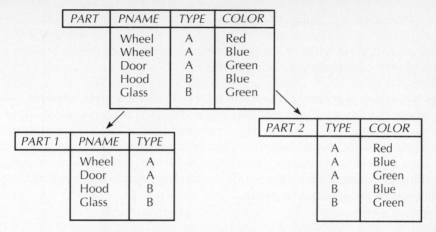

FIGURE 5.7 Binary decomposition of PART

the relations of Fig 5.6 does not allow the system to retrieve the unique quality of a wine. Similarly joining the relations of Fig. 5.7 does not retrieve the color of each part. Thus it appears that too small relations (such as binary relations or, even worse, unary relations) may lead to information loss.

In summary, a relation that does not represent a unique entity or relationship of the real world seems to suffer from information redundancy, potential inconsistencies, and insertion and deletion anomalies. In addition, designing relations that represent as several tables an entity or a relationship generally fails to give correct answers to queries. Thus the design of canonical relations, corresponding to real-world entities and relationships, appears important to relational databases.

5.5.2. Universal Relation Assumption

Before studying relation design theory, it is necessary to specify the meaning of column names in different relations. Similar to [Kent81], it is possible to ask the following questions: Does the occurrence of the same column name in two relations mean the same? Is it necessary to define them over the same domain? Are they necessarily joinable? A simple approach to these problems is to assume that column names have global meaning. Thus if two columns in a database have a different meaning, they must be renamed. For instance, if DATE appears twice for designating the date of birth of a drinker and the date of an excess then one should define two attributes BIRTH_DATE and EXCESS_DATE. Under this hypothesis — that attributes mean the same wherever they occur—it is possible to assume the existence of a universal relation.

> **Definition 5.7 Universal relation**
> Relation U whose schema is composed of the union of all database
> attributes, such that any relation instance in the database is a projec-
> tion of U over the relevant attributes.

The hypothesis that there exists a universal relation for a given database (which is usually the join of all the relations in the database) is known as the *universal instance assumption*. It is a strong assumption. Note that a relaxation of the universal instance assumption, the *weak instance assumption,* has been shown to have interesting properties [Honeyman82, Mendelzon84]. The weak instance assumption assumes the existence of a universal relation whose projections contain each of the database relations.

5.5.3 Decomposition and Synthesis Approaches

Two methods have been proposed to design relational databases without anomalies or information losses. The first is *schema decomposition,* proposed by Codd [Codd71], theoretically developed in [Rissanen73], and generalized by Fagin [Fagin77] and Zaniolo [Zaniolo81]. Schema decomposition starts from a universal relation schema composed of all the database attributes. The approach consists of decomposing by successive projections the universal relation into subrelations (Fig. 5.8). The decomposition process stops when no more decomposition can be done without losing certain desirable properties, such as the possibility of recomposing the initial universal relation instance by joins. With the decomposition process, designers hope to obtain relations that do not suffer from anomalies. Decomposition algorithms are generally based on a formal description of dependencies between attributes.

The second approach is *schema synthesis* [Bernstein76]. This approach starts with a set of independent attributes. Based on semantic properties and links

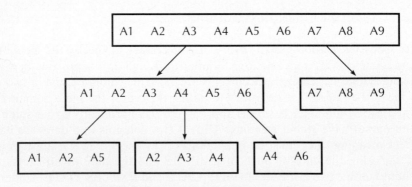

FIGURE 5.8 A decomposition approach

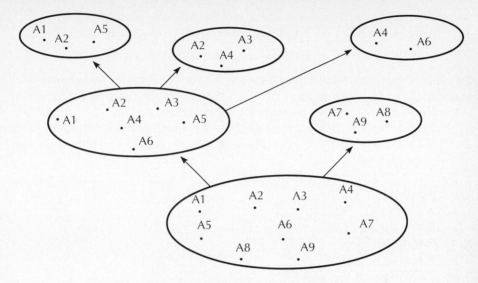

FIGURE 5.9 A synthesis approach

between these attributes, relations are composed in such a way that they do not suffer from the previously mentioned anomalies. Synthesis algorithms are generally based on a graph representing the links between attributes (Fig. 5.9).

We now present a decomposition and a synthesis algorithm to design relations without anomalies. Because such algorithms require a deep knowledge of semantics links between attributes, it is necessary to introduce concepts to capture and describe these links. The fundamental concepts are based on the notion of functional dependency.

5.5.4 Functional Dependencies

Definition and Examples
The notion of functional dependency was introduced by Codd [Codd70]. The goal was to characterize relations presenting potential anomalies. Such relations should be decomposed in two relations.

> **Definition 5.8 Functional dependency**
> A functional dependency is a constraint on a relation schema $R(A1, A2, \ldots, An)$ of the form $X \rightarrow Y$, where X and Y are subsets of $\{A1, A2, \ldots, An\}$, which guarantees that for every instance r of relation R, a value of X uniquely determines a value of Y.

More formally, if a relation schema R satisfies a functional dependency $X \to Y$, if $t1, t2$ are tuples of r and π denotes the projection operation:

$$X \to Y \text{ if } \pi_X(t1) = \pi_X(t2) \Rightarrow \pi_Y(t1) = \pi_Y(t2).$$

In other words, the relationship between the set of X values and the set of Y values defined by any instance r of R is a function if the functional dependency $X \to Y$ holds. In that case, we say that X determines Y.

To illustrate the definition, let us give a few functional dependencies. In the DRINKER-OF-WINE relation of Fig. 5.4, we can isolate the following functional dependencies:

```
W# → VINEYARD
W# → VINTAGE
W# → QUALITY
W# → REGION
W# → COUNTRY
REGION → COUNTRY
VINEYARD,VINTAGE → QUALITY
D# → NAME
W#,D#,DATE → QTY
```

On the contrary, the functional dependencies given below do not hold:

```
D# → W#
W# → D#
QUALITY → VINEYARD
W# → QTY
```

In the SUPPLY-OF-PART relation of Fig. 5.5, the following dependencies hold:

```
C# → CNAME
P# → PNAME
S# → SNAME
PNAME → TYPE
PNAME → COLOR
C#,P# → S#
C#,P#,S#,DATE → QTY
```

The following functional dependencies do not hold:

```
C# → P#
COLOR → PNAME
S# → QTY
```

A functional dependency (FD) is an assertion on a relation schema. Thus it characterizes a property of all possible instances, not only the current relation state. In other words, a functional dependency is an intentional property of a relation schema. It can never be inferred from a given relation instance. To determine whether a functional dependency holds between two sets of attributes, one must analyze carefully the attribute meanings. FDs capture essential links between attributes, which explains their importance for relational database design.

Properties of Functional Dependencies
It is always possible to find all the FDs that a relation schema satisfies. One way is to compare all subsets of attribute of the relation schema and to determine if one subset functionally depends on the other. This approach is time-consuming. Knowing certain functional dependencies, it is possible to derive others. Indeed functional dependencies satisfy a set of inference rules known as the *Armstrong axioms* [Armstrong74]. Three basic deduction rules form an independent basis that permits one to obtain all dependencies inferred from a given set. These three rules are the following ($X \subset Y$ denotes that the set X is included in the set Y with possible equality):

Reflexivity: If $Y \subset X$ then $X \rightarrow Y$. This rule affirms that a set of attributes determines any subset of itself (including itself).

Augmentation: If $X \rightarrow Y$ and $W \subset Z$, then $XZ \rightarrow YW$. This rule means that if X determines Y and W is a subset of Z, then the two sets of attributes X and Y may be augmented, respectively, by Z and W

Transitivity: If $X \rightarrow Y$ and $Y \rightarrow Z$, then $X \rightarrow Z$. This rule is the most useful. It allows one to obtain a new dependency from two dependencies having a common right and left side.

Using these rules, new ones can be obtained:

Union: If $X \rightarrow Y$ and $X \rightarrow Z$, then $X \rightarrow YZ$.

Pseudo-transitivity: If $X \rightarrow Y$ and $WY \rightarrow Z$, then $WX \rightarrow Z$.

Decomposition: If $X \rightarrow Y$ and $Z \subset Y$, then $X \rightarrow Z$.

These rules allow the designer to generate all FDs implied by a given subset. However, most FDs are not useful for schema design. We can restrict ourselves to a simple class of FDs called *elementary FDs* [Delobel73, Zaniolo81].

Definition 5.9. Elementary functional dependency
Functional dependency of the form $X \rightarrow A$, where A is a single attribute and X a set of attributes that does not include A such that there does not exist X' strictly included in X satisfying $X' \rightarrow A$.

In other words, an elementary functional dependency is an FD in which the right-hand side is a single attribute and the left-hand side is minimum. Inference axioms among elementary FDs can be reduced to a unique axiom, the pseudo-transitivity rule: If $X \to Y$ and $WY \to Z$, then $WX \to Z$. Pseudo-transitivity is a complete inference rule for elementary FDs. This results from the fact that reflexivity cannot be used to infer elementary FDs; reflexivity and pseudo-transivity derive augmentation ($W \subset Z$ implies $WY \subset ZY$; thus reflexivity implies $ZY \to WY$; but $X \to Y$ and $ZY \to WY$ implies by pseudo-transitivity $ZX \to WY$, which is augmentation); and pseudo-transitivity obviously implies transitivity (simply by making $W = \phi$ in pseudo-transitivity definition). Thus being given a set of elementary FDs, all elementary FDs that may be inferred from this set are those derived by pseudo-transitivity. Only elementary dependencies are actually used by the schema design procedure presented below. Thus, from now on, we mean elementary FD for FD, and we shall consider only the pseudo-transitivity inference rule, which is complete for elementary FDs.

Graphical Representation of Functional Dependencies

Given a set of attributes $\{A_1, \ldots, A_n\}$ and a set of FDs $\{X_i \to A_j\}$ where X_i is a subset of $\{A_1, \ldots, A_n\}$, we can try to represent these FDs by a graph to visualize them. When all left parts of the FDs (X_is) are single attributes, the functional dependency graph is simply a direct graph with $\{A_1, \ldots, A_n\}$ as set of vertices and $\{X_i \to A_j\}$ as set of edges. Each attribute corresponds to a vertex; a functional dependency $A_i \to A_j$ is represented by an edge from A_i to $A_{j.}$ For example, the set of FDs

$$\{W\# \to \text{VINEYARD}, W\# \to \text{VINTAGE}, W\# \to \text{REGION},$$
$$\text{REGION} \to \text{COUNTRY}, D\# \to \text{NAME}\}$$

is represented by the FD graph of Fig. 5.10.

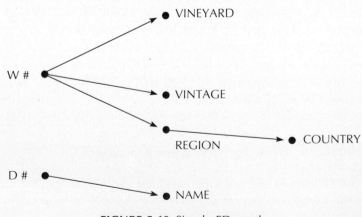

FIGURE 5.10 Simple FD graph

More generally, elementary FDs may include several attributes on the left-hand side. In that case, bipartite graphs (graphs with two types of nodes) are necessary. The FDs are of the form $X_i \rightarrow A_j$, where $X_i = \{A_{i1}, \ldots, A_{ip}\}$. Auxiliary composed vertices must be introduced to the dependency graph to represent sets of attributes as X_i. A dependency of the form $A_{i1}, \ldots, A_{ip} \rightarrow A_j$ is then modeled by a set of edges going from A_{ik} to the composed vertex X_i, for $k = 1$ to p, and by an additional edge going from X_i to A_j. To distinguish auxiliary composed-vertices, we shall draw them using small rectangles (readers familiar with Petri nets may see them as transitions). The FD graph of the DRINKER-OF-WINE relation schema is given in Fig. 5.11. That of the SUPPLY-OF-PART relation schema is given in Fig. 5.12. More formally we define a FD graph as in [Ausiello83].

> **Definition 5.10 Functional dependency graph**
> Given a set of attributes $\{A_i\}$ and a set of FDs $\{X_i \rightarrow A_j\}$, the FD graph is a directed bipartite graph such that:
> For every attribute A_i, there is a simple vertex labeled by A_i.
> For every FD $X_i \rightarrow A_j$ in which $X_i = \{A_{i1}, \ldots, A_{ip}\}$ with $p > 1$, there is an auxiliary vertex labeled by X_i and a set of edges going from A_{i1} to A_j, ..., A_{ip} to A_j.
> For every FD $X_i \rightarrow A_j$ there is an edge from X_i (a simple or composed vertex) to Aj.

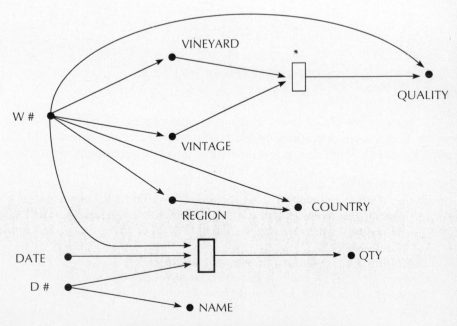

FIGURE 5.11 DRINKER-OF-WINE FD graph

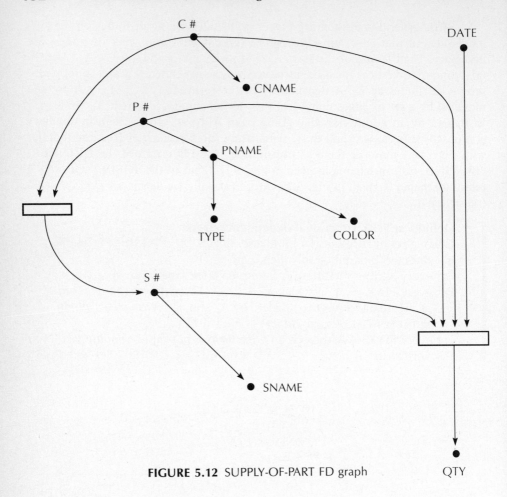

FIGURE 5.12 SUPPLY-OF-PART FD graph

FD graphs are useful representations to analyze a set of functional dependencies. Well-known operations on FD graphs such as closures derive valid FDs from a set of FDs. However, a few difficulties appear due to composed vertices.

Closure and Minimal Cover
Considering a set of elementary FDs, it is possible to derive all elementary FDs that are inferable from this set using the pseudo-transitivity axiom. Thus it is useful to define the *pseudo-transitive closure* of a set of FDs.

Definition 5.11 Pseudo-transitive closure of FDs
Given a set of FDs *F*, the pseudo-transitive closure of this set is *F* union the set of FDs that may be inferred from *F* using the pseudo-transitivity axiom.

For example, the pseudo-transitive closure of the set of FDs

$$F = \{W\# \rightarrow \text{VINEYARD}, W\# \rightarrow \text{VINTAGE}, W\# \rightarrow \text{REGION},$$
$$\text{REGION} \rightarrow \text{COUNTRY}, D\# \rightarrow \text{NAME}\}$$

is

$$F^+ = F \cup \{W\# \rightarrow \text{COUNTRY}\}.$$

The pseudo-transitive closure corresponds to the classical transitive closure on the dependency graph when this graph does not include composed nodes. For example, the (pseudo-)transitive closure of the graph of Fig. 5.10 is portrayed in Fig. 5.13. It corresponds to the FD graph of F^+, as defined above.

More generally, when an FD graph G contains composed vertices, to construct the FD graph G^+ representing the pseudo-transitive closure of G is a complex operation. This may be done by defining the concept of reach on the FD graph G. An attribute A_j is reachable from a set of attribute $\{A_{i1}, \ldots, A_{ip}\}$ if one of the following conditions holds:

1. A_j belongs to $\{A_{i1}, \ldots, A_{ip}\}$.
2. There exists a predecessor of A_j in G that is a simple node reachable from $A_{i1}, \ldots, A_{ip}$.
3. There exists a predecessor of A_j in G that is a compound node and whose predecessors are reachable from $A_{i1}, \ldots, A_{ip}$.

The concept of reach can be understood by deriving a Petri net from the FD graph. Such a Petri net is obtained by considering composed vertices as transitions and by adding transitions on edges that link two simple vertices. Then a transition $A_{i1}, \ldots, A_{ip} \rightarrow A_j$ belongs to G^+ iff A_j is reachable from $A_{i1}, \ldots,$

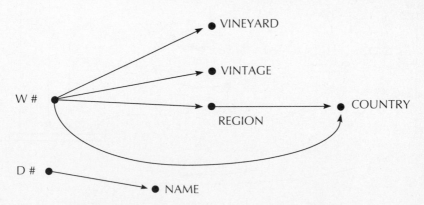

FIGURE 5.13 Transitive closure of Fig. 5.10 graph

A_{ip} in G. With this method, we can derive the pseudo-transitive closure of the SUPPLY-OF-PART relation schema (Fig. 5.14).

From the notion of pseudo-transitive closure, it is possible to determine if two sets of elementary FDs represent the same semantics knowledge of the relation schema. Two sets of elementary FDs are said to be equivalent if they have identical pseudo-transitive closure. To design relational schemas, it is interesting to consider minimal sets of FDs able to generate all FDs of the pseudo-transitive closure. Such minimal sets are called *minimal cover* [Delobel73].

> **Definition 5.12 Minimal cover**
> Set F of elementary FDs associated to a set of attributes A, which satisfies the following properties:
> 1. No FD in F is redundant (that is, for all f in F, $F - \{f\}$ is not equivalent to F).
> 2. All elementary FDs between subsets of A are in the pseudo-transitive closure of F.

Any set of FDs has a minimal cover; however, in general, a set of FDs may have several minimal covers (Fig. 5.17). Fig. 5.15 portrays the minimal cover of the DRINKER-OF-WINE dependencies; there is a unique minimal cover in that case. Fig. 5.16 gives a minimal cover of the SUPPLY-OF-PART dependencies.

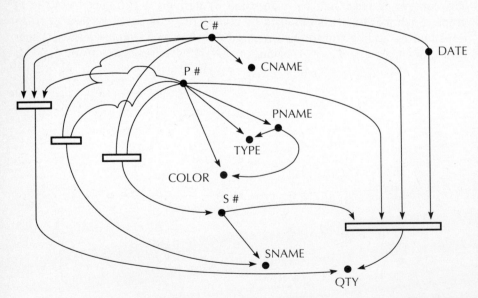

FIGURE 5.14 Pseudo-transitive closure of the SUPPLY-OF-PART dependencies

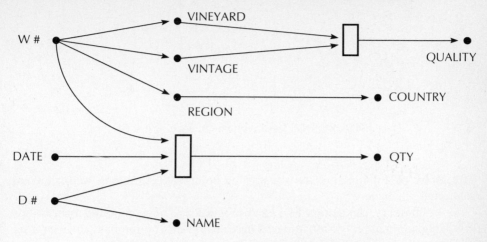

FIGURE 5.15 Minimal cover for DRINKER-OF-WINE

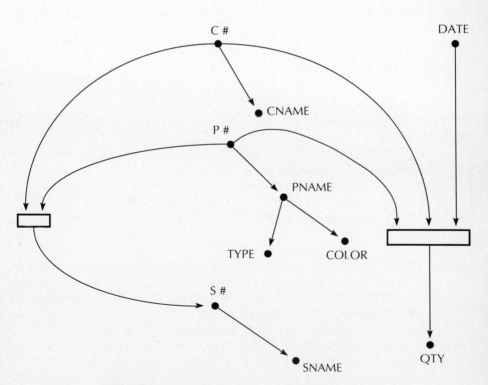

FIGURE 5.16 Minimal cover for SUPPLY-OF-PART

FIGURE 5.17 Two minimal covers of *R(A,B,C)*

The choice of a minimal cover is a starting point in the design of well-behaving relational schemas.

In summary, elementary FDs can be regarded as noncompound associations involving minimal sets of attributes. There always exists a minimal cover of a set of FDs composed of elementary FDs. All elementary FDs can be generated from a minimal cover using pseudo-transitivity. Any other nontrivial dependency (of the form $X \rightarrow Y$ where *Y* is a subset of *X*) is, in fact, obtained by adding some attributes to an elementary one and/or by combining them according to the union law [Zaniolo81]. From the concept of FD, it is possible to introduce normal forms for relations. A normal form is a condition on the relation schema that precludes update anomalies.

5.5.5 Third Normal Form

Candidate Keys
The definition of normal forms requires a good understanding of the concept of *candidate key*.

> **Deninition 5.13 Candidate key**
> Subset *X* of the attributes of a relation schema $R(A1, A2, \ldots , An)$ such that *X* determines all attributes of $R: X \rightarrow A1$, $X \rightarrow A2, \ldots, X \rightarrow An$; and there is no proper subset *Y* of *X* that determines all attributes of *R*.

In other words, a candidate key is a minimal set of attributes that determines all attributes. For example, {W#,D#,DATE} is the unique candidate key for the relation schema DRINKER-OF-WINE. {C#,P#,DATE} is the unique candidate key for the relation schema SUPPLY-OF-PART.

A relation schema may have several candidate keys. In general, one candidate key is selected among all possible as the relation key. We shall use the word *key* for candidate key. A *superkey* is a set of attributes including a key. If an attribute *A* belongs to some key of a relation schema *R*, then *A* is said to be *prime* in *R*. Otherwise *A* is *nonprime* in *R* [Beeri79]. For example, in the relation schema SUPPLY-OF-PART, DATE is prime, but PNAME and S# are nonprime. That an attribute belongs to a superkey does not imply that it is prime.

Definition of Third Normal Form
E. Codd introduced *first normal form* to avoid relations with nonatomic values as attribute values.

> **Definition 5.14 First normal form**
> A relation schema is in first normal form (1NF) if the values of all domains are atomic.

Because atomicity of a value means that one cannot consider parts of it, first normal form is a matter of point of view. If one precludes dealing with part of domain values, 1NF always holds. For instance, consider a set-valued domain in which sets are regarded as nonatomic (we can query or update part of them): COMPOSED COLOR = {∅, {BLUE}, {RED}, {BLUE,RED}}. Then the relation of Fig. 5.18 is not in 1NF. This relation would be in 1NF if the sets were considered atomic. In general one does not consider sets of values as atomic; thus 1NF precludes set-valued attribute. More simply, 1NF prevents considering part of attribute values. The advantages of 1NF are that domain values appear as elementary building blocks for relations and that updating an attribute value requires replacing it with a new value in a nonambiguous way.

Second normal form has been introduced to avoid anomalies that appear when a nonprime attribute depends only on a part of a key. The values of this attribute are then repeated for all the different values of the other part of the key. More formally, we say that an attribute A fully depends on X if it is not dependent on any proper subset of X. Thus if $X \rightarrow A$ is an elementary FD, A is fully dependent on X.

> **Definition 5.15 Second normal form**
> A relation schema R is in second normal form (2NF) if each of its nonprime attributes is fully dependent on each of its keys.

PART	P#	COLOR
	100	∅
	200	{Blue}
	300	{Blue, Red}

FIGURE 5.18 A non-1NF relation

For example, the relation SUPPLY(C#, P#,SNAME,PNAME) is not in 2NF since the nonprime attribute PNAME is determined by the attribute P#. Thus PNAME does not fully depend on the key. As another example, the relation DRUNK(W#,DATE,D#,NAME,QTY) is not in 2NF since the nonprime attribute NAME depends on D#. Thus NAME does not fully depend on the key < W#,DATE,D#>. Similarly the DRINKER-OF-WINE relation is not in 2NF.

2NF is not sufficient protection against update anomalies. Certain relations may include nonprime attributes that determine other nonprime attributes. In that case, the values of the second group of nonprime attributes may be duplicated for each value of the first group. To avoid such redundancy, *third normal form* (3NF) has been introduced [Codd72]. Let R be a relation schema, let X be a subset of the set of attributes of R, and let A be any attribute of R. Attribute A is *transitively dependent* on X if there exists Y such that $X \rightarrow Y$, $Y \rightarrow A$, Y does not determine X, and A does not belong to Y [Beeri79]. For example, if $K1,K2,K3 \rightarrow A1$ and $K1,K2,A1 \rightarrow A2$, in the transitive closure of the dependencies, we have $K1,K2,K3 \rightarrow Y$ and $Y \rightarrow A2$ where Y is $K1,K2,A1$; thus, $A2$ is transitively dependent on $K1,K2,K3$. In most cases the notion of transitive dependency is from the key and means that a nonprime attribute is determined by another nonprime attribute [Beeri79].

> **Definition 5.16 Third normal form**
> A relation schema is in third normal form (3NF) if none of its nonprime attributes is transitively dependent on any of its keys.

If a nonprime attribute is partially dependent on a key, it is also transitively dependent on that key. Thus every relation schema in 3NF is also in 2NF.

Let us give examples of relations not in 3NF. The relation LOCATION (W#,REGION,COUNTRY), giving the location of a wine number, is not in 3NF. The nonprime attribute COUNTRY is transitively dependent on W#, which is the key. Indeed, we have: W# → REGION → COUNTRY. In a similar way, the relation SUPPLY(C#,P#,S#,SNAME) is not in 3NF as C#,P# → S# → SNAME. More difficult to see is the fact that $R(K1,K2,K3,A1,A2)$ is not in 3NF if $K1,K2,K3 \rightarrow A1$ and $K1,K2,A1 \rightarrow A2$.

Properties of Third Normal Form
Given a relation that is not in 3NF, it is desirable to decompose this relation in several relations by projections. For example, the relation LOCATION(W#, REGION,COUNTRY) may be decomposed in two relations, LOC(W#,RE-GION) and GEO(REGION,COUNTRY), where:

$$LOC = \pi_{W\#,REGION}(LOCATION).$$
$$GEO = \pi_{REGION,COUNTRY}(LOCATION).$$

These two relations are in 3NF. Similarly, the relation SUPPLY(C#,P#, SNAME,PNAME) may be decomposed in SUP(C#,P#,SNAME) and PART (P#,PNAME) where:

$$SUP = \pi_{C\#,P\#,SNAME}(SUPPLY)$$
$$PART = \pi_{P\#,PNAME}(SUPPLY)$$

which are in 3NF.

It is always possible to decompose by projection a relation to obtain 3NF relations; for example, we may decompose in binary relations that are always in 3NF. The problem is to choose decompositions that do not lose information. Two types of decomposition are particularly interesting.

Definition 5.17 Lossless join decomposition
Decomposition of a relation R into a set $\{R1,R2, \ldots, Rn\}$ of projections such that $r = \pi_{R1}(r) \bowtie \pi_{R2}(r) \bowtie \ldots \bowtie \pi_{Rn}(r)$ for any instance r of R.

When there is no ambiguity, we shall say simply *lossless decomposition* for *lossless join decomposition*. The definition clearly means that we can reconstruct the initial relation by taking the natural join of the decomposed relations. Thus querying the decomposed relations using natural joins leads to the same results as querying the initial relation.

The other type of interesting decomposition is defined regarding FDs. When a relation schema R is decomposed by projections in relations $R1$, $R2$, $\ldots$, Rn, one may wonder if certain FDs are lost. Indeed, if an FD between two attribute sets $X \to Y$ that holds in the relation schema R is such that the set XY is split between different relations, then the FD is a priori lost. This is because $X \to Y$ cannot hold in a relation Ri if XY does not belong to the Ri schema. In fact, the problem is more complex as FDs' inference rules may regenerate the a priori lost FD. Let us recall that two sets of (elementary) FDs are equivalent if they have identical (pseudo-transitive) closure. This justifies the following definition.

Definition 5.18 Dependency-preserving decomposition
Decomposition of a relation schema R into projections $R1,R2,$ $\ldots, Rn$ such that the dependencies R are equivalent to the union of $R1,R2, \ldots, Rn$ dependencies.

For instance, the relation PART(P#,PNAME,TYPE,COLOR) may be decomposed in two relations, P1(P#,PNAME,TYPE) AND P2(TYPE,COLOR). This decomposition is not a lossless join decomposition, as shown by Fig. 5.19. Also it loses the dependencies PNAME $\to$ COLOR and P# $\to$ COLOR, as shown in Fig. 5.20.

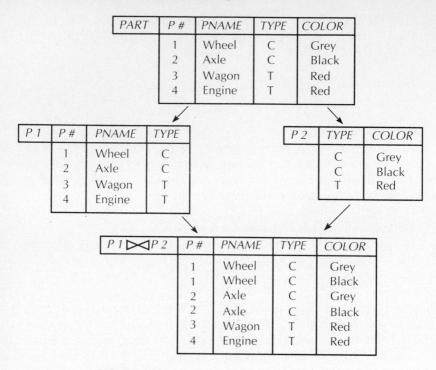

PART	P #	PNAME	TYPE	COLOR
	1	Wheel	C	Grey
	2	Axle	C	Black
	3	Wagon	T	Red
	4	Engine	T	Red

P 1	P #	PNAME	TYPE
	1	Wheel	C
	2	Axle	C
	3	Wagon	T
	4	Engine	T

P 2	TYPE	COLOR
	C	Grey
	C	Black
	T	Red

P 1 ⋈ P 2	P #	PNAME	TYPE	COLOR
	1	Wheel	C	Grey
	1	Wheel	C	Black
	2	Axle	C	Grey
	2	Axle	C	Black
	3	Wagon	T	Red
	4	Engine	T	Red

FIGURE 5.19 Nonlossless join decomposition

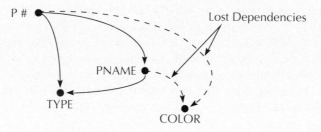

FIGURE 5.20 FD graph closure of PART, P1 and P2

Also consider the relation DRUNK(W#,DATE,D#,VINEYARD,NAME, QTY). Its FD graph is shown in Fig. 5.21. The relation may be decomposed into three relations: DR(D#,NAME),DN(D#,DATE,QTY), and WN(W#,VINE-YARD). The dependency graph of these three relations is shown in Fig. 5.22. The arc linking W# and the compound node being lost, this decomposition does not preserve the functional dependencies. Also it is easy to see that it is not a lossless join decomposition.

It is important to note that each relation schema not in 3NF has at least

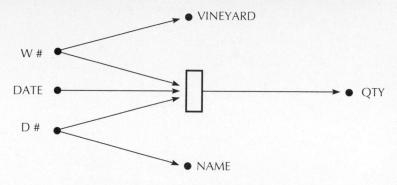

FIGURE 5.21 FD graph of the DRUNK relation

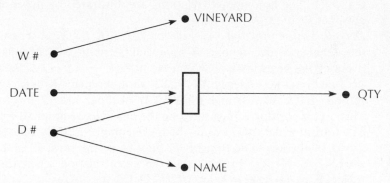

FIGURE 5.22 FD graph of the decomposition of DRUNK

one 3NF decomposition such that the decomposition is a lossless join decomposition and the decomposition is a dependency-preserving decomposition.

Decomposition Algorithm

The goal of a 3NF decomposition algorithm is to convert a relation schema that is not in 3NF into a set of relations. The input of the algorithm is a non-3NF relation schema and its set of dependencies. Because the relation is not in 3NF, either 2NF is violated or only 3NF is violated. In either case, one of the following decompositions must be applied. If both 2NF and 3NF are violated, we can apply any of the following decompositions.

1. *Decomposition of a non-2NF relation.* The relation schema is of the form $R(K1,K2,X,Y)$ where $K1,K2$ is the key and X and Y are sets of attributes such that $K1 \rightarrow X$. Because of the functional dependency $K1 \rightarrow X$, which asserts that R is not in 2NF, it is possible to replace R by its two projections $R1(K1,K2,Y)$ and $R2(K1,X)$, without loss of information. This decomposition is illustrated on the dependency graph of

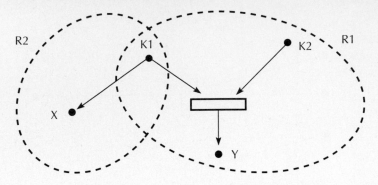

FIGURE 5.23 Non-2NF relation decomposition

Fig. 5.23. The decomposed relations are illustrated by hyper-edges in dot lines.

2. *Decomposition of a non-3NF relation.* Let $R(K,X1,X2,X3)$ be the relation schema to decompose. A nonprime attribute $X2$ depends transitively of the key K. Suppose that we have $K \to X1 \to X2$. Because of the functional dependency $X1 \to X2$, we can replace R by its two projections $R1(K,X1,X3)$ and $R2(X1,X2)$, without loss of information. This decomposition is illustrated on the dependency graph of Fig. 5.24. The transitive dependency may be more complex. Let us denote by $K1$ a part of the key. The transitivity may be of the form $K \to Y \to X2$ where $Y = K1,X1$. In that case, the given relation schema must be replaced by $R1(K,X1,X3)$ and $R2(K1,X1,X3)$.

The recursive application of these decompositions surely leads to relations in third normal form without loss of information. A decomposition algorithm looks like the procedure given in Fig. 5.25.

A Synthesis Algorithm
Another approach, the schema synthesis, has been proposed for elaborating 3NF relations [Beeri79]. The synthesis algorithm first builds a minimal cover of ele-

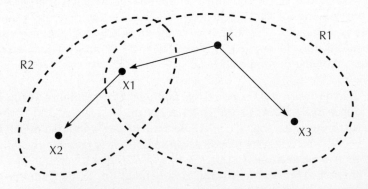

FIGURE 5.24 Non-3NF relation decomposition

Procedure decomposition (R,{FDi});
    begin
    if R is not in 2NF **then**
        begin
        apply decomposition (1) of a non-2NF relation;
        call decomposition (R1, {FD});
        call decomposition (R2, {FD});
        end
    else
        begin
        if R is not in 3NF **then**
            begin
            apply decomposition (2) of a non-3NF relation;
            call decomposition (R1,{FD});
            call decomposition (R2,{FD});
            end
        else output R;
        end;
    end;
  end.

FIGURE 5.25 A decomposition algorithm

mentary FDs. Let F be this minimal cover. Then F must be partitioned into groups Fi such that FDs in each Fi have the same left-hand side and no two groups have the same left-hand side. Each Fi then produces a 3NF relational schema composed with all the constituent attributes of Fi. This algorithm is given in Fig. 5.26. It also provides a nonloss dependency-preserving decomposition.

Procedure synthesis ({Ai}, {FD});
    begin;
    Find a minimal cover F of {FD};
    Reduce to elementary dependencies;
    Partition F into groups Fi according to FDs' left-hand side Xi;
    Merge group Fi and Fj having equivalent left-hand side (i.e., such
        that Xi →Xj and Xj →Xi);
    For each Fi **do**
        begin
        construct a relation with all attributes of the group;
        mark the FDs' left-hand side Xi as being the relation key;
        end;
    end;

FIGURE 5.26 A synthesis algorithm

5.5.6 Boyce-Codd Normal Form

Third normal form was introduced to solve update anomalies among nonprime attributes in a relation; however, it does not eliminate problems among prime attributes. For this reason, the stronger *Boyce-Codd normal form* (BCNF) was introduced [Codd74].

> **Definition 5.19 Boyce-Codd normal form**
> A relation schema R is in BCNF if, for any elementary functional dependency $X \to A$, X is a key of R.

In other words, a relation schema is in BCNF if it does not contain other elementary FDs than those of the form key → attribute. Another equivalent definition is as follows: a relation schema R is in BCNF if, for all disjoint nonempty sets of attributes X and Y in R, if $X \to Y$, then X is a superkey of R. For instance, the following relation is not in BCNF: WINE(VINEYARD,REGION,COUNTRY), if we assume the dependencies VINEYARD,COUNTRY → REGION and REGION → COUNTRY. The dependency graph and an instance of this relation are given in Fig. 5.27. There exist two candidate keys that overlap: VINEYARD,COUNTRY, and VINEYARD,REGION. Thus all attributes are prime, and the relation is in 3NF. Indeed 3NF is insufficient to capture redundancy in such a relation. BCNF is a normal form, which, in some sense, corrects 3NF deficiencies. The given WINE relation is not in BCNF.

A relation not in BCNF can be decomposed into relations in BCNF. The decomposition is a lossless join decomposition. However, it is not certain that the decomposition preserves all dependencies. For example, the relation WINE(VINEYARD,REGION,COUNTRY) may be decomposed into

WINE	VINEYARD	REGION	COUNTRY
	Julienas	Californie	USA
	Julienas	Beaujolais	France
	Morgon	Beaujolais	France
	Chablis	Bourgogne	France
	Chablis	Californie	USA

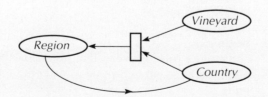

FIGURE 5.27 Instance and dependency graph of a non-BCNF relation

WINE1(VINEYARD,REGION) and WINE2(REGION,COUNTRY). In this decomposition, the FD VINEYARD,COUNTRY → REGION is lost. However, as REGION → COUNTRY, the decomposition is a lossless join one.

5.5.7 Multivalued Dependencies and Fourth Normal Form

Motivation and Definition
We introduced the concept of functional dependency to decompose relations and avoid update anomalies. This led us to 3NF and BCNF. Unfortunately 3NF and BCNF are insufficient to eliminate data redundancy and update anomalies. For example, the relation STUDENT(S#,COURSE,SPORT), shown in Fig. 5.28, is in 3NF and in BCNF (there is no FD). However, there is a lot of data redundancy. Also if student 100 gives up the database course, several updates have to be performed. In fact, for one given value of S#, there exist several values of COURSE and several values of SPORT, and these two sets of values are independent. This example shows the weakness of the notion of functional dependency, which does not permit one to capture the independence between COURSE and SPORT. This independence entails data redundancy. To capture such anomalies, the concept of *multivalued dependencies* was proposed [Fagin77] [Zaniolo81].

> **Definition 5.20 Multivalued dependency (MVD)**
> Given a relation schema $R(A1,A2, \ldots , An)$, X and Y two subsets of $\{A1,A2, \ldots , An\}$ whose complement is $Z = \{A1,A2, \ldots , An\} - (X \cup Y)$, there is a multivalued dependency $X \twoheadrightarrow Y$ (we say X multidetermines Y) iff, in any instance r of R, for any two tuples $t1$ and $t2$ in r with $\pi_X(t1) = \pi_X(t2)$, there exists a tuple $t3$ in r such that $\pi_X(t3) = \pi_X(t2)$, $\pi_Y(t3) = \pi_Y(t1)$ and $\pi_Z(t3) = \pi_Z(t2)$.

The symmetry of $t1$ and $t2$ in the definition implies that there exists also a tuple $t4$ in r such that $\pi_X(t4) = \pi_X(t1)$, $\pi_Y(t4) = \pi_Y(t2)$ and $\pi_Z(t4) = \pi_Z(t1)$. In other

STUDENT	S#	COURSE	SPORT
	100	Database	Tennis
	100	Database	Football
	200	Database	Bicycle
	200	Artif. Int.	Bicycle

FIGURE 5.28 An example of a BCNF relation with redundancies

words, the values of Y that correspond to a given X also correspond to each combination of the given X with the possible values of Z. Or any value of X corresponds to a set of associated value of Y independent of the values of the rest of the relation $Z = \{A1, A2, \ldots, An\} - (X \cup Y)$. An MVD can be viewed as an inference rule: the MVD $X \twoheadrightarrow Y$ states that if tuples $<x,y,z>$ and $<x,y',z'>$ appear in r, then tuples $<x,y,z'>$ and $<x,y',z>$ also appear in r. This inference rule is illustrated in Fig. 5.29.

Let us point out some link between MVD and FD. If $X \to Y$, then for any two tuples $<x,y,z>$ and $<x,y',z'>$ in r, we have $y=y'$. Thus the tuples $<x,y',z>$ and $<x,y,z'>$ are also in r. This means that the MVD $X \twoheadrightarrow Y$ holds in r.

Properties of Multivalued Dependencies

As for functional dependencies, there exist inference rules for MVDs. Let $W, X, Y,$ and Z be subsets of attributes of a relation schema R. XY denotes the union of the two sets X and Y. A complete set of axioms for MVDs (a set of rules that permit deducing all MVDs from a given sample) is the following:

> *Reflexivity:* $X \twoheadrightarrow X$.
> *Augmentation:* If $X \twoheadrightarrow Y$, then $XZ \twoheadrightarrow Y$.
> *Additivity:* If $X \twoheadrightarrow Y$ and $X \twoheadrightarrow Z$, then $X \twoheadrightarrow YZ$.
> *Projectivity:* If $X \twoheadrightarrow Y$ and $X \twoheadrightarrow Z$, then $X \twoheadrightarrow Y \cap Z$ and $X \twoheadrightarrow Y-Z$.
> *Differential-transitivity:* If $X \twoheadrightarrow Y$ and $Y \twoheadrightarrow Z$, then $X \twoheadrightarrow Z-Y$.
> *Pseudo-transitivity:* If $X \twoheadrightarrow Y$ and $WY \twoheadrightarrow Z$, then $XW \twoheadrightarrow Z-WY$.
> *Complementation:* If $X \twoheadrightarrow Y$ and $Z = R - XY$, then $X \twoheadrightarrow Z$.

To mix FDs and MVDs, it is necessary to add two more axioms to get complete inference axioms (inference rules that generate all possible FDs and MVDs from a given set of FDs and MVDs):

> *Replication:* If $X \to Y$, then $X \twoheadrightarrow Y$.
> *Coalescence:* If $X \twoheadrightarrow Y$ and $Z \to W$ and $W \subset Y$ and $Y \cap Z = \phi$, then $X \to W$.

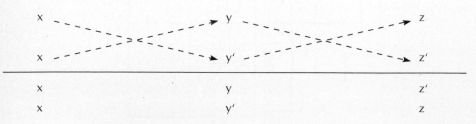

FIGURE 5.29 The MVD $X \twoheadrightarrow Y$ as an inference rule

As for functional dependencies, it is possible to introduce the notion of elementary multivalued dependency to avoid considering trivial MVDs (MVDs of the form $X \twoheadrightarrow Y$, which holds for any relation including XY in its schema).

Definition 5.21 Elementary multivalued dependency
Multivalued dependency in a relation schema R of the form $X \twoheadrightarrow Y$ such that there are other attributes in R ($X \cup Y \neq R; Y$), and X are disjoint: $Y \cap X = \phi$; and there exists no distinct MVD $X' \twoheadrightarrow Y'$ in R where $X' \subset X$ and $Y' \subset Y$.

Thus an elementary MVD is a nontrivial MVD where the rest of the relation is not empty and possesses minimal left and right sides.

Let us give a few more examples of MVDs. Let us consider a relation DRINKER(D#, VINEYARD, GIRL-FRIEND), which means that drinker of number D# likes wines of given vineyard (he drinks some at least once) and is in love with the girl of given name. An instance of such a relation is given in Fig. 5.30. The MVD D# $\twoheadrightarrow$ VINEYARD,GIRL-FRIEND is a trivial one. The MVDs D# $\twoheadrightarrow$ VINEYARD and D# $\twoheadrightarrow$ GIRL-FRIEND are elementary ones. The MVD D#,VINEYARD $\twoheadrightarrow$ VINEYARD is not elementary. Another example holds in the relation FLIGHT(F#,PLANE,PILOT), where F# is a flight number, PLANE a plane reference, and PILOT a pilot name. The MVDs F# $\twoheadrightarrow$ PLANE and F# $\twoheadrightarrow$ PILOT holds in FLIGHT if any pilot flies any plane on any flight; in other words, PLANE and PILOT must be independent.

Fourth Normal Form
Fourth normal form may be seen as a generalization of BCNF to MVDs. It has been introduced to decompose BCNF relations that still present update anomalies.

DRINKER	D#	VINEYARD	GIRL-FRIEND
	100	Chablis	Jane
	100	Chablis	Mary
	100	Volnay	Jane
	100	Volnay	Mary
	200	Volnay	Mary
	200	Medoc	Mary

FIGURE 5.30 Example of a relation with MVDs

Definition 5.22 Fourth normal form
A relation schema R is in fourth normal form (4NF) if for any elementary MVD of the form $X \twoheadrightarrow Y$, X is a superkey of R.

Thus a relation is not in 4NF if one can find an elementary MVD that does not include a key on the left-hand side. For example, the relation STUDENT (S#,COURSE,SPORT) is not in 4NF because, in the elementary MVD S# $\twoheadrightarrow$ COURSE, S# is not a key. In the same way, the relations

>DRINKER(D#, VINEYARD, GIRL-FRIEND)
>FLIGHT(F#,PLANE,PILOT)

whose keys are underlined, are not in 4NF.

Decomposition of a Relation in Fourth Normal Form
To avoid update anomalies, a relation that is not in 4NF must be decomposed in 4NF relations. The decomposition may be performed using recursively the decomposition rule.

>*Fourth normal form decomposition rule.* Let $R(XYZ)$ be a non-4NF relation schema. Let $X \twoheadrightarrow Y$ be the elementary MVD, which is not of the form KEY $\twoheadrightarrow$ ATTRIBUTES. Then this relation is decomposed by projection in two relations $r1$ and $r2$ of schemas $R1(XY)$ and $R2(XZ)$, respectively, such that: $r1 = \pi_{XY}(r)$ and $r2 = \pi_{XZ}(r)$.

It can be shown from the MVD definition that $r = r1 \bowtie r2$. Thus the previous decomposition is a lossless join decomposition. For example, relations:

>STUDENT(S#,COURSE,SPORT)
>DRINKER(D#, VINEYARD, GIRL-FRIEND)
>FLIGHT(F#,PLANE,PILOT)

are respectively decomposed in:

>STUDENT1(S#,COURSE), STUDENT2(S#,SPORT)
>DRINKER1(D#,VINEYARD), DRINKER2(D#,GIRL-FRIEND)
>FLIGHT1(F#,PLANE), FLIGHT2(F#,PILOT)

which are in 4NF.

Embedded Multivalued Dependencies
Let us assume a relation DRINKER(D#, VINEYARD, GIRL-FRIEND,LOVER), where LOVER contains the girlfriend's lovers who also like the wine of a given vineyard. An instance of this relation is portrayed in Fig. 5.31. The relation has

DRINKER	D#	VINEYARD	GIRL-FRIEND	LOVER
	100	Chablis	Jane	Peter
	100	Chablis	Mary	John
	100	Volnay	Jane	Peter
	100	Volnay	Mary	John
	100	Volnay	Mary	Michael

FIGURE 5.31 4NF relation with redundancy

much redundant information. However, the multivalued dependency D# $\twoheadrightarrow$ VINEYARD does not hold because the tuple $<100,\text{Chablis,Mary,Michael}>$ is missing in Fig. 5.31 (Michael does not like Chablis). In the same way, the MVD D# $\twoheadrightarrow$ VINEYARD, GIRL-FRIEND does not hold. Indeed, there is no multivalued dependency in DRINKER. However, there is one in its projection DRINKER (D#,VINEYARD,GIRL-FRIEND). To avoid such anomalies, embedded MVDs have been introduced. An embedded dependency is denoted $X \twoheadrightarrow Y // Z$, where Z is the attributes to keep with X and Y in the projection where the MVD holds. For example, in the DRINKER relation, there exists the embedded MVD: D# $\twoheadrightarrow$ VINEYARD // GIRL-FRIEND. This notion of embedded MVD is not general enough to solve all problems. We need to introduce the more general concept of join dependency [Fagin79].

5.5.8 Join Dependencies and Project-Join Normal Form

Insufficiency of Binary Decompositions

Functional and multivalued dependencies allow us to decompose a relation of schema R in its projections $R1,R2, \ldots, Rn$ without loss of information. Indeed, for every instance r of R of which $R1,R2, \ldots, Rn$ is a valid decomposition, we have:

$$r = \pi_{R1}(r) \bowtie \pi_{R2}(r) \bowtie \ldots \bowtie \pi_{Rn}(r).$$

The problem is that the decomposition rules introduced so far do not capture all possible lossless decompositions of a relation by projections. A counterexample is the relation DBWINE(DRINKER,VINEYARD,PRODUCER). An instance of this relation is given in Fig. 5.32. Indeed, this relation is the join of its three projections, $R1$(DRINKER,VINEYARD), $R2$(DRINKER,PRODUCER), $R3$(VINEYARD,PRODUCER), but two of them are insufficient to reconstruct by join the initial relation DBWINE. It appears that functional and multivalued

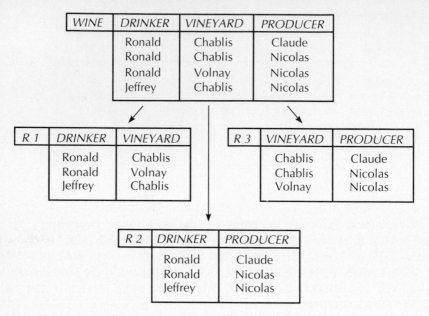

FIGURE 5.32 A decomposable 4NF relation

dependencies are not sufficient to isolate lossless decomposition into more than two relations.

Join Dependency

To capture possible lossless join decomposition into three or more relations, the concept of join dependency may be introduced.

> **Definition 5.23 Join dependency (JD)**
> Let $\{R1,R2, \ldots, Rp\}$ be a set of relation schemas and R a relation schema union of $R1,R2, \ldots, Rp$. R satisfies the join dependency $*\{R1,R2, \ldots, Rp\}$ if, for every instance r of R, the equality $r = \pi_{R1}(r)$ $\bowtie$ $\pi_{R2}(r) \bowtie \ldots \pi_{Rp}(r)$ holds.

In other words, the join dependency $*\{R1,R2, \ldots, Rp\}$ holds in R if $R1,R2,$ $\ldots, Rp$ is a lossless join decomposition of R. As a consequence, a relation schema R satisfies the join dependency $*\{R1,R2, \ldots, Rp\}$ when the following condition holds for every instance r of R:

If a set of tuples $\{t1,t2, \ldots, tp\}$ of r is such that $\pi_{Ri \cap Rj}(ti) = \pi_{Ri \cap Rj}(tj)$ for all i and $j \in [1,p]$, then the tuple t with $\pi_{R1}(t) = \pi_{R1}(t1)$, $\pi_{R2}(t) = \pi_{R2}(t2), \ldots, \pi_{Rp}(t) = \pi_{Rp}(tp)$ also belongs to r.

For example, the DBWINE relation of Fig. 5.32 satisfies the join dependency: $*\{$(DRINKER,VINEYARD), (DRINKER,PRODUCER), (VINEYARD,

PRODUCER)}. If $<d,v>$, $<d,p>$ and $<v,p>$ are, respectively, tuples of
$R1$(DRINKER,VINEYARD), $R2$(DRINKER,PRODUCER), $R3$(VINEYARD,
PRODUCER), then $<d,v,p>$ is a tuple of DBWINE.

Join dependencies are generalizations of multivalued dependencies. Indeed
the multivalued dependency $X \twoheadrightarrow Y$ in a relation $R(X,Y,Z)$ corresponds to the
join dependency *$\{(XY),(XZ)\}$. Conversely the join dependency *$\{R1,R2\}$ corresponds to the multivalued dependency $R1 \cap R2 \twoheadrightarrow R1 - R1 \cap R2$ ($\cap$ and $-$
being operations on attribute sets).

Similar to embedded multivalued dependency, we can also introduce *embedded join dependencies*. An embedded join dependency is like a join dependency except that its schemas do not cover R. Thus an embedded join dependency
is satisfied by a relation schema R if for every instance r of R, the equality $\pi_{R'}(r)$
$= \pi_{R1}(r) \bowtie \pi_{R2}(r) \bowtie \ldots \pi_{Rp}(r)$ holds where $R' = R1 \cup R2 \ldots$
$\cup Rp$. For example, in the relation DRINKER(D#, VINEYARD, GIRL-
FRIEND,LOVER), of Fig. 5.31, the embedded join dependency *$\{($D#,VINE-
YARD$),($D#,GIRL-FRIEND$)\}$ holds. For further reading on join dependencies,
consult [Rissanen78], [Fagin79], and [Yannakakis81].

Project-Join Normal Form
Decomposition should also take into account JDs. For that, a new normal form
has been introduced [Fagin79]. It requires the notion of *trivial join dependencies*.
They are those of the form *$\{R1,R2, \ldots, Rp\}$ where one of the Ri is the whole
relation schema R. Given a set of functional dependencies and a set of join dependencies $F = \{FD, JD\}$, it is possible to determine all the join dependencies implied by F [Fagin79]. The *project-join normal* form may then be defined.

> **Definition 5.24 Project-join normal form (PJNF)**
> A relation schema R is in project-join normal form iff any join depen-
> dency *$\{R1,R2, \ldots, Rp\}$ that holds in R is either trivial or contains
> a superkey of R (that is, some Ri is a superkey of R).

For instance, the DBWINE relation is not in project-join normal form because
the JD

    *$\{$(DRINKER,VINEYARD),(DRINKER,PRODUCER),
        (VINEYARD,PRODUCER)$\}$

does not include a superkey of R. Indeed the unique key of R is {DRINKER,
VINEYARD,PRODUCER).

When a join dependency that does not include a superkey has been isolated,
decomposition is performed in a straightforward manner by projections according to the problematical join dependency. Project-join decomposition does not
solve the problem of embedded join dependencies; however, it has been shown
that project-join normal form is the ultimate normal form in the sense that a
relation in PJNF cannot be decomposed further without loss of information us-

ing projections [Fagin79]. It appears that decomposition by projection is not sufficient to eliminate data redundancy and update anomalies in database relations.

5.5.9 Further Dependencies

Many kinds of dependencies may induce data redundancy in relations, such as FDs, MVDs, embedded MVDs, JDs, and embedded JDs. Therefore it is interesting to find a general representation of dependencies that allows the description of the previously studied dependencies in a uniform way. Such a representation is possible using algebraic dependency and template dependency. In the remainder of this section, we introduce these generalized kinds of dependencies and an important procedure, the chase. This procedure determines if a given dependency can be inferred from a given set of dependencies. For a more thorough presentation of these aspects, consult [Maier79] and [Yannakakis80]. The latter introduced the class of *algebraic dependencies,* which are set inequalities on algebraic expressions formed with projection and equijoins.

> **Definition 5.25 Algebraic dependency**
> Let R be a relational schema and r any instance of R. R satisfies the algebraic dependency $\phi\{R1, R2, \ldots, Rp\}$ iff $r \supset \phi(\pi_{R1}(r), \pi_{R2}(r), \ldots, \pi_{Rn}(r))$ where ϕ is a relational expression that may be composed of projections and equijoins.

Such algebraic dependencies are very general — probably too general to be practical. The study of a restricted class of algebraic dependencies requires the comparison of project-join relational expressions. A useful tool for comparing expression is the *tableau* [Aho79]. We used a simplified definition here, similar to [Maier79].

> **Definition 5.26 Tableau**
> A tableau $T(A1, A2, \ldots, Ak)$ is a relation over a universal schema U where the domain of each attribute Ai is a set of symbols $\{ai, bi1, \ldots, bin\}$.

ai are called *distinguished symbol* and *bij nondistinguished*. ai and bij represent variables. A variable may appear in only one column. Furthermore only one distinguished variable may appear in each column. Thus the columns are typed with a unique domain.

An example of a tableau is given in Fig. 5.33. A tableau T defines a target schema $trs(T)$, which is the set of attributes such that the corresponding distinguished symbol occurs in T. For example, the tableau of Fig. 5.33 has for target schema $\{A1, A2, A3\}$.

	A1	A2	A3	A4
T =	a1	b21	b31	b41
	b11	a2	b32	b42
	a1	b22	a3	b43

FIGURE 5.33 Example of a tableau

A *valuation* $\beta(T)$ of a tableau T is a function that transforms the tableau in a relation by assigning a value to each symbol of T. A valuation $\beta(T)$ is compatible with a relation instance u if $\beta(T)$ is included in u. Such a valuation of the tableau consists of replacing each line by tuples of u having the same pattern for the corresponding attributes. The *summary t* of a tableau T is the tuple composed of distinguished symbols. Thus a tableau T defines a mapping ϕ_T from relations over U to relations over $trs(T)$. The image of a given relation instance u of schema U is a relation instance $\phi_T(u)$ whose tuples are the possible valuations of the tableau summary t, for all compatible valuations of T with u; formally: $\phi_T(u) = \{\beta(t) \backslash \beta$ is compatible with $u\}$.

By definition, two tableaux with same target schemas are equivalent if they define the same mapping for all relation instances. Some of the basic results of the theory of tableaux are the following [Aho79]:

1. For every project-join expression F over a relation schema R, there is a tableau T such that, for every instance r of R: $F(r) = \phi_T(r)$.
2. Each tableau T has a minimal subset T^* equivalent to T; T^* is unique up to renaming of nondistinguished symbols.
3. Let X be the target schema of a tableau T; then for any relation u of schema U, $\pi_X(u)$ is included in $\phi_T(u)$.

It results from properties 1, 2, and 3 that tableaux are useful tools to compare algebraic expressions: Two project-join expressions are equivalent if their corresponding tableaux are equivalent. Tableaux are also useful to define *template dependency*, a very general kind of dependency.

Definition 5.27 Template dependency (TD)
A template dependency of the form T/t, where T is a tableau with summary t and target schema X, is satisfied by a relation schema R iff, for every instance r of R: $\phi_T(r) = \pi_X(r)$.

Clearly a template dependency states that in any instance r of R, for each collection of tuples $\{t1, t2, \ldots, tn\}$ with values corresponding to T symbols, there should exist a subtuple corresponding to the corresponding value of t. It is an inference rule that states the presence of a subtuple derived from the tableau summary whenever the tableau pattern is met in the relation. A few examples of template dependencies are illustrated with:

1. *Multivalued dependency* $A1 \twoheadrightarrow A2$ in $R(A1,A2,A3)$:

$A1$	$A2$	$A3$
$a1$	$a2$	$b31$
$a1$	$b21$	$a3$
$a1$	$a2$	$a3$

2. *Join dependency* $*\{(A1,A2), (A2,A3), (A1,A3)\}$ in $R(A1,A2,A3)$:

$A1$	$A2$	$A3$
$a1$	$a2$	$b13$
$b11$	$a2$	$a3$
$a1$	$b21$	$a3$
$a1$	$a2$	$a3$

The definition of template dependency can be slightly generalized by replacing the summary t by a constraint c that must be enforced by distinguished symbols. Then all types of dependencies studied so far may be represented as template dependencies. Furthermore the notion of template dependency is more general and permits representing other kinds of dependencies.

5.5.10 The Chase of Dependencies

One question that often arises in the normalization process is whether a set F of dependencies implies a given dependency d. We say that $F \models d$ (d can be inferred from F and is, in some sense, redundant with F) if d holds in every relation satisfying F. A procedure for testing if d can be inferred from F is the chase [Maier79]. Tableaux are useful tools to solve this problem.

The basic idea is to start with a tableau representing the dependency to infer d without summary or constraint. Then by applying successive transformation rules to that tableau corresponding to the dependencies in F, we try to generate the summary $<a1,a2, \ldots >$ (or the constraint c) that gives the desired dependency. The rules may be applied either up to generating the desired dependency or up to saturation. In the latter case, d cannot be inferred from F. The transformation rules for tableaux are the following:

Rule for functional dependency. If $X \rightarrow Y$ is a FD in F and there exists $t1$ and $t2$ in T such that $\pi_X(t1) = \pi_X(t2)$ and $\pi_Y(t1) \neq \pi_Y(t2)$ then the variables $v1$ in $\pi_Y(t1)$ and $v2$ in $\pi_Y(t2)$ are identified by the following renaming rule: (1) if one of the variables is distinguished, the other one is renamed to that distinguished variable, (2) if both are nondistinguished,

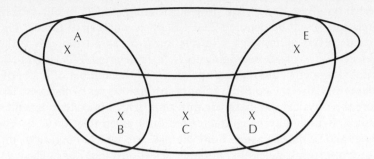

FIGURE 5.34 Cyclic hypergraph for a join dependency

the variable with the larger subscript is renamed to be the variable with
the smaller subscript.

Rule for join dependency: If *{R1,R2, . . . , Rp} holds in R, then
$T := \pi_{R1}(T) \bowtie \pi_{R2}(T) \bowtie \ldots \bowtie \pi_{Rn}(T)$.

Because multivalued dependency is a particular case of join dependency, the second rule is valid for MDs. It can also be applied in the case of embedded join
(or multivalued) dependencies. Finally the transformation rules may be applied
while they change the tableau *T.* As the procedure has the Church-Rosser property (the rules are confluent to a unique tableau), the result does not depend on
the order of rule applications.

   Dependency theory goes further than template dependencies. An interesting
discussion is the existence of a unique universal relation for a given set of attributes. This property is related to the acyclicity of the hypergraph that represents
the set of join dependencies. Given a set of attributes and a JD, we can associate
a hypergraph whose nodes are attributes and whose edges are sets of nodes; an
edge represents a group of attributes pertaining to the JD. For example, the JD
*{(A,B),(B,C,D),(D,E),(A,E)} is portrayed by the hypergraph of Fig. 5.34. This
is a cyclic hypergraph. Relations with cyclic hypergraphs may determine several
universal relations. Readers may consult [Maier83] for a fuller discussion of cyclic database schema and dependency theory in general.

5.6 Internal Schema Optimization

5.6.1 Load and Cost Evaluations

The optimization of the internal schema requires an evaluation of the database
contents and activities. Several models have been proposed to capture these parameters [Cardenas75, Sevcik81, Whang81, Carlis84, Schkolnick85]. In general,
the cost model is system dependent. However, to state the main parameters of

the internal database design, we present a simple model. In our model, the size of the relation R will be denoted TUPLE(R), in number of tuples. The number of different entries in an index of a relation R on an attribute Ai is the number of different values of Ai belonging to $R;$ it is denoted VALUE(R,Ai). A more sophisticated model would require knowledge of the number of pages of relations and indexes and also the consideration of different types of indexes. To simplify, we ignore the physical database organization, which is system dependent.

User activities may be characterized on a given relation R by considering the queries and updates classes. For example, five typical operations may be distinguished: insertions, deletions, updates, selections, and joins. The cost of selections being dependent on the given attributes, we shall further distinguish a type of selection per attribute name. Thus frequencies may be assigned to each of the four first operation classes as follows:

$F_I(R)$ is the frequency of insertions of instances of a relation R per time unit (for example, a week or a day).

$F_D(R)$ is the frequency of deletions of instances of a relation R per time unit.

$F_U(R)$ is the frequency of updates of instances of a relation R per time unit.

$F_S(R,Ai)$ is the frequency of selections of instances of a relation R through attribute $Ai,$ per time unit.

For a given relation $R,$ the insertion, deletion, and update costs generally depend on the number of indexes I(R) in a linear way but are independent of the relation size. Thus, we may assume:

$$COST_I(R) = \lambda_I \cdot I(R) + \mu_I.$$
$$COST_D(R) = \lambda_D \cdot I(R) + \mu_D.$$
$$COST_U(R) = \lambda_U \cdot I(R) + \mu_U.$$

The cost of selecting by attribute Ai depends greatly on the presence or absence of an index on attribute Ai. Let $IND(R,Ai)$ be a value equal to 0 if Ai is indexed and to 1 otherwise. The selection cost may be roughly approximated by (λ_{SS} is the scan cost per tuple while λ_{SI} is the indexed cost per tuple):

$$COST_S(R,Ai) = IND(R,Ai) \cdot \lambda_{SS} \cdot TUPLE(R) + (1 - IND(R,Ai)) \cdot \lambda_{SI} \cdot$$
$$(TUPLE(R)/VALUE(R,Ai)).$$

Moreover, we also need to evaluate join operations frequencies and costs. Let us denote $F_J(R1,R2)$ the join frequency of relations $R1$ and $R2$. Join processing requires a time that is, in the worst case, of the order of the product of the relation sizes (see Chapter 9):

$$COST_J(R1,R2) = \mu_J \cdot TUPLE(R1) \cdot TUPLE(R2).$$

Using all the previous parameters, the total cost of a given activity on a database schema DB = $\{R1, R2, \ldots, Rn\}$ may be computed. It is given by the following formula:

$$COST = \Sigma_R \{F_I(R) \cdot COST_I(R) + F_D(R) \cdot COST_D(R) + F_U(R) \cdot COST_U(R)$$
$$+ \Sigma_A F_S(R,A) \cdot COST_S(R,A) + \Sigma_{R'} F_J(R,R') \cdot (COST_J(R,R'))\}$$

The internal database design may be seen as the computation of the best schema that minimizes the COST function. This is a rather complex problem that we oversimplified and is generally solved in two steps, called *logical* and *physical design*. Logical design consists of choosing the relations to implement and physical design in generating the indexes.

5.6.2 Choice of Base Relations

The first step, logical database design, consists of optimizing the relational schema without considering the access paths. Such optimization is DBMS independent because data placement and access paths are omitted. Thus in our model, the indexes will be omitted ($I(R)$ will be set to 0 and $IND(R,A)$ will be set to 1). The cost formula becomes, by denoting $F_S(R)$ the selection frequency on relation R:

$$COST = \Sigma_R\{F_I(R) \cdot \mu_I + F_D(R) \cdot \mu_D + F_U(R) \cdot \mu_U$$
$$+ TUPLE(R) \cdot (\lambda_{SS} \cdot F_S(R) + \mu_J \cdot \Sigma_{R'} F_J(R,R') \cdot TUPLE(R'))\}$$

Again this formula is oversimplified; however, it shows that logical design depends only on the relation schema — that is, the relation sizes and activities. A normalized schema tends to minimize the number of tuples in each relation *(TUPLE(R))*, but it maximizes the number of relations and the join frequencies. A universal schema (if possible) gives a unique relation with a lot of tuples and very high operation frequencies.

Between these two extreme alternatives, the optimized logical schema may be determined starting from a normalized conceptual schema and proceeding by synthesis. The search space of feasible logical schema is described from the conceptual schema by performing successive joins of relations. This procedure corresponds to the step called *denormalization*. An exhaustive search may be applied to obtain the best logical schema. During the search, each possible solution is generated from a previous one by joining two relations having a possible natural join; the minimum-cost selected schema is kept as the logical schema. Another approach to searching the large search space is to use a stochastic algorithm. An approximately minimum cost schema can be found by picking randomly a large number of schemas from the search space and choosing the minimum-cost one. This number can be reduced by using a stochastic technique as simulated annealing [Ioannidis87].

Whatever search strategy for the minimum cost schema is used, denormalization allows the design tool to generate integrity constraints. During the search process, it is interesting to keep track of the join dependencies and the keys of the relations generated. These integrity constraints must be generated with the logical schema. Also referential integrity constraints are useful and must be included in the logical schema. They are generally derived from an E/R perception of the normalized schema. In summary, let us recall that a direct implementation of a 3NF schema may result in unnecessary join costs. Thus denormalization is a necessary step for good performance.

5.6.3 Access Path Generation

The next step is the generation of access paths, the main part of physical database design. It is greatly dependent on the DBMS, which may or may not implement hashing access methods, clustering methods, or even indexes. With our simplified models, access path generation is simply the generation of indexes in the logical schema relations. Index generation should not be based only on the cost formula, including the IND parameter. Keys and referential integrity constraints should be considered. Depending on the DBMS, it might be a good heuristics to generate indexes on all key attributes and all foreign key attributes. Other indexes might be generated in order to minimize the cost formula. In addition, indexes are good tools to improve join performances (the join cost is dependent on the existence of indexes on the join attributes — see chapter 9). In summary, access path generation is a complex process, which tries to optimize the database according to a DBMS-dependent cost formula.

5.6.4 Tuning and Improvements

The database design can and must always be improved. It is true for the conceptual schema. It is even more important for the internal schema. Most DBMSs supply tools to audit database requests and to monitor performance. Some vendors have developed software aids for performance studies. Such tools can help in detecting database bottlenecks at run time. For example, a join between two relations may be detected as a critical issue. Thus these two relations may be grouped to suppress the join cost. This entails a revision of the logical schema. Many other alternatives are possible. The important point is to remember that a database design can always be improved in terms of data semantics and system performance.

5.7 Conclusion

This chapter presented an overview of the relational database design process. It includes practical and theoretical considerations. Clearly practitioners and design tools need the support of the normalization theory to perform good design. Relational database design is not an easy task. However, it is not true that understanding relational theory clearly is always a necessary condition to use relational DBMSs. It may even be dangerous; relations that are normalized may yield bad performances.

The current knowledge on database design includes theoretical and practical rules with optimization heuristics. Moreover, database design needs to capture user requirements. It is more an art than a science, even if an underlying theory is used in certain steps of the design. A few researchers [Bouzeghoub83, Rolland86, Tucherman85] have proposed the development of expert system–based tools for supporting automatic database design. An expert system for database design could encompass the whole design process, starting from the capture of user requirements and going through view integration, conceptual design, logical design, and physical design. The knowledge base of the expert system would include the database design rules and heuristics.

Such an expert system for database design has been developed at the University of Paris VI, in cooperation with an industrial partner [Bouzeghoub85]. The system, called SECSI, is written in PROLOG and run on PCs and UNIX stations. This automatic design tool offers an incremental knowledge base, accepts incomplete specifications, and justifies and explains its results. It generates first a normalized relational schema and then an optimized internal schema. A first version of this system has been released on the French market. Similar tools are developed elsewhere [Tucherman85, Rolland86]. Expert systems could become successful automatic and intelligent database designers.

5.8 References and Bibliography

[Aho79] Aho A. V., Beeri C., Ullman J. D. "The Theory of Joins in Relational Databases," ACM Transactions on Database Systems, V4, N3, September 1979, pp. 297 – 314.

[Armstrong74] Armstrong W. W. "Dependency Structures of Database Relationships," IFIP World Congress 1974, North-Holland ed., pp. 580 – 83.

[Ausiello83] Ausiello G., D'Atri, Sacca D. "Graph Algorithms for Functional Dependency Manipulation," Journal of the ACM, V30, N4, October 1983, pp. 752 – 66.

[Batini84] Batini C., Lenzerini M. "A Methodology for Data Schema Integration in the Entity-Relationship Model," IEEE Transactions on Software Engineering, V10, N6, November 1984, pp. 650 – 64.

[Beeri79] Beeri C., Bernstein P. "Computational Problems Related to the Design of Normal Form Schemas," ACM Transactions on Database Systems, V4, N1, March 1979.

[Bernstein76] "Synthesizing Third Normal Form Relations from Functional Dependencies," ACM Transactions on Database Systems, V1, N4, December 1976, pp. 277 – 98.

[Bouzeghoub83] "Design of an Expert System for Database Design," ICOD-2 Workshop on *New Applications of Data Bases,* Academic Press, 1983.

[Bouzeghoub85] Bouzeghoub M., Gardarin G., Metais E. "Database Design Tools: An Expert System Approach," Proc. 11th Very Large Data Bases, Stockholm, 1985, pp. 82 – 95.

[Bouzeghoub86] Bouzeghoub M., Gardarin G. "Tools for Database Design and Programming — A New Perspective," in *Relational Databases, State of the Art Report* 14:5, Pergamon Infotech Limited, 1986.

[Cardenas75] Cardenas A. F. "Analysis and Performance of Inverted Database Structures," Comm. ACM, V18, N5, May 1975, pp. 252 – 63.

[Carlis84] Carlis J. V., March S. T. "A Descriptive Model of Physical Database Design: Problems and Solutions," 1st Data Engineering Conference, Los Angeles, 1984, IEEE ed., pp. 253 – 60.

[Codd70] Codd E. F. "A Relational Model of Data for Large Shared Data Banks," Comm. ACM, V13, N6, June 1970, pp. 377 – 87.

[Codd71] Codd E. F. "Normalized Database Structure: A Brief Tutorial," ACM SIGFIDET Workshop on Data Description, Access and Control, November 1971, pp. 1 – 17.

[Codd72] Codd E. F. "Further Normalization of the Data Base Relational Model," in *Data Base Systems,* R. Rustin ed., Prentice-Hall, 1972.

[Codd74] Codd E. F. "Recent Investigations in Relational Database Systems," IFIP World Congress 1974, North-Holland ed., pp. 1017 – 21.

[Dayal84] Dayal U., HWang H. Y., "View Definition and Generalization for Database Integration in a Multidatabase System," IEEE Transactions on Software Engineering, V10, N6, November 1984, pp. 628 – 44.

[DeAntonellis83] De Antonellis V., Demo B. "Requirements Collection and Analysis," in *Methodology and Tools for Database Design,* S. Ceri ed., North-Holland, 1983.

[Delobel73] Casey R. G., Delobel C. "Decomposition of a Data Base and the Theory of Boolean Switching Functions," IBM J. Research Develop., V17, N5, December 1973, pp. 374 – 86.

[El-Masri79] El-Masri R., Wiederhold G. "Data Model Integration Using the Structural Model," ACM, 1979, pp.191 – 202.

[Fagin77] Fagin R. "Multivalued Dependencies and a New Normal Form for Relational Databases," ACM Transactions on Data Base Systems, V2, N3, September 1977, pp. 262 – 78.

[Fagin79] Fagin R. "Normal Forms and Relational Database Operators," ACM SIGMOD 1979, Boston, June 1979, pp. 153 – 60.

[Honeyman82] Honeyman P. "Testing Satisfaction of Functional Dependencies," Journal of the ACM, V29, N3, 1982, pp. 668 – 77.

[Ioannidis87] Ioannidis Y. E., Wong E. "Query Optimization by Simulated Annealing," Proc. 1987 ACM-SIGMOD, San Francisco, 1987.

[Kent81] Kent W., "Consequences of Assuming a Universal Relation," ACM Transactions on Data Base Systems, V6, N4, December 1981, pp. 539 – 56.

[Lum79] Lum V. Y. et al. "1978 New Orleans Data Base Design Workshop Report," 5th Very Large Databases Conference, Rio de Janeiro, October 1979, IEEE ed. pp. 328 – 39.

[Maier79] Maier D., Mendelzon A. O., Sagiv Y. "Testing Implications of Data Dependencies," ACM Transactions on Data Base Systems, V4, N4, December 1979, pp. 455 – 69.

[Maier83] Maier D. *The Theory of Relational Databases,* Computer Science Press, 1983.

[Mendelzon84] Mendelzon A. O. "Database States and Their Tableaux," ACM Transactions on Data Base Systems, V9, N2, June 1984, pp. 264 – 82.

[Navathe84] Navathe S., El-Masri R., Sahidar T. "Relationship Merging in Schema Integration," Proc. 10th Very Large Data Bases, August 1984, pp. 78 – 90.

[Reiner86] Reiner D. S. "Database Design — Theory and Practice," 12th Very Large Data Bases Tutorials, Kyoto, August 1986.

[Rissanen78] Rissanen J. "Theory of Relations for Databases — A Tutorial Survey," 7th Symposium on Math. Foundations of Computer Science, Springer-Verlag, Lecture in Comp. Science N. 64, pp. 537 – 51.

[Rissanen73] Rissanen J., Delobel C. "Decomposition of Files — A Basis for Data Storage and Retrieval," IBM Research Report RJ 1220, San Jose, Calif., May 1973.

[Rolland86] Rolland C., Proix C. "An Expert System Approach to Information System Design," IFIP World Conf. 1986, Dublin, October 1986.

[Schkolnick85] Schkolnick M., Tiberio P. "Estimating the Cost of Updates in a Relational Database," ACM Transactions on Data Base Systems, V10, N2, June 1985, pp. 163 – 80.

[Sevcik81] Sevcik K. "Data Base System Performance Prediction Using an Analytical Model," 7th Very Large Data Bases Conf., Cannes, France, September 1981, pp. 182 – 98.

[Tardieu83] Tardieu H., Rochefeld A., Colletti R. La Methode MERISE, ed. Organisation, 1983.

[Teichroew77] Teichroew D., Hershey E. A. "PSL/PSA: A Computer Aid Technique for Structured Documentation and Analysis of Information Processing Systems," IEEE Transactions on Software Engineering, SE-3, 1, January 1977.

[Tucherman85] Tucherman L., Furtado A., Casanova M. "A Tool for Modular Database Design," Proc. 11th Very Large Data Bases, Stockholm 1985.

[Whang81] Whang K-Y, Wiederhold G., Sagalowicz D. "Separability — An Approach to Physical Database Design," 7th Very Large Data Bases Conf., Cannes, France, September 1981, pp. 320 – 32.

[Yannakakis80] Yannakakis M., Papadimitriou C. H. "Algebraic Dependencies," Foundations of Computer Science Conference, 1980, IEEE Proc., pp. 328-32.

[Yannakakis81] Yannakakis M. "Algorithms for Acyclic Database Schemes," 7th Very Large Data Bases Conf., Cannes, France, September 1981, pp. 82 – 94.

[Zaniolo81] Zaniolo C., Melkanoff M. A. "On the Design of Relational Database Schemata," ACM Transactions on Data Base Systems, V6, N1, March 1981, pp. 1 – 47.

6
INTEGRITY, VIEWS, AND SECURITY

6.1 Introduction

A database system must guarantee database consistency, a condition that exists if the database satisfies a set of rules called semantic integrity constraints or simply *integrity constraints*. The rules may be explicitly declared in the data dictionary or implicit. For instance, an integrity constraint may state the equality of two values in the database (for example, a W# value in the DRINK relation must equal a W# value in the WINE relation) or state a complex assertion between multiple data (for example, the sum of the quantities in the DRINK relation should not exceed the sum of the quantities in the HARVEST relation). The problem of maintaining database consistency is the problem of rejecting updates that violate the integrity constraints. Such invalid updates may be caused by erroneous data entry, concurrent accesses to the database, software or hardware failures, or unauthorized data modifications. Thus maintaining database consistency requires semantic integrity control, concurrency control, reliability control, and protection against unauthorized accesses.

This chapter is devoted to the study of semantic integrity control and security enforcement methods. In addition, we study external views in relational databases, which can be used as a powerful security mechanism.

Semantic integrity control checks that integrity constraints are not violated by database update requests. It ensures database consistency by rejecting updates that lead to inconsistent database states or by executing specific actions compen-

183

sating the effect of the updates. An inconsistent database state is characterized by the fact that certain integrity constraints are false. Two methods have been proposed to avoid inconsistent database state. The *detection method* consists of verifying that all integrity constraints hold after one or more updates. If a constraint is violated, the updates are undone; thus data are reinstated to their former condition. The *prevention method* verifies, before updating the database, that no integrity constraint can be violated by the update. Thus it disallows updates that might violate the database consistency.

View mapping techniques are implemented primarily to derive external relations from internal relations stored in the database. Views are basically external schemas in the context of the relational model. Views ensure logical data independence. In addition, views protect the database against unauthorized accesses, as a user can manipulate only relations and attributes defined in his or her view. View mapping requires efficient algorithms to transform a query expressed on a view into a query expressed on the relations stored in the database. The main techniques for view mapping are query modification and view concretion. One difficult problem concerns view update — the transformation of an update expressed on a view to updates expressed on the internal relations.

Security protection refers to the control of permission for data retrieval, updating, deletion, insertion, and data administration. Although sophisticated techniques, such as data encryption and statistical database protection, can be applied to improve data security, we shall concentrate on the authorization mechanisms specific to relational databases. Security protection is a complex problem not fully treated in this book. Specific books are devoted to that problem such as [Fernandez81].

In this chapter, we first present a classification of the various types of integrity constraints as well as languages to specify integrity constraints. Then, we focus on the methods to enforce integrity assertions. Next, we concentrate on view mapping techniques. Finally, we study the problem of security protection.

6.2 Definition of Integrity Constraints

In this section, integrity constraints are classified according to their functions. At the highest level, integrity constraints are distinguished between structural and behavioral constraints. At the second level, several types of integrity constraints are considered. Most of these types have already been defined either in the chapter on the relational model (see Chapter 4 for structural constraints) or in the chapter on database design (see Chapter 5 for behavioral constraints).

6.2.1 Structural Integrity Constraints

Definition 6.1 Structural integrity constraint
Integrity constraint inherent in a data model expressing a specific semantic property of basic constructs using the data model.

A structural constraint is generally specified as part of the schema at database definition. With the relational model, there exist the following types of structural integrity constraints:

1. The *unique key constraint* specifies that a relation has a nonnull key composed of one or more attributes. For example, the wine number (W#) is the primary key of the WINE relation.
2. The *referential integrity constraint* specifies that part of a key in a relation is used as a key in another relation. For instance, the wine number W# in the DRINK relation references the primary key of the WINE relation.
3. The *domain constraint* restricts the values of one attribute to a specific set. We may distinguish type constraints that specify the domain format and operations (the attribute QUANTITY is of type real) and range constraints that restrict the possible values of a domain (for example, the attribute QUANTITY must range between 10 and 30).
4. The *nonnull constraint* removes the null value from the set of possible values for a specific attribute. For example, null is not allowed for the VINEYARD attribute in the WINE relation.

The choice of structural constraint type is somewhat arbitrary. Structural constraints were introduced in the relational model to extend semantics data modeling capabilities. The unique key constraint was introduced in the relational model to avoid duplicating tuples in a relation, that is, to capture real-world entities without ambiguity. One could envision a different relational model without keys. However, because tuple identification could be a problem in such a model, some form of tuple identification should be introduced. Tuple identifiers could be system generated and visible to the user. More simply, it was chosen to introduce user-specified attribute values as tuple identifiers (keys). Keys and domain constraints are insufficient to model real-world data semantics. In particular, they do not permit the capture of semantic links between two or more relations. It was only in 1981 that referential integrity was introduced as a structural constraint in the relational model [Date81]. Referential integrity allows the designer to declare foreign keys in a relation that captures semantic links between relations, in general E/R links.

6.2.2 Behavioral Integrity Constraints

Definition 6.2 Behavioral integrity constraint
Integrity constraint modeling a semantic property of the database that regulates the behavior of applications.

A behavioral integrity constraint is generally introduced in addition to the schema. With the relational model, several types of behavioral constraints have been introduced. Most of them can be expressed as first-order logic assertions. Behavioral constraints can express relationships internal to a relation such as:

Functional dependencies as defined in Chapter 5; for example, the wine number (W#) determines uniquely the vineyard.

Multivalued dependencies as defined in Chapter 5; for example, the classes taught by a professor are independent of the names of his children (PROF →→ CLASSES | CHILDREN) in a PROFESSOR (PROF,CLASSES,CHILDREN) relation.

Aggregate dependencies that restrict the possible values of an aggregate function in a relation; for example, the sum of quantities drunk per wine must not exceed 10.

They can also define interrelation links, such as:

Inclusion dependencies, which specify that one or more columns of a relation remain included in other relations; for example, a CITY in the DRINKER relation must appear as a CITY in the STATES relation.

Equational dependencies, which enforce equality or inequality of two arithmetic expressions computed from relations using attribute values or functions of attribute values (including aggregate functions); for instance, the quantity in stock for each wine must always be equal to the quantity purchased less the quantity drunk.

Another important type of behavioral integrity constraints concerns *equational invariance* under an update program. Such a constraint states that the result of an arithmetic expression computed from relations using attribute values or functions of attribute values (including aggregate functions) must not be changed by the update program (by a sequence of updates composing a transaction as defined in the next chapter). Thus, for example, the sum of the balances in the database of a bank must remain constant upon completion of the program "transfer." Finally it should be noted that certain integrity constraints are time dependent; thus, for example, they might state that only certain data changes are permitted at certain instants or relative to other changes. For example, an integrity constraint can state that the attribute PERCENT in the WINE relation can only decrease.

6.2.3 Integrity Constraint Manipulation Languages

In relational DBMSs, integrity constraints are manipulated using nonprocedural languages. In SQL, certain structural integrity constraints may be defined at relation creation, within the CREATE command as seen in Chapter 4. This includes unique key constraints, domain constraints, and nonnull constraints. SQL does not support referential integrity in its current version. In addition, a specific command:

ASSERT <assertion-name> **ON** [<operation> **OF**] <relation-name> : <search condition>

is included in certain versions of SQL to define behavioral constraints. An assertion-name is a name given to the constraint to refer to it in the data dictionary — for example, to destroy it. It is possible to specify constraints that must be enforced only when certain operations are performed on a given relation. The operation is a typical SQL modification operation — update, delete, or insert. The operation type is useful for integrity control optimization. A search condition is an SQL search condition as defined in Chapter 4. For example, the integrity constraint "average percent of the wines should not exceed 12" may be expressed as follows:

ASSERT AVG_WINE **ON** WINE: AVG(PERCENT) ≤ 12

As an additional example, it is possible to accept the deletion of a wine only if the corresponding quantities in the DRINK relation are 0 using the following command:

ASSERT DEL_WINE **ON** DELETION OF WINE:
(SUM(QUANTITY) FROM DRINK WHERE DRINK.W# = WINE.W#) = 0

It is also possible to use the key words OLD and NEW to specify time-dependent constraints, for example, a percentage can only decrease:

ASSERT UPD_WINE ON UPDATE OF WINE:
NEW PERCENT < **OLD** PERCENT

In the QUEL nonprocedural language of INGRES [Stonebraker76], a specific command is also used to define behavioral constraints:

DEFINE INTEGRITY ON <relation> **IS** <qualification>.

However, a qualification can only refer to a unique relation. Thus QUEL supports only monorelation integrity constraints.

A relational DBMS offering a complete integrity subsystem should support an extended integrity constraint manipulation language. Such a language has been implemented in the SABRINA system [Simon87]. This language allows one to specify, read, or drop integrity constraints. These constraints can be defined either at relation creation time or later. Constraint definitions are based on simple key words for the common constraints of the relational model. These are unique key constraints, referential, inclusion, functional, and multivalued dependencies. A more general constraint can be expressed by a qualification given in tuple relational calculus, possibly conditioned by another qualification. Variables of the qualification can be universally or existentially quantified. Each constraint is seen as a query qualification that must be satisfied by all tuples of the Cartesian product of the relations determined by the tuple variables. In fact, all constraints (unique key, referential, inclusion and so on) could be expressed using the general constraint form but often in a complex way. In a way similar to SQL, the key words NEW and OLD are introduced to express a specific kind of time-dependent constraints called *transition constraints*.

Fig. 6.1 illustrates the syntax of the integrity constraint manipulation language proposed here. The objectives of the language (similar to the language

ASSERT <constraint_name>	**AS** <Integrity constraint>
DROP <constraint_name>	
Integrity constraint ::=	unique key constraint | not null constraint | referential dependency | inclusion dependency | functional dependency | multivalued dependency
unique key constraint ::=	**UNIQUE** <attribute_list> **IN** <relation>
not null constraint ::=	**NOT NULL** <attribute_list> **IN** <relation>
referential dependency ::=	**REFERENCE** <relation> <attribute_list> **FROM** <relation> <attribute_list>
inclusion dependency ::=	**INCLUSION** <relation> <attribute_list> **IN** <relation> <attribute_list>
functional dependency ::=	**FD** <attribute_list> **TO** <attribute_list> **IN** <relation>
multivalued dependency ::=	**MD** <attribute_list> **TO** <attribute_list> **[INDEPENDENTLY OF** <attribute_list>] **IN** <relation>
general constraint ::=	**[DEFERRED] CONSTRAINT** **[IN** <relation>(variable] **[WITH** <relation>(variable)] . . . **[WHEN** <update-type>] <qualification> **[IF** <qualification>]

FIGURE 6.1 Example of an integrity constraint manipulation language

implemented in SABRINA) are simplicity and completeness, in the sense that all integrity constraints specified above can be defined with simple commands. As usual, a clause between brackets is optional <Attribute_list> is a list of one or more attributes separated by commas. <Update_type> is chosen among INSERT, DELETE, AND UPDATE. <Qualification> is a query qualification expressed in tuple relational calculus using the variables previously defined.

For simplicity, we consider that the effect of a constraint violation is always to reject the tuples that violate the constraint. However, some database systems may be more elaborated. For example, certain compensation actions can be specified in the constraint definition language. More generally, *triggers* [Astrahan76] could be combined with integrity constraints for specifying the effect of updates.

Definition 6.3 Trigger
Rule specifying an action to activate when a database condition is true.

A trigger is often expressed as a rule of the form **if** <search-condition> **then** <action>. The action is generally a database update, insert, or delete command. Thus triggers may be used to restore the database consistency after a constraint violation. For example, if W# in DRINK must refer to an existing wine in WINE (there exists a referential integrity constraint from DRINK to WINE), database integrity after deleting a wine in WINE can be reinstated by a trigger. The condition of the trigger could be the violation of the referential integrity constraint. The action of the trigger could be to delete all tuples in DRINK that do not refer to an existing tuple in WINE. Not too many existing relational DBMSs implement triggers. Thus we do not consider triggers further in this chapter.

Certain systems do not verify integrity constraints at each update but rather at the end of an update program. Such constraints are said to be *deferred*. Verifying constraints at program end allows the program to temporarily violate an integrity constraint during execution. This capability is necessary for supporting equational invariance and for avoiding mandatory order of updates in the case of referential integrity constraints. Indeed controlling integrity constraints at each update does not permit multiple updates that temporarily violate an integrity constraint but globally satisfy it. This motivates the key word DEFERRED in the general constraint specification language of Fig. 6.1. As an example, let us assume that W# in DRINK must refer to an existing wine in WINE (a referential integrity constraint from DRINK to WINE). At least two updates are necessary to insert a new wine with its consumption: one to insert the wine and the other to insert the consumptions. If the integrity constraint is controlled after each update, it is impossible to insert the consumptions before the wine. This is not true if the integrity control can be deferred at program end — that is, after the two updates.

Let us now give a few examples of constraints expressed with the language of Fig. 6.1, using the well-known wine database:

DRINKER (D#, NAME, FIRSTNAME, CITY)
WINE (W#, VINEYARD, VINTAGE, PERCENT)
DRINK (W#, D#, DATE, CITY, QUANTITY)

Unique key constraint
ASSERT UK **AS UNIQUE** W# **IN** WINE
Functional dependency
ASSERT FD **AS FD** W# **TO** VINEYARD **IN** WINE
This can also be expressed as:
ASSERT FD **AS CONSTRAINT IN** WINE (W) **WITH** WINE(V)
W.VINEYARD = V.WINEYARD **IF** W.W# = V.W#
General domain constraint
ASSERT GD **AS CONSTRAINT IN** WINE(W)
W.PERCENT > 10 AND W.PERCENT < 15
Transition constraint
ASSERT TC **AS CONSTRAINT IN** WINE(W) **WHEN UPDATE**
NEW W.PERCENT > **OLD** W.PERCENT
Referential integrity
ASSERT REFW **AS REFERENCE** WINE.W# **FROM** DRINK.W#
Another possible expression is:
ASSERT REFW **AS CONSTRAINT IN** WINE(W) **WITH** DRINK (E)
FOR ALL E **EXIST** W (E.W# = E.W#)
Constraint with aggregates
ASSERT AG **AS CONSTRAINT IN** WINE(W) **WITH DRINK** (E)
SUM(E.QUANTITY WHERE E.W# = W.W#) < 10
IF (W.VINEYARD = "BEAUJOLAIS")

6.3 Analysis of Integrity Constraints

Integrity constraints defined by a database administrator are first processed by a parser, which stores them in internal form in the data dictionary (the relational metabase). The parser should reject integrity constraints that contradict either the database or other integrity constraints. It is also desirable to analyze the integrity constraints to simplify them before using them. A logical simplification of integrity constraints will reduce the time required to control the database integrity when updates occur. To reject invalid updates, it is in first approximation necessary to evaluate integrity constraints against the database as normal queries. We define the evaluation cost of a constraint as the cost of verifying it. The evaluation cost of a set of integrity constraints is the sum of the evaluation cost of each constraint. The main goal of integrity constraint analysis is to prepare for efficient evaluation and thus reduce the estimated evaluation cost.

In this section, we study the following questions:

1. Are the integrity constraints noncontradictory?
2. Are the integrity constraints nonredundant?

3. Is it possible to simplify an integrity constraint to control the validity of an update by using the knowledge that it was satisfied before the update?
4. What integrity constraint must be verified for a given type of modification (insertion, deletion, and update)?

These questions should be answered during constraint analysis in order to store an optimized version in the dictionary. In certain systems, a constraint compiler generates optimized programs that will be run later to control the validity of an update.

6.3.1. Consistency Check

Let $I = \{I_1, I_2, \ldots, I_n\}$ be a set of integrity constraints to be satisfied by a database *DB*. For simplicity, we assume that each constraint I_i can be expressed as a first-order logic assertion in domain or tuple calculus. A logical analysis of the constraints may allow a sophisticated integrity constraint parser to detect contradictions between constraints. More precisely, we shall introduce the notion of *consistency* for a set of integrity constraints.

> **Definition 6.4 Integrity constraint consistency**
> A set of integrity constraints is consistent if there exists at least one database state DB_s that satisfies all integrity constraints in the set.

For example, the set of integrity constraints:

$I = \{$ASSERT I_1 AS CONSTRAINT IN WINE(W) W.PERCENT < 10;
      ASSERT I_2 AS CONSTRAINT IN WINE(W) W.PERCENT $> 12\}$

can be rewritten in tuple relational calculus as:

$$I = \{\forall W(WINE(W) \rightarrow W.PERCENT < 10);$$
$$\forall W(WINE(W) \rightarrow W.PERCENT > 12)\}$$

It is inconsistent; a wine cannot be of degree less than 10 and greater than 12.

To prove consistency of a given set I of constraints, the resolution method (see Chapter 1) may be applied. If one can infer the empty clause from the set of integrity constraints I, that exhibits a contradiction within the set; the integrity constraints are nonconsistent.

6.3.2 Redundancy Elimination

It may be that one or more integrity constraints can be proved to be true from the others. For example, the set of integrity constraints:

$$I = \{\text{ASSERT } I_1 \text{ AS CONSTRAINT IN WINE(W) W.PERCENT} < 14;$$
$$\text{ASSERT } I_2 \text{ AS CONSTRAINT IN WINE(W) W.PERCENT} < 16\}$$

is equivalently written in tuple relational calculus as:

$$I = \{\forall W(WINE(W) \rightarrow W.PERCENT < 14);$$
$$\forall W(WINE(W) \rightarrow W.PERCENT < 16)\}$$

The second integrity constraint is subsumed by the first one. Thus it can be eliminated since it is redundant with the first one.

In general, given a set of integrity constraints I, the problem is to find a logically equivalent set J such that I may be proved from J (denoted $J \models I$) and such that the cost of evaluating J against the database is less than the cost of evaluating I. This leads to the concept of minimal integrity constraint set.

> **Definition 6.5 Minimal set of integrity constraints**
> Being given a database DB with the integrity constraint set $I = \{I_1, I_2, \ldots, I_n\}$, a minimal set of integrity constraints for DB is $J = \{J_1, J_2, \ldots, J_k\}$ such that I may be proved from J and there does not exist J' with an evaluation cost less than J allowing to prove I.

For example, with the set of integrity constraints given in tuple relational calculus:

$$I = \{ \forall W(WINE(W) \rightarrow W.PERCENT < 14);$$
$$\forall W(WINE(W) \rightarrow W.PERCENT < 16);$$
$$\forall W(WINE(W) \rightarrow W.PERCENT > 10)\},$$

a possible minimal set may be:

$$J = \{\forall W(WINE(W) \rightarrow W.PERCENT > 10 \text{ AND W.PERCENT} < 14)\}.$$

More generally, to find a minimal set of integrity constraints from a given set I, the resolution method may also be applied. One can compute the closure I^+ of the given set I with all possible resolvents and select a complete but nonredundant set I^m with minimum evaluation cost. Then constraints must be grouped together to avoid scanning a relation several times. This procedure can be improved in many ways — for example, by not including in I^+ resolvent that subsumes an already existing clause. Resolution is practicable only in the case of integrity constraints without functions (for example, arithmetic operations are forbidden) because functions may lead to infinite sets (resolution is semidecidable).

In summary, logical processing of integrity constraints may allow the integrity parser to check for integrity constraint consistency and to simplify the integrity constraints. Although useful for efficient database integrity controls, such simplifications of integrity constraints are usually not implemented in most of the current systems.

6.3.3 Differential Simplification

Another simplification of an integrity constraint is possible to ensure that an update does not violate database integrity. The idea is to take advantage of the fact that the integrity constraint was satisfied before the update. Therefore it is necessary to evaluate the integrity constraint after the update only for the modified data. Thus it is possible to generate a simplified form of an integrity constraint that applies only to modified data. Such a form is called a *differential form*.

A more formal definition of the differential form can be given if one considers how an update is performed in most relational DBMSs. Let R be a relation. An insertion generally leads to the creation of a relation R^+ in which all tuples to be inserted in R are prepared. At update commit (at the end of an update program), the system generally performs $R = R \cup R^+$. Let I be an integrity constraint bearing on R that may be violated by the insertion. With first-order logic integrity constraints, I may be written as an expression of relational algebra operations denoted $I(R)$. R satisfies I before the insertion means that $R = I(R)$. To check if I is still satisfied after inserting the tuples in R^+, one must verify: $R \cup R^+ = I(R \cup R^+)$. If I does not include differences, one can distribute the I relational algebra operations in regard to the union, which yields: $R \cup R^+ = I(R) \cup dI(R,R^+)$. In simple cases $dI(R,R^+)$ is simply $I(R^+)$, but that is not always true, as I may include auto-joins of R. As $R = I(R)$ before the insertion, it is sufficient to control that $R^+ = dI(R,R^+)$. This simple result tells us that only the newly inserted tuples must be controlled. One has to be careful, however; such simplifications are not always so effective with complex integrity constraints.

To illustrate the simplification, let us consider an insertion of two tuples $\{<100,\text{Sancerre},1981,10.7>, <200,\text{Tokay},1978,10.5>\}$ in the WINE relation. R^+ is the relation composed of the two tuples while R is the old WINE relation. The integrity constraint:

ASSERT I_1 AS CONSTRAINT IN WINE(W) W.PERCENT < 14

is satisfied before inserting the new tuples means that:

WINE $= \sigma_{\text{PERCENT} < 14}(\text{WINE})$.

To control the integrity constraint after the insertion, one must verify:

WINE $\cup$ WINE$^+ = \sigma_{\text{PERCENT} < 14}(\text{WINE} \cup \text{WINE}^+)$

which gives, by distributing the restriction with regard to the union:

WINE $\cup$ WINE$^+ = \sigma_{\text{PERCENT} < 14}(\text{WINE}) \cup \sigma_{\text{PERCENT} < 14}(\text{WINE}^+)$.

Thus it is sufficient to control after the insertion that

$$WINE^+ = \sigma_{PERCENT < 14}(WINE^+)$$

which may be expressed as the integrity constraint:

ASSERT dl_1 AS CONSTRAINT IN WINE$^+$(W) W.PERCENT < 14

In the case of deletion, one models it as $R = R - R^-$, where R^- is the set of tuples to be deleted from R. Then in certain cases, it may be possible to simplify the relational algebra equation expressing an integrity constraint bearing upon a relation S and involving R. Such an integrity constraint can be expressed as $S = \emptyset\, I(S, R - R^-)$. It may be replaced by $dI(S, R^-) = \emptyset$. Thus it may appear sufficient to check a simplified condition on $dI(S, R^-)$.

Let us give an example with a referential integrity constraint, for instance:

ASSERT REFW AS REFERENCE WINE.W# FROM DRINK.W#.

With relational algebra, the integrity constraint considered for the DRINK relation may be expressed as:

$$DRINK = \pi_{W\#,D\#,DATE,CITY,QUANTITY}(DRINK \bowtie WINE).$$

Let us delete the wines { < 100,Sancerre,1981,10.7 >, < 200,Tokay,1978,10.5 > } first stored in WINE$^-$. One must control after deleting:

$$DRINK = \pi_{W\#,D\#,DATE,CITY,QUANTITY}(DRINK \bowtie (WINE - WINE^-))$$

which is obviously true if ($\emptyset$ denotes the empty relation):

$$DRINK \bowtie WINE^- = \emptyset$$

This simple equation expresses the idea that one should not delete tuples in WINE that correspond to existing tuples in DRINK.

More generally, an update can be modeled as deleting tuples stored in R^-, and then inserting tuples stored in R^+. Thus an update of R is modeled as $R = (R - R^-) \cup R^+$. This differential formula can be injected in equations such that $R = I(R)$ (constraints bearing on R) and $S = I(R,S)$ (constraints bearing on S but involving R) to try to simplify them, as done in the case of insertions or deletions. However, difficulties may arise due to the fact that relational operations such as selections and joins do not distribute with differences.

In general, typical simplifications lead to the concept of *differential test*, introduced in [Simon87].

> **Definition 6.6 Differential test**
> A differential test for an integrity constraint $I(R1,R2, \ldots, Rn)$, a selected relation Ri, and a modification mode m is an equation $Ri^* = dI(R1^*,R2^*, \ldots, Rn^*)$ such that:
>
> Rk^* is either Rk, Rk^+, Rk^-, or $\emptyset$.
> If the updated database satisfies the equation, then it satisfies I.
> The evaluation cost of dI is less than the evaluation cost of I.

The definition states that the differential test is sufficient to check the updated database consistency. More formally denoting (DB) a database state and $u(DB)$ the updated database state, it may be written: $\{(DB) \models I; u(DB) \models dI\} \Rightarrow \{u(DB) \models I\}$. A differential test is defined for a given modification mode (insert, delete, or update) of a relation and reduces the integrity constraint evaluation cost. For instance, with the wine database, a differential test for (WINE, INSERT, ASSERT I_1 AS CONSTRAINT IN WINE(W) W.PERCENT < 14) is WINE$^+$ = $\sigma_{\text{PERCENT} < 14}$(WINE$^+$). A differential test for (WINE, DELETE, ASSERT REFW AS REFERENCE WINE.W# FROM DRINK.W#) is $\emptyset$ = DRINK $\bowtie$ WINE$^-$. The notion of differential test can be applied to various types of integrity constraints to simplify their evaluation. See [Simon87] for detailed applications.

6.3.4 Operational Simplification

Certain integrity constraints can be violated only by some type of updates on a given relation. To avoid unnecessary integrity controls, it is important to determine which type of updates on which relation can violate a given integrity constraint. In general, one distinguishes insertion, deletion, and modification as update types. Therefore it is interesting to tag integrity constraints with couples $<R,U>$, R being a relation name and U an update type. The tagging rules for integrity constraints can be simply explained. For this purpose, integrity constraints must be written in tuple relational calculus, with quantifiers in front of the insertion. The tagging rules are the following [Simon87]:

1. If a variable on a relation R appears in an integrity constraint I quantified by $\exists$, then a $<R,\text{DELETE}>$ tag is generated for I.
2. If a variable on a relation R appears in an integrity constraint I quantified by $\forall$, then a $<R,\text{INSERT}>$ tag is generated for I.
3. If a variable on a relation R appears in an integrity constraint I, then a $<R,\text{MODIFY}>$ tag is generated for I.

For example, let E and R be two relations such that there exists a referential integrity constraint between the first attribute $E1$ of E and the first attribute $R1$ of R: $\forall r\ R(r)\ \exists e\ E(e)\ (r.R1 = e.E1)$. The integrity constraint must be tagged with the following couples, $<E,\text{DELETE}> <R,\text{INSERT}> <R,\text{MODIFY}>$

$<E,\text{MODIFY}>$, which means that the integrity constraint must be checked when inserting or modifying R and when deleting and modifying in E. Therefore there is no need to check it when inserting in E or deleting in R. Tagging integrity constraints saves useless verifications.

6.4 Data Integrity Enforcement

To enforce database integrity, the DBMS must assert that the integrity constraints are satisfied after each update. The main problem of integrity enforcement is performance. As a first approach, the control of a set of integrity constraints against a database generally requires running a complex query composed from the integrity constraints. However, it is possible to implement various strategies to ensure that the integrity constraints are not violated when performing an update. The simplest strategy is to verify that no tuple violates the integrity constraints after the update and to undo the update if the test fails. More elaborated strategies may prevent modifications of tuples that would violate an integrity constraint.

6.4.1 Detection Methods

Let us assume a database DB composed of relations $R1$, $R2$, . . . , Rn, which must satisfy an integrity constraint I (note that a set of integrity constraints may be replaced by a unique one composed as a conjunction of the first-order logic assertions expressing each integrity constraint). The simplest way to enforce the integrity constraint I is to perform the desired update u to the database state (DB) and then to control that I is satisfied by the new database state $u(DB)$. To check that $u(DB)$ satisfies I, the DBMS can execute the query:

```
SELECT*
FROM R1,R2, . . . , Rn
WHERE ¬ I
```

and control that the answer is empty. Otherwise the update u violates the constraint I, and the consistent database state (DB) should be reconstituted by undoing u.

Using the integrity constraint simplification strategies described in the previous section, it is generally possible to replace the previous query by a simpler one using a posttest.

Definition 6.7 Posttest
Pos(I) is a posttest for an integrity constraint *I*, a database *DB*, and an update *u* iff, for each state *(DB)* verifying *I* and image *u(DB)* of *(DB)* by *u*: *u(DB)* satisfies *I* is equivalent to *u(DB)* satisfies *pos(I)*.

Note that *I* is a posttest for *I*. To simplify the query, we shall use a simplified integrity constraint or a differential test as a posttest. A *detection method* is used to evaluate a posttest on the updated database.

> **Definition 6.8 Detection method**
> Method consisting of evaluating a posttest after updating the database and in undoing the update if the posttest appears to be violated.

Several optimizations for processing a constraint *I* can be used to elaborate an efficient posttest *pos(I)*. First, only those integrity constraints involved in modified relations must be checked. Second, integrity constraints may be replaced by differential tests. It is also worth noting that retrieving tuples satisfying $\neg pos(I)$ is more efficient than retrieving tuples satisfying *pos(I)* since no tuple will be retrieved if the constraint is satisfied. Assembling an empty answer is generally easier for a DBMS than assembling a huge answer. Also, a detection method retrieves all tuples that violate the integrity constraint. These tuples can be given to the user to explain the update rejection. If one does not need to return the incorrect tuples, a simple way is to count their number using a query of the form:

```
SELECT COUNT(*)
FROM Ri1,Ri2, . . . , Rik
WHERE ¬ pos(I)
```

Note that the relations involved in the FROM clause are only those necessary for evaluating the posttest. Moreover, the evaluation of integrity constraints with a detection method can be postponed to the end of the update program. The integrity subsystem applies a differential test only once to modified relations, thereby achieving better performance.

6.4.2 Prevention Methods

Basic Concepts
It is possible to prevent invalid modifications of tuples and thus the violation of some integrity constraint. Thus when an update is processed, a procedure can restrict the set of updated tuples to those that satisfy the integrity constraints. This will guarantee database consistency by filtering updates with conditions that guard the database against invalid updates. Such conditions are called *pretests*.

> **Definition 6.9 Pretest**
> Pre(I) is a pretest for an integrity constraint I, a database DB, and an update u iff, for each state (DB) verifying I and image u(DB) of (DB) by u, u(DB) satisfies I is equivalent to (DB) satisfies pre(I).

Note that I is not a pretest for I; however, a pretest can be derived from I. A method used to evaluate a pretest before updating the database is called a *prevention method*.

> ### Definition 6.10 Prevention method
> Method of evaluating a pretest before updating the database so as to prevent the update of tuples that violate the pretest.

The question is then to determine a pretest. A pretest can be derived from the integrity constraint by applying the inverse of the update to it. More formally, let u be an update applied to a relation Ri of a database state (DB) and $I(R1, \ldots, Ri, \ldots, Rn)$ an integrity constraint. Following [Simon87], the *modified integrity constraint* $I_u(R1, \ldots, u(Ri), \ldots, Rn)$ is the image of I obtained by replacing Ri by the result of updating Ri by u. The modified integrity constraint is a pretest for u. If one updates only the tuples of Ri that satisfy the modified integrity constraint, then the integrity constraint cannot be violated.

As an example, let us consider the integrity constraint:

$$I(WINE) = \{\forall W \ (WINE(W) \rightarrow W.PERCENT < 15)\}$$

and the update u expressed in SQL:

```
UPDATE W.PERCENT = W.PERCENT + 1
FROM WINE (W)
WHERE W.VINEYARD = "VOLNAY"
```

The modified integrity constraint is:

$$I_u(WINE) = \{\forall W \ (WINE(W) \rightarrow W.PERCENT + 1 < 15)\}.$$

Thus, W.PERCENT < 14 is a pretest for the given update and integrity constraint. It is obvious that if one increases by 1 only percentage of alcohol less than 14, no percentage can be greater than 15. Thus the pretest acts as a guard to avoid integrity constraint violation.

When given a set of integrity constraints $\{I1, \ldots, Ik\}$ and an update u, it appears that only certain integrity constraints are changed in the modified integrity constraint set $\{I1_u, \ldots, Ik_u\}$. These are the integrity constraints that may be violated by the update and may be used to build the pretest.

Update Modification

Update modification is the method implemented in INGRES [Stonebraker75] to prevent the updates of tuples that would violate integrity constraints. The language of INGRES is QUEL, a variation of the tuple relational calculus with an English syntax of the form:

```
[RANGE OF <variable> IS <Relation>] . . .
COMMAND <Result>
[WHERE <Qualification>]
```

The method consists of modifying any update u on a relation R by adding to the qualification (the search condition) the modified integrity constraints that may be violated by u. More precisely, an update of the form

```
REPLACE R = u(R)
WHERE Q
```

becomes

```
REPLACE R = u(R)
WHERE Q AND I1ᵤ(R) AND I2ᵤ(R) AND . . . AND Ikᵤ(R)
```

in which $Ik_u(R)$ denotes the search condition of the modified integrity constraint Ik.

For example, assuming the integrity constraint:

$$I(WINE) = \{∀W \ (WINE(W) \rightarrow W.PERCENT < 15)\}$$

and the update u expressed in QUEL as:

```
RANGE OF W IS WINE
REPLACE W.PERCENT = W.PERCENT + 1
WHERE W.VINEYARD = "VOLNAY"
```

the modified update will be:

```
RANGE OF W IS WINE
REPLACE W.PERCENT = W.PERCENT + 1
WHERE W.VINEYARD = "VOLNAY" AND W.PERCENT + 1 < 15
```

The method is clearly preventive. Only tuples that satisfy the update qualification and the modified integrity constraints will be updated. For instance, in the previous example, only VOLNAY with PERCENT less than 14 would be updated. Thus the system must never undo updates because no integrity constraint can be violated. A problem with this method is that the user does not know what tuples are not updated. For instance, in the wine database, if a user increases the percentage of alcohol by 100 percent, he or she will not be notified that probably no tuple will be modified (as a wine has generally a percentage greater than 7.5). Also the method is limited to integrity constraints in which all variables are universally quantified [Simon84], so it cannot be used for referential integrity constraints, for example.

Pretest Optimization

In the update modification method of INGRES, pretests are built directly by using the modified integrity constraints that are added to the update qualification. Indeed pretest can be optimized in several ways. Although it is sometimes possible to transform them using some logical method (such as resolution), it is generally more efficient to consider operation semantics. For example, if the update decreases the percentage of a wine, it is not necessary to add the pretest PERCENT $-$ 1 $<$ 15 to the update qualification. More generally, if the update is embedded in a program (for example, written in Pascal/R), one can benefit from the program semantics to elaborate pretests. In [Gardarin79], a technique to elaborate pretests in database programs was developed using Hoare's axiomatic approach to program correctness. The idea was to simplify the pretest by leaving out the conditions not threatened by the program statements. A precompiler of a database programming language can greatly improve pretests.

Another method to elaborate pretests consists of maintaining redundant aggregate data [Bernstein80]. For example, if a constraint states that every value in column A must be less than every value in column B, maintaining the minimum value of column B allows the system to elaborate an efficient pretest $u(A)$ $<$ MIN(B), where u is an update applied to A. More generally, data redundancy is often useful to elaborate pretests, particularly for integrity constraints with aggregates. Redundancy can also be used to simplify the integrity constraints to be checked in the case of a detection method.

Differential Pretest

A method that can be considered intermediate between prevention and detection has been implemented in the SABRINA DBMS. The method has two steps: (1) prepare the update by constructing the differential relation R^+ and R^- and (2) for each threatened integrity constraint, use a *differential pretest* to control that the update will not violate the integrity constraint.

Definition 6.11 Differential pretest

ΔPre(I) is a differential pretest for an integrity constraint I, a database DB, and an update u of a relation R iff, for each state (DB) verifying I and image $u(DB)$ of (DB) by u, $u(DB)$ satisfies I is equivalent to (DB), R^+, R^- satisfies Δpre(I).

Informally the concept of differential pretest pursues two objectives. The first is to allow a preventive strategy of integrity control; that is, the differential pretest does not depend on the updated database state but rather on both the before-update database state and the differential relations. The second objective is to obtain a simplified expression; the evaluation of a differential pretest for an integrity constraint I and an update u should cost less than the evaluation of I. The notion of simplified expression is based on the simple heuristics that enforcing dI will generally involve smaller relations than enforcing I, as R^+ and R^- are smaller than the base relation.

For each integrity constraint and update type, it is possible to find a differential pretest. For example, let E and R be two relations such that there exists a referential integrity constraint between the first attribute $E1$ of E and the first attribute $R1$ of R: $\forall r\ R(r)\ \exists e\ E(e)\ (r.R1 = e.E1)$. Let us consider the following update: INSERT INTO R VALUES t. A differential pretest for the given integrity constraint is: $\forall r\ R^+(r)\ \exists e\ E(e)\ (r.R1 = e.E1)$. As R^+ only contains t, it appears that this differential pretest will be very efficient. With the following update:

```
DELETE *
FROM E (e)
WHERE e.E1 = "alpha"
```

a differential pretest will be: $\forall e\ E^-(e)\ \forall r\ R(r)\ (r.R1 \neq e.E1)$. The pretest can be even more elaborated and replaced by $\forall r\ R(r)\ (r.R1 \neq \text{"alpha"})$. Sophisticated algorithms used to discover pretests are given in [Simon87]. The principle of construction is updating the integrity constraint in replacing R by $(R - R^-) \cup R^+$ and then simplifying the assertion by considering that it is true on R (before updating).

6.5 View Management

6.5.1 View Definition

To offer a high degree of data independence, DBMSs provide external schemas. The external schema of a relational database is defined through the concept of *view* (see Chapter 2).

> **Definition 6.12 View**
> A view is a virtual database whose schema and contents are derived from an existing database through a mapping specified as a set of relational queries.

In fact, each query in the mapping defines a *derived relation* in the view, which in turn appears as a set of derived relations. Often a view is composed of a unique derived relation; thus the concepts of view and derived relation are synonymous for most database specialists.

Many relational DBMSs offer a specific command to define a view from existing relations. For example, INGRES supplies the following command:

DEFINE_VIEW <view_name> (<attribute list>) **WHERE** <Qualification>.

System R supports the similar command:

DEFINE_VIEW <view-name> [<attribute list>]
AS [**LIKE** <relation-name> [**EXCEPT** <attribute>.<characteristics> = <value>] . . .] <Query>.

For example, a view DRINKER_OF_BEAUJOLAIS giving all names and types of drinkers having drunk Beaujolais wine could be defined as (in SQL):

DEFINE_VIEW DRINKER_OF_BEAUJOLAIS **AS**
    SELECT NAME, TYPE
FROM DRINKER(D), WINE(W), DRINK(E)
WHERE D.D# = E.D# **AND** E.W# = W.W#
AND W.VINEYARD = "BEAUJOLAIS"

The LIKE expression allows the user to change the characteristics of the view attributes — for example, the unit or the format of a value.

It is possible to use any query to define a view. For example, an aggregate can be used to specify a view giving the quantity of wine drunk per drinker, as follows:

DEFINE_VIEW QUANTITY_DRUNK **AS**
    SELECT NAME, TYPE, SUM(QUANTITY)
    FROM DRINKER(D), DRINK(E)
    WHERE D.D# = E.D#
    GROUP BY D.D#

When a view has been defined, it must behave as a normal relation. In particular, an authorized user must be allowed to query the derived relation. Two techniques have been proposed to query views. One is to apply the view definition mapping at each query. It is called *query modification*. The other one is to materialize the view. It is called *view concretion*. It is important to understand that a view is a dynamic window over a database and must reflect all changes made in the database.

6.5.2 Query Modification

The query modification method, as proposed by the INGRES designers, is a general tool to process views, integrity, and authorizations. We have already studied a variation (update modification) as a prevention method for integrity control.

We now study query modification for views. Given a query Q applied to a derived relation V defined from base relations $R1, R2, \ldots, Rn$ using a mapping $F(R1, \ldots, Rn)$, the query modification method may be defined as follows.

> **Definition 6.13 Query modification**
> Technique that transforms a query $Q(V)$ applied to a view V into an equivalent query $Q(F(R1, \ldots, Rn))$ applied to the corresponding base relations.

The query modification algorithm works directly on the query before query optimization. When a view is defined, the view specification is recorded in a metabase relation named VIEW. The view specification can then be used to map a user query on views into a query on base relations. Given a QUEL query with tuple variables $V1, V2, \ldots, Vn$ and a qualification Q, the query modification technique can be summarized by the algorithm given in Fig. 6.2 [Stonebraker75].

An illustration of the algorithm is given with a view that gives all names and types of drinkers having drunk Beaujolais wine (in QUEL):

> **DEFINE_VIEW** DRINKER_OF_BEAUJOLAIS **AS**
>   **RANGE OF** D **IS** DRINKER
>   **RANGE OF** E **IS** DRINK
>   **RANGE OF** W **IS** WINE
>   **RETRIEVE** D.NAME, D.TYPE
>   **WHERE** D.D# = E.D# **AND** E.W# = W.W#
>   **AND** W.VINEYARD = ''BEAUJOLAIS''

and the query giving the heavy drinkers of Beaujolais' names:

> **RANGE OF** B **IS** DRINKER_OF_BEAUJOLAIS
> **RETRIEVE** B.NAME
> **WHERE** B.TYPE = ''Heavy''

> **Procedure** Modify_Query ({V1, . . . , Vn}, Q)
>   **For each** variable Vi **do**
>   **Begin**
>   Retrieve the view definition VDi for the relation referenced by Vi;
>   Replace Vi's range definition by the ranges appearing in VDi;
>   Add the VDi qualification to the query qualification (with AND);
>   Replace each attribute Vi.Aj by the corresponding attribute (or aggregate) in VDi;
>   **End;**
>   **End;**

FIGURE 6.2 Overview of the query modification algorithm

First, the range of the view definition replaces B's range, and the query becomes:

> **RANGE OF** D **IS** DRINKER
> **RANGE OF** E **IS** DRINK
> **RANGE OF** W **IS** WINE
> **RETRIEVE** B.NAME
> **WHERE** B.TYPE = "Heavy"

Then the view qualification is added to the query, which yields:

> **RANGE OF** D **IS** DRINKER
> **RANGE OF** E **IS** DRINK
> **RANGE OF** W **IS** WINE
> **RETRIEVE** B.NAME
> **WHERE** B.TYPE = "Heavy"
> **AND** D.D# = E.D# **AND** E.W# = W.W#
> **AND** W.VINEYARD = "BEAUJOLAIS"

Next attributes are mapped to base relations using the view definition; that is, B.NAME is replaced by D.NAME, and B.TYPE is replaced by D.TYPE, which yields the modified query:

> **RANGE OF** D **IS** DRINKER
> **RANGE OF** E **IS** DRINK
> **RANGE OF** W **IS** WINE
> **RETRIEVE** D.NAME
> **WHERE** D.TYPE = "Heavy"
> **AND** D.D# = E.D# **AND** E.W# = W.W#
> **AND** W.VINEYARD = "BEAUJOLAIS"

Another way to transform a query on a view to a query on base relations has been developed in System R. The method proceeds from a relational algebra tree as defined in Chapter 4, resulting from a first level of the query compilation. When defined, the view is also compiled in a relational algebra tree. Mapping the query to base relations consists of replacing each nonbase relation in the query tree by the relational algebra tree defining it. The resulting tree must be optimized to get the final optimized tree query, which is run against the database.

We illustrate the method with the query giving the names of the heavy drinkers expressed on the view giving all names and types of drinkers having drunk Beaujolais wine. The view definition tree and the query tree are portrayed in Fig. 6.3. The tree resulting from the merge of both trees is also given in Fig. 6.3. This tree must be optimized by the query optimizer.

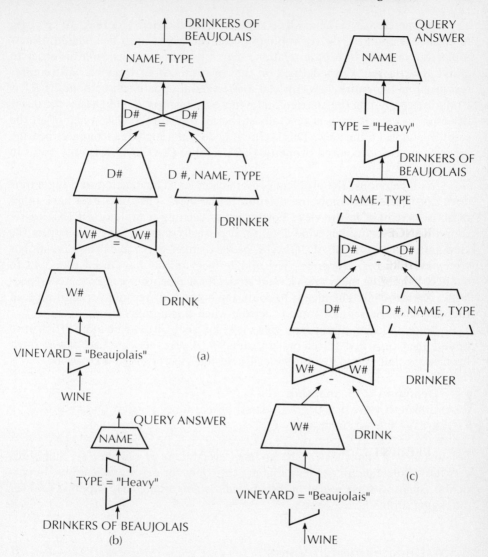

FIGURE 6.3 Query transformation by merging trees

6.5.3 View Concretion

Another approach to view management consists of materializing the derived relations in the database. Such views are called *concrete views*.

> **Definition 6.14 Concrete view**
> One or more derived relation(s) whose extension is computed and sorted permanently in the database.

A concrete view is generally computed when the view is defined. When base relations are updated, the corresponding concrete views must be updated. If new tuples are inserted in a base relation, they too must be considered in order to derive the concrete views defined on that relation. At first glance, this requires recomputing the entire view. Instead a differential update can be done. If R^+ is a relation containing the inserted tuples in a base relation R and $Q(R)$ is the query defining the view, then it is generally sufficient to compute $Q(R^+)$ and insert the resulting tuples in the view. This is true if Q does not include differences bearing on R because the required property $Q(R \cup R^+) = Q(R) \cup Q(R^+)$ only holds in that case.

With deletions, the problem is more complex. The deletion of a tuple in R does not necessarily imply the deletion in the view. The tuple may have other reasons to remain in the view. For instance, deleting a tuple of DRINK corresponding to a Beaujolais wine does not necessarily remove the drinker from the view DRINKER_OF_BEAUJOLAIS, as the drinker may have drunk Beaujolais wine several times. Concrete view update mechanisms have been proposed to avoid recomputing the whole view under database deletions using counters [Nicolas82, Kerherve86]. The idea is to count the number of reasons for each tuple in the view to be present. A tuple is deleted when this number becomes zero.

Since updating of concrete views may be costly, it may be more efficient to update them only in deferred mode [Adiba80]. A concrete view becomes an intelligent copy that is updated periodically. Such a view is called a *snapshot*.

Definition 6.15 Snapshot
Concrete view that is not updated in real time (at each update program end) but periodically.

For instance, a snapshot can be updated every hour or once a day. Snapshots provide obsolete database views that are sufficient for many applications. In particular, snapshots are useful in distributed systems where they supply a tool for managing sophisticated copies.

6.5.4 Update through Views

As views are the relational implementation of external schemas, it is necessary to allow a user to update the database through views. Unfortunately it is not always possible to propagate the updates on a view to the database. The propagation can entail undefined values or inconsistencies in the database. For example, inserting a new drinker in the view DRINKERS_OF_BEAUJOLAIS does not define which tuple must be inserted in the DRINK relation. In fact, the view only contains the name and type of the drinker, and it is difficult to derive a tuple of DRINK from the given data (for example, from the tuple < "Patrick," Heavy >, how can the tuples in DRINK be derived?). A more difficult example is an update through the view QUANTITY_DRUNK as defined above because it does not determine which are tuples to update in the DRINK relation.

A formal treatment of the view update problem is given in [Bancilhon81]. The concept of *view complement* may be informally defined.

> **Definition 6.16 View complement**
> The complement of a view V is a view W such that W contains enough information to derive the whole database as a view of V and W.

For example, the view:

NOT_DRINKER_OF_BEAUJOLAIS =
$\sigma_{\text{VINEYARD} \neq \text{"BEAUJOLAIS"}}$(DRINKER $\bowtie$ DRINK $\bowtie$ WINE)

is a complement of the view:

DRINKER_OF_BEAUJOLAIS =
$\sigma_{\text{VINEYARD} = \text{"BEAUJOLAIS"}}$(DRINKER $\bowtie$ DRINK $\bowtie$ WINE).

Both views are defined using relational algebra, more specifically restrictions and external joins (a join that does not lose information).

A *minimal complement* of a view is a complement that does not include a smaller complement. A minimal complement describes the information not visible within the view. In general, a minimal complement is not unique. Choosing a view complement that must remain constant under a view update defines an update policy. It is not necessary to choose a minimal complement, although such a choice permits more updates to be accepted. Informally a method to solve the view update problem can be summarized as follows [Bancilhon81]:

1. Choose a (minimal) complement for the given view.
2. Check if the given view update might leave the chosen complement invariant; if not, reject the update.
3. Associate with each update u the database update that leaves the complement invariant.

However, the search of a complement is an NP-hard problem, which makes the algorithm not practical.

In practice, updates through views are supported in certain systems under certain restrictive conditions. In System R, only monorelation views can be updated under the conditions that no duplicate tuples are eliminated when computing the view and no aggregate function appears in the view definition. In other words, only views defined as selections of relations in which a key attribute remains in the projection may be updated. In INGRES, updates are tolerated if there does not exist any function using multiple variables in the view definition;

the view update does not change the attributes appearing in the view qualification; and the translated update bears upon a unique relation. In both systems, an update is accepted only if it belongs to the view and if it does not violate the database integrity. Those restrictions enable a simple and efficient treatment of view updates.

6.6 Data Security

Views play an important role in protecting data [Chamberlin75]. When a database access is performed through a view, a user may have access only to the data described in the view(s) he or she is allowed to access. Furthermore the view restricts the possible accesses to certain attributes of the base relations by hiding some attributes or values. Unfortunately views are insufficient to ensure a good level of data security. Additional support is needed.

6.6.1 Identification and Authorization

A DBMS guarantees data security by rejecting nonauthorized operations. To perform an operation, there is a subject that executes the operation and an object on which the operation is done [Hoffman77]. In a DB7S, the subjects are user application programs and the objects are the data. First subjects must be *identified*.

Definition 6.17 Identification
Action consisting of associating to a subject a name or a number that uniquely identifies him or her.

A simple way to violate data security is for a subject to pretend to be another one. To avoid this problem, subjects must be *authenticated*.

Definition 6.18 Authentication
Action that checks that a subject is actually who he or she pretends to be.

The best-known authentication method is the use of a password. A password is a character string known only by the subject and the object and provided by the subject in order to be authenticated. More sophisticated methods include the use of badges, questionnaires, and the execution of algorithms known only by the subject and the object.

An authenticated subject can then proceed to certain operations on certain objects according to the operation rights granted by the system administrators or by other subjects.

Definition 6.19 Authorization
Right of executing an operation by a subject on an object.

The attribution of an authorization may depend on the subject (for example, his or her access privileges or the terminal employed), the object (for example, its name, its current state, its content, its value), or the operation (for example, read or write).

6.6.2 Control of Authorization

There are several ways to control authorization. One way is the use of an *authorization matrix*. An authorization matrix is a matrix in which the rows correspond to subjects and the columns to objects, defining for each couple < subject-object > the authorized operations. For example, let us consider two relations describing the objects student NAME and RESULT, and subjects student, secretary, and professor. The operations that can be accomplished on objects NAME and RESULT are read and write. The authorizations can be coded by two bits, the first for read right and the other for write right. Fig. 6.4 depicts the matrix corresponding to this example, 0 meaning denied access and 1 meaning authorized access.

In practice, the authorization matrix can be stored in several ways:

By row: With each subject is associated the list of objects he or she may access and his or her access rights.
By column: With each object is associated the list of subjects who can access it with the access rights.
By element: With each couple "subject-object" is associated the access rights of the subject on the object. The matrix is often stored by element as a relation with three attributes < subject, object, right >.

A simpler way to control authorizations is to associate an authorization level to the subjects and the objects. An *authorization level* is a number attached to each object and each subject. An access is authorized only if the level of the subject is greater than or equal to the level of the object assessed. For example, let us consider the subjects and objects introduced above with the authorization

	Name	Result
STUDENT	01	01
SECRETARY	11	01
PROFESSOR	11	11

FIGURE 6.4 Example of authorization matrix

	Name	Result
STUDENT	11	01
SECRETARY	11	00
PROFESSOR	11	11

FIGURE 6.5 Matrix of authorizations with levels

levels: student (1), secretary (2), professor (3), name (1), result (3). The corresponding matrix is illustrated in Fig. 6.5.

The drawback of authorization levels is the loss of the concept of operation. Nonetheless, this solution is simple to implement and permits the combination of levels. If a subject of level s_1 accesses data through an equipment of level s_2, the subject will get the level $s = \min (s_1, s_2)$—for example, if there is a terminal in free access with level 1 and a terminal in the office. This method can be extended to a more complete model with partially ordered level classes [Denning79].

6.6.3 Object Definition

The choice of the objects to protect is an important problem. The first DBMSs restricted the protectable objects to the object types. CODASYL recommends protection by key at any level of object type described in the schema. IMS permits the protection of subsets of fields in a segment. On the contrary, relational systems enable the protection of sets of tuple occurrences defined by predicates. In most systems, an object is defined by a selection query. Thus it is a content-dependent part of a relation (base or view relation).

6.6.4 Subject Definition

Defining the subjects is not a problem since any user can be considered a subject; however, to simplify data administration, it is useful to handle user groups. The group notion is hierarchical. A group inherits all the authorizations of its hierarchical descendants. It is also possible to superimpose several hierarchies [Fernandez81]. Finally a subject can be a set of predefined transactions. The access by these transactions must also be protected.

6.5.5 Right Attribution

The attribution of rights to subjects over objects is another important problem. It is necessary to define who grants the rights. Two extreme approaches are possible. The first approach is decentralized, as in System R [Griffiths76]. The creator of an object becomes its owner and is granted all privileges on it. He or she can use the following primitive to authorize the access on his or her objects: GRANT <operation type> ON <object> TO <subject>. A user can also revoke the rights he or she has given using the primitive: REVOKE <operation type> FROM <object> TO <subject>. When a right is withdrawn from a given user *u,* the system must also withdraw this right to all users having received the right from *u*. That explains why most systems keep track of the giver of each right.

The second approach is centralized as in INGRES. The database administrators have all privileges and can grant some privileges to other users. The centralized approach is simpler to implement. Hybrid solutions [Chamberlin78] are also possible if several subject groups are given predefined privileges.

6.6.6 Authorization Control

Controlling of rights must be performed before accepting an operation on an object. The main issues in the implementation of right control are avoiding excessive overhead and preventing possible bypass. If rights are stored in the system metabase as a relation with schema RIGHT (USER, OBJECT, RIGHT, GIVER), this relation must not be accessed at each command. It is preferable to bring into main memory all the rights of a user when he or she logs into the system. To avoid bypassing, the system should prevent the modification of rights by a user program; for example, when rights are in main memory, they should remain in a safe working area where the user cannot access them. In summary, attributing and controlling authorizations is not too difficult, although one should avoid excessive overhead and keep rights from unauthorized accesses.

6.7 Conclusion

In this chapter, we studied some integrity problems. They cover several aspects as the one of ensuring that the data in the database are accurate or cannot be deliberately falsified. However, the latter is rather a problem of security. Other problems of integrity will be studied in the following chapter. These aspects are physical integrity problems; in this chapter, we studied semantic integrity problems. Semantic integrity is one of the most important issues to guarantee the correct use of a database.

Not many DBMSs support efficient semantic integrity control. The design of an integrity subsystem was first discussed in [Stonebraker75] for INGRES and in [Eswaran75] for System R. Specific optimization techniques were proposed in [Hammer78], [Gardarin79], and [Bernstein80]. Both optimization techniques and an integrity subsystem design are discussed in [Simon87]. Many others have contributed to the development of semantic integrity in theory and practice.

Another important problem developed in this chapter is that of view mapping. While querying through a view is a well-understood process, updating through views is not yet well understood. View complements provide insight into the theory of view update translation [Bancilhon81], but requiring that a complement be chosen that remains constant may be too restrictive [Keller87]. Furthermore most relational DBMSs strongly restrict the conditions under which a view update can be accepted. More research is clearly needed.

6.8 References and Bibliography

[Adiba80] Adiba M., Lindsay B., "Database Snapshots," Proc. VLDB Conf., Montreal, October 1980.

[Adiba81] Adiba M., "Derived Relations: A Unified Mechanism for Views, Snapshots and Distributed Data," Proc. VLDB Conf., Cannes, France, September 1981.

[Astrahan76] Astrahan M. M. et al., "System R: Relational Approach to Database Management," ACM TODS, V1, N2, June 1976.

[Bancilhon81] Bancilhon F., Spyratos N., "Update Semantics and Relational Views," ACM TODS, V4, N6, December 1981, pp. 557 – 75.

[Bernstein80] Bernstein P., Blaustein B., Clarke E. M., "Fast Maintenance of Semantic Integrity Assertions Using Redundant Aggregate Data," Proc. of 6th VLDB Conf., Montreal, October 1980.

[Blaustein81] Blaustein B., "Enforcing Database Assertions. Techniques and Applications," Ph.D. thesis, Harvard University, 1981.

[Brodie78] Brodie M. L. "Specification and Verification of Database Semantic Integrity," Ph.D. thesis, University of Toronto, 1978.

[Buneman79] Buneman O. P., Clemons E. K., "Efficiency Monitoring Relational Databases," ACM TODS, V4, N3, September 1979.

[Chamberlin75] Chamberlin D., Gray J., Traiger I., "Views, Authorization and Locking in a Relational Database System," Proc. National Computer Conference, 1975, pp. 425 – 30.

[Chamberlin78] Chamberlin D. D. et al., "Database System Authorization," in [DeMillo78].

[Date81] Date C. J., "Referential Integrity," Proc. VLDB Conf., Cannes, France, September 1981.

[Dayal82] Dayal U., Bernstein P., "On the Correct Translation of Update Operations on Relational Views," ACM TODS, V8, N3, September 1982.

[DeMillo78] DeMillo R. A., Dobkin D. P., Jones A. K., Lipton R. J. (eds.), *Foundations of Secure Computation,* Academic Press, 1978.

[Denning79] Denning D. E., Denning P. J., "Data Security," ACM Computing Survey, V11, N3, September 1979.

[Eswaran75] Eswaran K. P., Chamberlin D. D., "Functional Specifications of a Subsystem for Data Base Integrity," 1st VLDB, Int. Conf., Framingham, September 1975.

[Fernandez81] Fernandez E. B., Summers R. C., Wood C., *Database Security and Integrity,* Addison-Wesley, 1981.

[Gardarin79] Gardarin G., Melkanoff M., "Proving Consistency of Data Base Transactions," Proc. 5th VLDB Conf., Rio de Janeiro, September 1979.

[Griffiths76] Griffiths P. P., Wade B. W., "An Authorization Mechanism for a Relational Data Base System," ACM TODS, V1, N3, September 1976.

[Hammer75] Hammer M., McLeod D. J., "Semantic Integrity in a Relational Database System," Proc. 1st VLDB Conf., Framingham, 1975.

[Hammer78] Hammer M., Sarin S. K., "Efficient Monitoring of Data Base Assertions," Proc. ACM-SIGMOD Conf., Austin, June 1978.

[Hoffman77] Hoffman J. L., *Modern Methods of Computer Security and Privacy,* Prentice-Hall, 1977.

[Hong81] Hong Y. C., Su Y. W., "Associative Hardware and Software Techniques for Integrity Control," ACM TODS, V6, N3, September 1981.

[Hsu85] Hsu A., Imielinski T., "Integrity Checking for Multiple Updates," Proc. ACM-SIGMOD Int. Conf., Austin, (Tex.), May 1985.

[Keller87] Keller M. A., "Comments on Bancilhon and Spyratos's Update Semantics and Relational Views," ACM TODS, V12, N3, September 1987, pp. 521 – 23.

[Kerherve86] Kerhervé B., "Relational Views: Implantation in Centralized and Distributed DBMS," Doctorat thesis, Paris VI University, March 1986.

[Morgenstern84] Morgenstern M., "Constraint Equations: Declarative Expression of Constraints with Automatic Enforcement," Proc. 10th VLDB Conf., Singapore, August 1984.

[Nicholas82] Nicholas J. M., "Logic for Improving Integrity Checking in Relational Data Bases," Acta Informatica, July, 1982.

[Simon84] Simon E., Valduriez P., "Design and Implementation of an Extendible Integrity Subsystem," Proc. of ACM-SIGMOD Int. Conf., Boston. Also in SIGMOD RECORDS V14, N2, June 1984.

[Simon87] Simon E., Valduriez P., "Design and Analysis of a Relational Integrity Subsystem," MCC Technical Report Number DB-015-87, January 1987.

[Stonebraker75] Stonebraker M., "Implementation of Integrity Constraints and Views by Query Modification," Proc. ACM-SIGMOD Conf., San Jose, 1975.

[Stonebraker76] Stonebraker M., Wong E., Kreps P., Held G., "The Design and Implementation of INGRES," ACM TODS, V1, N3, 1976, pp. 189 – 222.

[Weber83] Weber H., Sticky W., Kartszt J., "Integrity Checking in Data Base Systems," Information Systems, V8, N2, 1983.

7
CONCURRENCY CONTROL

7.1 Introduction

This chapter discusses one of the most controversial problems arising in databases, concurrency control, and presents the basic techniques proposed to resolve it. Concurrency control is that part of the DBMS that ensures that simultaneously executed transactions produce the same results as if they were executed in sequence. In other words, concurrency control makes transaction data sharing completely transparent to the users. It is easy to develop a DBMS with simple though effective concurrency control algorithms that would lock the whole database during the execution of each transaction; such a system would rapidly degrade with increasing number of users and become completely unacceptable. Thus we are led to seek simple though effective methods that allow a high degree of concurrency in order to achieve satisfactory performance.

The first goal of this chapter is to present the various concurrency control techniques. The second is to introduce basic concurrency control principles and to derive from them proofs of the algorithms. In summary, we seek to give a unified view, precise algorithm descriptions, and formal proofs of concurrency control techniques.

The chapter is divided into six sections. Section 7.2 presents key definitions concerned with data integrity. It also describes how simultaneous executions of transactions in database systems may create conflicts that lead to lost operations, currency confusion, or database inconsistency. Section 7.3 analyzes the requirements of conflict-free execution. Having defined a schedule for a set of transactions as a sequence of the actions making up the transactions, we show that certain schedules introduce conflicts. Thus the goal of concurrency control is to allow the execution of solely those schedules that do not lead to such situations. This may be accomplished by requiring that data management systems generate only serializable schedules (those that yield the same results as a serial schedule). The next question is how to verify serializability of schedules. It turns out that a sufficient condition for a schedule to be serializable is that its associated precedence graph be circuit-free. Three types of approaches have been developed to satisfy this condition. They are shortly summarized below and presented in details in Sections 7.4, 7.5, and 7.6.

The first approach consists of two steps: (1) ordering and marking transactions before they are executed and (2) verifying that conflicting accesses take place in the original order; if two transactions are found out of order, one of them is aborted and restarted later. Three types of algorithms have been proposed to accomplish these functions. Total ordering algorithms order all transactions despite the permutability of certain pairs of operations (like read and read). Partial ordering algorithms, which order only nonpermutable operations, are clearly preferable. Multiversion partial ordering algorithms avoid excessive transaction restarts by maintaining several versions of the data to be accessed.

The second approach resembles the first, although it is based on a new type of transaction ordering; the transactions are now ordered according to their termination time. More precisely, transactions are divided into two phases: a process phase and a so-called commit phase during which the database is updated. The ordering is defined at the beginning of the commit phase; if it turns out that it has been violated during preparation for the actual update, then the transaction is aborted.

The third approach is derived from the classical operating system method for allocating resources to tasks. Various portions of data may be viewed as resources, which may therefore be allocated (locked) or deallocated (unlocked) to transactions. However, this method by itself is not sufficient because of the presence of integrity constraints. Thus it is necessary to restrict the locking rules so that a transaction cannot unlock any portion of the data until it has locked all the data it intends to access. These principles are incorporated in a generalized two-phase locking algorithm, which we present and prove through the application of precedence graphs. Unfortunately deadlock now appears through data locking. Avoidance of deadlock is difficult because the method requires advanced knowledge of the data to be accessed, information that is not available in the database context, which allows ad hoc queries. Deadlock detection may be accomplished by algorithms that check for the presence of circuits in the waiting graph of the transaction set of interest. Detected deadlock is then broken by aborting one or more transactions. Another possible difficulty is the so-called phantom problem wherein a transaction arrives too late to access a recently inserted data item it requires; this problem, which can occur in all the methods presented, may be solved by locking logical parts of the database defined by predicates.

7.2 Definitions and Problem Statements

7.2.1 Database Consistency

Let us recall first some basic definitions. A *schema* (or *database scheme*) includes both a description of the data and the integrity constraints that qualify that data. The collection of integrity constraint is said to be *self-consistent* if it contains no contradictions. A database instance is said to be *consistent* if its integrity constraints are self-consistent and its data do not violate the constraints.

The purpose of concurrency control is to maintain database consistency when multiple users are updating the database. Each user performs a sequence of retrieve and update commands (a *transaction*) that, if executed alone, would keep the database consistent. Problems arise because transactions from different users may interfere in such a way that either certain command effects may be lost or certain integrity constraint may become false.

7.2.2 Concurrency Problems

Lost Operations
A well-known example of the problems arising from the simultaneous execution of user programs in a DBMS is the *lost operations*. The most common situation concerns a lost update [Engles76]. This problem arises from the following sequence of events: during the execution of a transaction T_1 an operation a_i may read a data item X into a buffer location x_1; then the transaction modifies the object in x_1 through a subsequent operation $a_j(j > i)$, utilizing the value previously input x_1. In the meantime, another transaction, T_2, has taken place, updating the same data item X through the operation a_k, which occurs between a_i and a_j. The effect of operation a_k is then erased when x_1 is rewritten into the database; thus a_k is lost. This situation is depicted in Fig. 7.1. A similar situation arises from currency confusion [Engles76], which takes place when a transaction maintains a reference to a data item destroyed by another transaction.

Inconsistencies
Another type of problem is due to the presence of integrity constraints. This is the problem of *inconsistency* [Eswaran76], which arises each time a transaction accesses or, worse, modifies a transitional state of the database characterized by the fact that an integrity constraint is not verified. The example shown in Fig. 7.2 illustrates inconsistent outputs. Let us assume that two data items A and B must satisfy the integrity constraint $A = B$. Transaction T_2 prints out A after

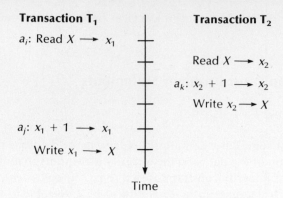

Transaction T₁

a_i: Read $X \longrightarrow x_1$

a_j: $x_1 + 1 \longrightarrow x_1$

Write $x_1 \longrightarrow X$

Transaction T₂

Read $X \longrightarrow x_2$

a_k: $x_2 + 1 \longrightarrow x_2$

Write $x_2 \longrightarrow X$

Time

FIGURE 7.1 Example of lost operations

it has been modified by T_1 and B before it has been modified by T_1. Thus the printed values of A and B are different.

The example in Fig. 7.3 is worse yet, for it illustrates the possible destruction of the database consistency. Again we assume the integrity constraint $A = B$. Transaction T_2 now updates a transitory inconsistent state wherein $A \neq B$ because A has been updated by T_1 and B has not yet been updated by T_1. At the end, A and B are no longer equal.

An inconsistency can also be generated by a transaction wherein the same read operation might be repeated with different results. A transaction may read the same data item twice in a row yet find two different values due to a modifica-

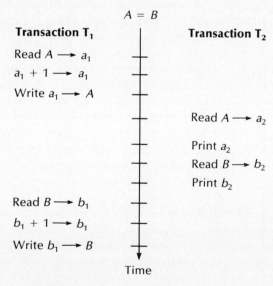

$A = B$

Transaction T₁

Read $A \longrightarrow a_1$

$a_1 + 1 \longrightarrow a_1$

Write $a_1 \longrightarrow A$

Read $B \longrightarrow b_1$

$b_1 + 1 \longrightarrow b_1$

Write $b_1 \longrightarrow B$

Transaction T₂

Read $A \longrightarrow a_2$

Print a_2

Read $B \longrightarrow b_2$

Print b_2

Time

FIGURE 7.2 Example of inconsistent outputs

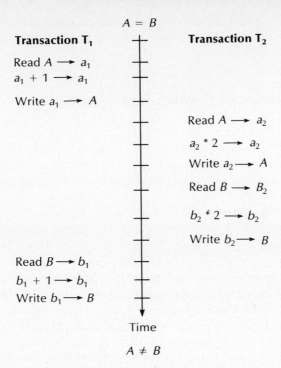

FIGURE 7.3 Example of introduction of inconsistencies in the database

tion of the data item caused by a concurrent transaction occurring between the two read operations. This situation is illustrated in Fig. 7.4; transaction T_1 prints out two different values for the data item A. It is known as the *nonreproducibility of read* problem.

In summary, the simultaneous execution of transactions may create conflicts that lead to operation losses or inconsistencies. (Both types of conflict are

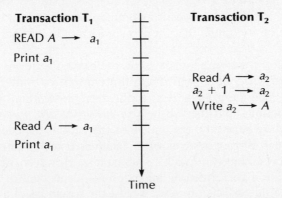

FIGURE 7.4 Nonreproducible read operations

often referred as inconsistencies.) The problem is to construct control algorithms that permit only the simultaneous execution of transactions that do not cause inconsistencies.

7.3 Characteristics of Conflict-free Executions

7.3.1 Basic Concepts

The DBMS controls accesses of transactions to portions of the database; such a portion is called a *concurrency control granule,* or simply a *granule.*

> **Definition 7.1 Granule**
> A unit of data that is individually controlled by the concurrency control subsystem.

In many systems, a granule is a page. In a few others, it is a tuple. The size of the granule is an important choice, greatly influencing the performances of the concurrency control mechanism; it is also a controversial point [Ries77, Ries79]. It may vary from a single record of a local database to a page or even a whole file. Small granules favor parallelism but require more time for control. In practice it is often desirable to provide variable-sized data granules to cater more closely to the data needs of various transactions.

A granule must obey certain internal integrity constraints. Indeed during a database update, the granules generally are modified by a number of primitives constituting functional units that must respect the internal consistency of granules, that is, the integrity constraints that qualify the data contained in the granules [Gardarin76, Schlageter79]. Such functional units are called *actions* [Eswaran76].

> **Definition 7.2 Action**
> A primitive indivisible processing command executed on behalf of a single user on a granule that enforces the granule internal integrity.

Thus for example, if the granule is a page, the basic operations are often taken as *read_page* and *write_page,* which constitute primitive (indivisible) actions in many systems. When the granule is a record, *read_record* and *write_record* are generally basic actions, but then so may be *insert_record, modify_record,* and delete_record. More generally, the choice of the actions depends on the system designers, although certain systems offer facilities (such as semaphores) to the user to define new actions (indivisible commands). However, we always assume that the computation performed by an action is independent of side effects and does not produce side effects; in other words, the semantics of an action is independent of other granule states and has no effect on other granules.

Having introduced the concept of actions, it is possible to define more precisely the notion of *transaction* [Eswaran76] from a database point of view.

> **Definition 7.3 Transaction**
> A sequence of actions $\{a_1, a_2, \ldots, a_n\}$ executed for a given user that respects the database consistency.

In general, the execution of a transaction is triggered by one or more input messages, thereby generating one or more output messages. It may also be triggered by an internal event (such as a clock). Note that between two actions a_i and a_{i+1} that act on the database, other computations may be performed; however, the performed operations must not interact with the database. A transaction T may be seen as a function transforming a database consistent state S (a state S that satisfies all integrity constraints I) to a new consistent state $T(S)$. Let $T = \{a_1, a_2, \ldots, a_n\}$ be a transaction; denoting by $S \models I$ the fact that I can be proved from S, we may write formally:

$$S \models I; \quad T(S) = a_n(a_{n-1}(\ldots (a_2(a_1(S))))); \quad T(S) \models I,$$

which means that the application of T is the sequential application of the actions a_1, a_2, a_{n-1}, a_n. S and $T(S)$ allow one to prove the integrity constraints I. This is generally not true for an intermediate state $S_i = a_i(\ldots (a_2(a_1(S))))$ where $i < n$: $S_i \not\models I$. The inconsistency of the intermediate states is the source of concurrency control problems.

Obviously the application of an action to a granule yields a result in the sense that it changes the database state and/or the transaction environment (its own memory or its output). We may define the result of an action a_i applied to a database state S as follows: The result of an action a_i applied to a database state S is the new database state $a_i(S)$ together with the side effects (if any). Thus for example, the result of the action read is the value of the input buffer following execution. The result of a write action modifying a database consists of the modified granule.

7.3.2 Scheduling of Transactions

In a centralized system, a scheduler controls the simultaneous execution of a set of transactions $\{T_1, T_2, \ldots, T_n\}$. Thus it is convenient to introduce the concept of a *schedule* for the transactions; it has also been called a *history* or an *audit* [Gray78].

> **Definition 7.4 Schedule**
> A schedule for a set of transactions $\{T_1, T_2, \ldots, T_n\}$ is a sequence of actions constructed by merging the actions of $T_1, T_2, \ldots, T_n$ while respecting the order of the actions making up each transaction.

A set of transactions can give rise to many diverse schedules for these transactions. However, each of these schedules maintains the order of the actions making up each transaction. Consider transactions T_1 and T_2 depicted in Fig. 7.5 that modify data items A and B linked by the integrity constraint $A = B$. We shall assume that A and B are individual granules, thereby maximizing the possibilities of concurrency. Two schedules for transactions T_1 and T_2 are shown in Fig. 7.6. Schedule (a) is acceptable, schedule (b) is unacceptable because it leads to operation losses.

TRANSACTION T_1	*TRANSACTION T_2*
Read $A \to a_1$	Read $A \to a_2$
$a_1 + 1 \to a_1$	$a_2 * 2 \to a_2$
Write $a_1 \to A$	Write $a_2 \to A$
Read $B \to b_1$	Read $B \to b_2$
$b_1 + 1 \to b_1$	$b_2 * 2 \to b_2$
Write $b_1 \to B$	Write $b_2 \to B$

FIGURE 7.5 Two examples of transactions

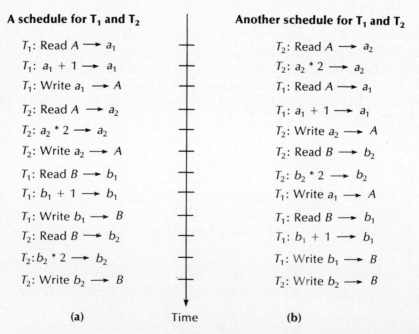

A schedule for T_1 and T_2

T_1: Read $A \longrightarrow a_1$

T_1: $a_1 + 1 \longrightarrow a_1$

T_1: Write $a_1 \longrightarrow A$

T_2: Read $A \longrightarrow a_2$

T_2: $a_2 * 2 \longrightarrow a_2$

T_2: Write $a_2 \longrightarrow A$

T_1: Read $B \longrightarrow b_1$

T_1: $b_1 + 1 \longrightarrow b_1$

T_1: Write $b_1 \longrightarrow B$

T_2: Read $B \longrightarrow b_2$

T_2: $b_2 * 2 \longrightarrow b_2$

T_2: Write $b_2 \longrightarrow B$

(a)

Another schedule for T_1 and T_2

T_2: Read $A \longrightarrow a_2$

T_2: $a_2 * 2 \longrightarrow a_2$

T_1: Read $A \longrightarrow a_1$

T_1: $a_1 + 1 \longrightarrow a_1$

T_2: Write $a_2 \longrightarrow A$

T_2: Read $B \longrightarrow b_2$

T_2: $b_2 * 2 \longrightarrow b_2$

T_1: Write $a_1 \longrightarrow A$

T_1: Read $B \longrightarrow b_1$

T_1: $b_1 + 1 \longrightarrow b_1$

T_1: Write $b_1 \longrightarrow B$

T_2: Write $b_2 \longrightarrow B$

(b)

Time

FIGURE 7.6 Examples of schedules for the two transactions of Fig. 7.5

7.3.3 Serializable Schedules

Certain schedules introduce operation losses or inconsistencies. The problem of concurrency control is to allow the execution of only those schedules that exclude them. Clearly a sequential execution of transactions (excluding simultaneous transactions) corresponds to a special schedule that has no loss of operation or inconsistencies. Such a schedule is called a *serial schedule* [Eswaran76].

> **Definition 7.5 Serial schedule**
> A schedule S of a set of transactions $\{T_1, T_2, \ldots, T_n\}$ is a serial schedule if there exists a permutation π of $\{1, 2, \ldots, n\}$ such that $S = <T_{\pi(1)}, T_{\pi(2)}, \ldots, T_{\pi(n)}>$.

In order to guarantee lack of conflict, it is convenient to allow only those schedules that read and update granules similarly to a serial schedule [Eswaran76, Papadimitriou77]. Such schedules are said to be *serializable*.

> **Definition 7.6 Serializable schedule**
> A schedule of a set of transactions $T_1, T_2, \ldots, T_n$ is serializable if it yields exactly the same result as a serial schedule of $\{T_1, T_2, \ldots, T_n\}$.

Thus the problem of concurrency control may be resolved by requiring that the system generates solely serializable schedules, which is a sufficient although not a necessary condition to guarantee absence of conflict [Gardarin77].

7.3.4 Properties of Actions

In certain situations, the order in which two actions are performed may affect their results; in others, this is not the case. Thus we are led to the concept of *permutable actions*.

> **Definition 7.7 Permutable actions**
> Two actions A_i and A_j are permutable if every execution of A_i followed by A_j yields the same result as the execution of A_j followed by A_i.

For example, two read actions are permutable, whereas read and write are not when they bear on the same granule. Two actions bearing on different granules are always permutable since the execution of the first action does not affect the result of the second, and vice-versa. It is interesting to note that write and write actions bearing on the same granule are generally not permutable. The effect of the sequence $\{<T_1:\text{write}(g)>, <T_2:\text{write}(g)>\}$ is the same as the action

$<T_2:\text{write}(g)>$, while the effect of the sequence $\{T_2:\text{write}(g)>, <T_1:\text{write}(g)>\}$ is the same as the action $<T_1:\text{write}(g)>$. Thus the last write is always predominant.

It is interesting to analyze the permutability of insert operations when performed in a file index. Let $e1$ and $e2$ be two entries in a file index. Let us consider two sequences of actions: $\{T_1:\text{insert}(e1)>, <T_2:\text{insert}(e2)>\}$ and $\{<T_2:\text{insert}(e2)>, <T_1:\text{insert}(e1)>\}$. Are these two sequences equivalent in the sense that they give the same results? In other words, are insertions in an index permutable actions? The answer depends on the index structure [Michel87]. If the index is a B-tree, the operations in general are not permutable because the split operations of a B-tree leaf may be acomplished differently according to the insertion order. If it is a data structure that splits in a way independent of the insertion order in a leaf (for example, the predicate tree structure introduced in Chapter 2), insert actions are permutable. As we shall see, the permutability of all actions performed on an object is an important property that avoids concurrency control on that object. Thus certain kinds of index (such as predicate trees) do not require heavy concurrency control algorithms.

7.3.5 Characterization of Serializable Schedules

In order to bring out the characteristics of serializable schedules, we shall introduce a basic transformation of transaction schedules. The permutation of two permutable actions a_i and a_j that are executed by different transactions consists of exchanging the order of execution of these operations. Thus, for example, the sequence $\{a_i,a_j\}$ is replaced by the sequence $\{a_j,a_i\}$. It is then possible to give a sufficient condition for a schedule to be serializable.

Proposition
A sufficient condition for a schedule to be serializable is that it can be transformed through permutation of permutable actions into a serial schedule.

Proof
By definition the results are invariant under permutations. If the schedule can be transformed into a serial schedule, it yields the same result as this serial schedule, and therefore it is serializable. The condition is not necessary. For example, the schedule $\{ <T_1:a=2>, <T_2:a=3>, <T_1:a=2> \}$ yields the same result as the serial schedule $\{ <T_2:a=3>, <T_1:a=2>\}$; thus it is serializable. However, $<T_1:a=2>$ and $<T_2:a=3>$ are not permutable actions; thus this schedule cannot be transformed in a serial schedule by permutation of permutable actions.

Consider schedule (a) depicted in Fig. 7.6. Representing only the additions and multiplications operations, this schedule may be written more simply:

T_1: $A + 1 \rightarrow A$
T_2: $A * 2 \rightarrow A$
T_1: $B + 1 \rightarrow B$
T_2: $B * 2 \rightarrow B$.

Operations $A * 2 \rightarrow A$ and $B + 1 \rightarrow B$ are permutable, for they bear upon different granules A and B. Therefore the schedule may be transformed into:

T_1: $A + 1 \rightarrow A$
T_1: $B + 1 \rightarrow B$
T_2: $A * 1 \rightarrow A$
T_2: $B * 2 \rightarrow B$

which is a serial schedule of T_1 and then T_2. Therefore the schedule depicted in Fig. 7.6 (a) is serializable.

7.3.6 Precedence Relation

The notion of nonpermutable operations allows one to define a relation between transaction called *precedence*.

Definition 7.8 Precedence
T_i precede T_j in a schedule $S = \{T_1, T_2, \ldots, T_n\}$ if there exist two nonpermutable actions a_i and a_j such that a_i is executed by T_i before a_j is executed by T_j.

The precedence relation denoted $<$ may be represented by a graph [Trinchieri75, Bernstein82], which characterizes the possible relationships among transactions during execution.

Definition 7.9 Precedence graph
A precedence graph of a schedule is an oriented graph whose set of vertices is the set of transactions and such that there exists an arc from T_i to T_j if T_i precedes T_j ($T_i < T_j$).

It is now possible to demonstrate the following proposition:

Proposition
A sufficient condition for a schedule to be serializable is that its associated precedence graph has no circuit.

Proof
Let us consider a schedule S with a circuit-free precedence graph. This precedence graph represents all precedence relationships among transactions due to nonpermutable actions. With the circuit-free precedence graph, it is possible to define among the transactions a partial order that respects precedence relationships due to nonpermutable actions. Such a partial order may be extended arbitrarily into a complete order $< T_{i1}, T_{i2}, \ldots, T_{in} >$. All the other operations being permutable, they may be rearranged to fit this order. Thus schedule S can be transformed through permutation of permutable actions into a serial schedule. It is a sufficient condition to be serializable according to the previous proposition.

An application of the proposition is shown in Fig. 7.7, which depicts the precedence graphs corresponding to the schedule shown in Fig. 7.6. Graph (a) has no circuit, confirming the fact that schedule (a) is serializable. Graph (b) has a circuit, explaining the fact that schedule (b) is not serializable.

An important special case of application arises when there exist only two possible actions on a granule of the database:

1. READ (granule).
2. WRITE (granule).

These operations must be seen as atomic (indivisible) actions. This is generally done by means of semaphore-like synchronization mechanisms [Dijkstra68, Courtois71] permitting exclusion of simultaneous execution of read/write operations on the same granule. In general, all other actions may be built from the read and write actions and mutual exclusion mechanism (such as semaphores). Henceforth and unless stated otherwise, we shall restrict ourselves to the types of systems found in practice where there are two basic actions: READ (granule) and WRITE (granule). Moreover, a granule will be generally assimilated to a page.

Permutation of operations bearing on different granules is always possible. Only certain permutations of operations bearing on the same granules are impossible. More precisely, if g is a granule, we have the following:

1. $< T_i$: READ $(g)>$ and $< T_j$: READ $(g)>$ are permutable operations.

(a)   (b)

FIGURE 7.7 Example of precedence graphs

2. $< T_i$: READ $(g)>$ and $< T_j$: WRITE $(g)>$ are nonpermutable operations. Therefore when T_i reads a granule before T_j writes it, $T_i < T_j$.
3. $< T_i$: WRITE $(g)>$ and $< T_j$: WRITE $(g)>$ are nonpermutable operations. There when T_i writes a granule before T_j writes it too, $T_i < T_j$.

In summary, precedences are created by read/write and write/write conflicts bearing on the same granule. The concurrency control algorithms we will study will all impose an order of transactions that must be followed by all precedences created by read/write and write/write conflicts. The transaction order can be induced by the transaction starting times (initial ordering algorithm), by the order of arrival of the first conflict (locking algorithm), or by the transaction ending time (validation ordering algorithm). Many variations of these basic strategies are possible, thus inducing various orders and algorithms.

7.4 Initial Timestamp Ordering Algorithms

7.4.1 Timestamps

One method to prevent the production of nonserializable schedules is to order the transaction when they are launched into execution and to ensure that conflicting acccsscs to granules take place in the transaction-given order. Such a method was first introduced in the concurrency control algorithms of the SDD.1 distributed system [Bernstein80]. To control the transaction ordering, it is necessary to associate with each transaction a unique identifier called a *transaction timestamp* [Rosenkrantz78].

Definition 7.10 Transaction timestamp
A numerical value assigned to a transaction that allows it to be ordered with respect to other transactions.

In a centralized system, the generation of transaction timestamps is a trivial problem. A counter managed by the system and increased by one at each transaction start is a possible solution. The system clock may also be used.

In order to ensure that the transactions operate on the granules in the order defined by the transaction timestamps, it is necessary to remember the timestamp of the last transaction that operated on a granule. This is done by means of a granule timestamp [Thomas79]. A *granule timestamp* is a numerical variable associated with a granule that stores the timestamp of the last transaction operating on that granule. It is possible to distinguish between a *read granule timestamp* (value of the transaction timestamp of the last transaction having done a read on that granule) and a *write granule timestamp* (value of the transaction timestamp of the last transaction having done a write on that granule).

The processing of granule timestamps as a means for controlling concurrent access may be carried out by reserving storage space in each granule. Such a strategy has two disadvantages: (1) the amount of utilized storage space may be nonnegligible (for example, several bytes per page) and (2) updating the granule timestamp may demand additional I/O operations, especially during read operations since these may require updating the granule timestamp on the disk. These problems may be circumvented by keeping timestamps in main memory and "forgetting" timestamps that are too old. Timestamps can be kept in page buffers, in directory entrances, or in special tables. Since access conflicts can occur only among current transactions, it is not necessary to preserve the timestamps corresponding to transactions that are not simultaneous with current transactions. Granule timestamps can also be stored in limited size tables of the main memory [Bernstein80]. An entry in such a table consists of the granule identifier and the corresponding granule timestamp. In addition to this table, one also needs a variable containing the value m of the largest granule timestamp value that has been expurgated from the table. In order to determine a granule timestamp value, the controller seeks that granule in the table. If that granule is found, its timestamp is also found in the table; otherwise the value of m is taken as the value of the timestamp of the sought granule. This ensures secure controls regardless of the size of the table and of the strategy utilized to eliminate timestamp from the table since the actual value of the timestamp of the sought granule is necessarily smaller or equal to m.

7.4.2 Total Timestamp Ordering Algorithm

This algorithm consists of verifying that transactional access to the granules takes place in the order initially assigned to transactions and indicated by the transaction timestamp. Whenever two transactions, T_i having timestamp i and T_j having timestamp j where $i < j$, operate on the same granule, the scheduler controlling access to this granule makes sure that T_i precedes T_j. If this is not the case, the scheduler aborts one of the transactions, which will be restarted later. It must be emphasized that this algorithm does not distinguish among read and write operations that are permutable and therefore nonconflicting. On the other hand, it needs only one type of granule timestamp.

Fig. 7.8 depicts the total ordering algorithm. Here g denotes the granule accessed by the transaction T_i having transaction timestamp i. $S(g)$ is the granule timestamp of granule g. ABORT is a procedure causing restart of transaction T_i or T_j.

The problem of restarting transactions following abort can be treated differently depending on whether the aborted transaction is T_i, the one that requests an operation, or T_j, the one that has already performed the operation that led to the conflict. In the first case T_i must be restarted with a new transaction time-

Procedure READ (T$_i$: transaction,g: granule);
    if (S(g) ≤ i)
    then
          begin
            "carry out the read";
            S(g) := i;
          end
    else ABORT;
end READ;

Procedure WRITE (T$_i$: transaction, g: granule);
    if(S(g) ≤ i)
    then
          begin
            "carry out the write";
            S(g) := i;
          end
    else ABORT;
end WRITE;

FIGURE 7.8 Total timestamp ordering algorithm

stamp i' greater than j in order to eliminate the conflict with T_j. However, T_i may now be in conflict with a new transaction, say $T_{j'}$. Thus T_i may be aborted again, and this process may continue indefinitely. One might try to halt these repeated aborts by assigning arbitrarily to the aborted transaction a sufficiently large transaction timestamp [Bernstein80]; however, another aborted transaction may still create repeated conflicts.

In the second case, T_j may be restarted with the same transaction timestamp. Indeed an older transaction (having a smaller transaction timestamp value) takes priority; therefore there is no danger of continuous restart of the transaction. A restart of T_j requires the restoration of all granules updated by T_j and reverification that the order of the conflicting access of T_i respects the order implied by the transaction timestamps. If this is not the case, it is necessary to restart the transaction preceding T_j. A difficult problem, known as the *domino effect* [Menasce78], may arise in this method. The domino effect problem arises when the updates of T_j were read by other transactions; these transactions must also be restarted. In other words, aborting a transaction T_j may lead to a situation where an earlier update of T_j is undone while its effect remains visible on a subsequent transaction, say T_k. This may require an abort of T_k, which in turn may lead to the abort of yet another transaction, and so on. Such a set of circumstances leads to ordering the transactions' commits according to the values of their transaction timestamp.

7.4.3 Partial Timestamp Ordering Algorithm

The preceding algorithm orders all operations on granules. Actually it is only necessary to order nonpermutable operations (read/write and write/write). The algorithm we present here consists of verifying that the sequences $<$ READ, WRITE $>$, $<$ WRITE, READ $>$, and $<$ WRITE, WRITE $>$ are performed in the order assigned initially and defined through the transaction timestamps. Two types of granule timestamps are utilized: SR, the read granule timestamp that is the timestamp of the most recent transaction (the transaction whose timestamp has the greatest value) having executed a read operation; and SW, the write granule timestamp that is the timestamp of the last transaction having executed a write operation. When a transaction executes a READ, the scheduler controls the correct sequence of the read with respect to the last write (the timestamp of the reading transaction must be greater than the value of the write granule timestamp). For instance, if a granule has been updated by transaction T_2, we have $SW = 2$; if it has been read by the youngest transaction T_7, we have $SR = 7$. In this situation ($SW = 2$ and $SR = 7$), any transaction with a timestamp equal to or greater than 2 can read without a problem.

When a transaction executes a write, the scheduler controls the correct sequence of the write with respect to the previously executed read and write. Thus the timestamp of the writing transaction must be equal to or greater than the value of the write granule timestamp and that of the read granule timestamp. For instance, with $SW = 2$ and $SR = 7$, only transactions with timestamp equal or greater than 7 can write. Fig. 7.9 shows the partial ordering algorithm. Apart from the granule timestamps of the granule g, which are denoted $SR(g)$ and $SW(g)$, the notations are the same as those of Fig. 7.8. The partial ordering algorithm suffers from the same problems as those afflicting the preceding total ordering algorithm, except that it aborts less transactions.

7.4.4 Multiversion Timestamp Ordering Algorithms

The strategy described may be improved by preserving several versions of the same granule. For each granule g, the system should preserve a set of write granule timestamps $\{SW_i(g)\}$ with the associated granule version values $\{V_i(g)\}$ and a set of read granule timestamps $\{SR_i(g)\}$. Thus a granule version i is defined by a triple $<SW_i(g), SR_i(g), V_i(g)>$. A granule version i is created for each update of g by a transaction T_i. For example, the granule represented by a rectangle in Fig. 7.11 has been successively updated by T_1, T_5, and T_{10}. There exist three successive versions: version 1, version 5, and version 10.

It is then possible to ensure the proper order of read operations with respect to write operations without ever restarting a transaction. To do this, it suffices to provide transaction T_i requesting to read granule g with the version whose

Procedure READ (T_i: transaction, g: granule);
    if SW(g) ≤ i
    then
            begin
              "carry out the read";
              SR(g) := MAX (SR(g),i);
            end
    else ABORT;
end READ;

Procedure WRITE (T_i: transaction, g: granule);
    if(SW(g) ≤ i) ∧ (SR(g) ≤ i)
    then
            begin
              "carry out the write";
              SW(g) := i;
            end
    else ABORT;
end WRITE;

FIGURE 7.9 Partial timestamp ordering algorithm

write granule timestamp is immediately below or equal to i. Therefore T_i shall always precede all transactions of higher timestamps writing on the granule in question and shall follow all transactions with lower timestamps. Thus T_i will be in proper order. Everything will take place as if T_i had requested to read just after the write of the version having an immediately lower granule timestamp. The control algorithm for the READ operation, including a device for multiversion partial ordering, is depicted in Fig. 7.10. For instance, if T_6 requires reading the granule, version 5 will be delivered to T_6 (Fig. 7.11).

It is also possible to force an ordering of the writing operations of transactions by inserting a new version created by a transaction T_i just after that having a write granule timestamp immediately below it, say $V_{i'}$. For instance, if T_8 writes on granule g of Fig. 7.11, a new version (version 8) will be created between version 5 ($V_{i'}$ is version 5) and version 10. If, however, before the T_i write actions, a transaction T_k having a timestamp higher than that of T_i ($k > i$) has read the version V_i', then either T_k or T_i must be aborted. It is impossible to write in the past (that is, to redo it) without redoing its consequences if any (that is, if this past was seen). However, T_k can be aborted only if it is not yet terminated. Therefore it is preferable to restart T_i with a new timestamp i' greater than k, thus avoiding redoing a committed past. These two possibilities are illustrated in Fig. 7.11 with $i = 6$, $k = 7$, and $j = 5$: T_6 tries to write upon g. In case (1), T_7 is aborted, T_6 creates a new version, and the restarted T_7 reads this version. In case (2), T_6 is aborted and restarted with timestamp 12. The control algorithm for the

Procedure READ (T_i: transaction, g: granule);
      j := "index of the last version of g";
      while $SW_j(g) > i$ **do** j := index of the previous version of g;
      "carry out the read of g version j";
      $SR_j(g) := MAX(SR_j(g),i)$;
end READ;

Procedure WRITE (T_i: transaction, g: granule);
      j := "index of the last version of g";
      while $SW_j(g) > i$ **do** j := index of the previous version of g;
      if $SR_j(g) > i$ **then** ABORT
      else "execute the write inserting a new version i of g after version
          j";
end WRITE;

FIGURE 7.10 Multiversion timestamp ordering algorithm

Version 1   Version 5   Version 10

Original
situation

(a)

Assume now that T_6 performs a WRITE upon g. Possible resequencing following
ABORT are shown below:

(1) ABORT of T_7 and restart with timestamp of 7 for T_7 after performing T_6
write yields the following:

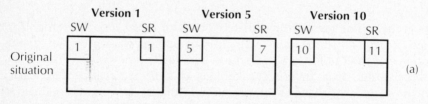

(b)

(2) ABORT of T_6 and restart with timestamp of 12 for T_6:

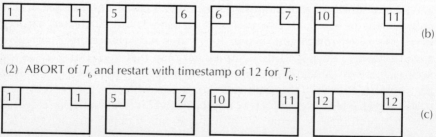

(c)

FIGURE 7.11 Illustration of possible sequences of operations controlled by the
multiversion timestamp ordering algorithm

operation WRITE is presented in Fig. 7.10. The notations are the same as in Fig. 7.9 with the addition of an index representing the various versions.

7.4.5 Further Timestamp Ordering Algorithms

Several variations of the previous algorithms have been proposed. First, the transaction timestamp does not need to be known before a first conflict arises. A method based on a dynamic allocation of transaction timestamps has been proposed [Bayer81]. The principle of this method is the following. A transaction starts with an unknown timestamp, say i; while this transaction does not access a granule that has also been accessed by an active transaction for a conflicting operation, the transaction is not given a timestamp; when a conflict appears, a timestamp is attached to the transaction in such a way that a serialization order can be achieved, if possible. This leads to a rather complex algorithm, but the frequency of transaction abort is reduced.

Another improvement is to apply *Thomas' rule* [Thomas79]. The idea is that the last write performed on a granule is the only one that remains visible when only one version is kept in the database. Thus if a write from a transaction T_i is performed on a granule g after this granule has been written by a transaction T_j with $j > i$, it is possible to ignore it without redoing the transaction T_i. This is not possible if g has been read by a transaction of timestamp greater than i and less than j because of the incorrect reading. Thus the partial timestamp ordering algorithm can be improved by not aborting a writing transaction T_i such that $SR(g) \leq i < SW(g)$; in that case, the write is simply ignored.

7.5 Optimistic Algorithms

Timestamp ordering algorithms verify correct transaction ordering at each granule access. We shall see that locking algorithms act more or less in a similar way. If a system designer is optimistic and believes that not too many conflicts arise, he or she will not implement such strong a priori control. Rather it may be desirable to let transactions go and control them a posteriori. This is the idea of optimistic methods [Kung81]; they control transactions not during execution but at commit time. More precisely, an optimistic algorithm considers that all transactions first prepare their updates in private buffers during execution. At transaction end, before committing the transaction updates in the database, a *certification* (also called *validation*) is introduced.

Definition 7.11 Certification
Special action that controls that committing the updates of a transaction in the database preserves serializability.

READ PHASE   CERTIFICATION   WRITE PHASE
(Execution)   (Validation)   (Commit)

|_____|_____|_____|

FIGURE 7.12 Transaction phases with optimistic concurrency control

If the transaction is successfully certified, its prepared updates are written in the database, and modifications are made visible to other transactions. If certification fails, the transaction is aborted; this is done by deleting the transaction.

In summary, with optimistic concurrency control, a transaction is composed of three phases: a read phase where updates are prepared in a private workspace, a certification phase, and a possible write phase. These phases are illustrated in Fig. 7.12.

One of the main issues of the design of an optimistic method is the choice of the certification algorithm. In most schemes, the serialization order is determined by the certification order. At transaction certification, it must be checked that the validating transaction T_i has seen all the modifications of the previously certified transactions. For all the transactions terminated when T_i starts, this is obvious. Thus the certification algorithm must check only that all granules read by T_i have not been written by any concurrent transaction T_j certified between the beginning of T_i and the certification of T_j. In the original proposal [Kung81], a transaction certification counter is maintained to determine the transactions against which a transaction has to be certified. Also for each transaction T_i, the system keeps track of read granule identifiers in the read set $RS(T_i)$ and of written granule identifiers in the write set $WS(T_i)$. The certification algorithm accepts the validation of T_i if the read set $RS(T_i)$ does not intersect with the write set $WS(T_j)$ of any transaction T_j certified during the read phase of T_i. A more precise specification of the corresponding algorithm is given in Fig. 7.13.

The proposed certification algorithm may reject a transaction that does not violate the serializability order. Indeed if a transaction T_2 reads a granule g written by a concurrent transaction T_1 committed before T_2 reads g, T_2 will be rolled back at certification time because its read set interferes with T_1's write set. Thus the certification algorithm can be improved to reject fewer transactions by using granule timestamps [Thomasian85]. Despite the sophistication of the certification scheme, optimistic concurrency control algorithms suffer from rollbacks performed at transaction end. In addition, they can suffer from a lack of fairness; long transactions can be restarted permanently if they always conflict with short transactions. Thus optimistic methods seem to be acceptable only for short transactions in the context of a low probability of conflicts; however, they can be mixed with other methods.

Procedure BEGIN_TRANSACTION (T_i : transaction);
        $RS(T_i) := \emptyset$;
        $WS(T_i) := \emptyset$;
        after(T_i) := certification_counter;
end BEGIN_TRANSACTION;

Procedure CERTIFY(T_i: transaction);
        for t = after(T_i) + 1 **to** certification_counter **do**
                if WS(t) $\cap$ RS(T_i) $\neq$ $\emptyset$ **then** ABORT(T_i);
        if "T_i not aborted" **then**
        begin
                certification_counter := certification_counter + 1;
                COMMIT(T_i);
        end;
end CERTIFY;

Procedure COMMIT(T_i: transaction);
        for each (g) of WS(Ti) **do**
                write(g);
end COMMIT;

FIGURE 7.13 Possible certification algorithm

7.6 Two-phase Locking Algorithms

7.6.1 Locking Principles and Protocol

The strategies already examined permit execution of transactions while verifying that conflicting accesses to the same granule are executed in either the order initially defined when launching the transactions or the order of transaction validation. If this order is not respected, one of the conflicting transactions is restarted. Therefore these strategies may be described as detecting nonserializable schedules that are corrected by restarting certain transactions. In contradistinction locking-type strategies avoid generating incorrect schedules by delaying one of the transactions that attempts to execute conflicting operations on the same granule.

The goal of locking algorithms is to allow simultaneous execution of only those operations that are compatible — that is, composed of permutable actions. More precisely, an operation is a sequence of actions performed by a transaction on an object. In general, an operation corresponds to a DBMS command, such as SELECT, UPDATE, or INSERT. Such operations entail several read and write actions, as defined. The possible simultaneous execution of operations on a granule is captured by the concept of *operation mode*.

Definition 7.12 Operation mode
A property that characterizes an operation by determining its compatibility with other operations.

The most common operation modes are the *retrieval* and *update* modes. The retrieval mode characterizes every operation that performs read actions only, whereas the update mode corresponds to every operation that performs a write, insert, or modify action; it also allows read actions. It is possible to distinguish more operation modes, as done by the DBTG [Codasyl71]. For example, nonprotected retrieval (also called *dirty read*), protected retrieval, insertion, deletion, and modification modes can be distinguished. The compatibilities between operation modes may be specified using a compatibility matrix. It is a square binary matrix C having as many rows and lines as distinguished operation modes. $C(i,j)$ is set to 1 if mode i is compatible with mode j and to 0 otherwise. For example, for modes $M0 = $ selection and $M1 = $ update, we obtain:

$$C = \begin{bmatrix} 1 & 0 \\ 0 & 0 \end{bmatrix}$$

Locking all the granules accessed while performing an operation on an object is required to avoid conflicts. Similarly, it is necessary to indicate to the scheduler controlling a granule that an operation is completed. To accomplish this, a locking protocol composed of two special actions is introduced:

● LOCK (g,M) permits a transaction to signal to the scheduler controlling granule g the start of an operation of mode(s) defined by M; when successful, it *locks* the granule for the requesting transaction in mode(s) M.
● UNLOCK (g) permits a transaction to signal to the scheduler controlling granule g the end of the current operation bearing on g; it *unlocks* granule g for all modes held by the requesting transaction.

The proposed protocol requires the execution of two additional actions per granule accessed: LOCK and UNLOCK. In relational systems, the interface seen by the transactions does not generally include locking requests; they are automatically generated by the DBMS. However, certain systems lock granules only in retrieval mode and require explicit locking in the update mode. Many systems automatically perform the unlocking actions either at the end of transactions or at certain intermediate points where the database is consistent. Thus it is no longer necessary to request the unlocking of each granule. This also facilitates restarts in case of failures. Even if the interface LOCK/UNLOCK is invisible to the user, there exists at least an equivalent logical interface within the system.

7.6.2 Locking Algorithms

In order to permit simultaneous execution on the same granule of compatible operations only, it is necessary to record the operation modes currently locked on every granule. This may be achieved in different ways — for example, with counters of locked operation modes stored in the heading of each granule. However, because it is necessary to memorize what transaction possesses a lock to be able to release the lock and also because storing locks inside a granule may induce overhead if the granule is released from the main memory, we prefer to manage a lock table. The table may contain for each pair $<$ granule g, transaction $T_i >$, where T_i operate on g, the bit vector

$$A(g,i) = \begin{bmatrix} a_1 \\ \cdot \\ \cdot \\ \cdot \\ a_j \\ \cdot \\ \cdot \\ \cdot \\ a_k \end{bmatrix}$$

where $a_j = 1$ if the granule g is locked in mode M_j by the transaction T_i and 0 otherwise. Similarly we assume that the modes requested by the action LOCK (g,M) are defined through a bit vector:

$$M = \begin{bmatrix} m_i \\ \cdot \\ \cdot \\ \cdot \\ m_j \\ \cdot \\ \cdot \\ \cdot \\ m_k \end{bmatrix}$$

where $m_j = 1$ if the mode M_j is requested and 0 otherwise. It is now possible to elaborate a general locking algorithm applicable for any set of operation modes, based on logical Boolean operations. We shall use the following Boolean operators:

   $\vee$ logical union of two Boolean vectors (logical OR) or more.
   $\wedge$ logical intersection of two Boolean vectors (logical AND) or more.
   $\neg$ logical negation of a Boolean vector.
   $\supset$ logical inclusion of Boolean vectors.

* Boolean matrices product (this corresponds to the usual matrix product where the add operation is replaced by logical union and the multiply operation is replaced by logical intersection).

Proposition

The operation modes requested during a primitive operation LOCK (g,M) executed for a transaction T_p are compatible with the operations modes currently locked upon granule g by the other transactions if:

$$\neg\, (\neg C^* \vee A\,(g,i)) \supset M$$
$$i \neq p$$

Proof

$\vee A\,(g,i)$ for $i \neq p$ is a bit vector whose j bit is 1 if M_i, is an operation mode locked on granule g by a transaction other than T_p. $\neg C$ is the complement of the compatibility matrix. Therefore, $\neg C * \vee A\,(g,i)$ for $i \neq p$ is a bit vector whose j bit is 1 if the mode M_j is incompatible with an operation mode currently locked on granule g by a transaction other than T_p. Finally $\neg\, (\neg C * \vee A\,(g,i)$ for $i \neq p$ is therefore a bit vector representing all the operation modes compatible with the operation modes locked on granule g by a transaction other than T_p. Therefore every vector included within the latter corresponds to modes compatible with those currently locked on granule g by a transaction other than T_p.

A locking algorithm requires the definition of a strategy for the case when the requested operation modes during the execution of a primitive LOCK are not compatible with the modes of currently executed operations. The simplest strategy is to return the message ''granule busy'' to the calling process, which can then loop periodically on the LOCK request. In order to control the waiting stages, it is generally preferable to place the request in a waiting state and block the calling transaction until the requested granule becomes available. A waiting queue $Q\,[g]$ can then be associated with each busy granule. This queue contains the locking requests (consisting of the vector M and the transaction identifier), which are queued in order of priority, this coinciding generally with the order of their arrival. Fig. 7.14 depicts the locking/unlocking algorithm corresponding to such a strategy; T_p is supposed to be the active transaction.

7.6.3 Correctness of Locking

The locking algorithm allows the simultaneous execution on the same granule of compatible operations only. This may be achieved by restricting the usage of the actions LOCK and UNLOCK in the transactions [Eswaran76]. We now introduce this so-called two-phase restriction.

Procedure LOCK (g,M);
    if¬(¬C * ∨ A (g,i)) ⊃ M
        i ≠ p
   then A(g,p) := A(g,p) ∨ M
   else
       begin
        "insert (p,M) into Q[g]";
        "block transaction T_p";
       end;
end LOCK;

Procedure UNLOCK (g)
    A(g,p) := 0;
    for each (q,M') of Q[g] **do**
        if ¬ (¬C * ∨ A (g,i)) ⊃ M'
          i ≠ p
     then
         begin
         A(g,q) := A(g,q) ∨ M' ;
         "remove (q,M') from Q[g]";
         "unblock transaction T_q";
        end;
  end UNLOCK;

FIGURE 7.14 Proposed locking algorithm

Every transaction that respects the locking protocol as defined up to here must execute LOCK with the correct operation mode before executing an operation on a granule. It must also execute UNLOCK after the end of the execution of this operation. Henceforth all the transactions must possess the property of *well-formness*.

Definition 7.13 Well-formed transaction
Transaction that locks in correct operation modes all accessed granules before operating on them and unlocks them after operation.

It is not necessary for a transaction to lock just before it performs the operation or to unlock just after the operation is completed. Locking can be anticipated and unlocking can be delayed. *Two-phase transactions* generally delay unlocking.

Definition 7.14 Two-phase transaction
Well-formed transaction that does not execute a LOCK after it has executed an UNLOCK.

Thus a two-phase transaction must lock all the granules on which it operates before it begins to unlock. A typical curve depicting the variation in the number of granules locked by a two-phase transaction is shown in Fig. 7.15.

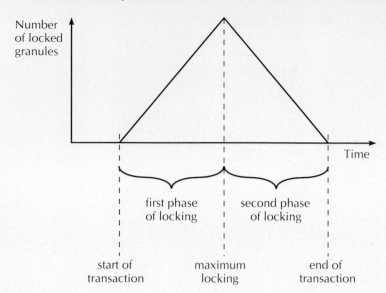

FIGURE 7.15 Variation of the number of granules locked by a two-phase transaction

The following proposition shows the importance of the two-phase restriction and demonstrates the correctness of a locking protocol used accordingly to the following rules:

R1: Every transaction must execute LOCK with the correct operation mode(s) upon the chosen granule before executing an operation on this granule.

R2: Every transaction must execute UNLOCK on the locked granules after operating on them.

R3: A transaction cannot execute LOCK after executing UNLOCK.

In most DBMSs granules are actually unlocked at the transaction end, which guarantees that transactions are two-phase and avoids the domino effect.

Proposition
Every schedule of a set of well-formed two-phase transactions is serializable.

Proof
A serializable schedule possesses a precedence graph with no circuits. Let us consider a schedule for the set $\{T_1, T_2, \ldots, T_n\}$ of two-phase transactions, and let us assume that there exists a precedence circuit $T_{i1} < T_{i2} < \ldots < T_{in} < T_{i1}$. It follows immediately that T_{i2} locks (through LOCK action) a granule g_{i1} after T_{i1} unlocks (through the UN-

LOCK action) that granule; T_{i3} locks a granule g_{i2} after T_{i2} unlocks that granule; and T_{i1} locks a granule g_{in}, after T_{in} unlocks that granule. Since each transaction T_{i2}, T_{i3}, . . . is two phase, it unlocks only after it has completed all its LOCK actions. Thus T_{i1} unlocks g_{i1} before executing the lock of g_{in}. Therefore T_{i1} is not two-phase, which contradicts the initial hypothesis.

Finally, two-phase locking requires each transaction to pass through a state of maximum locking wherein all the accessed granules are locked. It follows that the accessing order to the granules forced upon the transactions is that one in which the transactions reach this maximum locking state. Two-phase locking may therefore be considered an ordering of the transactions. This order is not constructed a priori as in the algorithms based on initial ordering; instead it is determined by the point in time when a transaction reaches its state of maximum locking. In most DBMSs it is the transaction end point (commit point).

7.6.4 The Deadlock Problem

A *dead*lock (or deadly embrace) *situation* arises when granules have been locked in such a sequence that a group of transactions cannot proceed because certain transactions are waiting for each other [Coffman71].

> **Definition 7.15 Deadlock situation**
> Situation in which a group of transactions satisfies the following properties: (1) Every transaction of the group is blocked, waiting for a granule, and (2) the completion of every transaction that does not belong to the group does not permit any transaction in the group to be unblocked.

Deadlock, a problem generated by locking, is difficult to resolve. Solutions are presented in Section 7.7.

7.6.5 Other Problems Due to Locking

Another problem due to locking is that of *starvation* [Courtois71], or *permanent blocking* [Holt72]. This problem appears as soon as a group of transactions effectively behaves as a coalition by carrying out mutually compatible operations (such as retrieval) in the presence of an individual transaction that intends to execute an operation incompatible with the former ones (for example, update). The individual transaction may then have to wait indefinitely. For instance, if transactions $R1,R2,R3,R4$, . . . , Rn, . . . are successively reading a granule g in such a way that the granule is always locked in read mode, a writing transaction W wanting to write upon g will wait forever. The solution to this problem is to line up requests for locks in order of arrival, letting through those that are compatible with all the requests that are ahead, including the one that is currently executing. Thus if W arrives before $R4$ and after $R3$, it will pass just after $R3$ and before $R4$.

The *phantom problem* has also been raised in [Eswaran76]. This arises when a granule is introduced in the database too late to be processed by a continuing transaction although it affects that transaction later. Consider the aircraft flight database shown in Fig. 7.16, which consists of a passenger list for each flight and some general flight information, including the number of passengers assigned a seat on the flight. Let us assume now the following transactions:

T_1 (part 1): List the passengers' names and numbers.
T_1 (part 2): List the flight information, including flight number and the number of passengers with reserved seats.
T_2: Add a passenger $<$ TOPPER,13 $>$ and increment the number of passengers in the flight information.

Let us assume that these transactions are executed in the following order: T_1 (part 1), T_2, T_1 (part 2). This is a possible schedule with locking since T_2 accesses an unlocked granule that does not even exist when T_1 performs the first part of its transaction. However, the result of T_1 is a list of three passengers while the number of passengers is printed as four. Thus Topper is a phantom for T_1.

This problem may be resolved be defining logical granules (in the example, this could be the logical relation PASSENGER) through special predicates [Eswaran76]. Locking through predicates also permits the defining of granules of variable size constructed according to the needs of various transactions. It requires special algorithms to determine whether two predicates are disjoint; this problem does not seem to have an efficient solution for generalized predicates. It should also be noted that the phantom problem is not peculiar to locking strategies and can also appear in the other approaches.

Another problem is the need for variable-sized granules, thus permitting locking at various levels, such as page, file, or even database. In order to ensure

PASSENGERS	
Name	Seat #
James	10
Mike	5
George	7
Topper	13

FLIGHT INFORMATION	
Flight #	Number of passengers
100	4

Topper is a phantom

FIGURE 7.16 Illustration of the phantom problem

compatibility among various levels, the notion of *intention mode* has been introduced [Gray78]. Within such a context, every granule can operate in two types of modes, normal modes and intention modes, which correspond to the intent to lock a subset of the granules under consideration. It has been shown [Gardarin78] that it is possible to define compatibilities among normal and intention modes starting from p initial modes through the following compatibility matrix:

$$C' = \begin{bmatrix} C & C \\ C & E \end{bmatrix}$$

where the first p modes of operations are the normal modes, the next p modes are the intention modes, and E is a matrix consisting of 1s. In order to lock a granule in mode $j,$ the algorithm locks all the granules containing the former in intention mode $p+j$ and then locks the granule in normal mode. Such an algorithm is particularly suitable to locking within hierarchies [Gray78].

7.7 Deadlock Solutions

7.7.1 Representation of Deadlock

First, we present an example of deadlock. Let us consider two transactions, T_1 and T_2. Transaction T_1 has succeeded in locking granule G_1 for update and is waiting to lock granule G_2 also for update. Transaction T_2 has succeeded in locking the same granule G_2 for update and is waiting to lock G_1 for protected retrieval (Fig. 7.17). The impossibility of executing simultaneously updates with other updates or protected retrievals upon the same granules results in the two transactions waiting for each other; it is a deadlock situation.

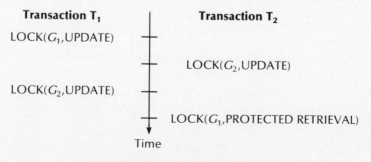

FIGURE 7.17 Example of deadlock

We present below two representations of deadlocks in terms of special graphs, the *waiting graph* [Murphy68] and the *allocation graph* [Holt72].

> ### Definition 7.16 Waiting graph
> Graph G (T,W) where T is the set of concurrent transactions $\{T_1,T_2, \ldots , T_n\}$ sharing granules $\{G_1,G_2, \ldots , G_m\}$, and W is the relation "waits" defined as follows: T_p waits for T_q if T_p demands locking a granule G_i and this request cannot be accepted because G_i has been locked by T_q.

[Murphy68] has presented the following proposition:

> ### Proposition
> There exists a deadlock if the waiting graph has a circuit.

Proof
If the waiting graph has a circuit, then there exists a group of transactions wherein: T_1 awaits T_2, T_2 awaits T_3, and $\ldots T_k$ awaits T_1. Every transaction in the group is therefore blocked waiting for a granule because this granule is utilized by another transaction of the group. Therefore completion of all the transactions not included in the group does not allow unblocking any transaction of the group. Vice-versa, the presence of deadlock implies the presence of at least one circuit. Otherwise every group of transactions would be such that the waiting subgraph it generates has no circuits. Following execution of all the transactions that do not block the group, it would therefore be possible to unblock a transaction of the group since a graph without a circuit has at least one terminal vertex.

Fig. 7.18 illustrates the application of the proposition to demonstrate that the situation in Fig. 7.17 is deadlocked. More generally, all the transactions belonging to a circuit are deadlocked. Furthermore a transaction waiting for a deadlocked transaction is itself deadlocked (Fig. 7.19).

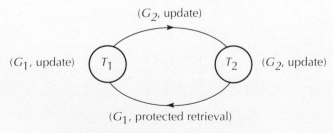

FIGURE 7.18 Waiting graph with circuit

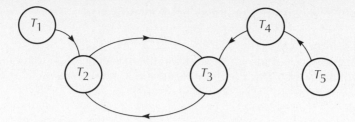

FIGURE 7.19 Transactions in various states of deadlock

It is interesting to establish the relationship between the waiting graph and the precedence graph. By definition, when a transaction T_i waits for a transaction T_j, this means that T_j has locked a granule G that T_i is requesting in an incompatible mode. Therefore the operation for which T_j has locked G should be performed before that requested by T_i since the two operations are incompatible and therefore composed of nonpermutable actions. Thus T_j precedes T_i with respect to G. However, the precedence relation does not generally imply the wait relation. Therefore reversing the arcs of the waiting graph yields a subgraph of the precedence graph. This implies that if the waiting graph has a circuit, then so does the precedence graph. Consequently a deadlock could not lead to a serializable schedule even if it was possible to complete the deadlocked transactions. We now introduce another representation of deadlocks.

Definition 7.17 Allocation graph
Graph composed of two sets of vertices corresponding to the set T of transactions and the set G of granules in which (1) an arc labeled with M links granule G_i to transaction T_p if T_p has succeeded in locking G_i in operation mode(s) M and (2) an arc labeled with M links transaction T_p to granule G_i if T_p has requested though not yet obtained locking of that granule in operation mode(s) M.

Fig. 7.20 depicts the allocation graph for the example shown in Fig. 7.18.

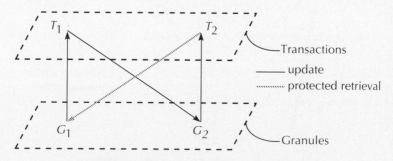

FIGURE 7.20 Example of allocation graph

The following proposition may be easily proved:

Proposition
A necessary condition for deadlock is the existence of a circuit in the allocation graph. This condition is generally not sufficient.

Proof
We shall demonstrate that if there are no circuits in the allocation graph, there cannot be any deadlock. Let T be an arbitrary set of transactions. Since the allocation graph has no circuit, the subgraph obtained after executing the transactions that do not belong to T also has no circuit. Therefore it has a terminal vertex. This vertex cannot be a granule since an unlocked granule cannot be waited for. Thus for every set of transactions T, the execution of all the transactions that do not belong to T would unblock a transaction belonging to T. Therefore there is no deadlock.

A simple example indicates that the condition is not sufficient. Let us consider three transactions T_1, T_2, T_3 sharing two granules G_1 and G_2 and utilizing the operation modes of retrieval, update, and insertion. Let us also assume that retrieval is compatible with retrieval and insertion, and update-update, update-insertion, and insertion-insertion are incompatible. The allocation graph depicted in Fig. 7.21 has a circuit, although there is no deadlock, as shown by the corresponding waiting graph, which appears in Fig. 7.22. We might note, however, that the condition is sufficient in the special case where the only modes are read and write, as illustrated in Fig. 7.20.

Generally there is no straightforward relationship between precedence graphs and allocation graphs. However, when the only existing operation modes are read and write, the presence of a circuit in the allocation graph is a necessary and sufficient condition for deadlock just like the presence of a circuit in the

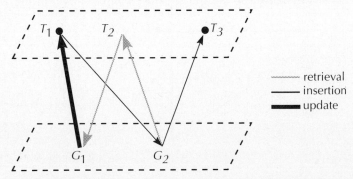

FIGURE 7.21 Allocation graph with circuit but without deadlock

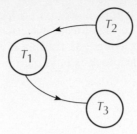

FIGURE 7.22 Waiting graph corresponding to Fig. 7.21

waiting graph. This in turn implies the presence of a circuit in the precedence graph.

7.7.2 Deadlock Prevention

Generally there are three ways to deal with deadlock: prevention, detection, and avoidance [Howard73]. Avoidance requires advanced knowledge of the granules that will be requested by transactions. This is not possible for a general ad hoc query system. Thus the first acceptable solution to the deadlock problem in the relational database context is deadlock prevention.

Deadlock prevention consists of eliminating one of the conditions that allows the possibility of deadlock when designing the concurrency control algorithm. One possible approach in the database context is the preordering of transactions using transaction timestamps. Such a preordering prevents the existence of cycles in the waiting graph. This approach has given two algorithms to prevent deadlock [Rosenkrantz78]: the so-called DIE-WAIT and WOUND-WAIT methods. These two methods impose a supplementary condition for a transaction to be accepted in the waiting list of a granule.

With the *DIE-WAIT method,* only an older transaction can wait for a younger one: T_i waits for T_j if $i < j$ and is aborted otherwise (dies). When a transaction dies, it is restarted with the same timestamp; thus sooner or later, it will become the oldest active transaction and will not die. This guarantees the absence of permanent rollback (starvation). With DIE-WAIT, a transaction can only wait for a younger one: this condition guarantees the absence of circuit in the waiting graph.

The *WOUND-WAIT method* is a symmetrical approach. Only a younger transaction can wait for an older: T_i waits for T_j if $i > j$. To avoid permanent rollback, the transaction requesting the locking of a granule held by a younger one does not abort but rather replaces the younger one, which is aborted. Thus if T_i requests a lock held by T_j, T_j is killed if $i < j$ and the lock is granted to T_i. This method can even be improved. Rather than killing T_j, it is possible only to wound it if the rule that a wound transaction cannot wait is imposed: a wound transaction that is waiting or wants to wait is aborted. In summary, the WOUND-WAIT method gives priority to the older transaction when a conflict occurs. The younger one either waits or is wounded. Thus an older transaction can never wait for a younger one, and no deadlock is possible.

7.7.3 Deadlock Detection

A deadlock detection algorithm may be constructed from a circuit detection algorithm for waiting graphs. We shall present an algorithm that tests a graph for circuits by successive elimination of terminal vertices [Holt72].

In a waiting graph, a vertex is terminal if the transaction that it represents is not waiting to lock any granules. Thus let $N(k)$ be the number of granules that the transaction T_k is waiting to lock. An initial reduction of the graph may be obtained by eliminating its terminal vertices — those for which $N(k) = 0$. The problem is to recompute the values of the $N(k)$ following the reduction in order to carry out the next reduction. This may be done by counting the requests that can be satisfied after each reduction, decrementing $N(k)$ for each such request of transaction T_k. This method has two special requirements:

1. It is necessary to mark the counted requests in order not to count them more than once.
2. It is necessary to utilize a special procedure to test whether a request is satisfied, taking into account the locking states of the transactions that have not yet been eliminated from the waiting graph.

Therefore let TENTATIVE-LOCK (G_i,R,k) be a Boolean procedure that tests whether request R of transaction T_k for granule G_i can be satisfied taking into account the locking of granules by the transactions T_j such that $N(j)$ is different from 0 (transactions that still wait). This procedure yields *true* if the request can be satisfied and *false* otherwise. The program for the procedure is analogous to that of the LOCK algorithm except that the locking states are not modified. Fig. 7.23 depicts a procedure DETECT that yields the answer *true* if there is deadlock and *false* otherwise.

When deadlock is detected, the problem is to select a transaction for restart. The detection algorithm presented yields the list of deadlocked transactions. One of these must therefore be selected and restarted. However, all solutions are not equally satisfactory, as indicated by Fig. 7.19, where it appears that restarting T_1,T_5, or T_4 does not resolve the deadlock. A possible solution to this problem may be to restart a transaction that blocks the greatest number of transactions — that is, one corresponding to the vertex having the greatest number of in-coming arc in the waiting graph.

In order to reduce the cost of detection, it is advisable to involve the detection algorithm only when a transaction has been waiting a lock for a long time

Boolean procedure DETECT
begin
      $T := \{$set of transactions T_j such that $N(j) \neq 0\}$;
      $L := \{$set of granules locked by the transactions $\epsilon\ T\}$;
      for each $G \in L$ **do**
            for each "nonmarked request R of T_k waiting for G_i" **do**
                  if TENTATIVE_LOCK $(G_i, R, k) =$ **true**
                then begin
                    "mark R";
                    $N(k) := N(k) - 1$;
                    if $N(k) = \phi$
                    then begin
                        "remove T_k from T";
                        "add the granules locked by T_k to the
                            set L";
                      end;
                  end;
              end;
          end;
      if $T = \phi$
      then DETECT := **false**
      else DETECT := **true**
   end DETECT;

FIGURE 7.23 Deadlock detection algorithm

(say a few seconds) rather than invoking the algorithm whenever a transaction just starts waiting for a lock. With such an approach, deadlock detection seems to be an acceptable solution to the deadlock problem, which can even be extended to distributed systems.

7.8 Conclusion

It appears that the various methods for concurrency control considered in this chapter may be divided into three general classes: timestamp ordering, certification, and locking. In the two former cases, the transactions are ordered either at launching time or at commitment time. In the last case, the requirement of maximum locking before unlocking defines the ordering; thus, the transactions are ordered during their executions, in a dynamic manner.

Performance requirements have motivated much of the recent work on concurrency control. Therefore it is fitting that the methods presented here be compared in this regard. We may consider this point with respect to degree of parallelism and time and space overhead. As far as parallelism is concerned, the various algorithms discussed here seem generally similar, for optimization through parallel operations in all cases is the main drive as all algorithms considered seek serializability. Time cost overhead considerations must include I/O and CPU time. On these aspects, performance evaluation results are inconclusive and sometimes contradictory. Further study is clearly in order, although many mathematical models have already been developed (mostly in the distributed database context — see, for example, [Wolfson87]) that seem to demonstrate the superiority of locking.

The basic principles of concurrency control are fairly well understood. Additional concurrency control algorithms can easily be constructed by varying the time at which ordering is defined, by delaying certain types of actions, or by combining the various methods. What is lacking is the availability of reliable performance evaluation based on detailed theoretical analysis and extensive experimentation.

7.9 References and Bibliography

[Adiba78] Adiba M., Chupin J. C., Demolombe R., Gardarin G. and Le Bihan J., "Issues in Distributed Data Base Management Systems: A Technical Overview," 4th Int. Conf. on Very Large Data Bases, Berlin, September 1978.

[Agrawal85] Agrawal R., DeWitt D. J., "Integrated Concurrency Control and Recovery Mechanisms: Design and Performance Evaluation," ACM TODS, V10, N4, 1985, pp. 529 – 64.

[Badal80] Badal D. Z., "The Analysis of the Effects of Concurrency Control on Distributed Data Base System Performance," 6th Int. Conf. on Very Large Data Bases, Montreal, October 1980.

[Bayer81] Bayer R. et al., "Dynamic Timestamp Allocation and Its Application to the BEHR Method," Technical Report, Munich University, July 1981.

[Bernstein80] Bernstein P. A., Goodman N., "Timestamp-Based Algorithms for Concurrency Control in Distributed Database Systems," 6th Int. Conf. on Very Large Data Bases, Montreal, October 1980.

[Bernstein81] Bernstein P. A., Goodman N., "Concurrency Control in Distributed Database Systems," Computing Surveys, V13, 1981, pp. 198 – 221.

[Carey84] Carey M. J., Stonebraker M. R., "The Performance of Concurrency Control Algorithms for DBMS," 10th Int. Conf. on Very Large Data Bases, Singapore, 1984.

[Codasyl71] CODASYL Committee, "Data Base Task Group Report," ACM, New York, April 1971.

[Coffman71] Coffman E. G., Elphick M. J., Shoshani A., "System Deadlocks," Computing Surveys, V3, N2, 1971, pp. 67 – 78.

[Courtois71] Courtois P. J., Heymans F., Parnas L., "Concurrent Control with Readers and Writers," Com. of the ACM, V14, N10, October 1971, pp. 667 – 68.

[Dijkstra68] Dijkstra E. W., "Cooperating Sequential Processes," in *Programming Languages,* Genuys (ed.), Academic Press, 1968.

[Ellis77] Ellis C. A., "A Robust Algorithm for Updating Duplicate Databases," Second

Berkeley Workshop on Distributed Data Management and Computer Networks, Berkeley, May 1977, pp. 146 – 58.

[Engles76] Engles R. W., "Currency and Concurrency in the COBOL Data Base Facility," IFIP Conf. on Modeling in DBMS, Freudenstadt, 1976.

[Eswaran76] Eswaran K. P., Gray J. N., Lorie R. A., Traiger L. L., "The Notion of Consistency and Predicate Locks in a Database System," Com. of the ACM, V19, N11, November 1976, pp. 624 – 33.

[Gardarin76] Gardarin G., Spaccapietra S., "Integrity of Databases: A General Locking Algorithm with Deadlock Avoidance," IFIP Conf. on Modelling in DMBS, Freudenstadt, January 1976.

[Gardarin77] Gardarin G., Lebeux P., "Scheduling Algorithms for Avoiding Inconsistency in Large Data Bases," 3d Int. Conf. on Very Large Data Bases, Tokyo, October 1977.

[Gardarin78] Gardarin G., "Résolution des conflits d'accès simultanés à un ensemble d'informations-applications aux bases de données réparties," Thèse d'état, University of Paris VI, April 1978.

[Gardarin80] Gardarin G., "Integrity, Consistency, Concurrency and Reliability in Distributed Data Base Management Systems," Int. Conf. on Distributed Data Bases, Paris, 1980.

[Goldman77] Goldman B., "Deadlock Detection in Computer Networks," MIT thesis, 1977.

[Gray78] Gray J., "Notes on Data Base Operating Systems," IBM Research Report, RJ 2188 (30001), San Jose, February 1978. Also in *Operating Systems, An Advanced Course,* Lecture Notes in Computer Science, Springer-Verlag, 1978.

[Gray81] Gray J., "The Transaction Concept: Virtues and Limitations," 7th Int. Conf. on Very Large Data Bases, Cannes, September 1981.

[Gray85] Gray J. et al., "One Thousand Transactions per Second" IEEE Spring Compcon, 1985.

[Holt72] Holt R. C., "Some Deadlock Properties of Computer Systems," Computing Surveys, V4, N3, September 1972, pp. 179 – 96.

[Howard73] Howard J. H., "Mixed Solutions for the Deadlock Problem," Com. of the ACM, V16, N7, July 1973, pp. 427 – 30.

[Kung81] Kung H. T., Robinson J. T., "On Optimistic Methods for Concurrency Control," ACM TODS, V6, N2, June 1981, pp. 213 – 26.

[Lamport78] Lamport L., "Time, Clocks and the Ordering of Events in a Distributed System," Com. of the ACM, V21, N7, July 1978, pp. 558 – 65.

[LeLann78] LeLann G., "Algorithm for Distributed Data Sharing Which Use Tickets," 3d Berkeley Workshop on Distributed Data Management and Computer Network, Berkeley, August 1978.

[Lindsay79] Lindsay B. G. et al., "Notes on Distributed Databases," IBM Research Report RJ 2571 (33471), San Jose, July 1979.

[Menasce78] Menasce D. A., "Coordination in Distributed Systems: Concurrency, Crash Recovery and Data Base Synchronization," Ph.D. dissertation, UCLA, December 1978.

[Menasce80] Menasce D. A., Popek G. J., Muntz R. R., "A Locking Protocol for Resource Coordination in Distributed Databases," ACM Transactions on Database Systems, V5, N2, June 1980.

[Menasce82] Menasce D. A., Nakanishi T., "Optimistic versus Pessimistic Concurrency Control Mechanisms in DBMS," Information Systems, V7, N1, 1982, pp. 13 – 27.

[Michel87] Michel R., "Le Controle de concurrence et la resistance aux pannes dans une architecture bases de données mono et multi processeurs," These doctorat, University of Paris VI, 1987.

[Murphy68] Murphy J. E., "Resource Allocation with Interlock Detection in a Multi-task System," AFIPS-FJCC, V33, 1968, pp. 1169 – 76.

[Obermarck82] Obermarck R., "Distributed Deadlock Detection Algorithm," ACM TODS, V7, N2, June 1982.

[Papadimitriou79] Papadimitriou C. H., "Serializability of Concurrent Updates," J. of the ACM, V26, N4, October 1979, pp. 631 – 53.

[Pradel86] Pradel U., Schlageter G., Unland R., "Redesign of Optimistic Methods: Improving Performance and Applicability," 2d Data Engineering Conf., 1986, IEEE ed.

[Ries77] Ries D. D., Stonebraker M. R., "Effects of Locking Granularity in a Database Management System," ACM Transactions on Database Systems, V2, N3, September 1977, pp. 233 – 46.

[Ries79] Ries D. D., Stonebraker M. R., "Locking Granularity Revisited," ACM Transactions on Database Systems, V4, N2, June 1979, pp. 210 – 27.

[Rosenkrantz78] Rosenkrantz D. J., Stearns R. E., Lewis P. W., "System Level Concurrency Control for Distributed Database Systems," ACM Transactions on Database Systems, V2, N3, September 1977, pp. 233 – 46.

[Schlageter79] Schlageter G., "Enhancement of Concurrency in Database Systems by the Use of Special Rollback Methods," IFIP Conf. on Data Base Architecture, Venice, June 1979.

[Schlageter81] Schlageter G., "Optimistic Methods for Concurrency Control in Distributed Database Systems," 7th International Conf. on Very Large Data Bases, Cannes, September 1981.

[Schlageter82] Schlageter G., "Problems of Optimistic Concurrency Control in Distributed Database Systems," ACM Sigmod Record, V12, N3, 1982, pp. 62 – 66.

[Severance76] Severance D. G., Lohman G. M., "Differential Files: Their Applications to the Maintainance of Large Database Systems," ACM Transactions on Database Systems, V1, N3, September 1976, pp. 256 – 367.

[Stonebraker78] Stonebraker M. R., "Concurrency Control and Consistency of Multiple Copies of Data in Distributed INGRES," 3d Berkeley Workshop on Distributed Data Management and Computer Network, Berkeley, August 1978.

[Thomas79] Thomas R. H., "A Majority Consensus Approach to Concurrency Control for Multiple Copy Databases," ACM Transactions on Database Systems, V4, N2, June 1979, pp. 180 – 209.

[Thomasian85] Thomasian A., Ryu I. K., "Analysis of Some Optimistic Concurrency Control Schemes Based on Certification," Proc. ACM SIGMETRICS 1985.

[Traiger82] Traiger I. L. et al., "Transactions and Consistency in Distributed Database Systems," ACM TODS, V7, N3, September 1982.

[Trinchieri75] Trinchieri M., "On Managing Interference Caused by Database Sharing," Alta Frequenza, V44, N11, 1975, pp. 641 – 50.

[Viemont82] Viemont Y., Gardarin G., "A Distributed Concurrency Control Algorithm Based on Transaction Commit Ordering," 12th FTCS, IEEE Ed., Santa Monica, June 1982.

[Wolfson87] Wolfson O., "The Overhead of Locking (and Commit) Protocols in Distributed Databases," ACM TODS, V12, N3, September 1987.

8
RELIABILITY

8.1 Introduction

The implementation of the transaction concept is central to maintaining database consistency. An important responsibility of a DBMS is to execute transactions in a reliable way. Transaction reliability is achieved through fault-tolerance techniques that recover from many kinds of failures. Those techniques are implemented in a DBMS module traditionally called the *recovery manager*. Since it is a low-level module that manipulates physical (versus logical) storage structures, the recovery manager of a relational system may not be different from that of a nonrelational system. In this chapter, we will review the major algorithms developed for recovery managers.

We assume a simplified model of a DBMS consisting of transactions, a computer system, and data storage. Storage generally includes three different media with an increasing degree of reliability: main memory, disk, and tape. Main memory is volatile storage that typically does not survive power failures. Disk provides on-line nonvolatile storage. Compared to main memory, disk is more reliable and much cheaper but slower by about three orders of magnitude. Magnetic tape is an off-line nonvolatile storage that is far more reliable than disk and fairly inexpensive but provides only sequential access. Transactions manipulate data in storage through specific actions (read, write, and so on). Those actions are performed by the system in main memory, which is the most efficient. However, since the entire database cannot reside in main memory, those actions also generate disk accesses.

In a computer system, failures can be caused by human errors, transaction programming errors, or hardware component crashes. Human errors (or malicious intentions) and transaction programming errors can be detected and, it is hoped, corrected by better data protection and semantic integrity control. The most important types of failure that the recovery manager is concerned with are transaction, system, and media failures [Gray78]. A *transaction failure* occurs when a transaction cannot proceed because of an action failure, a deadlock situation, an incorrect ordering of concurrent accesses, or some other problem. The transaction must be aborted and may be reinitiated. A *system failure* occurs because of a serious error in a system table or a hardware crash (such as a power failure). The system must be stopped and restarted. The content of main memory is assumed to be entirely lost because of system restart. Secondary memory is not affected by a system failure. A *media failure* occurs with a nonrecoverable error on disks. Media failures can be due to a hardware problem (such as head crash) or a software error that make the disks unreadable. A subset of data on disk is lost. This is the most serious type of failure.

A transaction failure can occur several times per minute. A system failure can occur several times per month. A media failure can arise only several times per year but may be nonrecoverable. Transaction failures can be easily detected by the run-time environment that interprets transaction code. However, the detection of system and media failures is more complex. It is based on additional software to check system tables and specific error correction codes to check the validity of data on disk. Failure detection is beyond the scope of this chapter.

The objective of reliability is to recover a consistent database state after failure while minimizing user interaction. Ideally recovery should be transparent to the user. The single principle on which all reliability algorithms are based is *data duplication:* corrupted or lost data should always be recoverable from the redundant copies. Managing this duplication is expensive, for it can well increase the number of disk accesses to process updates. Therefore various reliability algorithms have been devised to minimize this overhead. Overall the recovery manager is a complex subsystem that is not independent of other important functions such as concurrency control, buffer management, and file management.

This chapter is organized as follows. Section 8.2 introduces the basic concepts for reliability, including the main data structures to manage data duplication. Section 8.3 presents the four classes of reliability algorithms. Section 8.4 details the two main techniques used to implement updates in a reliable manner. Finally, Section 8.5 describes the most popular algorithm to process transaction commit in an atomic fashion. For a more detailed treatment of reliability, the reader is referred to [Bernstein87].

8.2 Basic Concepts

The basic concepts introduced in this chapter describe the data structures that permit recovery from failure, the basic rules that ensure transaction atomicity, and the different types of recovery procedures.

8.2.1 Transaction Atomicity

The transaction is generally considered the atomic unit of processing, or unit of restart [Gray81a]. The recovery subsystem guarantees that either all actions of the transaction or none of them are actually performed. For example, consider a debit-credit transaction that transfers the amount x from account A to account B. Either both actions $<A := A - x; B := B + x>$ or neither of them are entirely processed.

Transaction atomicity can be achieved if atomicity is provided at a lower level of the system. The recovery manager typically assumes that the action of writing in secondary storage is stable. The physical write action in stable storage is atomic. A physical object is either correctly and entirely written or is not written at all; it cannot be partially written. Since the main database repository is magnetic disk, we will assume that a physical object is a disk page (one or more disk sectors).

Definition 8.1 Stable storage
Secondary storage divided into pages in which a page write is either correctly executed or not executed at all.

The realization of a stable storage is not obvious. Techniques such as redundancy codes and double writes are generally employed. In the following, we consider that secondary memory is stable.

The atomicity property implies that a transaction has only two possibilities: commit or abort. Commit indicates normal transaction termination; all the transaction's updates will definitely be integrated into the database.

Definition 8.2 Transaction commit
Execution of a special atomic action (called COMMIT), generally at the end of transaction, that integrates all the updates of the transaction in the database.

The commit action can also be used by a recovery procedure. Abort indicates abnormal transaction termination; none of the transaction's updates should be integrated in the database. All objects updated by the transaction are left in their initial state.

Definition 8.3 Transaction abort
Execution of a special atomic action (called ABORT), generally after a transaction failure, inducing the abortion of all database updates done by the transaction.

The abort action may also be executed by a recovery procedure. In some cases, aborting one transaction may lead to the abortion of other transactions [Hadzilacos83]. A transaction is said to be active if it has begun execution but is not yet in a final state (aborted or committed).

8.2.2 Data Structures

The most popular data structures managed by a recovery manager are logs and backup copies that provide the data duplication necessary for recovery [Verhofstad78]. A log records information regarding the state of update transactions and the updated pages. A log can record logical entities (tuples, attributes), physical entities (pages), state changes (old data values, new data values), or operations (transactions and parameters). To simplify our presentation, we assume pages are logged. Therefore the main types of information recorded in the log are *before-images* and *after-images*.

Definition 8.4 Before-image
The page value before update.

Definition 8.5 After-image
The page value after update.

The update of a single page may generate an after-image that consists of more than one page — for example, if a large object has been inserted in that page. To simplify the presentation, we will assume that after-images are one page.

Definition 8.6 Log
System file containing the before-images and after-images of the updated pages in order of update time, labeled with the identifiers of the update transactions and containing the records of transaction begin, commit, and abort.

The log can be divided between two separate files: a before-image log and an after-image log. Since, however, it records a history of the transactions, a log is generally implemented as a single sequential file. This facilitates the recovery procedure. Fig. 8.1 illustrates a log record containing both before-images and after-images. The log is generally recorded in a reserved area on disk or on separate disks. The basic assumption is that the log never fails (this can be achieved

| Transaction Identifier |
| Modification Time |
| Modified File |
| Address of Modified Page |
| Before-Image |
| After-Image |

FIGURE 8.1 Example of log record

by duplexing or triplexing the log on several disks [Gray86]). To reduce the size of the logs, differential images (as opposed to complete images) can be supported. A *differential image* is the difference with the previous page value. Furthermore the log can be periodically pruned from some records. A log record for page P modified by transaction Ti can be removed if Ti has aborted or there exists a committed transaction $Ti+1$ that modified P after Ti.

After a media failure, the part of the database that is lost must be reconstituted from external archives. For this purpose, *backup copies* are periodically made on magnetic tapes.

Definition 8.7 Backup copy
Copy of a database done periodically while the database is in a consistent state.

Backup copies can be prepared several times a day. To simplify concurrency control, they are generally done while there are no running transactions, although they can also be done during normal processing of transactions using a specific locking or multiversion mechanism [Reed79].

After a normal or abnormal termination of the system, it is necessary to restart from a correct system state. *System checkpoints* are used for that purpose.

Definition 8.8 System checkpoint
Consistent state of the system context, independent of the current state of the database, saved on secondary memory from which it is possible to restart.

Another frequent definition includes backup copies [Haerder83], stressing that checkpoints are most useful to reduce the recovery time from media failure.

The information saved on disk includes generally an image of the main memory, the state of current programs, and the pointers to files, in particular the logs. A record system checkpoint is written in the log. A restart procedure starts from the last system checkpoint. The more recent the checkpoint is, the least

costly the restart is. But taking checkpoints too frequently can significantly reduce system throughput. Optimizing the frequency of system checkpoints is a
difficult problem [Gelenbe79].

8.2.3 Basic Rules

In all systems, page updates are first written in main memory buffers. Buffers
are volatile; their contents are lost or contaminated in case of system failure (system failure includes power failure). The pages that have been updated in buffer
but are not yet in stable storage are called *dirty pages*. The buffer contents are
ultimately flushed to disk at commit time. To guarantee transaction atomicity, a
reliability algorithm must enforce two fundamental rules: the *commit rule* and
the *log-ahead rule* [Bernstein83].

> **Definition 8.9 Commit rule**
> All the dirty pages produced by a transaction must be written in stable
> storage before the actual commit.

If this rule is not followed, a system failure after the transaction commit would
lose the last after-images.

> **Definition 8.10 Log-ahead rule**
> If a database object is physically modified before the end of transac-
> tion, its before-image must have been previously recorded in the log.

This rule enables a transaction to be undone in case of abort by reconstituting
the before-image from the log. The application of these two rules is illustrated
in Fig. 8.2. For high performance in transaction processing systems, a common

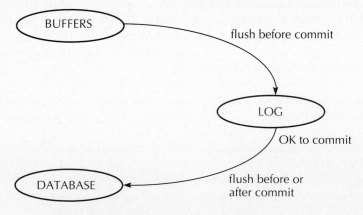

FIGURE 8.2 Integration of updates before commit

technique is group commit, by which log records are written to a disk block for a group of transactions. Group commit reduces the number of disk writes to the log [Gawlick85].

8.2.4 Recovery Procedures

The procedure executed to start the system after normal termination or failure is called the *recovery procedure* (or the *restart procedure*). The recovery procedures are based on the log, on-line backups, and eventually the tape archives. Their objective is to reach a consistent database state while minimizing the amount of lost work.

> **Definition 8.11 Recovery procedure**
> System procedure executed at system restart time to reconstruct the most recent consistent database state before termination or shutdown.

In order to achieve this goal, a recovery procedure must be able to undo or redo a transaction's updates. *Undoing* an update is the action of writing in the database the before-image of the updated page from the log. *Redoing* an update is the action of writing in the database the after-image of the updated page from the log.

Three types of recovery procedures can be distinguished: recovery after normal termination, system failure, or media failure. *Normal recovery* is used after normal termination of the system. At termination time, a system checkpoint is written as the last record in the log. Normal recovery consists of restoring the execution context saved at the last checkpoint. Such a procedure is run when the last log record is a system checkpoint.

Recovery after system failure is often called *warm recovery*. Recall that a system failure leads to the loss of main memory content without the loss of data in secondary storage. For simplicity, we assume that all updates done by a committed transaction are in stable storage and therefore cannot be lost in the system failure. In this case, the recovery procedure restores the state of the system from the last checkpoint. The log is processed forward from the beginning in order to determine the committed and noncommitted transactions, called, respectively, winners and losers [Gray81b]. Then the log is processed backward to undo the updates of the noncommitted transactions (the losers). Note that there might be uncommitted transactions that started before the last checkpoint and therefore must be undone. This procedure is illustrated in Fig. 8.3. It is executed at system restart when the last log record is not a checkpoint and no media failure has been detected.

Recovery after media failure is often called *cold recovery*. The cold recovery procedure is used when a subset of the database on disk is lost or when the data-

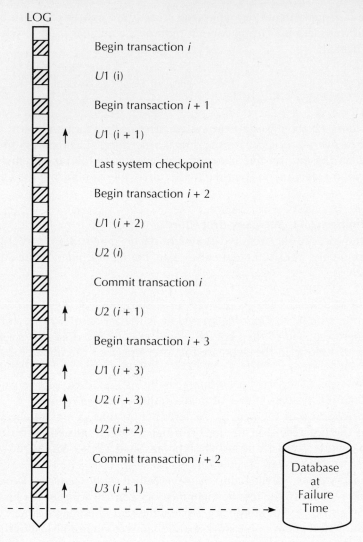

FIGURE 8.3 Example of warm recovery. Transactions i and $(i + 2)$ are winners while $(i + 1)$ and $(i + 3)$ are losers. Uj (i) designates the jth update of transaction i. Undone updates are marked ↑.

base has become inconsistent because of software errors. In this case, a consistent snapshot of the database is reconstituted from the most recent backup copy. It is likely, however, that transactions have been processed after the last backup copy. Therefore the log of subsequent activities must also be used to reconstruct a consistent database. The assumption is that the log is consistent. The recovery procedure processes the log forward from the system checkpoint corresponding to the time of the last backup copy and applies all after-images to redo the committed transactions. When the log has been entirely processed, the warm recovery procedure is generally executed.

Warm and cold recovery procedures must be idempotent. Idempotence ensures that the same procedure can be applied many times and produce the same result. This property is necessary since a failure may occur when the system is already recovering from a previous failure, which leads to restarting the recovery procedure from the beginning. Idempotence is achieved by careful (and difficult) programming of the recovery procedures.

These recovery procedures are not used with catastrophic failures, which occur when part or all of the log on stable storage is lost. Most systems avoid this type of failure by duplexing or triplexing the log. In the event of catastrophic failure, the only solution is to write special transactions for testing the database consistency and interacting with the database administrator to compensate the effects of lost transactions or go back to earlier states on old tape archives.

8.3 Algorithms

There are four classes of reliability algorithms, essentially characterized according to the time they flush to stable storage the dirty pages generated by an active transaction. Each type of algorithm can be described by the specification of the five following interface primitives to the recovery manager. For simplicity, we ignore the cold recovery procedure, although in Section 8.3.5, we will show how to extend the following primitives to include provision for cold recovery.

BEGIN (T) introduces transaction *T* to the transaction manager.
READ (T, P, B) reads the page *P* into buffer *B* for transaction *T*.
WRITE (T, P, B) writes the buffer *B* into page *P* for transaction *T*.
COMMIT (T) commits transaction *T*.
ABORT (T) aborts transaction *T*.
RESTART recovers from a system failure.

The types of reliability algorithms differ in their ability to undo or redo a transaction's updates. Undoing an update is the basic action for aborting a transaction. Redoing an update is the basic action for restart. By combining the ability of undo and redo, four types of algorithms may be devised: undo/no-redo, no-undo/redo, undo/redo and no-undo/no-redo. The classification of reliability algorithms based on their undo and redo capabilities is due to [Bernstein83] and [Haerder83].

For each type of algorithm, we present a simplified algorithm that uses three lists of transactions: the list of active transactions (*La*), the list of aborted transactions (*Lb*), and the list of committed transactions (*Lc*). Those lists are assumed to be nonvolatile (they should be included in the log).

We assume that a subset of the database is cached in an area of main memory, called *buffer pool*. The buffer pool is managed by a specific module, the buffer manager, to provide fast access to frequently accessed pages. Requesting a page that is not present in buffer pool induces a page fault. In such a case, the buffer manager selects one page slot in the buffer pool, fetches the requested page from disk, and inserts it in that slot. The selection of a page slot is based on a page replacement policy such as least recently used [Effelsberg84]. If the page selected for replacement is dirty, it is swapped out to disk.

The log does not reside in buffer pool but in stable storage. Therefore each insertion in the log is done directly in stable storage at the expense of a disk access.

8.3.1 Undo/No-redo

In this class of algorithms, redoing a transaction to recover from a system failure is never necessary. Thus no after-images are required in the log. This capability is provided by flushing to stable storage all dirty pages of an active transaction before commit. Therefore the updates of a committed transaction cannot get lost by a system failure. Restart is thus very inexpensive. However, since all updates must be flushed to the database before commit, these algorithms preclude the buffering of writes and thus hurt response time. Aborting a transaction (during normal operation or recovery) requires undoing its updates. This type of algorithm is generally used in conjunction with a pessimistic concurrency control algorithm that rarely aborts transactions. The undo/no-redo paradigm has been implemented in the Adaplex database system [Chan82]. Since it is identical in all algorithms, only the BEGIN procedure is described below.

```
procedure BEGIN (T);
begin
   La := La ∪ {T};
end;
procedure READ (T, P, B);
begin
   read P from buffer pool into B; { may generate a page fault }
end;
procedure WRITE (T, P, B);
begin
   insert the before-image of P from buffer pool in the log; { a page fault is
        possible }
   write P to buffer pool from B;
end;
```

```
procedure COMMIT (T);
begin
   for each page P updated by T do
      if P is in buffer pool then flush P to disk;
   Lc := Lc ∪ {T}; { T becomes committed }
   La := La − {T};
end;
procedure ABORT (T);
begin
   Lb := Lb ∪ {T};
   for each page P updated by T do
      read the before-image of P from the log into buffer pool;
   La := La − {T};
end;
procedure RESTART;
begin
   for each T ∈ La do
      ABORT (T);
end;
```

8.3.2 No-undo/Redo

In this class of algorithms, undoing a transaction is never necessary. Thus no before-images are required in the log. This capability is provided by flushing to stable storage all dirty pages of an active transaction after commit. Before commit, the before-images of the pages updated by the transaction are still on disk. If the transaction aborts, its after-images are simply discarded. Abort is thus very inexpensive. This type of algorithm is generally used in conjunction with an optimistic concurrency control algorithm, which tends to abort transactions often in case of conflict. The updates of a committed transaction may not have been propagated to disk before a system failure. Therefore the restart procedure may have to redo the updates of committed transactions. No-undo/redo algorithms are described in [Bayer83, Lampson76]. The no-undo/redo paradigm has been used in the university version of the INGRES database system.

```
procedure READ (T, P, B);
begin
   if P has been updated by T
      then read the after-image of P into B
      else read P from buffer pool into B; { may generate a page fault }
end;
```

```
procedure WRITE (T, P, B);
begin
   insert B in the log; { inserts the after-image of P }
end;
procedure COMMIT (T);
begin
   Lc := Lc ∪ {T}; { T becomes committed }
   for each page P updated by T do
      write the after-image of P to disk from the log;
   La := La − {T};
end;
procedure ABORT (T);
begin
   Lb := Lb ∪ {T};
   La := La − {T};
end;
procedure RESTART:
begin
   for each T ∈ La do
      if T ∈ Lc
         then COMMIT (T)
         else ABORT (T);
end;
```

8.3.3 Undo/Redo

This class of algorithms combines the undo capability of the algorithm of Section 8.3.1 with the redo capability of the algorithm of Section 8.3.2. Therefore dirty pages may be flushed to disk before, during, or after commit. The decision to flush to disk is entirely left to the buffer manager, which can do better scheduling of disk accesses to improve performance. Abort and restart are both relatively expensive, however, they optimize the normal case at the expense of abort and restart. This type of algorithm is better when abort and restart are rare (the normal case). It works better with a pessimistic concurrency control algorithm. The undo/redo paradigm is due to [Bjork73] and elaborated in [Gray78]. Most systems use it.

The READ and RESTART procedures are identical to those of Section 8.3.2. The WRITE procedure is identical to that of Section 8.3.1.

```
procedure COMMIT (T);
begin
   Lc := Lc ∪ {T}; { T becomes committed }
   for each page P updated by T do
```

```
        if P is dirty then write the after-image of P to disk from the log;
    La := La − {T};
end;
procedure ABORT (T);
begin
    Lb := Lb ∪ {T};
    for each page P updated by T do
        if the after-image of P is on disk
            then read the before-image of P from the log into buffer pool as a
                    dirty page;
    La := La − {T};
end;
```

8.3.4 No-undo/No-redo

A no-undo algorithm requires flushing all dirty pages to disk after commit. Conversely a no-redo algorithm requires flushing all dirty pages to disk before commit. Therefore a no-undo/no-redo algorithm must flush neither after commit nor before commit. Thus the only possibility is to flush at commit time in a single atomic action. Making the commit procedure an atomic action is not obvious but feasible using a particular implementation of shadowing. We will detail such a technique in Section 8.4. The no-undo/no-redo paradigm is due to [Lorie77].

The interface primitives to the recovery manager may be specified as follows. The primitives READ, WRITE, and ABORT are the same as in Section 8.3.2, and the RESTART primitive is identical to that of Section 8.3.1. Conceptually the COMMIT procedure can be viewed as follows:

```
    procedure COMMIT (T);
    begin
    < <
        for each page P updated by T do
            write the after-image of P to disk from the log;
        La := La − {T};
    > >
    end;
```

< < instructions > > indicates that the instructions are executed atomically. Note that the list of committed transactions (*Lc*) needs not be maintained. This type of algorithm is suitable for any type of concurrency control algorithm since ABORT and RESTART are fairly inexpensive, but the normal case is expensive so it is not often used [Gray81b].

8.3.5 Support of Media Recovery

The specification of reliability algorithms ignored the cold recovery procedure; however, it is easy to extend them to include provision for recovering from media failure. The basic information for cold recovery includes a backup copy of the database, the last system checkpoint, and the log of after-images. The after-images are useful for redoing the transactions that committed after the last system checkpoint. Therefore a reliability algorithm that does not redo transactions for system restart must still support redo for cold recovery. This can be supported by extending the WRITE primitive to always write to the log the after-images of the updated pages.

8.4 Implementation of Updates

There are two basic techniques for implementing disk page updates in conjunction with a reliability algorithm: update-in-place and shadowing. Each technique is more efficient under different conditions.

8.4.1 Update-in-Place

Update-in-place tries to keep the updated objects at their original location.

Definition 8.12 Update-in-place
Technique that places the after-image of an updated page, whenever possible, in its original location on disk.

The after-image can be placed in the original location only if the update does not require more space than the original page. In general, this situation occurs when the update is a deletion or a modification. If however, the after-image is larger than the original page (such as after an insertion), only part of the after-image may be placed at the original location. The remaining page(s) of the after-image must be placed in a new location allocated by the clustering algorithm of the DBMS.

Update-in-place may be used by all reliability algorithms except the no-undo/no-redo algorithm. The latter requires that the integration of all updates in stable storage be done in a single atomic action at commit time. Realizing that single atomic action is possible only with some form of shadowing.

The update-in-place technique exhibits three significant advantages. First, there is no need to allocate new disk space if the after-image of the updated page has only one page. Second, index pages that point to the updated pages need not be updated unless an updated page overflows (its after-image has more than one page). Thus updates and locks to index pages are minimized, saving disk accesses and maximizing the degree of concurrency. Third, only a single mechanism is necessary for accessing a page for the first time or after it has been updated within the same transaction. This simplifies DBMS code. Shadowing requires two different mechanisms.

8.4.2 Shadowing

Shadowing never keeps the updated objects at their original location.

> **Definition 8.13 Shadowing**
> Technique that always places the after-image of an updated page in a new location on disk.

The updates of a transaction are done not in place but rather in new pages, whose old versions are called *shadow pages* [Lorie77]. A new page is private to a transaction; it cannot be seen by other transactions and becomes public when the transaction commits. The after-image pages of a transaction constitute the transaction's private workspace. Every page request first has to check the transaction workspace in case the page has already been updated by the same transaction. Until the transaction actually commits, the shadow page of each updated page is still available to all other transactions. Therefore there is no need to manage a before-image log in order to undo a transaction.

Shadowing may be used with any reliability algorithm; however, it is the only technique that enables implementation of the no-undo/no-redo algorithm. A particular form of shadowing permits the integration in stable storage of all new pages of a transaction in a single atomic action [Lorie77]. To simplify the presentation of this technique, let us assume that each file in the database has a file descriptor that points to a page table in which each entry contains a disk page address. In general, the page table has a complex organization, such as a B-tree or a hashed index. When a transaction updates a file for the first time, the file page table is duplicated within the transaction workspace, and the addresses of the new pages replace the shadow page addresses. This private version of the page table will reflect the current state of the file being updated. Undoing a transaction requires ignoring the transaction workspace without additional work. At commit time, the new page table and all the pages pointed to are on disk. The transaction commit consists of updating the file descriptor to point to the new page table. Since a single write is involved, this action is atomic. This mechanism is illustrated in Fig. 8.4.

For small updates (such as modifying a few bytes in a page), the shadow page mechanism incurs much useless duplication, which wastes some main memory space. The reason is that the difference between the new page and the shadow page is small. Another form of shadowing, based on differential files [Severance76], is more efficient for small updates. Only the new values of objects up-

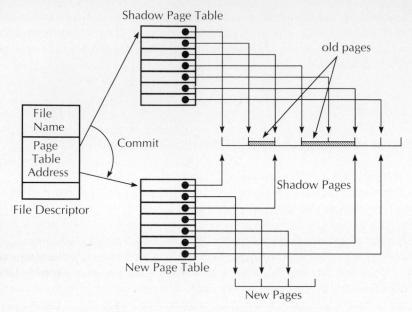

FIGURE 8.4 Commit by switching the page table

dated by a transaction are recorded into a differential file, in general smaller than a set of new pages. This approach, however, suffers from a number of drawbacks. Similar to the shadow page technique, the differential file has to be searched for each page access by the transaction. Since the objects are of variable size, searching a differential file is less efficient than searching fixed-size page addresses. Furthermore the integration of differential objects into pages at commit time is difficult. Finally, this approach does not support the no-undo/no-redo algorithm.

The shadowing technique exhibits two significant advantages. First, while new pages may be flushed to disk any time before commit by the buffer manager, there is no need for a before-image log. This saves some disk accesses. Second, shadowing is the only technique that supports the no-undo/no-redo algorithm. But shadowing also has two serious drawbacks. First, physical clustering of data pages on disk gets lost with updates. Second and more important, the use of the no-undo/no-redo algorithm requires that concurrency control be applied to the page table, which limits the degree of concurrency.

8.5 Transaction Commit

In Section 8.3, we examined the transaction commit procedures for the four types of reliability algorithms. The implicit assumption underlying their presentation was that a transaction is implemented as a single process controlled by one system, the DBMS. In general, this assumption is not true. A single transaction may well deal with several systems (such as DBMS, mail system, or communication system) running on the same computer. Therefore a transaction consists of several processes, each controlled by a different system. For example, a transaction initiated under CICS might interact with both SQL/DS (a relational DBMS) and DL/1 (a hierarchical DBMS). All processes of the same transaction may actually perform updates, each under the control of a different system. This situation is similar to a distributed database system in which a transaction consists of several subtransactions, each running at a different site.

An obvious way of committing a multiprocess transaction is to consider each process a transaction. Thus any process may commit independent of others. However, some processes may commit their updates while some others may abort. The updated database becomes inconsistent. This approach obviously does not ensure the atomicity of the multiprocess transactions. The problem is the absence of synchronization or protocol among all processes participating in the transaction. The solution is to use an atomic commit protocol. The simplest and most popular protocol is the *two-phase commit protocol* [Lampson76, Gray78, Skeen81], which has been devised for distributed systems.

In the two-phase commit protocol, synchronization of the transaction processes, called *participants* (or *slaves*), is managed by a new process, called *coordinator* (or *master*). In practice, the coordinator is one of the transaction processes that plays both roles. For simplicity, we assume that this is not the case. The protocol ensures that all participants either commit or abort, despite any failure. The decision to commit or abort is taken by the coordinator after the first phase.

In the first phase, the *precommit* phase, the coordinator requests that all participants prepare for the commitment. In the second phase, the *commit phase,* the coordinator signals to all participants to commit, if all of them successfully completed the first phase, or abort.

The protocol is illustrated in Fig. 8.5. During application of the protocol, the various states reached by the coordinator and the participants are logged so that in the event of a failure, the recovery procedure can apply the necessary phase(s) of the protocol. We assume that the coordinator and each of the participants has a separate log. We also assume that communication between coordinator and participants is done via messages over a reliable network.

The coordinator triggers the precommit phase by writing a precommit record in the log and then asking all participants to prepare to commit. After completing its subtransaction and receiving the precommit message, each participant performs operations to ensure that it will be able to commit despite any failure. These operations include reliability operations (such as recording in the log all before-images and after-images of the updated pages) and eventually concurrency control operations. If the participant is able to commit, it writes a "ready" record in the log and indicates "ready" to the coordinator. Otherwise it writes a "not ready" record in the log and indicates "not ready" to the coordinator. The

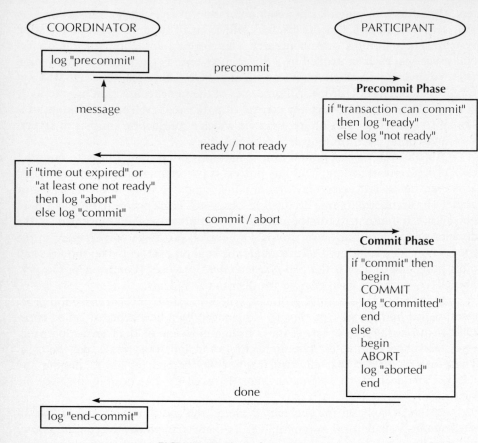

FIGURE 8.5 Two-phase commit

prepare-to-commit message is optional. Subtransactions can precommit and say "ready" to the coordinator asynchronously.

The coordinator takes the global decision of either committing or aborting the transaction. If it receives "ready" from all participants, the decision is to commit. If at least one of the participants replied "not ready" or a time-out expired, the decision is to abort. The expiration of the time-out (activated in the precommit phase) means that at least one participant has not replied because it failed. The global decision is recorded in the log and broadcast to all participants. On receipt of the decision, all participants either commit or abort and record the global decision in their log. Finally each participant informs the coordinator, with the message "done," that it completed the commit phase. On receipt of all "done" messages, the coordinator records an "end-commit" message.

The two-phase commit protocol achieves transaction atomicity despite all types of failure but the catastrophic one (in which the log is lost). The correctness of the protocol is given in [Baer81]. Fig. 8.6 illustrates various histories of two-

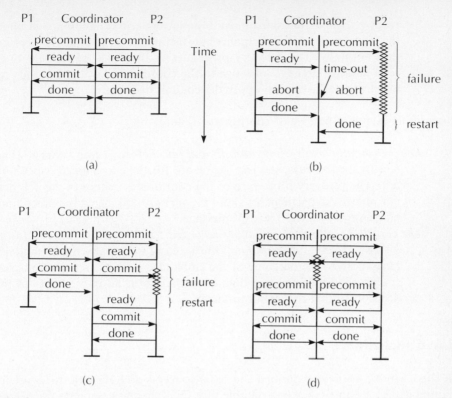

FIGURE 8.6 Different histories of two-phase commit. (a) Normal commit, (b) failure of P2 before precommit, (c) failure of P2 after precommit, and (d) failure of coordinator before getting "ready."

phase commits involving a coordinator and two participants $P1$ and $P2$. The normal operation case is shown in Fig. 8.6(a). The other histories illustrate the behavior of the protocol under abnormal conditions. We distinguish the situations between participant and coordinator failure. However, note that both the coordinator and a participant may fail at the same time. For example, the loss of power supply makes the coordinator and all participants fail. First, let us examine the case of participant failure.

A participant fails before precommit. The behavior of the protocol in this situation is illustrated in Fig. 8.6(b). The coordinator, which does not receive "ready" from the failed participant, decides to abort the transaction after expiration of the time-out. The recovery procedure of the failed participant will abort the participant because no "ready" record has been logged.

A participant fails after having completed the precommit phase (Fig. 8.6(c)). In this situation, the coordinator receives "ready" or "not ready" from all participants and therefore decides to commit or abort the transaction. All participants but the failed one termiate the transaction normally. The recovery procedure of the failed participant must send another "ready" message to the coordinator, which can then request the participant to apply the commit decision.

Now let us examine the case of coordinator failure.

> *The coordinator sends "precommit" and fails before getting "ready"* (Fig. 8.6(d)). In this case, the last log record for the coordinator is precommit. The recovery procedure of the coordinator reiterates the precommit phase. All participants that have already completed the precommit phase respond by a "ready" message.
>
> *The coordinator fails after having recorded "commit" or "abort" in the log but before "end-commit."* In this case, some participants may not have received the outcome of the global decision. Therefore the recovery procedure of the coordinator must inform all participants of the decision so that they can terminate.

8.6 Conclusion

In this chapter, we have described the basic concepts and algorithms for maintaining database consistency in a reliable way. This chapter completes the discussion on data integrity and security of Chapter 6 and concurrency control in Chapter 7.

The design of an efficient recovery manager is difficult since it is dependent on the implementation of other complex functions, such as concurrency control, buffer management, and file management. The major design choice relates to an efficient combination of reliability algorithm, update implementation, and concurrency control algorithm. Reliability algorithms may be essentially characterized by their ability to undo a transaction's updates since the redo capability is mandatory to support recovery after media failure. Optimistic concurrency control generates more aborts than pessimistic schemes and thus works best because the cost of undo is close to zero. Therefore a no-undo/optimistic scheme or an undo/shadowing/optimistic scheme are good combinations. Pessimistic concurrency control rarely aborts transactions and thus does not require an efficient undo capability. We believe that the most efficient scheme for centralized DBMSs is an undo/update-in-place/pessimistic scheme because there are fewer disk accesses in these schemes.

The single solution to data reliability is duplication. The management of such duplication affects performance. The traditional techniques based on logs and backup copies have two inherent problems. First, any data page update incurs at least two disk writes, one for the updated page and one for the log record.

Second, recovery after media failure is a slow process, perhaps unacceptably so for applications that require high data availability.

Those two problems may be overcome by using additional hardware (at additional cost) and different reliability techniques. The first problem stems from the volatility of main memory, which imposes to write updated data to disk before commit time. A solution is to use a small part of main memory, which is as stable as disk [Copeland86, Elhard84]. Stable main memory can be constructed using current random access memory with an uninterruptible power supply (UPS). Upon power failure, the stable main memory and the disk are switched to UPS battery power, and then the content of the stable main memory is written to disk. Transactions can commit after writing to stable main memory, which is much faster than writing to disk. A background task is responsible for migrating the updated pages to disk whenever the disk is idle. This solution has several strong advantages, including better scheduling of disk accesses and amortization of page updates; for example, a page may be written to disk only after n updates, thus saving $(n-1)$ disk accesses. Because of its increasing cost-effectiveness, stable main memory is more likely to be used by database systems in the near future.

Recovery after media failure is slow because a database snapshot must be reconstituted from the last archive, and then the redo log must be sequentially processed. An obvious solution that eliminates this painful reconstruction is to maintain two on-line copies of the database. Mirroring [Borr81], in which identical copies are stored on two separate disks, one being the mirror of the other, provides an adequate solution. Each page write must be done simultaneously on both disks. If one disk fails, the mirror disk remains accessible, thereby avoiding cold recovery. This solution requires additional hardware and software but also improves (read) access performance since a page can be retrieved from either disk (whichever one is idle at the time). Mirroring works best in multiprocessor architectures.

8.7 References and Bibliography

[Baer81] Baer J. L., Gardarin G., Girault C., Roucairol G., "The Two-Step Commitment Protocol: Modeling, Specification and Proof Methodology," 5th Int. Conf. on Software Engineering, San Diego, 1981, IEEE ed.

[Bayer83] Bayer R., "Database System Design for High Performance," Proc. IFIP 9th World Computer Congress, Amsterdam, September 1983.

[Bernstein83] Bernstein P. A., Goodman N., Hadzilacos V., "Recovery Algorithms for Database Systems," Proc. IFIP 9th World Computer Congress, Amsterdam, September 1983.

[Bernstein87] Bernstein P. A., Hadzilacos V., Goodman N., *Concurrency Control and Recovery in Database Systems,* Addison-Wesley, 1987.

[Bjork73] Bjork L. A., "Recovery Scenario for a DB/DC System," Proc. of ACM National Conf., ACM, 1973.

[Borr81] Borr A. J., "Transaction Monitoring in ENCOMPASS," Int. Conf. on VLDB, Cannes, France, September 1981.

[Chan82] Chan A., Fox S., Lin W. T. K., Nori A., Ries D. R., "The Implementation of an Integrated Concurency Control and Recovery Scheme," ACM SIGMOD Conf. on Management of Data, Orlando, June 1982.

[Copeland86] Copeland G., Krishnamurthy R., Smith, M. "Recovery Using Safe RAM," MCC Technical Report DB-403-86, Austin, Texas, December 1986.

[Effelsberg84] Effelsberg W., Haerder T., "Principles of Database Buffer Management," ACM TODS, V9, N4, December 1984.

[Elhard84] Elhard K., Bayer R., "A Database Cache for High Performance and Fast Restart in Database Systems," ACM TODS, V9, N4, December 1984.

[Gawlick85] Gawlick D., "Processing Hot Spots in High Performance Systems," Proc. IEEE Compcon, February 1985.

[Gelenbe79] Gelenbe E., "On the Optimum Checkpoint Interval," Journal of the ACM, V26, N2, April 1979, pp. 259 – 70.

[Gray78] Gray J. N., "Notes on Database Operating Systems," in *Operating Systems – An Advanced Course,* R. Bayer et al. (eds.), Springer-Verlag, 1978.

[Gray81a] Gray J. N., "The Transaction Concept: Virtues and Limitations," Int. Conf. on VLDB, Cannes, September 1981.

[Gray81b] Gray J. N., et al., "The Recovery Manager of the System R Database Manager," ACM Computing Surveys, V13, N2, June 1981, pp. 223 – 42.

[Gray86] Gray J. N., "Why Do Computers Stop and What Can Be Done about It?" Symp. on Reliability in Distributed Software and Database Systems, IEEE, 1986.

[Hadzilacos83] Hadzilacos V., "An Operational Model for Database System Reliability," ACM Symposium on PODS, Atlanta, Georgia, March 1983.

[Haerder83] Haerder T., Reuter A., "Principles of Transaction-Oreinted Database Recovery," ACM Computing Surveys, V15, N4, December 1983, pp. 287 – 317.

[Lampson76] Lampson B., Sturgis H., "Crash Recovery in a Distributed Data Storage System," Technical Report, Computer Science Laboratory, Xerox, Palo Alto Research Center, Palo Alto, 1976.

[Lorie77] Lorie R. A., "Physical Integrity in a Large Segmented Database," ACM TODS, V2, N1, March 1977, pp. 91 – 104.

[Reed79] Reed D. P., "Implementing Atomic Actions," 7th ACM SIGOPS Symposium on Operating System Principles, December 1979.

[Severance76] Severance D. G., Lohman G. M., "Differential Files: Their Applications to the Maintenance of Large Databases," ACM TODS, V1, N3, September 1976, pp. 167 – 95.

[Skeen81] Skeen D., "Non-blocking Commit Protocols," ACM SIGMOD Conf., 1981.

[Verhofstad78] Verhofstad J. S. M., "Recovery Techniques for Database Systems," ACM Computing Surveys, V10, N2, June 1978, pp. 167 – 95.

9
QUERY PROCESSING

9.1 Introduction

Relational database management systems (RDBMSs) offer high-level languages that are nonprocedural and use set-at-a-time operators. When querying a relational database, the user specifies the result desired without providing the access paths to the data. Hence the DBMS is responsible for determining how to access the data by applying a query processing algorithm that produces an access plan for a given query. This algorithm is implemented in the system by a query processing module that we will refer to as the *query processor*. Designing a query processor is a difficult and important task that has received considerable attention [Jarke84, Kim85]. The reason is that the efficiency of the query processor conditions the performance of the DBMS in performing high-level queries and thus its usability. The performance issue is critical with relational systems because queries are used to perform various tasks such as end-user retrieval and update queries, schema management, semantic integrity, and authorization management. The first RDBMSs were strongly criticized and unsuccessful because of their poor performance. Since then query processing methods have been designed and proved to be efficient first in prototypes and later in commercial products.

The objective of query processing is to execute queries in such a way that cost is minimized. The selection of the best access plan (which optimizes the cost function) is known to be computationally intractable for general queries [Ibaraki84]. Therefore heuristics are necessary for optimizing the cost function. This

275

cost function typically refers to machine resources such as disk space, disk input-output (IO), buffer space, and central processing unit (CPU) time. In current centralized systems where the database resides on disk storage, the emphasis is on minimizing the number of disk accesses. However, the recent availability of large main memory buffer space and the sophistication of user queries makes CPU time more critical. Therefore the cost measure typically includes IO and CPU costs.

All query processors have an optimization phase that exploits available access paths to the data. Therefore physical database design is an important issue related to query optimization. Nonrelational database systems such as IMS and System 2000 provide sophisticated ways of organizing the physical database structure. Current RDBMSs too provide efficient ways to organize data. Physical database design permits tailoring the underlying database structure to a given data access pattern. This pattern is deduced from the knowledge of database applications. Thus the power of the storage model provided by the DBMS and the accuracy of physical database design are crucial to the efficiency of query processing.

In this chapter, we will describe the state-of-the-art solutions to the query processing problem in a relational context. We limit ourselves to centralized database systems where the database system runs on a single processor. Query processing in distributed database systems is more complex [Ceri84, Sacco82, Yu84] because the solution space for query optimization is larger. Our presentation is done in the context of relational calculus and relational algebra because these are the basic languages of relational systems. Section 9.2 presents the problem and the objectives of query processing. Section 9.3 presents the main system parameters influencing query processing. Section 9.4 describes the design issues of a query processor and the various phases common to most query processing methods. The different phases are then detailed in subsequent sections. Section 9.5 presents the query decomposition phase. Section 9.6 presents the possibilities of algebraic restructuring of a query. Section 9.7 describes the query optimization phase. Finally, Section 9.8 provides the algorithms for performing the basic relational algebra operations.

9.2 Objectives of Query Processing

9.2.1 Problem

Given a user query expressed in relational calculus, there generally exist many possible strategies to perform it. These strategies may lead to significantly different execution times. The main objective of the query processor is to find the optimal strategy for executing a query. The problem is generally NP-complete in the number of relations involved and thus computationally intractable [Ibaraki84]. Therefore it is usually necessary to use heuristics to simplify the problem and find a quasi-optimal solution.

We illustrate by means of an example the importance of query processing and query optimization in particular. In this chapter, all examples are based on the following subset of the wine database scheme, introduced in Chapter 4:

WINE (W#, VINEYARD, VINTAGE, PERCENT)
PRODUCER (P#, NAME, REGION)
HARVEST (P#, W#, QTY)

where W# is the wine number and P# the producer number. Consider the following simple user query Q1: "names of wines which have been harvested by a producer in a quantity greater than 100." Expressed in tuple relational calculus, the query is (using SQL syntax):

(Q1)   SELECT   W.VINEYARD
         FROM   WINE W, HARVEST H
         WHERE   W.W# = H.W# AND
                  H.QTY > 100

There are many ways to translate this query into a sequence of relational algebra operations where the ordering of operations is dictated. The two following strategies, expressed in relational algebra, answer correctly the given query (many other strategies exist for such a simple query). For short, we use variable names instead of relation names.

Strategy 1:
         PROJECT (RESTRICT (W × H, W.W# = H.W# and H.QTY >
         100), W. VINEYARD)
Strategy 2:
         PROJECT (JOIN (H, RESTRICT (W, QTY > 100), W.W# =
         H.W#), W.VINEYARD)

Strategy 1 first composes the Cartesian product of the base relations W and H resulting in a temporary relation (W × H) and then restricts and projects the useful data from that temporary relation. Strategy 2 joins relation H with relation RESTRICT (W, QTY > 100), which is a subset of relation W that is useful to the answer and then projects the result of the join on VINEYARD.

In order to compare the expected performance of these strategies, we use the following simplifying assumptions. The database is stored on disk. The cardinality (number of tuples) of relation WINE (or W) is 500 and that of relation HARVEST (or H) is 1200. There are 100 tuples in H that satisfy the restriction predicate. Finally the execution time of a strategy is proportional to the sum of the cardinalities of intermediate results. This is generally true since temporary relations must be written by a producer operator and read by a consumer operator. Read and write operations may lead to disk IOs if the requested data are not in main memory.

Let us first evaluate strategy 1. It generates two temporary relations. The first is the Cartesian product of H and W, whose cardinality is 600,000. The second is the selection from this first temporary relation of tuples satisfying the restrict predicate, and its cardinality is 100. The execution time of strategy 1 is thus O (600,100), where O stands for "order of" (or "proportional to").

For strategy 2, the first temporary relation generated by the restriction on relation H has cardinality 100. Assuming that each wine is produced by five producers, the second temporary relation resulting from the join of the first temporary relation with H is 500. The execution time of strategy 2 is thus O (600). Therefore strategy 2 is better than strategy 1 by almost a factor of 1000.

This example, based on a simple query with only two relations and three operations, exhibits the importance of query optimization.

9.2.2 Function of the Query Processor

The role of the query processor is to map a query expressed in a high-level language (relational calculus) on a relational database into a sequence of lower-level operations (implementing relational algebra) acting on relations. (The different layers involved in this mapping will be detailed in Section 9.4.) As we saw in the previous example, many strategies (sequences of relational operations) exist for answering a single query. An important objective in doing this mapping is to select a strategy that minimizes cost, generally the total execution time of the query [Selinger79], which is the sum of all execution times of operations that participate in the query. Cost can also be the response time of the query [Valduriez84]; in this case, the goal is to maximize the parallel execution of operations. Some more recent optimization methods aim also at maximizing the throughput of the entire system as measured by the number of queries processed per time unit.

In a centralized database system, the total time to be minimized is the sum of IO and CPU times. The IO time is incurred in transferring data blocks between secondary memory, typically magnetic disks, and main memory, typically random access memory (RAM). This time can be minimized by using fast access methods to the data and a sufficiently large main memory. The CPU (time) is incurred in performing operations on data in main memory. Another cost function that could be significant but has received much less emphasis is the actual cost of storing data on secondary and main memory. For simple queries, the CPU time may be ignored since it is largely dominated by the IO time; however, CPU time becomes significant for complex queries or when large main memories are used.

9.3 Parameters Influencing Query Processing

A number of common assumptions underlie the design of query processing algorithms. In a centralized system, the most important assumptions are the physical storage model and the complexity of database operations.

9.3.1 Storage Model

The storage model prescribes the storage structures and algorithms supported by the system to map the conceptual schema into the physical (or internal) schema. In an RDBMS, conceptual relations are generally mapped into files based on two partitioning functions. Vertical partitioning maps relations into files where a file corresponds to an attribute, several attributes, or the entire relation. Horizontal partitioning clusters each file based on the values of a single or multiple attributes using a single or multiple attribute file organization.

Most relational systems employ an *n*-ary storage model (NSM) where each conceptual relation is stored in a single file. The key concept in NSM is that all attributes of a conceptual tuple are stored together. Thus the vertical partitioning function is very simple (1-1). The horizontal partitioning function clusters all conceptual tuples of a file based on one or more attributes. In addition, several secondary indexes (also implemented as files) might be defined on nonclustered attributes. Fig. 9.1(a) illustrates an example of storage representation for relation WINE (VINEYARD, VINTAGE, PERCENT). We assume that each conceptual tuple is assigned a surrogate for tuple identity, called TID (tuple identifier). A

TID	VINEYARD	VINTAGE	PERCENT
1	Chablis	1982	12
2	Chablis	1983	12
3	Bordeaux	1982	11

(a)

TID	VINEYARD
1	Chablis
2	Chablis
3	Bordeaux

TID	VINTAGE
1	1982
2	1983
3	1982

TID	VINEYARD
1	12
2	12
3	11

(b)

FIGURE 9.1 Alternative storage representations of relation WINE. (a) Storage with NSM and (b) storage with DSM.

TID is a globally unique value created by the system when a tuple is instantiated, which the system never modifies. TIDs permit efficient updates and reorganizations of files since references do not involve physical pointers. Most RDBMSs, including INGRES and System R, support the notion of tuple identifier. With NSM, attributes TID, VINEYARD, VINTAGE, and PERCENT are stored together for each tuple.

An alternative model to NSM is the decomposition storage model (DSM). The DSM stores all values of each attribute of a relation together in a separate file [Batory79, Copeland85]. Therefore DSM files are binary relations pairing each attribute value with the identifier of its conceptual tuple. Fig. 9.1(b) illustrates the DSM representation of relation WINE. Each DSM file can be clustered on the attribute value or on the tuple identifier or on both. If a DSM file is clustered on the attribute value, then run-length compression can be easily applied by associating all TIDs of tuples having the same atribute value. Run-legth compression provides both increased access and storage performance. Furthermore some secondary indexes can be added as copies of DSM files. For instance, the DSM file for (TID, VINEYARD) can have two copies: one clustered on TID and the other clustered on VINEYARD.

A detailed analysis of the performance trade-offs between NSM and DSM is provided in [Copeland85]. The NSM approach is best for queries that involve many attributes of the same relations; however, projection on a few attributes is inefficient if the number of attributes in the file is high. The DSM approach is best for complex queries involving many selections and projections on a few attributes. Projection on many attributes is inefficient relative to NSM since many DSM files must be joined based on the common TID. Although the performance advantages of NSM and DSM are clear for a given access pattern, most RDBMSs use NSM assuming that simple queries and projection on many attributes are predominant.

A model hybrid between DSM and NSM has also been proposed [Navathe84]. This storage model vertically partitions a relation based on the attribute affinities such that attributes used together frequently are stored in the same file. The knowledge about the most frequent queries in user workloads is thus exploited to organize storage structures for efficient access. Each file contains several attributes and an identifier of the corresponding tuple. Therefore the operations best supported are restrictions and projections on the groups of attributes that are frequently accessed together. The fact that this model is a hybrid of NSM and DSM provides a compromise of the advantages and disadvantages of both schemes. However, the accuracy of the vertical partitioning is a key factor for efficiency. In general, this model supports highly dynamic workloads only poorly.

In the rest of this chapter, we will assume the NSM for two reasons. First, the fact that each relation is implemented in a single file simplifies the description of the query processing algorithms. Second, most query processing algorithms available in the literature assume the NSM. We refer readers to [Khoshafian87] for a description of a query processing algorithm for DSM.

9.3.2 Complexity of Database Operations

Generally a query processor translates a relational calculus query into a program of relational algebra. The optimization of the ordering of relational algebra operations is based on cost functions associated with each operation. In order to understand the assumptions generally used by the query optimization algorithms, we briefly discuss the complexity of the relational operations. To simplify this section, the discussion is independent of any particular (and probably efficient) implementation. Complexity is defined with respect to relation cardinalities. We denote by $card(R)$ the cardinality of relation R. Furthermore we ignore the use of clustered or secondary indexes for performing relational operations.

Relational operations are basically either unary or binary. However, generalization to n-ary operations for efficiency purpose is possible. We also assume that the cardinalities of operand relations of binary operations are the same. The two basic unary operations are restriction and projection. Because the processing of a single tuple does not affect that of the others, the complexity of restriction is $O(card(R))$. If projection does not require duplicate elimination, its complexity is $O(card(R))$. However, duplicate elimination has a complexity similar to this of binary operations, and therefore hashing or sorting is necessary. By definition, the Cartesian product of two relations of cardinality n is $O(card(R)^2)$. Other binary operations (like join) can be optimized by using sorting or hashing [Bratbergsengen84]. Assuming that sorting is used, their complexity is $O(card(R)*\log card(R))$. Hashing can make the complexity of semijoin close to $O(card(R))$, but in order to be independent of particular implementations, we assume its complexity to be this of join. Other complex unary operations like group functions or projection with duplicate elimination can be also computed in time $O(card(R) \log (card(R)))$.

9.4 Issues in Designing a Query Processor

We now consider the design issues that are common to all query processing algorithms. In addition, we propose a layering of the different phases of query processing starting from a calculus query down to the execution of operations to produce the result. The space of solutions to the problem of query processing appears to be large because many parameters are involved. Therefore quite different query processing methods have been proposed in the context of centralized systems [Jarke84]; however, a number of common issues underlie the design of a query processor.

9.4.1 Type of Algorithm

Query processing algorithms can be divided into two main types characterized by exhaustive search of the solution space or use of heuristics. Exhaustive search, in which all possible strategies are enumerated and evaluated, can determine the optimal strategy to answer a query, provided that the appropriate timing is employed. The complexity of exhaustive search algorithms is combinatorial in the number of relations. However, it is often argued that it is cost-effective because the number of relations involved in a query is generally very small [Selinger79], defined as fewer than ten (typically between one and five). The number of relations involved in queries expressed in languages of higher expressive power than relational calculus can be extremely large [Krisnamarthy86]. Because of the combinatorial complexity of exhaustive search, a number of heuristics must be used. They restrict the search of the solution space and thus simplify the problem. The main heuristics are to regroup common subexpressions in order to avoid duplicate work, perform the operations that restrict the size of intermediate relations first, order the binary operations in such a way that minimizes the size of intermediate relations, and choose the best algorithm, if several exist, to perform individual operations.

9.4.2 Optimization Granularity

Most query processing algorithms optimize a single query at a time. The main reason is that the problem is sufficiently complex as is. However, this approach precludes repeated usage of intermediate results from one query to another. Optimizing multiple queries at a time allows the use of the results of one query in processing others and ordering them in such a way that throughput (number of queries per second) is maximized. However, the decision space is much larger and makes the cost of optimization prohibitive [Jarke85].

9.4.3 Optimization Timing

The time at which the query is optimized is an important factor affecting performance. Query optimization can be static, dynamic, or hybrid. *Static optimization,* used in most commercial systems, is done before execution of the query. It can be viewed as a compilation approach. Because it is difficult to determine precisely the size of intermediate results, static algorithms rely heavily on the accuracy of statistics and estimation formulas. Inaccurate statistics increase error propagation. The main advantage of the static approach is that query optimization, an expensive process, is done once for many executions of the same query. This is particularly important when database queries are embedded in applications programs. However the compilation into low-level access plans exploits the physical database structure. Any change to the database structure invalidates the access plans and requires recompilation. In practice, reorganization (dropping or adding indexes) is rare because it is expensive.

Dynamic optimization is done at run time. It can be viewed as an interpretation approach. The main advantage is that it provides exact information on the sizes of intermediate results. Coupled with the exhaustive search of the decision space at each step, dynamic optimization can determine the optimal strategy. Its main shortcoming is that optimization cannot be amortized over multiple executions of a repetitive query.

Some *hybrid strategies* have been proposed to combine the advantages of both approaches. The query is compiled using a static algorithm, but it can be partially reoptimized at run time if estimates of intermediate results appear to be incorrect. Although more complex, this approach, used in some commercial systems, is probably best.

9.4.4 Statistics

Static optimization methods rely on accurate statistics on the database to estimate the size of intermediate results generated by operations on base relations. There is a direct trade-off between accuracy of the statistics and their maintenance cost. Sophisticated statistics are more precise but expensive to maintain. The statistics used primarily apply to each relation and some important attributes in relations. Relation statistics are typically relation cardinality, size of a tuple, and sometimes proportion of tuples in one relation participating in the join with another relation. Attribute statistics are cardinality of the domain (number of possible distinct values) and actual number of distinct values. To simplify the use of these statistics in estimating intermediate results, two strong assumptions are traditionally made: independence between different attribute values and uniform distribution of attribute values within their domain.

9.4.5 Phases of Query Processing

The problem of query processing can be decomposed into several subproblems corresponding to various layers. These problems are not independent since decisions made for one subproblem may affect those made for another. However, to make this complex problem tractable, they are generally treated independently in a top-down fashion. In Fig. 9.2, we propose three phases for query processing, with each phase solving a well-defined problem. To simplify, we assume a static query processor that compiles a query before executing it. The input to the query processor is a query expressed in relational calculus and applied to the conceptual schema. Three main phases are involved in order to map the query into an optimized sequence of operations and to execute them to produce the result: decom-

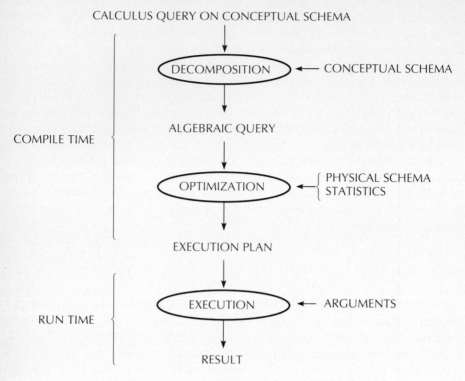

CALCULUS QUERY ON CONCEPTUAL SCHEMA

DECOMPOSITION ◄── CONCEPTUAL SCHEMA

COMPILE TIME

ALGEBRAIC QUERY

OPTIMIZATION ◄──{ PHYSICAL SCHEMA
STATISTICS

EXECUTION PLAN

EXECUTION ◄── ARGUMENTS

RUN TIME

RESULT

FIGURE 9.2 Three phases of query processing

position, optimization, and execution. The first two phases are done at compile time, and the third takes place at run time. The first phase decomposes the calculus query using the conceptual schema into a query expressed in relational algebra. Analysis and simpification of the query are done during this phase. The second phase consists of finding an optimal or quasi-optimal ordering of the relational operations and choosing the access paths to the data, as well as the algorithms for performing database operations. The decisions are based on the physical schema and on the statistics available on the relations. The output of this phase is an optimized query generally expressed in a low-level implementation of relational algebra and stored in an execution plan.

Definition 9.1 Execution plan
Optimized program of low-level database operations corresponding to a query

The execution plan of a query is generally saved for repetitive executions. The last step is the execution of the execution plan. If the query is parametric — that is, it contains variable parameters such as in the query "wines of vintage

X?'' — its arguments must be given at run time. Sometimes the algorithms to perform the relational operations are chosen during this last step (if not already done in the optimization phase).

9.5 Query Decomposition

This section presents the functions necessary to simplify an end-user query expressed in relational calculus into a query expressed in relational algebra on the conceptual schema. These functions correspond to the first layer of Fig. 9.2. Query decomposition can be divided into four steps: (1) rewriting of the query in a normalized form, (2) analysis of the normalized query, (3) simplification, and (4) algebraic restructuring using equivalence rules.

9.5.1 Normalization

The input query in relational calculus is first lexically, syntactically, and semantically analyzed and then transformed into a normalized form suitable for further optimization. Lexical and syntactic analysis is similar to these of programming languages. The validity of the query is checked against the grammar of the query language. The attributes and relations involved in the query are checked to be present in the schema. Furthermore type checking of the query qualification as well as of the result specification are done here.

If the query is correct until this point, it is rewritten in a normalized form. Most relational calculus languages like SQL require the query to be expressed in *prenex form*.

> **Definition 9.2 Prenex form query**
> Query where all quantifications precede a quantifier-free qualification
> (for example, the WHERE clause in SQL).

The query qualification can be transformed in two normal forms where one gives priority to the ANDs while the other gives priority to the ORs. A qualification in conjunctive normal form is as follows:

$$(P_{11} \text{ or } P_{12} \ldots \text{ or } P_{in}) \text{ and } \ldots (P_{m1} \text{ or } P_{m2} \ldots \text{ or } P_{mn}).$$

where P_{ij} is an atomic predicate.

A qualification in disjunctive normal form is as follows:

$$(P_{11} \text{ and } P_{12} \ldots \text{ and } P_{in}) \text{ or } \ldots (P_{m1} \text{ and } P_{m2} \ldots \text{ and } P_{mn}).$$

The AND predicates are mapped into join or restriction operations while the OR predicates are mapped into union operations. The use of the conjunctive normal form leads to doing unions first. The use of the disjunctive normal form allows considering the query as independent subqueries linked by unions. The translation of an arbitrary relational calculus query is done by applying a few transformation rules as shown in [Jarke84].

9.5.2 Semantic Analysis

The objective of semantic analysis is to refute incorrect queries. An incorrect query can be incorrectly formulated or contradictory. A query is incorrectly formulated if disjoint components of the query are useless. This arises frequently when some join specifications are missing. A query is contradictory if its qualification cannot be satisfied by any tuple. For example, the predicate PERCENT > 13 and PERCENT < 12 is contradictory. Incorrect queries can be recognized without accessing the base data. The interpretation of incorrect queries varies from one system to another. One simple way is to generate the value false for the incorrect part of the qualification. For example, the qualification ((PERCENT > 13 and PERCENT < 12) or VINTAGE > 1979) will become VINTAGE > 1979. Algorithms to determine query correctness exist only for a subset of relational calculus. All use various types of graphs. We will present the two types of graphs that are most used: the *relation connection graph* and the *attribute connection graph*. To illustrate these graph types, we consider the following query (Q2) on the WINES database: "Names of wines produced in Bourgogne in quantity equal to or greater than 100." The query expressed in SQL is:

```
(Q2)    SELECT   W.VINEYARD
        FROM     WINE W, PRODUCER P, HARVEST H
        WHERE    W.W# = H.W# AND
                 H.P# = P.P# AND
                 P.REGION = "Bourgogne" AND
                 H.QTY > = 100
```

The *relation connection graph* was introduced in [Wong76].

> **Definition 9.3 Relation connection graph**
> Graph where each node represents a base relation, where an edge between two nodes represents a join, and where an edge going to its source node represents a restriction. A node is added to represent the resulting relation (if any).

An example of a connection graph for the query Q2 is given in Fig. 9.3. This query is conjunctive and thus can be modeled as a single graph. Queries with join disjunctions must be modeled with several graphs; however, this type of query is

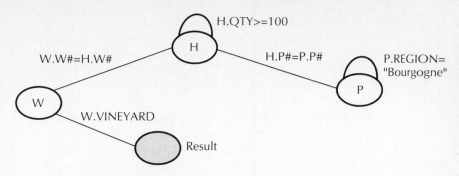

FIGURE 9.3 Relation connection graph of query Q2

less frequent. Several versions of such a graph exist—in particular, the query graph [Bernstein81] where only joins are depicted by an edge.

The relation correction graph is useful for recognizing a particular class of queries for which an efficient query processing algorithm may be applied. An important type of query that can be well optimized is tree queries (queries whose query graph is a tree). Queries exhibiting a cycle in their query graph are called *cyclic queries* and are more difficult to handle. For example, let us assume that both relations PRODUCER and WINE have an additional attribute AGE. The following SQL query, which searches the producers having the same age as at least one wine they have produced, is a cyclic query:

```
(Q3)    SELECT   P.NAME
        FROM     WINE W, PRODUCER P, HARVEST H
        WHERE    W.W# = H.W# AND H.P# = P.P#
        AND      P.AGE = W.AGE
```

The query graph of Q3 is portrayed in Fig. 9.4.

The *attribute connection graph* can be defined as follows.

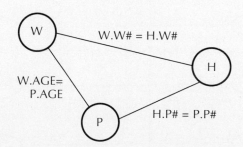

FIGURE 9.4 Cyclic query graph of query Q3

> **Definition 9.4 Attribute connection graph**
> Graph in which a node is associated to each reference of an attribute
> or of a constant, where a join is depicted by an edge between the
> participating attributes, and where a restriction is represented by an
> edge between an attribute and a constant.

Fig. 9.5 shows the attribute connection graph of query Q2.

An interesting variant is the normalized attribute connection graph as introduced in [Rosenkrantz80]. The normalized attribute connection graph is a directed graph where each node represents a reference to an attribute, or constant 0, where an arc between two attributes represents a join, and where an arc between an attribute and constant 0 represents a restriction. This graph is weighted: an arc from node x to node y weighted by c represents the inequality $x \leq y + c$. For example, the inequality $x \geq c$ is represented by an arc from node 0 to node x with weight $-c$. Fig. 9.6 gives an example of normalized attribute connection graph for query Q2.

For the particular case of conjunctive queries using only the comparison operators $=$, $<$, $>$, $\leq$, $\geq$ without negation (NOT), incorrect queries can be detected by applying the following:

1. A multivariable query is incorrectly formulated if its relation connection graph is not connected. In general, the reason is that a join predicate is missing, although different interpretations of the queries can be considered; for example, the Cartesian product may be assumed [Wong76].
2. A query is contradictory if its normalized attribute connection graph exhibits a cycle of which the valuation sum is negative [Rosenkrantz80].

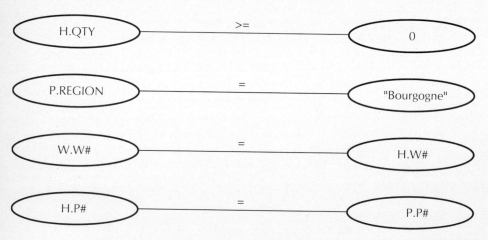

FIGURE 9.5 Attribute connection graph of query Q2

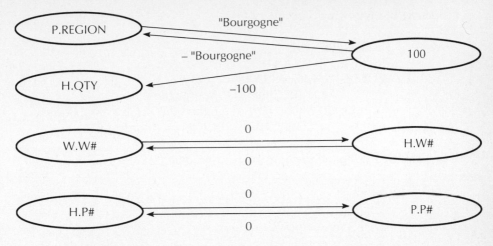

FIGURE 9.6 Normalized attribute connection graph of query Q2

9.5.3 Simplification

In relational calculus, different semantically equivalent expressions exist for a given query. Two query expressions are said to be equivalent if they give the same result for any database state.

> **Definition 9.5 Equivalent queries**
> Queries that produce the same effect for every possible state of the database.

Some expressions are preferable because they are simpler and thus candidates for better performance. Transformation rules can be used to simplify the query expressions. We will look at three types of simplification: elimination of redundancy, transitivity, and integrity rules.

A query qualification may contain redundant predicates. The execution of queries with redundant qualifications leads to duplicated work. Queries submitted to the query processor may contain redundant predicates because they generally result from a first translation of user queries by applying view, protection, and semantic integrity rules. Queries resulting from this translation may be unnecessarily redundant and can be simplified. A first (and good) optimization is to eliminate this redundancy by applying well-known idempotency rules of Boolean algebra — for example ($< ->$ denotes logical equivalence):

A and not (A) $< ->$ false
not (A or B) $< ->$ not (A) and not (B)
A or false $< ->$ A

For example the following SQL query Q4

    (Q4)   SELECT   REGION
               FROM   PRODUCER
               WHERE   NAME = "Dupont" OR
                         NOT (REGION = "Bourgogne") AND
                         (REGION = "Bourgogne" OR REGION = "Bordelais")
                             AND NOT (REGION = "Bordelais")

can be simplified using the previous rules to become:

    SELECT   REGION
    FROM   PRODUCER
    WHERE   NAME = "Dupont"

A query qualification may be transformed into an equivalent query qualification by applying the transitive closure of the normalized attribute connection graph. All subgraphs having the same transitive closure lead to equivalent qualifications. It is then possible to retain only the subgraphs that give qualifications that can be more efficiently processed. For example, let us consider the following qualification: $R.A = 10$ and $R.A = S.A$ and $S.A = T.A$. By transitivity, the following qualification is equivalent to the original qualification: $R.A = 10$ and $R.A = S.A$ and $S.A = 10$ and $R.A = T.A$. The transformation here has been twofold. First, the binding of $R.A$ to the constant 10 has been propagated to $S.A$. Thus only a subset of relation S is selected before the join. Second, the join predicate ($S.A = T.A$) has been replaced by ($R.A = T.A$). Choosing between these two join predicates is dictated by optimization considerations. Note that this type of transformation tends to lengthen the query qualification in order to provide more opportunities for optimization.

Finally, semantic integrity rules can be useful to simplify queries. Semantic integrity rules are assertions on all database states. If a query contradicts an integrity assertion, then its answer is void and the database need not be accessed. We illustrate this feature with a simple example. Assume we have a constraint saying that if the vintage of a wine is 1982 (predicate A), then its percentage is greater than 12 (predicate B). In tuple relational calculus, this integrity assertion is (not A or B):

    NOT (W.VINTAGE = 1982) OR (W.PERCENT > 12)

The following query expressed in SQL

    SELECT   W#
    FROM   WINE W
    WHERE   W.VINTAGE = 1982 AND
               W.PERCENT = 11

contradicts the integrity assertion and hence cannot be satisfied by any tuple of the database. Although it is attractive, the computation cost of this type of simplification can be prohibitive since the query must be matched against all integrity assertions having relations in common.

9.6 Algebraic Restructuring Methods

A query expressed in relational calculus can be mapped into a relational algebra program that provides a sequence of relational operations. An obvious and simple mapping method is to translate each individual predicate of the qualification in order of appearance into the corresponding relational operation (for example, join, selection) and to translate the target statement (for example, SELECT in SQL) of the query into the corresponding operation (for example, projection).

A graphical representation of a relational algebra program is useful for program manipulation. A relational algebra program can be described by a *relational algebra tree.*

> **Definition 9.6: Relational algebra tree**
> Tree describing a query where a leaf represents a base relation, an internal node represents an intermediate relation obtained by applying a relational operation, and the root represents the result of the query. The data flow is directed from the leaves to the root.

For example, query Q2 expressed in SQL can be mapped into the relational algebra tree given in Fig. 9.7. The mapping of the relational algebra tree into an execution plan is easy.

Different queries expressed in relational calculus may be equivalent. Similarly different relational algebra trees may be equivalent. Since relational operations have different complexity, some trees may provide much better performance than others. Important factors for optimization are the ordering of relational operations and the sizes of intermediate relations generated. Relational algebra trees can be restructured using transformation rules, introduced in [Smith75] and developed in [Ullman82]. Here we present the equivalence rules for transforming relational algebra trees. Proofs of the rules can be found in [Aho79]. We limit ourselves to the basic relational algebra operations: projection, restriction, join, Cartesian product, union, and difference. Similar rules can be deduced for other operations like semijoin, grouping, or transitive closure, but they are more complicated. We will illustrate graphically the eight most important rules to restructure relational algebra trees in Fig. 9.8. These eight rules permit substantial transformations that can optimize query execution. They allow the separation of unary operations, the grouping of unary operations on the same relation, the commutation of unary operations with binary operations, and the ordering of the binary operations. These rules can be applied by a simple restructuring algorithm that uses heuristics independent of statistics and physical infor-

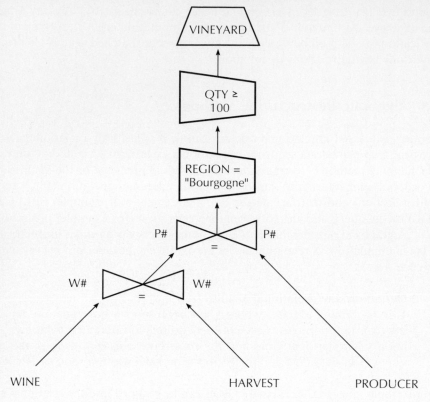

FIGURE 9.7 Relational algebra tree of query Q2

mation on the database. In the following, we present this simple algorithm. It uses a single heuristic: restriction and projection reduce the size of their operand relation and thus should be applied first.

The restructuring algorithm can be divided into the following sequential steps:

1. Separate restrictions with several predicates into subsequent restrictions of one predicate using rule 3.
2. Push restrictions down the tree as much as possible using rules 4, 5, and 6.
3. Group subsequent restrictions among the same relations using rule 3.
4. Push projections down the tree as much as possible using rules 7 and 8.
5. Group subsequent projections on the same relations and remove redundant projections.

Rule 1: Commutativity of joins

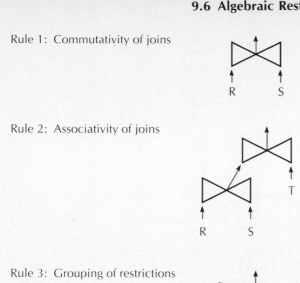

Rule 2: Associativity of joins

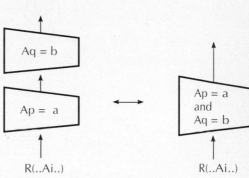

Rule 3: Grouping of restrictions

Rule 4: Commuting restriction
with projection

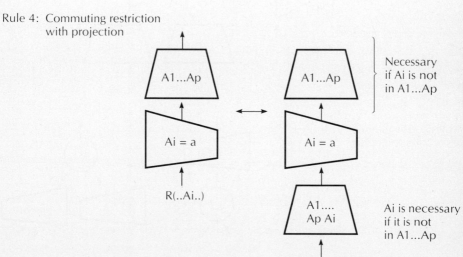

Necessary
if Ai is not
in A1...Ap

Ai is necessary
if it is not
in A1...Ap

FIGURE 9.8 Rules for transforming relational algebra trees

Rule 5: Commuting
restriction and join

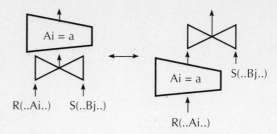

Rule 6: Commuting
restriction and union, or
restriction and difference

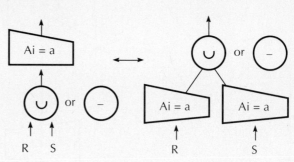

Rule 7: Commuting
projection and join

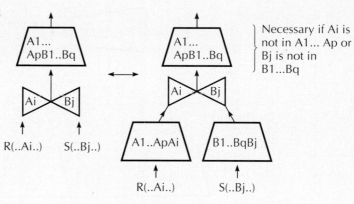

Necessary if Ai is
not in A1... Ap or
Bj is not in
B1...Bq

Rule 8: Commuting
projection and union

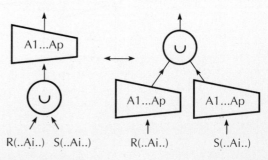

FIGURE 9.8 (*Continued*)

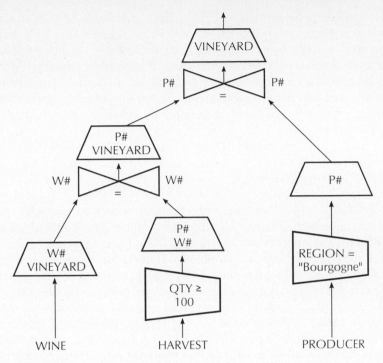

FIGURE 9.9 Equivalent relational algebra tree after restructuration

To illustrate the use of this algorithm, we applied it to the relational algebra tree of Fig. 9.7. The transformed tree is given in Fig. 9.9. Note that rules 1 and 2 are not used in the algorithm because it cannot order the binary operations (joins). The ordering of binary operations is typically done either at run time when sizes of intermediate results are known or, if statistical information about the database is available, at compile time.

9.7 Query Optimization

The algebraic restructuring rules permit the generation of many candidate algebraic trees for executing a single query. An important phase of query processing is to select a processing strategy that optimizes a given cost function. This optimization phase has for input an algebraic query involving conceptual relations and for output an execution plan of the query. This phase is in charge of decisions regarding the ordering of database operations, the access paths to the data, the algorithms for performing database operations, and the intermediate relations to be materialized. These decisions are undertaken based on the physical database schema and statistics about the database. A set of decisions that lead to an execution plan can be captured by a processing tree, which may be seen as a detailed algebraic tree. The accurate estimation of the cost of processing trees will enable choosing the "optimal" one. This cost is based on statistical information about base data and formulas for deriving the size of intermediate relations. After introducing the notion of processing tree and cost estimations of processing trees, we present three alternative techniques for generating the final processing tree: dynamic generation by reduction, generation by exhaustive search, and efficient optimization approaches.

9.7.1 Processing Trees

The decomposition phase of query processing produces an algebraic query expressed on conceptual schema. The subsequent optimization phase generates an access plan for the query based on the physical schema by selecting the optimal execution strategy. The conceptual-physical translation includes the mapping of relations into physical ones (stored in files) and the mapping of relational algebra operations to primitive database operations (directly implemented). Assuming the n-ary storage model, the conceptual-physical mapping of relations is trivial since a relation is stored in a single file. For efficiency, relational database systems rarely implement directly relational algebra operations that remain conceptual. Rather they support basic operations that minimize the accesses to relations. For instance, selection-projection without duplicate elimination can be performed directly by accessing the operand relation only once (compared to two successive operations with pure relational algebra). The following basic database operations are generally directly supported:

- Restriction-projection without duplicate elimination, called *selection*.
- Duplicate elimination.
- Join-project without duplicate elimination, called *join*.
- Set operations (Cartesian product, union, difference, intersections).
- Update operations (insert, delete, modify).

In addition, the following basic operations are always included for mapping non-relational algebra operations:

- Sorting.
- Aggregate functions.

Each basic operation can be implemented by several algorithms, each optimal under certain circumstances.

A query execution strategy dictates the access to base relations, the choice of algorithms for performing basic operations, and the ordering of these operations. There are many strategies for executing a given query. *Processing trees* as introduced in [Krishnamurthy86] are useful to model particular execution strategies.

Definition 9.7 Processing tree (PT)
Tree modeling an execution strategy where a leaf is a base relation and a nonleaf node is an intermediate relation materialized by applying a basic operation algorithm.

The algorithm for performing a basic operation includes the choice of the access paths (cluster index, secondary index) to base relations. Figure 9.10 illustrates an example of processing tree that corresponds to the algebraic tree of Fig. 9.9. A nonleaf node indicates the operation that produces the intermediate relation (for example, selection) and the algorithm for performing it (for example, selection$_1$ indicates that algorithm 1 is chosen for performing selection).

Processing trees can be classified into various classes based on important characteristics. A class of PTs defines a solution space for the optimization problem. To simplify the optimization phase, most relational systems are restricted to one or a few classes of PTs. Since join is generally considered the most expensive operation, an important subset of PTs is the *join PT*.

Definition 9.8 Join processing tree (JPT)
Processing tree where the only basic operations considered are joins.

The materialization of intermediate relations resulting from basic operations consumes important resources: buffer space and possibly disk space if the relation is too large to be kept in buffer. It is possible to avoid the materialization of some intermediate relations by applying an *n*-ary pipelined join algorithm [Niebuhr76,

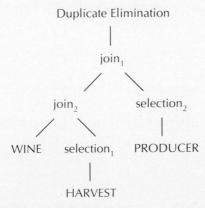

FIGURE 9.10 Example of processing tree

Kim80]. JPTs can model decisions regarding the materialization of intermediate relations by distinguishing between *binary* and *pipelined JPT.*

Definition 9.9 Binary JPT
JPT where each join has exactly two operand relations.

Definition 9.10 Pipelined JPT
JPT where a join can have an arbitrary number of operand relations.

Fig. 9.11 illustrates binary and pipelined JPTs corresponding to the processing tree in Fig. 9.10. The execution of a pipelined JPT will outperform the execution of a binary JPT if the intermediate relations produced by binary joins cannot be maintained in buffer, thereby inducing disk accesses for writing and reading them. Most existing relational systems consider PTs corresponding to binary JPTs. Furthermore the execution of the processing tree is assumed to be sequential. The advantage is that no more than two intermediate relations can coexist simultaneously so that they can be maintained entirely on main memory. The disadvantage is less parallel execution.

The optimization problem can be formulated as finding the PT of minimal cost. The PT can be generated dynamically if optimization takes place at run time. In this case, cost estimations for join operations are based on the exact size of operand relations since these are either base relations or intermediate relations materialized at the time of the decisions. If the optimization timing is static (the final PT must be generated before execution), estimation of the size of intermediate relations is of major importance for deriving the cost of a PT.

9.7.2 Cost Estimation of Processing Trees

The estimation of the cost of a PT is obtained by computing the sum of the costs of the individual basic operations in the PT. The cost measure is typically composed of CPU time and disk IO time. CPU time is sometimes ignored, and

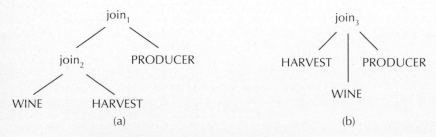

FIGURE 9.11 Examples of join processing trees (JPT).
(a) Binery JPT and (b) pipelined JPT.

the cost measure is approximated by the number of disk accesses [Blasgen77]. The cost of an individual operation with a specific algorithm is itself a monotonic function of the cardinalities of the operand relations. If the operand relations are intermediate relations, their cardinality must also have been estimated. Therefore for each operation of the PT, two numbers must be predicted: the individual cost of the operation and the cardinality of its result (except for the final result of the query). The accurate prediction of these two numbers is a prerequisite for query optimization. Therefore the cost function of each algorithm that implements a basic operation must be known to the system. In Section 9.8, we will review the cost functions of some well-known algorithms. The estimation of the cardinality of intermediate results is based on statistical information regarding the physical relations and formulas that predict the cardinality of the result of each operation type. The minimum statistics are:

- The cardinality of the domain of each attribute, A, denoted by *dom(A)*.
- The number of distinct values actually present for each attribute, A, denoted by *ndist(A)*.
- The minimum and maximum values of each numerical attribute.
- The cardinality of each relation, R, denoted by *card(R)*.

The *selectivity factor of a condition,* such as selection or join predicate, is defined as follows:

Definition 9.11 Selectivity factor of a condition
Proportion of tuples in the database that satisfy the condition.

The cardinality of the result of an operation based on a condition (selection or join) is a function of the cardinality of the operand relation(s) and of the selectivity factor of the condition, denoted by s. The cardinality of the result of a selection operation on relation R is $s * card(R)$. The cardinality of the result of the join of two relations R and S is $s * card(R) * card(S)$.

The accurate estimation of selectivity factors is difficult [Piatetsky84]. The traditional simplifying assumptions made by query processors are that attribute values are uniformly distributed within their domain and that attributes are independent. These assumptions are quite strong and often incorrect in the real world. For instance, there are many more people with the last name Smith than Valduriez (at least in the United States). Also, the attribute salary is not independent of attributes university degree and professional experience (at least in the United States). However, these assumptions enable simple estimations for selection operations.

The selectivity factor s of a selection predicate can be computed as follows [Selinger79]:

$$s\ (A=\text{value}) = 1/\ \text{ndist}\ (A)$$
$$s\ (A>\text{value}) = \max(A) - \text{value} / \max(A) - \min(A)$$

$$s\ (A < \text{value}) = \text{value} - \min(A) / (\max(A) - \min(A))$$
$$s\ (A \text{ in } \{\text{values}\}) = s\ (A = \text{value}) * \text{card}\ (\{\text{values}\})$$
$$s\ (P \text{ and } Q) = s\ (P) * s\ (Q)$$
$$s\ (P \text{ or } Q) = s\ (P) + s\ (Q) - (s\ (P) * s\ (Q))$$

More accurate estimations of selectivity factors for selection predicates require detailed statistical information, which permits relaxing the assumptions of uniform distribution of attribute values. These statistics include histograms and distribution steps [Pietetsky84].

The estimation of the selectivity factor of the join operation is impractical in general. Some systems use the upper-bound value of 1, which is tantamount to equating the join to a Cartesian product. This approach is incorrect. However, there exists a frequent case of join where the join selectivity factor can be simply computed. This case involves an equi-join based on the key of one relation, say $R1$, and the foreign key of another one, say $R2$. The join selectivity factor can be approximated as $1/\text{card}(R2)$, which is an upper bound (this assumes that each tuple of $R1$ participates in the join). Applying this rule to the join of relations PRODUCER and HARVEST on attribute P# will predict the cardinality of the join to be the cardinality of relation PRODUCER. It is the correct selectivity factor (and not an upper bound) if all producers have produced at least one wine.

Considering the major impact of joins on the performance of query processing, an important question is whether it is a good investment to maintain join selectivity factors for the important joins not on foreign keys as part of statistical information. A negative answer to that question is established in [Kumar87] in which experiments show that the optimal plan for most join queries is insensitive to the inaccuracy of the join selectivities. Therefore an important conclusion is that crude join selectivity estimates, as done by most query optimizers, are sufficient.

The estimation of the cardinalities of the result of other operations is often restricted to upper bounds, which are easy to compute. Duplicate elimination, which can reduce significantly the cardinality of an operand relation, is an interesting but difficult case [Gelenbe82].

9.7.3 Reduction Approach

The reduction approach dynamically generates and executes the query processing tree [Wong76]. An important characteristic of this approach is that all kinds of JPTs can be produced. This approach has been implemented in INGRES [Stonebraker76]. This algorithm uses simple heuristics in the choice of the first operations and takes into account the actual size of the intermediate results to order the subsequent operations. This algorithm need not manage statistical information for the evaluation of the execution plans.

The input to the algorithm is a calculus query. Thus the decomposition and optimization phases (shown in Fig. 9.2) are combined. The reduction algorithm first executes the unary (monovariable) operations and tries to minimize the sizes of intermediate results in ordering binary operations.

The basic assumption is that the cost of an operation is proportional to the size of the operand relations. The reduction algorithm replaces an N relation query Q by a series of queries $Q1 \rightarrow Q2 \rightarrow \ldots \rightarrow QN$, where each query Qi uses the result of the query $Qi - 1$. It is mainly based on two query transformation techniques, *detachment* and *substitution*.

Definition 9.12 Detachment
Transformation that divides a query into two subqueries, each having a single common relation.

With the detachment, a query Q may be decomposed into two successive queries Q' and Q'', each having only one relation in common, which is the result of Q'. The detachment enables the simpler operations to appear. These operations are selections and semijoins, the only operations that can be detached. The selections are easily recognized because they are monorelation. The semijoins are isolated by looking at the relation connection graph of the query. Any arc that divides the graph into two disjoint subgraphs enables the query processor to decompose the query into two subqueries linked by a semijoin.

Not all the queries can be decomposed by detachment. A query in which no detachment is possible is said to be *irreducible*. The semijoins are irreducible; a fortiori, the joins are irreducible. Furthermore cyclic queries are irreducible [Bernstein81]. Irreducible queries are converted into monorelation queries by *tuple substitution*.

Definition 9.13 Tuple substitution
Transformation of an N relation query Q in a set of queries of $(N - 1)$ relations by replacing one relation by its actual tuples.

The recursive application of tuple substitution until the chain of all queries is monorelation can be seen as a general nested-loop solution. For example, the application of tuple substitution to query Q $(R_1, R_2 \ldots, R_n)$, where R_i is a relation, can lead to the following nested-loop evaluation (described in Pascal-like formalism):

```
for each tuple t₁ in R₁
    for each tuple t₂ in R₂
        •
        •
        •
            for each tuple tₙ in Rₙ
```

$$\textbf{if } (P(t_1, t_2, \dots, t_n) \textbf{ then}$$
$$\text{apply } F(t_1, t_2, \dots, t_n)$$

where P is a predicate and F is the function defining the effect of Q.

Each step of application of tuple substitution corresponds to one "for each" statement. In order to generate the smaller number of subqueries, the relation chosen to be substituted is the one with the smaller cardinality. Since the processing tree is dynamically executed, the exact cardinalities of the operand relations (already computed) are available.

The reduction algorithm applied to a given query Q can be summarized as follows:

1. Detach all separable subexpressions in Q (selections and semijoins) into subqueries.
2. Execute all monorelation subqueries (selections) generated by step 1.
3. Apply tuple substitution recursively to the remaining n-relation subqueries by increasing order of substituted relation cardinalities.

We illustrate this algorithm with the following example query on the WINES database: "Names of wines produced in Bourgogne." The query expressed in SQL is:

(Q5)   SELECT W.VINEYARD
        FROM   WINE W, PRODUCER P, HARVEST H
        WHERE   W.W# = H.W# AND
                H.P# = P.P# AND
                P.REGION = "Bourgogne"

One selection can be detached, thereby replacing Q5 by Q51 followed by Q5′, where P1 is an intermediate relation.

(Q51)   P1 = SELECT P.P#
             FROM   PRODUCER P
             WHERE   P.REGION = "Bourgogne"

(Q5′)   SELECT W.VINEYARD
             FROM   WINE W, P1 P, HARVEST H
             W.W# = H.W# AND
             H.P# = P.P#

After successive detachments, query Q5′ may be replaced by the following two subqueries:

(Q52)   H1 = SELECT   H.W#
              FROM   P1 P, HARVEST H
              WHERE   H.P# = P.P#

(Q53)   SELECT   W. VINEYARD
              FROM   WINE W, H1 H
              WHERE   W.W# = H.W#

Query $Q5$ has been replaced by the sequence $Q51 \rightarrow Q52 \rightarrow Q53$. Query $Q51$ is monovariable and is executed as is. Queries $Q52$ and $Q53$, which are not monovariable, must be reduced further by tuple substitution.

The execution of monorelation queries generated by the reduction algorithm exploits the existing access paths to the relations. The result of a monovariable query may be stored with a particular file organization for optimizing the processing of the subsequent operation. For instance, the result of a selection operation followed by a join (generated by tuple substitution) will be stored in a file hashed on the join attribute so that a hash-based join algorithm may be used.

The reduction approach exhibits several advantages: it is relatively simple, it does not require statistics to be maintained about the database; and the dynamic ordering of joins based on exact cardinalities of relations minimizes the probability of generating a bad execution of a query. There are, however, serious problems with this approach. The systematic execution of selections before joins may lead to low performance (for example, if selections have bad selectivity). The main disadvantage is that decomposition and optimization, two expensive tasks that require access to schema information, are done at run time and must be repeated for every execution of the same query.

9.7.4 Exhaustive Search Approach

Exhaustive search of the solution space is the most popular approach because it is cost-effective. It was first developed in System R [Selinger79]. This approach performs static optimization based on statistical information. The originality of the algorithm proposed in [Selinger79] is threefold: (1) it takes into account IO cost, CPU cost, and existing access paths, (2) it does not apply systematically the heuristic that pushes all selections down the tree because it can have a dramatic effect on performance, and (3) it considers the ordering of the result tuples produced by an execution plan. In this section, we describe the algorithm in [Selinger79]. A calculus query is first decomposed into a relational algebra tree using the techniques presented in Section 9.5. The transformation rules presented in Section 9.6 are then used to generate alternative processing trees, each corresponding to an execution plan. The query processor attempts to choose the best execution plan for the query by predicting the cost of each candidate processing tree. Because the number of candidate trees can be large, some of them are ignored. A first heuristic is to eliminate all trees involving Cartesian products (the most expensive operation). Furthermore when two joins are equivalent by commutativity, only the cheapest one is kept. Finally selection operations must be done either before a join operation or during the processing of the join, in which case the selection predicate is tested when the join predicate is satisfied [Blasgen77]. The cost of each candidate execution plan is evaluated by the formula: Cost = IOs + W * instructions. This general cost function measures the disk access time (IOs) and the CPU time (instructions). W is a coefficient, adjustable according to the system, between IO time and CPU time. Thus the choice of the plan of minimal cost for processing a query minimizes resource utilization.

The calculation of cost takes into account index selectivity and access path properties. Statistics regarding relations, attributes, and indexes are used to assign a selectivity factor to each of the disjunctions of predicates of the query. The product of the selectivity factors by the cardinalities of the relations gives the cardinality of the query's result.

The exhaustive search approach can be viewed as searching for the best strategy among all possible strategies. The possible strategies for executing a query are generated by permutation of the join ordering. With n relations, there are $n!$ possible permutations. The algorithm can be conceptually seen as:

> **for each** n! permutations **do**
>   **begin**
>   build the best strategy to join $R_1, \ldots, R_n$
>   compute cost
>   **end**
>   select strategy of minimum cost

The System R algorithm does not actually generate all $n!$ permutations. The permutations are produced dynamically by constructing a tree of alternative strategies. For each pair of strategies for joining two relations equivalent by commutativity, the strategy of highest cost is dropped.

We now detail the System R algorithm. The query processor first takes into consideration the selection operation and determines the cheapest access path to a relation by evaluating each possible access path. The cost of each access path and the order it produces are predicted. This order is useful for queries whose results need to be sorted or grouped in that order or if duplicate elimination is required for the final projection. Two access paths of minimal cost are then considered: the cheapest access path, which gives the sorted tuples in a useful order, and the cheapest access path, which does not generate any order. The cost of an access path requires the calculation of the selectivity factor based on statistics shown in Section 9.7.2.

If the query is monorelation and the order of the result is unimportant, the cheapest access path is chosen. If the order of the resulting tuples is required or if the query contains joins, the cost of the cheapest access path that gives a useful order is to be compared with the cost of the cheapest access path added to the cost of sorting the resulting tuples. The cheapest alternative is selected in the execution plan.

The optimization then takes into consideration the joins so as to choose between two algorithms to process them, one of which is optimal in a given context. These two algorithms are the nested-loop join algorithm and the sort-merge join algorithm.

The evaluation of the cardinality of a join result is simple and is calculated in the same way as the product of the operand cardinalities divided by the constant 10. That amounts to assuming that the result of a join is large but still smaller than the result of the Cartesian product. This estimation can be largely inaccurate.

In the dynamic construction of alternative join orderings, first, the join of each relation based on its best monorelation access path with every other relation is considered. For each pair of equivalent binary joins (R, S) and (S, R), the one of minimum cost is kept. Then joins of three relations are considered. For each pair of joins (R, S, T) and (R, T, S), the one of minimum cost is kept. The algorithm proceeds until joins of n relations have been treated.

We illustrate this algorithm by applying it to query Q5 from Section 9.7.3. Let us assume the following indexes on the relations involved in Q5:

WINE: index on W#,
PRODUCER: index on P#, index on REGION,
HARVEST: index on W#, index on P#.

Let us assume that the best monorelation access paths to these relations for Q5 are

WINE: sequential scan,
PRODUCER: index on REGION,
HARVEST: sequential scan.

There are 3! possible join orders for that query:

1. WINE × PRODUCER ⋈ HARVEST
2. PRODUCER × WINE ⋈ HARVEST
3. HARVEST ⋈ WINE ⋈ PRODUCER
4. HARVEST ⋈ PRODUCER ⋈ WINE
5. WINE ⋈ HARVEST ⋈ PRODUCER
6. PRODUCER ⋈ HARVEST ⋈ WINE

Strategies 1 and 2 are ignored by the algorithm because they contain a Cartesian product. Among the remaining strategies, all strategies but number 6 require a sequential scan of the first relation and indexed access to the other relations. Only strategy 6 has indexed access to all three relations. Assuming that the predicate REGION = "Bourgogne" has good selectivity, strategy 6 is chosen by the query processor.

The exhaustive search approach is used in many commercial systems because it is cost-effective. The compile time optimization of a query can be amortized over multiple executions. The algorithm, however, is complex. For a query involving n relations, the worst-case time complexity of the algorithm is $O(n!)$, which is prohibitive when n is large (e.g., n equals 10). The use of dynamic programming and heuristics, as in System R, reduces the complexity to $O(2^n)$, which is still significant. Current relational DBMSs assume n to be small, which makes this approach practical. To handle the case of complex queries, the optimization process itself must be efficient.

9.7.5 Efficient Optimization Approach

Recently approaches to efficient query optimization have been proposed [Ibaraki84, Krishnamurthy86] in order to handle complex queries with a large number of relations without incurring the complexity of the exhaustive search approach. As with the exhaustive search approach, the objective is to perform static optimization at compile time. In this section, we illustrate the approach by introducing the algorithm in [Krishnamurthy86]. This algorithm determincs the optimal join order for an important subset of queries, the tree queries, in time $O(n^2)$ where n is the number of relations. Furthermore it can handle cyclic queries.

To simplify the presentation, we limit the description of the basic algorithm to the case of linear join processing trees (LJPTs). A LJPT is a JPT with a linear structure where each join has at most one temporary relation as input. Fig. 9.12 shows an example of an LJPT. An LJPT provides a total order of the joins, called the *LJPT sequence*. The cost of each join algorithm is assumed to be of the form card($R1$) * g (card($R2$)), where g is peculiar to the join algorithm. As we shall see in Section 9.8, some algorithms cannot be captured with this generic cost function. Again this assumption is for ease of presentation. An interesting consequence of the assumptions of tree query and this generic form of g function is that the choice of a join algorithm for a given node can be done independent of the choices for other nodes.

The optimization problem can be seen as searching the query processing tree with minimum cost. We denote by s_i the selectivity factor of the join of Ri with its parent. For instance, in Fig. 9.12, s_2 is the selectivity factor of the join of $R1$ and $R2$. The cost of an LJPT for a query Q on n relations is [Krishnamurthy86]:

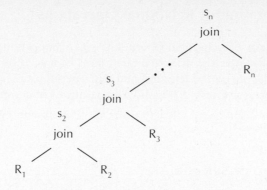

FIGURE 9.12 Example of linear JPT

$$\text{cost of LJPT (Q)} = \sum_{j=2}^{n} \left(\prod_{i=1}^{j-1} [s_i * \text{card } (R_i)] \quad * g_j(\text{card}(R_j)) \right).$$

The recursive rewriting of this equation is shown to satisfy the adjacent sequence interchange property (ASI property in [Monma79]). A consequence is that the ordering of two subsequences of joins can be decided independent of the rest of the sequence. The decision is based on a rank function defined only for the subsequences. The rank of a subsequence measures the increase in the intermediate result, normalized by the cost of doing the joins in the subsequence. For optimality, this rank must be minimized. Because of the ASI property of the cost function, an optimal sequence for the LJPT can be obtained in $O(n^2 \log n)$ time [Ibaraki84]. The method consists of computing the cost of the processing tree for each choice of the root of the tree. However, the method of [Ibaraki84] assumes only one join algorithm (the nested-loop join algorithm). The more general and efficient method in [Krishnamurthy86] exploits the commonalities between two choices for the root and avoids duplicate work. This method has an $O(n^2)$ time complexity.

Finally, the latter method extends to other classes of PTs, including other operations. It can be extended with heuristics to handle cyclic queries as well. In this case, the algorithm does not necessarily select the optimal solution but avoids the worst solution.

Although the time complexity of the algorithm is appealing, the performance of the algorithm is traded off against generality. The two main limitations of the algorithm are the linearity of the cost function (*g* function) and the heuristics for handling cyclic queries. Note that the reduction and exhaustive search approaches do not have such limitations. Research is ongoing to extend the applicability of efficient optimization methods.

9.8 Implementation of Relational Operations

The implementation of relational operations is an important aspect of query processing since these are the primitive operations of a relational system. In this section, we concentrate on the selection and join operations. The implementation of other operations is not very different. All operations of complexity O(card (R) * log card (R)) as shown in Section 9.3.2 can be implemented in a way similar to join [Bratbergsengen84].

9.8.1 Execution of Selections

The clustering of data in a file is generally done in a way that optimizes the selection operation. The efficiency of the selection operation relies heavily on the presence of indexes on the attributes involved in restriction predicates. However, there are cases where indexes are not useful. A good example is when the selection has bad selectivity (75 percent tuples satisfy the restriction qualification). The access of tuples through indexes would incur more IOs than scanning sequentially the pages containing the tuples. Furthermore the file containing the selected relation may be sequential. Thus we can distinguish two different algorithms for performing selection: sequential scanning and use of indexes.

Selection without Index
Sequential scanning requires that every tuple of the operand relation be compared with the selection qualification. If the qualification is true, then the useful attributes are kept in an intermediate relation. This method implements restriction and projection (without duplicate elimination). Filter processors have been proposed to accomplish such an operation as the data are read either from disk or main memory [Bancilhon80, Faudemay85].

Selection with Index
We now consider the case where indexes on selection attributes are useful. We keep the presentation independent of the index implementation. The only assumption is that an index associates attribute values with addresses (logical or physical), which we will refer to as tuple identifiers (TIDs).

  If all the attributes of the qualifications are indexed, then the execution of selection is done by intersections and unions of lists of TIDs. Consider relation WINE assuming that each attribute has a (secondary or clustered) index. The following selection:

(VINEYARD = "Chablis") and (VINTAGE > 1980) and (PERCENT = 12)

can be processed by the following set operations on lists of TIDS:

$$C \cap (V1 \cup V2) \cap P$$

where

C is the list of TIDs of wine "Chablis"
V1 is the list of TIDs of wines "1981"
V2 is the list of TIDs of wines "1982"
P is the list of TIDs of wines with "percent = 12"
there are no wines after 1982.

The intersection operations have to be performed in order of increasing sizes of lists in order to reduce execution time [Apers82].

When not all attributes are indexed, the best algorithm is first to access the indexes in order to find the TIDs of potential tuples and then to access these tuples in order to test the remaining predicates; however, this is not feasible when a predicate on a nonindexed attribute is in disjunction of all other predicates.

9.8.2 Execution of Joins

As with selection, we can distinguish between two types of algorithms depending on the presence of indexes on the join attribute. In the following, we review the principles of the basic join algorithms without index and with index. We consider the join of two relations R_1 and R_2 on attributes A from R_1 and B from R_2. We will denote by $|R_1|$ and $|R_2|$ the number of pages in relations R_1 and R_2, respectively. Also we will assume that $|R_1| < |R_2|$.

Join without Index

In the absence of an index on join attribute, there are four methods to perform join: nested loop, sort-merge, hashed, and semijoin method.

The nested-loop join algorithm [Gotlieb75] is the simplest. For each tuple of relation R_1, each tuple of relation R_2 is sequentially accessed, and a joined tuple is formed if the two tuples match. The IO time of this algorithm is the time to read entirely R_1 and, for each page of R_1, the time to read entirely R_2. Therefore its IO time is:

$$|R_1| + (|R_1| * |R_2|)$$

which is prohibitive when R_1 and R_2 are large. The nested-loop join algorithm can be easily extended to a pipelined n-ary join algorithm [Kim80]. For each tuple of relation R_1, for each tuple of relation R_2, . . . , for each tuple of relation R_{n-1}, each tuple of R_n is accessed, and a joined tuple is formed if the n-ary join predicate is satisfied. This algorithm has the value of not generating temporary relations.

The sort-merge join algorithm [Blasgen77] consists of sorting both relations on the join attribute and completing the join operation by a merge-type operation. The IO time of this algorithm is:

$$2 * |R_1| * \log |R_1| + 2 * |R_2| * \log |R_2| + |R_1| + |R_2|$$

Because of its logarithmic complexity, the sort-merge join algorithm is efficient relative to other algorithms when the sizes of the operand relations are large [Valduriez84].

The hashed join algorithm, as introduced in [Stonebraker76], consists of two phases. In the first, one of the operand relations is hashed on the join attribute. Such a hashed relation can be the output of a previous selection operation. In the second phase, the other relation is sequentially scanned, and for each tuple, the hashed relation is accessed using its join attribute value, and the matching tuples are thus retrieved. Assuming that each data page contains k tuples and that the time to create the hashed relation (supposed to be R_1) is $2 * |R_1| * IO$, the IO time of this algorithm is:

$$(2 * |R_1|) + |R_2| + (k * |R_2|)$$

If k is not high, the hashed join algorithm has linear complexity.

The second phase of this algorithm can be optimized by using bit arrays [Babb79] constructed during the first phase. An array of n bits is initialized to 0. Each bit addressed by a hashed function $g(A)$ is marked to 1. During the second phase, the hashed relation is accessed only if $g(B) = 1$. If j is the average number of matching tuples per page of R_2, the IO time of this algorithm becomes:

$$(2 * |R_1|) + |R_2| + (j * |R_2|)$$

This optimization is obviously worthwhile if $k > j$, which is often the case.

The join algorithm using semijoins [Valduriez82] replaces the join of the relations R_1 and R_2 by the join of their semijoins. The value of this algorithm is that semijoin operations can be implemented efficiently in a way similar to selection. Therefore the join operation, which is more costly, processes only useful tuples. Like the use of bit arrays, this algorithm is better than others when the join has good selectivity.

Join with Index

We present the join algorithms that have been proposed in case of the presence of an index on join attribute of one relation, indexes on join attributes of the two relations, and join index [Valduriez87].

When one of the operand relations has a (secondary or clustered) index on join attribute, two algorithms exist. The first [Blasgen77] is similar to the hashed join algorithm, except that the hashed file is now an indexed file. The relation whose attribute is not indexed is sequentially scanned, and for each tuple, the other relation is accessed through the index on join attribute. The number of accesses per tuple depends on the implementation of the index (see Chapter 2).

The second algorithm [Gotlieb75] works when there is a secondary index on the join attribute of one relation. The idea is to build dynamically a secondary index for the other relation, ordered like the existing index. Then the two indexes can be merged to produce a set of couples (TID1, TID2) such that TID1 and TID2 are identifiers of tuples of R_1 and R_2 that satisfy the join predicate. The join operation is completed by accessing relations R_1 and R_2 based on the TIDs (used as addresses). This algorithm is efficient when the join has good selectivity (the set of (TID1, TID2) is small). The cost of dynamically creating a secondary index is estimated to be 25 percent of the cost of the operation [Gotlieb75].

When both relations have an index on join attribute, a simple algorithm [Blasgen77] consists of merging the two indexes (sorted on join attribute) to produce a set of couples (TID1, TID2) of matching tuples. The join operation terminates as in the previous algorithm.

All the preceding join algorithms with index try to take advantage of indexes primarily designed for optimizing selection operations. In [Valduriez87a], we proposed a simple data structure, called a join index, designed solely for optimizing joins. A join index on relations R_1 and R_2 is a relation of couples (TID1, TID2) where TID1 and TID2 are identifiers of matching tuples of R_1 and R_2, respectively. An example of a join index is given in Fig. 9.13. The small size and simplicity of join indexes provide opportunities for efficient implementation. Join indexes appear to be efficient for performing complex relational queries involving joins [Valduriez87a], for performing recursive queries [Valduriez86a], and for supporting complex objects [Valduriez86b]. Further they allow efficient

WINE

TID1	W#	VINEYARD	VINTAGE	PERCENT
1	121	VOLNAY	1978	12
2	110	CHABLIS	1980	12.5
3	150	TOKAY	1982	11.5
4	101	VOLNAY	1979	12

HARVEST

TID2	P#	W#	QTY
1	10	110	500
2	15	101	200
3	20	150	800

JOIN INDEX

TID1	TID2
2	1
3	3
4	2

FIGURE 9.13 Example of join index

processing of complex queries where the most complex part of the query can be done on indexes (smaller than the base relations) [Valduriez87b].

9.9 Conclusion

In this chapter, we have presented the basic concepts and algorithms for query processing. This study has been done in the context of queries expressed in relational calculus or relational algebra. Because of its complexity, query processing is divided into three main phases: decomposition, optimization (which can be followed by access plan generation), and execution.

The objective function is generally a combination of IO time and CPU time. Although IO time is the dominating factor affecting performance, CPU time becomes significant when in the presence of large memories and complex queries. Performance evaluation of System R's optimizer [Mackert86] has shown the significant impact of CPU time on performance.

Important inputs to the query optimization problem are database statistics and formulas to estimate the size of intermediate results. There is a direct trade-off between the accuracy (and cost of maintenance) of statistics and performance. The critical operation is generally the join of relations. For most frequent joins not on foreign keys, join selectivity factors are of great benefit. The use of statistics can be avoided by applying heuristics to transform a query. However, it has long been recognized [Epstein80] that exhaustive search of the solution space, based on statistics, significantly outperforms the heuristics approach. The overhead incurred by exhaustive searches is rapidly amortized if the query is complex or frequently executed. The main drawback of the exhaustive search approach is the combinatorial complexity of the algorithm, which is impractical for queries on a large number of relations. Approaches to efficient optimization have been recently proposed [Krishnamurthy86].

An important component of query optimization is join ordering. We have seen techniques that take advantage of existing access paths. Distributed database systems use extensively the semijoin operator to help processing joins. Semijoins are beneficial only when the join has good selectivity, in which case they act as powerful size reducers. Semijoin has been shown to be useful also in relational database systems implemented on multiprocessor architectures in [Valduriez82, Valduriez84]. Another promising approach for solving join queries is through the use of auxiliary and small data structures, called join indexes [Valduriez87a], that can minimize both CPU time and IO time.

We have concentrated on join queries for two reasons: they are the most frequent queries in the relational framework, and they have been extensively studied. Furthermore the number of joins involved in queries expressed in languages of higher expressive power than relational calculus can be extremely large, making the join ordering more crucial [Krishnamurthy86]. The optimization of

general queries containing joins, unions, and aggregate functions is a more difficult probem [Selinger80].

9.10 References and Bibliography

[Aho79] Aho A. V., Sagiv Y., Ullmann J. D., "Equivalence among Relational Expressions," SIAM Journal of Computing, V8, N2, May 1979, pp. 218 – 46.

[Apers82] Apers P. M. G. "Query Processing and Data Allocation in Distributed Database
Systems," Thesis, Vrije Universiteit, Amsterdam, 1982.

[Babb79] Babb E., "Implementing a Relational Database by Means of Specialized Hardware," ACM TODS, V4, N1, March 1979.

[Bancilhon80] Bancilhon, F., Scholl, M., "Design of a Back-end Processor for a Database
Machine," ACM-SIGMOD Conf., Los Angeles, May 1980.

[Batory79] Batory D. S., "On Searching Transposed Files," ACM TODS, V4, N4, December 1979.

[Bernstein81] Bernstein P. A., Chiu D. M., "Using Semi-Joins to Solve Relational Queries," Journal of the ACM, V28, N1, 1981.

[Blasgen77] Blasgen M. W., Eswaran K. P., "Storage and Access in Relational Data
Bases," IBM Systems Journal, V16, N4, 1977.

[Bratbergsengen84] Bratbergsengen K., "Hashing Methods and Relational Algebra Operations," Int. Conf. on VLDB, Singapore, 1984.

[Ceri84] Ceri S., Pelagatti G., *Distributed Databases: Principles and Systems,* McGraw-
Hill, 1984.

[Copeland85] Copeland G., Khoshafian S., "A Decomposition Storage Model," ACM
SIGMOD Conf., Austin, Texas, May 1985.

[Epstein80] Epstein R., Stonebraker M., "Analysis of Distributed Data Base Processing
Strategies," Int. Conf. on VLDB, Montreal, 1980.

[Faudemay85] Faudemay P., Valduriez P., "Design and Analysis of a Direct Filter with
Parallel Composators," Int. Workshop on DBM, Bahamas, March 1985.

[Gelenbe82]Gelenbe E., Gardy D., "The Size of Projections of Relations Satisfying a
Functional Dependency," Int. Conf. on VLDB, Mexico, September 1982.

[Gotlieb75] Gotlieb L. R., "Computing Joins of Relations," ACM SIGMOD Conf., San
Jose, California, May 1975.

[Ibaraki84] Ibaraki T., Kameda T., "On the Optimal Nesting Order for Computing N-
Relation Joins," ACM TODS, V9, N3, September 1984.

[Jarke84] Jarke M., Koch J. "Query Optimization in Database Systems," ACM Computing Surveys, V16, N2, 1984.

[Jarke85] Jarke M., "Common Subexpression Isolation in Multiple Query Optimization,"
in [Kim85].

[Khoshafian87] Khoshafian S., Boral H., Copeland G., Jagodits T., Valduriez P., "A
Query Processing Strategy for the Decomposition Storage Model," Data Engineering Conf., Los Angeles, February 1987.

[Kim80] Kim W., "A New Way to Compute the Product and Join of Relations," ACM
SIGMOD Conf., Santa Monica, California, May 1980.

[Kim85] Kim W., Reiner D. S., Batory D. S., *Query Processing in Database Systems,*
Springer-Verlag, 1985.

[Krishnamurthy86] Krishnamurthy R., Boral H., Zaniolo C., "Optimization of Non-Recursive Queries," Int. Conf. on VLDB, Kyoto, 1986.

[Kumar87] Kumar A., Stonebraker M., "The Effect of Join Selectivities on Optimal Nesting Order," ACM SIGMOD Record, V16, N1, March 1987.

[Mackert86] Mackert L. F., and Lohman G., "R* Optimizer Validation and Performance Evaluation for Local Queries," ACM SIGMOD Conf., Washington, D.C., 1986.

[Monma79]Monma C. L., Sidney J. B., "Sequencing with Series-Parallel Precedence Constraints," Mathematical Operations Research, N4, 1979.

[Navathe84] Navathe S., Ceri S., Wiederhold G., Jinglie D., "Vertical Partitioning Algorithms for Database Design," ACM TODS, V9, N4, December 1984.

[Niebuhr76] Niebuhr K. E., Smith S. E., "N-ary joins for Processing Query by Example," IBM Technical Disclosure Bulletin, V19, N2, 1976.

[Piatetsky84] Piatetsky-Shapiro G, Connell C., "Accurate Estimation of the Number of Tuples Satisfying a Condition," ACM SIGMOD Conf., Boston, 1984.

[Rosenkrantz80] Rosenkrantz D. J., Hunt H. B., "Processing Conjunctive Predicates and Queries," Int. Conf. on VLDB, Montreal, October 1980.

[Sacco82] Sacco, M. S., Yao S. B., "Query Optimization in Distributed Data Base Systems," in *Advances in Computers,* V21, Academic Press, 1982.

[Selinger79] Selinger P. et al., "Access Path Selection in a Relational Database Management System," ACM SIGMOD Conf., Boston, May 1979.

[Selinger80] Selinger P. G., Adiba M., "Access Path Selection in Distributed Data Base Management Systems," First Int. Conf. on Data Bases, Aberdeen, 1980.

[Smith75] Smith J. M., Chang P. Y., "Optimizing the Performance of a Relational Algebra Database Interface," Comm. ACM, V18, N10, 1975.

[Stonebraker76] Stonebraker M. et al., "The Design and Implementation of Ingres," ACM TODS, V1, N3, September 1976.

[Ullman82] Ullman J. D., *Principles of Database Systems,* Computer Science Press, 1982.

[Valduriez82] Valduriez P., "Semi-join Algorithms for Multiprocessor Systems," ACM SIGMOD Conf., Orlando, Florida, June 1982.

[Valduriez84] Valduriez P., Gardarin G., "Join and Semi-Join Algorithms for a Multiprocessor Database Machine," ACM TODS, V9, N1, 1984.

[Valduriez86a] Valduriez P., Boral H., "Evaluation of Recursive Queries Using Join Indices," EDBS Int. Conf., Charleston, 1986.

[Valduriez86b] Valduriez P., Khoshafian S., Copeland G., "Implementation Techniques of Complex Objects," Int. Conf. on VLDB, Kyoto, 1986.

[Valduriez87a] Valduriez P., "Join Indices," ACM TODS, V12, N2, June 1987.

[Valduriez86b] Valduriez P., "Optimization of Complex Queries Using Join Indices," Database Engineering, IEEE, V9, N4, Special Issue on Query Optimization, December 1987.

[Wong76] Wong E., Youssefi K., "Decomposition — A Strategy for Query Processing," ACM TODS, V1, N3, September 1976.

[Yy84] Yu C. T., and Chang C. C., "Distributed Query Processing," ACM Computing Surveys, V16, N4, 1984.

10

DEDUCTIVE
DATABASES

10.1 Introduction

In this chapter, we study the extension of the relational model to support deductive capabilities. Relational database technology is now well mastered, and relational DBMSs are being used successfully in industry, banking, and administration. Relational databases are increasing in size and complexity, and programs written around the database using classical languages or fourth-generation languages are more and more numerous and intelligent. To facilitate application development, to avoid multiple developments of similar programs with closed functionalities, and to provide reasoning capabilities on symbolic data, it is often desirable to integrate into the database a definition of common knowledge shared by different users. The database then becomes a knowledge base although a knowledge base often includes complex objects (see Chapter 11) and not just classical relations.

The common knowledge to be integrated in the database may be expressed as rules. Rules define deduced (also called derived) relations. Deduced relations are a generalization of the view concept studied in Chapter 6. A rule is a conditional statement of the form if <condition> then <deduced relation>. The tuples stored in the database relations constitute the extensional database; the rules define the intensional database, which is composed of deduced relations. The objective is to integrate as much knowledge as possible in the intensional database in such a way that application programs necessary to perform a given task remain small and easy to write. Sharing the rules in the database is a rational way to share the enterprise knowledge.

Another point of view that may be considered is derived from logic programming, a programming art (or science) characterized by rule-based languages, mainly PROLOG. PROLOG may be seen as a Horn clause–based programming language or simply as a language to declare subprograms calling each other in a top-down manner. The idea of deductive databases is to introduce the logic programs in a common knowledge base shared by the different users, as the database is. A deductive DBMS will have to manage both the shared rules and data in a consistent and efficient way. It should supply easy and safe commands to update and query the extensional relations, the intensional relations, and also the meta-data, including the rules.

Managing large knowledge bases, with thousands of rules and gigabytes of facts, is not easy. Complex research problems must be solved. These problems are at the crossroads of artificial intelligence and databases. They are both theoretical and practical. From a theoretical point of view, the approaches using logic entail a good understanding of data and rule models. From a practical point of view, the approaches with prototypes should yield important developments that can be used to experiment with knowledge base management systems (KBMSs) that support not only relations and rules but also complex objects.

In this chapter, we examine deductive DBMSs and the research being done to extend relational technology with rules. This chapter requires a good understanding of logic (see Chapter 1). First, we clarify what a deductive database is. Second, we concentrate on the rule definition language. Third, we introduce deductive query processing and present an overview of connection graphs proposed to model rule executions. Fourth, we concentrate on recursive rule processing and introduce the various methods devised to optimize recursive queries. In the last section, we describe the possible architectural approaches to extend a relational DBMS with deductive capabilities. In conclusion, we point out a number of problems.

10.2 What Is a Deductive Database?

10.2.1 From Logic to Deductive Databases

Historically a relational database was considered a model of a first-order logic (FOL). In this view, the *model theoretic approach,* FOL formulas represent queries or integrity constraints [Gallaire78]. A predicate name in a formula corresponds to a relation name. The database values are understood as a set of constants that satisfies the FOL formulas.

> **Definition 10.1 Model theoretic approach**
> Logical comprehension of a database as a model of a set of first-order logic formulas.

Thus the database is a set of predicate instances that corresponds to an interpretation of the first-order language. For example, the wine database will be understood as three predicates: WINE(. . .), DRINK(. . .), and DRINKER(. . .). A given database instance corresponds to a logical interpretation of these three predicates as given in Fig. 10.1. Queries are treated as expressions that are true or false with respect to the database. More precisely, as detailed in Chapter 4 (Section 4.6), a query is an expression of the form $\{X|W(X)\}$ where X is a vector (or tuple) of domain variables and $W(X)$ an FOL formula in which X are the only free variables. The semantics of the query is to find all X values in the interpretation that satisfy W. For example, the query:

$$\{X|WINE(X) \wedge X.VINEYARD = \text{"VOLNAY"}\}$$

retrieves all the X tuples satisfying the formula (being a WINE of vineyard Volnay). Although the model theoretic approach is simple, it is limited, notably to model views, null values, negative queries (i.e., queries with a negative predicate, such as $\{X|\neg DRINKER(X)\}$, and disjunctive information (for example, the wine 100 is of vineyard VOLNAY or CHABLIS).

Inference techniques developed in first-order logic found applications in the relational database area. For this purpose, it appeared necessary to model a database as a set of logic formulas that can be used for inferring new formulas. This yields the *proof theoretic approach* [Reiter78, Gallaire78].

Definition 10.2 Proof theoretic approach
Logical comprehension of a database as a set of axioms of a first-order theory.

In this approach, the database is seen as a set of FOL axioms that defines a generalized relational theory. At first glance, the theory corresponding to the wine database instance of Fig. 10.1 would be the following set of formulas:

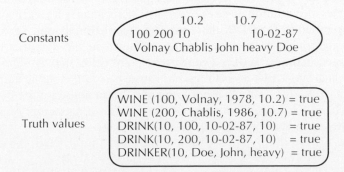

Constants	10.2 10.7 100 200 10 10-02-87 Volnay Chablis John heavy Doe
Truth values	WINE (100, Volnay, 1978, 10.2) = true WINE (200, Chablis, 1986, 10.7) = true DRINK(10, 100, 10-02-87, 10) = true DRINK(10, 200, 10-02-87, 10) = true DRINKER(10, Doe, John, heavy) = true

FIGURE 10.1 Database instance as a logical interpretation

WINE(100,Volnay,1978,10.2)
WINE(200,Chablis,1986,10.7)
DRINK(10,100,10-02-87,10)
DRINK(10,200,10-02-87,10)
DRINKER(10,Doe,John,heavy)

To be complete and support general proof methods such as resolution, the theory requires additional axioms. Although a deep knowledge of the additional axioms is not necessary for building deductive DBMSs, it is useful to know that, in addition to encoding the extensional database, the axioms define in particular the equality and uniqueness of names in the database (that is, if two constants are different, they mean different things; for example, a VOLNAY is not a CHAMPAGNE). More precisely, the whole set of the theory axioms [Reiter84] includes:

1. A subset of axioms that are true for every database, called the *initial axioms* (denoted IA). It is composed of (c_1, . . . , c_n denote the database constants):

    a. The *reflexivity, commutativity,* and *transitivity* axioms to define the equality predicate denoted $=(x,y)$ together with an axiom for the substitution of equal terms for each predicate of the FOL (equality must be defined for values and vectors of values).

    b. The *unique name axiom,* which states that names of constants are nonambiguous: $\neg=(c_i,c_j)$ for all i,j.

    c. The *domain closure axiom,* which states that no other value than those recorded in the database domains exists: $\forall x \, (=(x,c_1) \lor \ldots \lor =(x,c_n))$.

2. A subset of axioms that defines the *extensional database.* This is basically a set of formulas of the form $\{A1,A2, \ldots , An\}$, where Ai is a positive ground atomic formula (an atomic formula without variables such as $P(c_1,c_2)$). Disjunctive information and null values are also possible [Reiter84] (formulas such as $P(c_1,c_2) \lor P(c_3,c_4)$, $P(c1,\omega)$ where ω is the null value). The extensional database set of formulas (EDB) constitutes the relation instance axioms. Associated with each predicate P specified in the EDB, there exists a completion axiom. Such an axiom states that no other tuples are contained in the database than those listed in the EDB. It is a generalization of the *closed world assumption,* which states that everything that is true is recorded in the database — in other words, that a fact not known in the database is false [Gallaire84]. Therefore the generalization of the closed world assumption is *the completion axiom,* which is defined as follows:

    a. If $t1,t2, \ldots , tn$ are tuples given for P in the EDB, the completion axiom is: $(\forall X \, P(X)) \rightarrow (=(X,t1) \lor =(X,t2) \lor \ldots \lor =(X,tn))$.

    b. If no tuple is given for P in the EDB, the completion axiom is: $\forall X \, \neg P(X)$.

It has been shown [Reiter84] that every generalized relational theory as defined above is consistent.

A generalized relational theory may be enriched with nonground formulas (formulas with noninstantiated variables) that define the *intensional database* (IDB). A deductive database is the union of an extensional database (a classical one) and of an intensional database.

Definition 10.3 Intensional database
Set of virtual relations defined as logic predicates derived from extensional database predicates using nonground logical formulas.

The IDB may include formulas that define already existing EDB predicates. For simplicity, such formulas are considered integrity constraints, although it could be possible to use them to produce information. The IDB may also include formulas that define new predicates. Such formulas are considered inference rules defining deduced relations. In the simplest languages, Horn clauses of the form

$$Q1 \wedge Q2 \wedge \ldots \wedge Qm \leftarrow P1 \wedge P2 \wedge \ldots \wedge Pn$$

where $m, n \geq 0$ are used to define the intensional database.

Let us give a classical example of a deductive relational database. We assume an extensional database composed of two predicates, one unary predicate defining the domain PERSON and a binary one defining the PARENT relation, the first attribute being the parent of the second. An extensional database may be composed of the following axioms (which represents in logical form the table of contents):

PERSON(John)
PERSON(Paul)
PERSON(Jim)
PERSON(Mary)
PERSON(Julie)
PARENT(John,Paul)
PARENT(Paul,Jim)
PARENT(Mary,Jim)
PARENT(Jim,Julie)

together with the domain closure axioms that state that nothing else is in the database. A possible intentional database may include:

1. Integrity constraints stating that every parent and every child is a person:

$$PERSON(x) \leftarrow PARENT(x,y)$$
$$PERSON(y) \leftarrow PARENT(x,y)$$

2. A deductive axiom defining the grandparent relation:

$$\text{GRANDPARENT}(x,y) \leftarrow \text{PARENT}(x,y) \wedge \text{PARENT}(y,z)$$

3. Two deductive axioms defining the ANCESTOR relation:

$$\text{ANCESTOR}(x,y) \leftarrow \text{PARENT}(x,y)$$
$$\text{ANCESTOR}(x,z) \leftarrow \text{PARENT}(x,y) \wedge \text{ANCESTOR}(y,z).$$

Given a deductive database that includes an extensional part EDB and an intensional part IDB, a query may be considered a theorem to demonstrate. More precisely, a query expressed with relational calculus is of the form $q = \{X \mid W(X)\}$ where X is a vector of variables $x1, x2, \ldots$ The *query answer* is the set of all instances of X for which $W(X)$ may be proved, using the proof theoretic view axioms of the database.

Definition 10.4 Query answer
Set of instances of the free variables $x1, x2 \ldots$ in a formula $W(x1, x2, \ldots)$ representing the query, for which $W(x1, x2, \ldots)$ can be proved using the database axioms.

Formally we may define the answer to the query $q = \{x \mid W(X)\}$ as follows:

$$\text{Answer}(q) = \{X \mid DB \models W(X)\}$$

DB being the set of axioms $IA \cup EDB \cup IDB$.

Theoretically it becomes possible to implement a deductive DBMS as a theorem prover based on a general proof method, such as resolution. To answer a query, the DBMS would have to generate all possible proofs for a given query formula. Two consequences derive from logical proof methods:

1. If the relational language includes infinite domains or function symbols (more precisely, if the Herbrand universe is infinite), the problem of finding the answers to a query might be semidecidable. Thus a deductive DBMS could loop forever if the design does not limit possible values to finite sets.
2. If some axioms in the deductive database are not consistent, it is theoretically possible to infer anything from a deductive database. Thus integrity is important in deductive databases.

Generally the main problem of deductive DBMS technology is designing and implementing inference methods that are more efficient than resolution and work with practical applications.

10.2.2 Practical Importance of Deductive Databases

Since the notion of deductive database is well understood [Gallaire84], system designers have tried to build practical deductive DBMSs. One of the most important problems is to design and implement inference algorithms that are more efficient than resolution to answer queries with large EDBs (fact bases) and large IDBs (rule bases). The objective is the extension of current relational DBMSs with AI technology to supply integrated tools for new applications [Gardarin84].

There are several classes of potential application. Some require the full support of knowledge bases including an intensional database and complex objects. Among the possibilities are CAD/CAM applications, intelligent document management, intelligent training systems, cartography, robot planning, medicine, and military applications. In general, expert system applications with large fact bases are possible candidates for deductive DBMSs.

10.2.3 Functions and Problems of Deductive DBMSs

A deductive DBMS is first a DBMS. Consequently it should supply a data description language to describe fact bases. Such a language allows the database administrator to describe the base predicates (that is, the extensional database relations) $B1$, $B2$, Bn, . . . as well as the associated integrity constraints. A deductive DBMS also offers a data manipulation language that offers functions to query the deductive databases and to update the base predicates (and sometimes the derived predicates). In general, a deductive DBMS (as a classical one) should offer various data description and manipulation language syntaxes. Among them, SQL is a possible candidate.

The new interface offered by a deductive DBMS is mainly a *rule definition language*.

Definition 10.5 Rule definition language
Language to define the deduced relations composing the intensional database.

This language allows the knowledge engineer to specify logical rules to derive deduced relations. In general, rules are grouped in sets called *rule modules* that define one or more deduced relations. After being defined, deduced relations may be queried by end users as classical relations. Such a language may be perceived as an extension of the view definition command of a classical relational DBMS. This extension is important because, in addition to the classical relational algebra with aggregate and arithmetic computations, several new functions are supported:

- Multiple layers of virtual relation derivations.
- Recursion, which allows one to define a relation as a function of itself.
- Negation, which permits one to refer to nonexisting facts.
- Set-valued variables, with nesting and unnesting to transform single values in sets, and conversely.
- Functions, which may be applied to multiple values and defined by the users.
- Updates of multiple relations.
- Metarules and arrangement of rules in successive modules.

The first may already be supported with classical relational DBMSs offering several levels of views, and the third may be partly supported with the inequijoin. However, deductive database technology will extend these. The goal is to automate the programming process to a new extent, allowing the sharing of large sets of knowledge rules among various users. In a sense, these rules should encode under a logical and extendable form all the knowledge currently included in transaction programs. We could even envision that tedious programming tasks will be replaced by knowledge rule definitions.

The design and implementation of a deductive DBMS as an extension of a relational DBMS poses difficult problems. First, a rule language must be chosen. Next, algorithms to maintain the knowledge base consistency when axioms are updated must be devised. Last, it is desirable to answer queries in an efficient way, using rules and facts to infer the responses, without generating useless or redundant facts and also without losing relevant tuples. The efficiency of the inference process with a large volume of rules and facts is probably the most difficult problem. Finally, the system architecture must be specified.

10.3 Rule Definition Language for Databases

10.3.1 Motivations and Informal Presentation

Integrating deductive functionalities within a DBMS requires the development of a rule definition language. Nonprocedural data manipulation languages have been invented to facilitate set-oriented database processing and to avoid navigation in the database structure. Thus a rule language should also be, as much as possible, nonprocedural and set oriented. It should also be easy to interface with a relational DBMS; for instance, a rule program should be directly translatable into relational algebra or tuple relational calculus, extended with programming control structures. In this section, we present a basic rule definition language and then various desirable extensions. The basic language is a pure Horn clause language, without function symbols, called *DATALOG* [Ullman85].

> **Definition 10.6 DATALOG**
> Rule-definition language to specify deduced relations based on Horn
> clauses without function symbols.

For logic programmers, DATALOG may be seen as a variation of PROLOG
with a set-oriented semantics. This semantics makes the result of a program independent of the order of the clauses in the program. It is a completely nonprocedural language based on Horn clauses. A Horn clause is a rule of the form
$Q \leftarrow P1 \wedge P2 \wedge \ldots \wedge Pn$ where Q and Pi are positive literals. It is a disjunction
of literals with a unique positive one (Q) and 0 to n negative ones ($P1$, $P2$, . . . ,
Pn).

Various extensions of DATALOG have been proposed to support:

- Function symbols in the arguments of predicates (DATALOG^{fun}).
- Explicit negation of Pi predicates (DATALOG^{neg}).
- Set-oriented arguments of predicates (DATALOG^{set}).
- Explicit database updates in a rule (DATALOG^{upd}).
- General non-Horn conditions with disjunctions and quantifiers
  (DATALOG^{non}).

We shall study all these extensions. They should be integrated in a unique rule
language DATALOG$^{neg+fun+set+upd+non}$. The LDL1 [Beeri86] and RDL1 [Maindre-
ville87] languages are attempts at forming such an integrated rule language.

10.3.2 Syntax and Semantics of DATALOG

In its basic form, DATALOG is a pure Horn clause language without function
and negation. The definition presented is derived from [Lloyd87].

Syntax of DATALOG
The language alphabet consists of:

Constants a, b, c, . . .
Variables x, y, z, . . .
Relational predicates $R1$, $R2$, . . .
Evaluable predicates denoted by special symbols such as $=$, $<$, $\leq$, $>$,
$\geq$, . . .
Connectives $\vee$, $\wedge$, $\leftarrow$
Punctuation symbols (,), ",", . . .

We assume that there exist a finite number of elements in each class, and at least
one.

From this alphabet, well-formed formulas may be defined inductively. Here we are interested only in Horn clauses, which are special well-formed formulas. A *term* is either a constant or a variable. An *atom* (also called an *atomic formula* or *positive literal*) is an expression of the form $P(t1,t2, \ldots, tn)$ where P is an *n*-ary predicate and $t1,t2, \ldots, tn$ are terms. $<t1,t2, \ldots, tn>$ is called a *tuple* of P. A *ground atom* is an atom not containing variables. Finally, a *rule* is an expression of the form $Q \leftarrow P1 \wedge P2 \wedge \ldots \wedge Pn$, with $n \geq 0$, where Q is an atom built with a relational predicate and Pi are atoms built with any predicate. Q is called the *rule head* (or conclusion), and $P1 \wedge P2 \wedge \ldots \wedge Pn$ is called the *rule body* (or premises). Each Pi is called a *subgoal*, while the conjunction of the Pi is a *goal*. A rule is said to be *recursive* if the head predicate also appears in the body. To simplify rule writing, we shall often replace "$\wedge$" by ",".

Let us give a few examples. John and Peter, 1,2,3 may be constants. PARENT(x,y) is an atom. ANCESTOR(John,Peter) is a ground atom. Examples of rules are:

PARENT(John,Peter) $\leftarrow$
ANCESTOR(x,y) $\leftarrow$ PARENT(x,y)
ANCESTOR(x,y) $\leftarrow$ PARENT(x,z) $\wedge$ ANCESTOR(z,y)
COUSIN(x,y) $\leftarrow$ ANCESTOR(x,z) $\wedge$ ANCESTOR(y,z)

As shown in the examples, a rule may be reduced to a rule head. If all terms are constants in the rule head, it is a fact; for example, PARENT(John,Peter) $\leftarrow$ is a fact. The third rule is recursive as the ANCESTOR predicate of the rule head also appears in the body.

A *DATALOG program* is a set of rules as defined above. We denote a DATALOG program between brackets, with a semicolon separating two rules. The order of the rules is irrelevant. Relational predicates are generally classified into base predicates, instances of which are stored in the extensional relational database, and deduced (or derived) predicates, which are those corresponding to the intensional database. DATALOG allows the user to define both rules and facts. Although the extensional database might be defined with DATALOG, we generally assume that it is specified as an existing relational database; thus DATALOG will be mainly used to specify rules with heads and bodies. The collection of the extensional and the intensional database is called a *logic database* (a deductive database written in logic).

Semantics of DATALOG
The semantics of a DATALOG program may be defined using a declarative or a procedural method. The former method is based on the model theoretic approach, and the latter is derived from resolution [Lloyd87]. In this section, we shall present the least model approach.

An interpretation of an FOL consists of a nonempty set D called the interpretation domain, an assignment for each constant of the alphabet to a corresponding element of *D*, and an assignment for each *n*-ary predicate symbol to a mapping from D^n to {true,false}. A variable assignment with respect to a given interpretation of an FOL is an assignment of each variable to an element of *D*. Being given an interpretation of a FOL and a variable assignment, any formula in FOL (and a rule as such) can be given a truth value (true or false) using classical truth tables [Lloyd87].

A *model* of a logic database is an interpretation in which all rules and facts are true. That means that:

- For each tuple $<t1,t2, \ldots , tn>$ in a relation *B*, $B(t1,t2, \ldots , tn)$ is true in the interpretation.
- For each rule $R(t1,t2, \ldots , tn) \leftarrow P1 \land P2 \land \ldots \land Pn$ and for any variable assignment θ with respect to the interpretation, if $\theta(P1 \land P2 \land \ldots \land Pn)$ is true in the interpretation, then $\theta(R(t1,t2, \ldots , tn))$ is also true.

In other words, a model of a logic database is a set of predicate instances that contain all the tuples of the database and all the tuples that can be inferred from the previous one using the rules.

An interesting property of any DATALOG program is that the intersection of a set of models is still a model. Thus any DATALOG program admits a *least model*, which defines the canonical semantics of the program [Van Emden76].

Definition 10.7 DATALOG program least model
Canonical semantics of a DATALOG program defined as the set of predicate instances that can be inferred from the program and no more.

A simple procedure is available to compute the least model of a DATALOG program [Van Emden76]. The procedure starts with the set *I* of the given facts in the program. Then *I* is augmented by successive applications of a rule. While a rule body can be instantiated with facts in *I* (if there exists a variable assignment θ, which maps the rule body predicate to facts of *I*), the fact corresponding to the instantiated rule head (variables must be replaced by their assigned values) is generated and added to *I*. When no new element can be added to *I*, it is the least model. For example, let us consider the DATALOG program *P*:

$$\{PARENT(John,Peter) \leftarrow; PARENT(Peter,Julie) \leftarrow;$$
$$ANCESTOR)(x,y) \leftarrow PARENT(x,y)\}$$

We can compute successively:

$I = \{$ PARENT(John,Peter), PARENT(Peter,Julie)$\}$
$I = \{$ PARENT(John,Peter), PARENT(Peter,Julie), ANCESTOR(John,Peter)$\}$
$I = \{$ PARENT(John,Peter), PARENT(Peter,Julie), ANCESTOR(John,Peter), ANCESTOR(Peter,Julie) $\}$

As no new element can be produced in I, the least model of P is:

{ PARENT(John,Peter), PARENT(Peter,Julie), ANCESTOR(John,Peter),
ANCESTOR(Peter,Julie) }.

Any derived predicate defined with DATALOG may be queried as a base relation using a classical query language. However, a query may always be defined as a special rule whose head is written "?" and whose body defines the query. As it is always possible to introduce intermediate derived predicates to compute an answer, queries are generally restricted to rules of the form $? \leftarrow R(t1,t2, \ldots , tn)$. The answer to such a query is the set of tuples $\{\theta(t1,t2, \ldots , tn) \mid \theta$ is an assignment of the variables of $t1, t2, \ldots , tn$ and $\theta(t1,t2, \ldots , tn)$ is a tuple of R in the least model of the DATALOG program defining $R\}$. To simplify notation, we shall denote queries simply with a question mark, as follows: $?R(t1,t2, \ldots , tn)$. We may introduce a query in a DATALOG program to specify exactly what must be computed. Indeed a query is a rule with an implicit head to list on the screen.

In conclusion, if one compares DATALOG to relational calculus, it appears that DATALOG includes the power of recursion but not the possibility of negation, while relational calculus includes negation but not recursion. DATALOG has been extended to support negation. Before studying DATALOG with negations, we consider DATALOG^{fun}, the extension of DATALOG with functions to get more expressive power and to be able to develop more interesting examples.

10.3.3 Extending DATALOG with Functions

To increase the expressive power of DATALOG, it is desirable to extend DATALOG with functions that may be invoked in a rule body or a rule head. Examples of functions are system-defined functions such as arithmetic function $(+, -, /, *)$ or more generally mathematical functions (for example, exp and log) or user-defined functions, which can be specified with a functional language such as LISP [Kiernan87] or any other. Functions are important because they lend themselves to complex object manipulation and complex operations; for example, geometric figures can be manipulated using functions. In general, functions allow the system designer to implement abstract data types [Stonebraker86].

From a logical point of view, the extension consists of introducing a new class of elements in the alphabet called function symbols and denoted $f,g,h, \ldots$ Each function symbol has a given arity n, which means that it accepts n parameters. New terms are then built recursively of the form $f(t1,t2, \ldots , tn)$ where each ti is itself a term (which may be built using function symbols). Terms may be used as previously, inside a predicate as an argument. The resulting rule language is called *DATALOG^{fun}*.

> **Definition 10.8 DATALOG with functions (DATALOG^{fun})**
> Extended version of DATALOG in which a predicate argument can be
> a term defined as a constant, a variable, or a function applied to a
> term.

Thus predicates such as $P(a,x,f(x),f(g(x,a)))$, where f is a one-place function and g a two-place function are now possible. The semantics of DATALOG must be extended to support functions. This is done by assigning to each n-ary function symbol a mapping from D^n to D, where D is the interpretation domain.

One problem that becomes important with DATALOG^{fun} is the finiteness of a query answer. A DATALOG query is *safe* if it has a finite answer independent of the database domains (they may be finite or not). The safety problem already exists in pure DATALOG. If domains can be infinite, a simple DATALOG program may return an infinite answer. An example is the following program, where salaries are integers:

$$\{SALARY(100);SUPERIOR(x,y) \leftarrow SALARY(X),x < y; ?SUPERIOR(x,y)\}.$$

To avoid such a confusing program in DATALOG, a syntactic characterization of safe programs (programs that return only safe answers) has been introduced [Zaniolo86] based on the notion of range restricted rules. A rule is *relation range restricted* if all variables of the rule head appear in a relation predicate in the rule body. For example, the rule $SUPERIOR(x,y) \leftarrow SALARY(x)$, $x < y$ is not range restricted because y does not appear in a relation predicate in the rule body. If all rules of a program are relation range restricted, the program is safe. This holds because relation predicates have finite interpretations.

With DATALOG^{fun}, the problem of safety is more fun. For example, the program

$$\{INTEGER(0); INTEGER(X + 1) \leftarrow INTEGER(X) \}$$

is not safe because it generates an infinite predicate (the positive integer); however, it is range restricted. Note, however, that the query ? INTEGER(10) is safe. The answer is true. A method for determining if a query is safe can be found in [Zaniolo86].

It is interesting to compare DATALOG^{fun} with relational algebra. It is straightforward to introduce functions in relational algebra [Zaniolo85]. Indeed it is necessary to include functions in restriction and join qualifications, which are then of the form $s_Q(R)$ and $R1 \bowtie_Q R2$ where Q is a well-formed formula of logic with possible functions (the variables in Q refer to attributes of R, resp. of R_1 and R_2). It is also necessary to include function computations in the projection criteria; thus a projection is of the form $\pi_{t1,t2}, \ldots, {}_{tn} (R)$ where $t1,t2, \ldots, tn$ are terms possibly with functions in logic. The least model of a safe DATALOG^{fun} program can be computed using loops of relational algebra expressions with functions but without difference. Thus DATALOG^{fun} has the power of relational algebra with functions but without difference, plus recursion. It does not have the power of negation.

10.3.4 Extending DATALOG with Negations

There are several reasons to add negation in DATALOG: to improve the expressive power of the language so that it can express relational difference and to represent inferences by default or exceptions [Artificial Int.80]. For example, being given a graph described by a relation GRAPH(ORIGIN,EXTREMITY,LABEL), a recursive rule such as:

$$\text{TRAVEL}(x,y,t) \leftarrow \text{GRAPH}(x,z,t1),\text{TRAVEL}(z,y,t2), t = t1 + t2$$

allows a programmer to perform a graph traversal with label summation. This rule uses a function (+). If we assume that edges recorded in a FORBID (ORIGIN, EXTREMITY) relation cannot be crossed, negation permits us to cross only authorized edges using the following rule:

$$\text{TRAVEL}(x,y,t) \leftarrow \text{GRAPH}(x,z,t1),\text{TRAVEL}(z,y,t2), t = t1 + t2, \neg\text{FORBID}(x,z).$$

More generally, the introduction of negation allows one to write rules of the form $Q \leftarrow L1 \wedge L2 \wedge \ldots \wedge Ln$, where Q is a positive literal and $L1,L2, \ldots, Ln$ are positive or negative literals. A negative literal is of the form $\neg P(t1,t2, \ldots, tn)$, where P is a predicate and $t1,t2, \ldots, tn$, are terms. An extended DATALOG language that supports rule with negated predicate(s) in the rule body is called *DATALOG^{neg}*.

> **Definition 10.9 DATALOG with negations (DATALOG^{neg})**
> Extended version of DATALOG allowing the use of negated predicates in rule bodies.

The semantics of a DATALOG^{neg} program is not easy to define because the least model is dependent on the order of applying the rules during the computation. It is not true that a DATALOG^{neg} program has a unique least model. Indeed it may have several least models. The problem of choosing one to define the canonical semantics of a DATALOG^{neg} program then arises. Let us give a simple example. The program:

$$\{\text{BIRD(Pegase)}; \text{FLY}(x) \leftarrow \text{BIRD}(x), \neg\text{PENGUIN}(x)\}$$

admits two least models: {BIRD(Pegase); PENGUIN(Pegase)} and {BIRD (Pegase);FLY(Pegase)}. Indeed, using logic equivalence, the second rule may be rewritten as $\text{FLY}(x) \vee \text{PENGUIN}(x) \leftarrow \text{BIRD}(x)$, which means that we introduced disjunctive rules; thus there is an ambiguity. There is no rigorous way to eliminate the ambiguity because the intersection of the two models {[BIRD(Pegase)} is not a model for the given program.

Under certain syntactic conditions, it is possible to admit DATALOG^{neg} programs and to define a canonical semantics for them. The basic idea is to divide a logic program with negations into strata, each stratum having a unique least model [Apt86, Naqvi86, Przymusinski86]. A module in DATALOG has been defined as a set of rules. Thus a *stratified program* can be defined as follows.

> ### Definition 10.10 Stratified DATALOG program
> DATALOG program divided in an ordered set of modules $\{S1, S2, \ldots, Sn\}$ called strata, in such a way that each stratum Si enriched with the least model of the previous stratum (if any) has a unique least model.

The idea is simple. Under the condition that negation does not cross a recursion (there cannot exist a predicate A defined from $\neg B$, B being itself defined from A), it is possible to compute the least model of negated predicates (predicate B) without using their negation and then to interpret the negations as a nonmembership test ($\neg B(x)$ will be interpreted as "x does not belong to the instance of B"). In other words, the programmer can use only a literal $\neg B$ in a rule body if B has been completely defined in other rules, independent of the considered rule head. Thus it is possible to divide the program in strata $S_1, S_2, \ldots, S_n$ such that in stratum S_i only predicates defined in strata $S_1, S_2, \ldots, S_{i-1}$ can be negated. It is not possible to stratify a DATALOG^{neg} program when recursion crosses negation.

Let us give a few examples. The programs $\{P(x) \leftarrow \neg P(x)\}$, $\{Q(x) \leftarrow \neg P(x); P(x) \leftarrow \neg Q(x)\}$ are not stratifiable because recursion crosses negation. With these programs, one cannot compute P (or Q) without using $\neg P$ (or $\neg Q$). Indeed, recursion crosses negation. The program $\{Q(x) \leftarrow R(x); P(x) \leftarrow P(x), \neg Q(x)\}$ is stratifiable; two strata are $S1 = \{Q(x) \leftarrow R(x)\}$ and $S2 = \{P(x) \leftarrow P(x), \neg Q(x)\}$. $S1$ computes Q without using $\neg Q$, then $S2$ computes P using $\neg Q$.

Stratifiable programs have a least model that can be characterized in a unique way by defining a predicate order of computation. The order corresponds to a least-model computation stratum by stratum using the closed world assumption at each level. The naturalness of the choice of a least-model model is discussed in [Bidoit86]. Let us give an example of a stratifiable program least model computation. The program $\{R(a); S(b); Q(x) \leftarrow R(x); P(x) \leftarrow \neg Q(x), S(x)\}$ is stratifiable. Predicate P must be computed after Q. Two possible strata are $S1 = \{R(a); Q(x) \leftarrow R(x)\}$ and $S2 = \{S(b); P(x) \leftarrow \neg Q(x), S(x)\}$. The least model of $S1$ is $\{R(a); Q(a)\}$. Starting with this set of facts, we may compute the second stratum $S2$ using the transformed program (negation is interpreted as "not belonging to"): $S2 = \{R(a); Q(a)\} \cup \{S(b); P(x) \leftarrow Q(y), x \neq y, S(x)\}$. The chosen least model of the program is $\{R(a); Q(a); S(b); P(b)\}$.

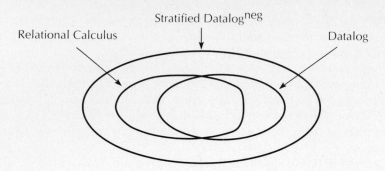

FIGURE 10.2 Comparative power of DATALOG, DATALOG^{neg}, and relational algebra

A comparison of DATALOG^{neg} for stratified programs, pure DATALOG and relational algebra yields the diagram shown in Fig. 10.2. Clearly DATALOG^{neg} is a superset of DATALOG and of relational algebra.

10.3.5 Extending DATALOG with Sets

One interesting feature of relational database languages is the ability to manipulate sets and functions over sets through aggregate operations. Recently several authors have tried to introduce sets in rule languages [Zaniolo85, Beeri86, Kuper86a, Abiteboul87a]. The goal is the ability to manipulate sets of objects, as in non-1NF relations. DATALOG extended with sets is called *DATALOG^{set}*.

> **Definition 10.11 DATALOG with sets (DATALOG^{set})**
> Extended version of DATALOG to manipulate sets of constants referred with set variables.

Let us consider the PART(PART#,SUBPART#) relation expressing the fact that one part is composed of another. To find all the subparts of each part in a relation with two attributes COMPOSED(PART#,SET_OF_SUBPART#) is a useful operation, called *nesting*. The reverse operation is *unnesting*. An example of nest/unnest is given in Fig. 10.3.

There are several ways to build sets with rules. First, we may introduce new domains in the database to support sets of constants. If one tolerates sets of sets, problems with infinite worlds may arise. Thus it is wise to limit domains to one-level sets or at least to a finite number of levels of sets. To avoid confusing set variables and nonset ones, we will use capital letters for sets and lowercase letters for normal element variables, as in [Kuper86a] (this is not necessary but useful for the beginner). To perform the nesting operation, a specific operator, called *grouping,* may be introduced as in [Beeri86]. Grouping puts in a set all values of the variables given in arguments that satisfy the rule body condition. Applied to

PART	TID	ASSEMBLY	SUBASSEMBLY	QTY
	1	locomotive	big	2
	2	locomotive	small	1
	3	big	axle	1
	4	big	big wheel	2
	5	small	axle	1

NEST ↓   ↑ UNEST

PART	TID	ASSEMBLY	<SUBASSEMBLY, QTY>
	1	locomotive	<big, 2> <small, 1>
	2	big	<axle, 1><big wheel, 2>
	3	small	<axle, 1>

FIGURE 10.3 Nesting and unnesting of the part relation

a variable x, it is denoted $<x>$. Thus the nesting of the part relation may be performed using the rule COMPOSED$(x, Y) \leftarrow$ PART(x,y), $Y = <y>$. Given sets and elements, a predicate "member of" (denoted ϵ) may be introduced. Using the "member of" predicate, unnesting is performed by the rule PART(x,y) $\leftarrow$ COMPOSED(x, Y), $y \epsilon Y$. Other predicates may also be introduced, such as strict set inclusion, denoted by $\supset$. Functions on sets are also possible, such as unary aggregate functions (COUNT, MIN, MAX, AVG, . . .) and binary union ($\cup$), intersection ($\cap$), and difference ($-$) functions.

Grouping does not provide more power than functions and negations to the rule language. Indeed if we define the unary interpreted function $\{\} : x \to \{x\}$, which maps an element to the set composed of this element and the binary interpreted function $\cup : X, Y \to X \cup Y$, it is possible to perform nesting as follows.

SPART$(x, Y) \leftarrow$ PART(x,y), $Y = \{y\}$;
SPART$(x, Y) \leftarrow$ SPART(x,Z), SPART(x,T), $Y = Z \cup T$;
COMPOSED$(x, Y) \leftarrow$ SPART(x, Y), $\neg$SPART(x,Z), $Z \supset Y$

Clearly using grouping is a simpler way to express nesting. Also if the system offers a special grouping operator, it has a good chance to be more efficient for performing nesting than if it does not have such an operator.

To conclude, note that the introduction of sets in a DATALOG program requires stratification to define the semantics of the program unambiguously. This is due to the fact that sets are a particular case of negation. The meaning of the necessary stratification may be stated as "compute sets before using them." Thus rules must be partially ordered in strata where grouping operations are performed at first.

10.3.6 Extending DATALOG with Updates

DATALOG is limited in the sense that it is based on Horn clauses. Thus rule heads are limited to a single positive predicate. It is possible to extend heads to include several predicates. There is no difficulty if the predicates appearing in the multiple head are positive. A rule with multiple heads is interpreted as several rules with the same body, one for each head. Another possibility is to tolerate a negative predicate in the head. A possible interpretation for such a predicate is a deletion of tuples corresponding to the instantiated variables satisfying the rule condition. Supporting both multiple heads and negative predicates in the head yields a full support of relation updates in the rule language. We call such a language *DATALOG$^{upd.}$*

| **Definition 10.12 DATALOG with updates (DATALOG^{upd})**
| Extended version of DATALOG to support multiple heads with possible negation in the head.

The following rule is a DATALOG^{upd} rule defined over the database schema {PARENT(ascendant, descendant),ANCESTOR(ascendant, descendant)}: ANCESTOR(x,z),$\neg$ANCESTOR(z,x) ← PARENT(x,y), ANCESTOR(y,z). This rule generates new ancestors but also removes certain possible cyclicities in families (if x is the parent of y and y is the ancestor of z, then x is the ancestor of z and z is not the ancestor of x).

An interpretation of DATALOG^{upd} is possible based on production rules, very popular in expert systems. A *production rule* is an expression of the form condition → action expression. An *action expression* is a sequence of actions where each action may be either a database update or a side effect (for example, send message or execute a procedure). A *condition* is any well-formed formula. When evaluation order is significant, rules are evaluated in an order given by a metarule; for example, choose a priority order given by the rule sequence. Thus a production rule language is not completely declarative but may contain a procedural aspect through the sequence of rules.

A DATALOG^{upd} program may be understood as a production rule system [Maindreville86]. Each production rule is executed up to saturation for each successive instantiation of the variables by tuples appearing in the database satisfying the condition; an execution consists of simultaneously deleting tuples appearing as arguments of negative actions and inserting tuples appearing as arguments of positive actions. The semantics of an action expression $R(r1)$, $R(r2)$, . . . ,$\neg R(s1)$, $\neg R(s2)$ . . . with conflicting updates over the same relation R, is more precisely defined by: $R := R - [\{si\} - \{ri\}] \cup [\{ri\} - \{si\}]$. Thus the order of actions is not important. A DATALOG^{upd} action may delete tuples in predicates that are used in another rule. To avoid ambiguous semantics, we may use an implicit metarule similar to the stratification rule: A deleting rule is evaluated only when all nondeleting rules cannot produce new tuples. Also the programmer can impose an order for rule evaluation, which introduces some procedurality.

10.3.7 Extending DATALOG with Non-Horn Conditions

A classical query language offers disjunctive conditions and quantifiers. Thus there is no reason to limit the body of a rule to a conjunction of predicates. The body can be extended to a general condition. A non-Horn condition over a database schema S is simply a formula of the relational calculus whose predicates are relation schema in S or comparison predicates $<, \leq, =, \geq, >$. The resulting extension of DATALOG is referred to as $DATALOG^{non}$.

> **Definition 10.13 Datalog with non-Horn conditions (DATALOG^{non})**
> Extended version of DATALOG to support formula of the relational calculus in the body of any rule.

In summary, with a fully extended DATALOG, a rule over a database schema S is a sentence of form $A \leftarrow C$ where:

1. C is a relational calculus condition with possibly negated predicates and set variables over the database schema S; the condition part $\leftarrow C$ may be omitted in case of unconditional rules. The relational calculus may use both tuple variables and domain variables.
2. A is an action expression over the database schema S.
3. The only free variables of C are variables of A that must appear in a positive predicate in C.
4. All the quantifiers occurring in C are type-restricted quantifiers (of the form $\forall X \in R$ or $\exists X \in R$.

To simplify the writing of conditions, we introduce *an implicit quantifying* procedure: Any variable that is free in C and does not appear in A is considered existentially quantified. Such an implicit quantification is common in query languages.

For example, to demonstrate the power of a fully extended DATALOG, we solve an electrical circuit problem requiring tuple deletions. This example assumes a relational database composed of a unique relation describing a set of electric circuits as follows: CIRCUIT(Name, Wire, Origin, Extremity, Impedance). *Name* is the name of a given circuit; *Wire* is the number identifying a given wire in a given circuit; the origin and extremity of this wire are given by the two corresponding attributes, and its impedance is defined by the last attribute. The key of the relation CIRCUIT is the couple of attributes {Name, Wire}. A typical problem will consist of computing the impedance of a given circuit. For simplicity, we assume that only the parallel and serial transformations are sufficient to

MODULE WIRE(Name, Wire, Origin, Extremity, Impedance);

   { Copy of the CIRCUIT relation in the WIRE relation for transformation }
   WIRE(X) ← CIRCUIT(X);

   {Parallel transformation rule }
   ¬WIRE(X), ¬WIRE(Y),
   WIRE(X.name, X.wire, X.origin, X.extremity, (X.impedance*
      Y.impedance)/(X.impedance + Y.impedance))
   ← WIRE(X) ∧ WIRE(Y) ∧ X.origin = Y.origin ∧ X.extremity = Y.extremity ∧
      X.wire ≠ Y.wire ∧ X.name = Y.name;
   {Serial transformation rule}
   ¬WIRE(X), ¬WIRE(Y), WIRE(X.name, X.wire, X.origin, Y.extremity,
      X.impedance + Y.impedance)
   ←WIRE(X) ∧ WIRE(Y) ∧ X.extremity = Y.origin ∧ X.name = Y.Name ∧
      COUNT(<X>) = 1 ∧ COUNT(<Y>) = 1;

END.

FIGURE 10.4 Example of a DATALOG$^{set+upd+non}$ program

compute the impedances of all the circuits. These rules consist of replacing two serial wires of impedance $Z1$ and $Z2$ by a unique one of impedance $Z1 + Z2$ and two parallel wires of impedance $Z1$ and $Z2$ by a unique one of impedance $(Z1*Z2 / Z1 + Z2)$. Assuming that the rule language supports the aggregate function COUNT on sets, a module of rules that compute a unique wire for each circuit with the circuit origin, extremity, and impedance is given in Fig. 10.4. The computed relation schema follows the MODULE declaration.

10.4. Deductive Query Processing and Modeling

10.4.1 Bottom-up Query Processing

The simplest solution to evaluating a query answer has two steps: Computing the least model of the DATALOG program and filtering the least model with the query. In the first step, the computation starts from the base predicates containing the facts and generates facts in the derived predicates by successive application of the rules. To apply a rule, the rule variables are instantiated with known facts. This requires the system to evaluate the condition composing the rule body on the known facts; for each instance of variables satisfying the condition, the action (a generation of a new fact) defined by the head predicate is performed. The generation procedure is applied up to saturation of all the derived predicates — that is, up to the point where no rule can produce new facts. Such a

While "There exists a nonsaturated derived relation R" **do**
    begin
                select some rule, r, whose actions apply to R;
                for each database tuples satisfying the condition of r **do**
                        perform the actions of r;
    end;

FIGURE 10.5 Forward-chaining generation process

procedure is known in artificial intelligence as a forward-chaining generation process [Nilsson80]. In Fig. 10.5, we summarize such a process.

During the second step, the query is applied to the generated derived predicate instance as a classical selection This approach starts from the base predicates to compute the instances of the derived predicate and to answer the query. For this reason, it is called a *bottom-up approach*.

Definition 10.14 Bottom-up evaluation
Evaluation technique starting from the database tuples and applying the rules using forward chaining to generate the query answer.

A bottom-up evaluation technique (Fig. 10.6) computes the least model of the logic program; thus it generates the intensional database. The query is applied to this intensional database. The order in which rules are applied is important for at least two reasons:

1. It may change the performance of the generation process. Because rules may interact in various ways (the result of applying one rule may change the condition of another), it is desirable to order them. In the case of a pure DATALOG program, the problem of rule ordering is an extension of query optimization.
2. In case of rules with negations or sets, it is necessary to generate each stratum in the stratification order to obtain a correct model. Moreover, with production rule languages (rules having database updates in rule heads), the result may depend on the order of rule applications.

10.4.2 Top-down Query Processing

Instead of starting from the extensional databases to generate query answers, it is possible to start from the query. The idea is to use the result pattern (predicate name and constants) given in the query and to push it through the rule in backward direction up to the database to see how it can be generated. Such a procedure is known in artificial intelligence as backward chaining [Nilsson80]. If data-

DATALOG PROGRAM WITH QUERY
(r1) PARENT(x,z) ⟵ MOTHER(x,z)
(r2) PARENT(x,z) ⟵ FATHER(x,z)
(r3) GRANDPARENT(x,z) ⟵ PARENT(x,y) ∧ PARENT(y,z)
(q)   ? GRANDPARENT(x,John)

DATABASE

MOTHER	ASC	DESC
	Mary	John
	Julie	Mary
	Julie	Jack

FATHER	ASC	DESC
	Peter	Chris
	Ted	Mary
	Ted	Jack
	Jef	Peter

APPLICATION OF r1

PARENT	ASC	DESC
	Mary	John
	Julie	Mary
	Julie	Jack

APPLICATION OF r2

PARENT	ASC	DESC
	Mary	John
	Julie	Mary
	Julie	Jack
	Peter	Chris
	Ted	Mary
	Ted	Jack
	Jef	Peter

APPLICATION OF r3

GRANDPARENT	ASC	DESC
	Julie	John
	Ted	John
	Jef	Chris

APPLICATION OF QUERY

GRANDPARENT	DESC	ASC
	Julie	John
	Ted	John

FIGURE 10.6 Bottom-up query evaluation

base facts are retrieved using backward chaining, the query is satisfied. Thus a yes/no answer can be given easily. Moreover, moving constants from the query to the database determines *relevant facts* to generate the query answer.

Definition 10.15 Relevant facts
Extensional database tuples that participate in the generation of at least one tuple of the query answer.

Relevant facts may then be used to generate all of the query answer if needed, as with a bottom-up evaluation. However, the technique is very different from bottom-up evaluation because it starts from the query, not the database. The method goes from the user query to the database; thus it is called a *top-down approach*.

Definition 10.16 Top-down evaluation
Evaluation technique starting from the query and applying the rules using backward chaining to derive the query answer from the database.

A top-down evaluation of the query PARENT(x,John) is represented in Fig. 10.7. The query GRANDPARENT(x,John) of Fig. 10.6 is more difficult to evaluate. In the first approach, all facts will be determined as relevant due to rule r3 (at first, no variable can be instantiated in the first occurrence of the PARENT predicate). The problem of determining precisely the relevant facts is difficult and will be studied in Section 10.5.

Top-down evaluation is formally based on the principles of SLD resolution [Lloyd87], a resolution method for definite clauses with a linear selection function. Let $? \leftarrow R(a,y)$ be a query on a derived predicate R. Any rule of the type $R(x,y) \leftarrow B1,B2, \ldots , Q1,Q2, \ldots$ whose rule head may be unified by a substitution μ with the query determines a resolvent for the query; that is, after unification, the rule body may be interpreted as a subquery that must be solved to generate the query answers. More precisely, for each rule of the given type, the subquery $\{B1,B2, \ldots , Q1,Q2, \ldots \}_{[\mu]}$ must be solved. Using a PROLOG-style evaluation, a subquery is solved in depth first search; thus the subgoals $B1_{[\mu]}$, $B2_{[\mu]}, \ldots , Q1_{[\mu]}, Q2_{[\mu]}, \ldots$ are successively evaluated using backward chaining. Where no recursive relation appears in the rules, the process always converges toward subqueries bearing on base predicates $B1$, $B2, \ldots$ Such subqueries may

DATALOG PROGRAM WITH QUERY
(r1) PARENT(x,z) ← MOTHER(x,z)
(r2) PARENT(x,z) ← FATHER(x,z)
(q) ? PARENT(x,John)

DATABASE

MOTHER	ASC	DESC
	Mary	John
	Julie	Mary
	Julie	Jack

FATHER	ASC	DESC
	Peter	Chris
	Ted	Mary
	Ted	Jack
	Jef	Peter

RELEVANT FACT FROM QUERY
PARENT(?, John)
RELEVANT FACT FROM r2
FATHER(?, John) gives no fact (empty relation)
RELEVANT FACT FROM r1
MOTHER(?, John) gives

MOTHER	ASC	DESC
	Mary	John

Thus, the query answer is Mary.

FIGURE 10.7 Top-down query evaluation

be directly evaluated by the DBMS. Collecting the subqueries' results yields the answer to the initial query.

In summary, it appears that a top-down derivation moves constants from the query to the base predicates through the rules to determine relevant facts. The determination of relevant facts, which are the only ones necessary to generate a query answer, is not simple. It requires understanding the connections between rules in a rule program, that is, the possible unifications between the rules' predicates. For this purpose, several representations of rules with graphs and nets have been proposed.

10.4.3 Modeling Rules with Graphs and Nets

It is important to understand the connection between the various rules of a rule program. A graph model, which captures the possible unification between the rule's head and the rule's body predicates, is often introduced. It is useful for performing rule consistency analysis and supporting certain rule evaluation strategies. For example, rules might be contradictory (in case of DATALOG with negation) or organized in such a way that certain virtual relations may never receive tuples. A graph model is generally relevant for introducing sufficient conditions for detecting such inconsistencies. Also certain query evaluation strategies are based on graph models [Ullman85]. In this section, we present the most popular graph models and then develop a PrTN model, which was introduced in [Gardarin85].

AND/OR Tree

The best-known model derives from articial intelligence where it is used to represent a set of rules. It is called an *AND/OR tree*.

> **Definition 10.17 AND/OR tree**
> Tree composed of OR nodes representing predicates and AND nodes representing rules in which the root of the tree represents a query and the edges represent top-down query evaluation.

Given a pure DATALOG rule program including a query, an AND/OR tree of the involved predicate occurrences is built as follows. Each predicate occurrence is represented by an OR node, meaning that each of its children (if any) is a possible contribution to the answer. A rule corresponds to an AND node. The root of the tree is the query predicate (therefore an OR node). The children of an OR node, which is not an extensional database relation, are all rules whose heads unify with the corresponding predicate. An extensional database relation does not have children. The children of a rule are all the predicate occurrences that appear in its body. To specify the unification performed when going from a rule to another, the substitution that unifies the rule with its parent predicate may be specified as a label on the edge going from the rule to its head predicate.

For example, let us consider the following DATALOG program (with a query), where MOTHER and FATHER are the extensional database relations (*t* stands for the date of parenthood in the MOTHER and FATHER relations that we introduce to show graphs with nonbinary predicates):

{ (r1) PARENT(x,z) ← MOTHER(x,t,z);
(r2)PARENT(x,z) ← FATHER(x,t,z);
(r3)GRANDPARENT(x,z) ← PARENT(x,y),PARENT(y,z)
(q) ?GRANDPARENT(x,John) }.

The associated AND/OR tree is portrayed in Fig. 10.8. An AND node is portrayed as a rectangle and an OR node as a circle.

An AND/OR tree shows the propagation of constants using backward chaining. Constants migrate from the root to the leaves. Unfortunately, in the case of recursive rules, an AND/OR tree may be infinite as new rule occurrences are added to develop nodes that correspond to recursive relations. We shall develop recursive query processing in the next section; however, it already appears that more sophisticated graphs are desirable to represent recursion.

Predicate Connection Graphs

The purpose of *predicate connection graphs* (PCGs) [McKay81] is to help in retrieving all predicates unifiable with a given query, even in the case of recursive rules.

> **Definition 10.18 Predicate connection graph**
> Oriented graph composed of complex nodes representing rules as ordered sets of predicates and edges corresponding to all possible unifications between a head's predicate and a body's predicate.

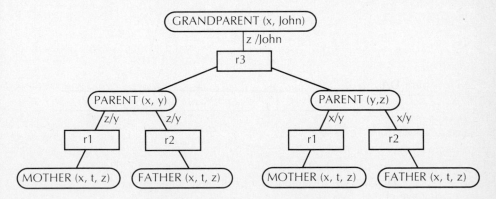

FIGURE 10.8 Example of AND/OR tree

Each node of a PCG is composed of the rule's head predicate and the rule's body predicates. Following [Chang81], we shall represent them as rectangles divided in two parts by a double line, a left part representing the rule head and a right one representing the rule body; predicates in the rule body part are separated by lines. Edges connect predicates that may be unified. Any edge of type $P{\rightarrow}Q$ is labeled by a substitution p/q, which is the substitution to apply to P to transform it to Q (to make the arguments identical). Fig. 10.9 gives the predicate connection graph for the DATALOG program (without query):

> { (r1) PARENT(x,z) ← MOTHER(x,t,z);
> (r2) PARENT(x,z) ← FATHER(x,t,z);
> (r3) ANCESTOR(x,z) ← PARENT(x,z);
> (r4) ANCESTOR(x,z) ← ANCESTOR(x,y),PARENT(y,z) }

An *active predicate connection graph* is derived from a predicate connection graph and a query. It corresponds to a traversal of the predicate connection graph from a singular node representing a query.

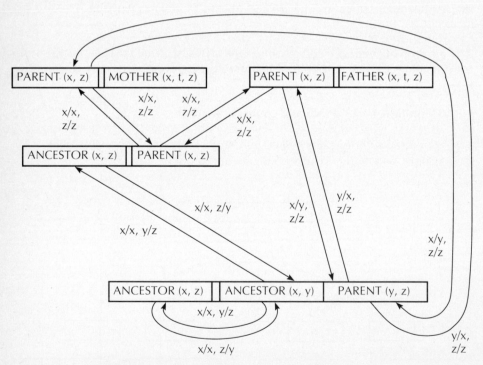

FIGURE 10.9 Example of a predicate connection graph

Definition 10.19 Active predicate connection graph
Subgraph of the predicate connection graph composed with the rules and the query considered as a singular rule without head, obtained by keeping only the unification edges required for a top-down evaluation of the query.

Fig. 10.10 represents the active predicate connection graph associated with the predicate connection graph of Fig. 10.9 and the query ANCESTOR (x, John). In [McKay81], active connection graphs are represented with intermediate goal nodes, which make them very similar to rule/goal graphs.

Rule/Goal Graphs
Like an AND/OR tree, a rule/goal graph [Ullman85] has two sets of nodes: predicate nodes and rule nodes. We represent predicate nodes with circles and

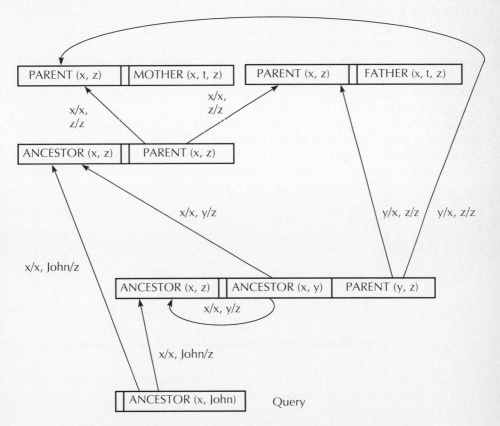

FIGURE 10.10 Example of an active predicate connection graph

rule nodes with rectangles. A rule/goal graph is associated with a query that specifies the predicate to evaluate. The only arcs in a rule/goal graph are defined by the following rule: If there is a rule *r* of the form *P* ← *P*1,*P*2, . . . , *Pn* in the intensional database, then there is an arc going from node *r* to node *P*, and for each predicate *Pi* there is an arc from node *Pi* to node *r*. In its simplest form, a rule/goal graph may also be defined as a variation of a AND/OR tree.

> **Definition 10.20 Rule/goal graph**
> Graph representing a set of rules derived from an AND/OR graph by replacing the expansion of any derived predicate already expanded in the tree by a cyclic arc going to the expanding rule.

Thus, a rule/goal graph cannot be infinite. In the presence of recursive rules, a rule/goal graph contains just a cycle. Fig. 10.11 portrays the rule/goal graph associated with the ANCESTOR predicate derived from the MOTHER and FATHER extensional database relation.

Extended Predicate Transition Nets

Here we present a model based on predicate transition nets that was introduced in [Gardarin85] and extended in [Maindreville87]. The model applies to a fully extended DATALOG, with functions, sets, negations, updates, and non-Horn clauses. A model with a few similarities called system graphs has been proposed in [Lozinskii85]. The notion of predicate transition net (PrTN) derives from Petri nets [Peterson81]. PrTNs have been shown to be a powerful tool for modeling production rules in expert systems [Giordana85]. Their main difference from Petri nets is that tokens are structured objects carrying values similar to database

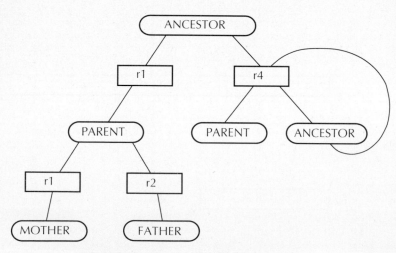

FIGURE 10.11 Example of rule/goal graph

tuples and that transition firing can be controlled by imposing conditions on the token values. A formal definition of PrTN can be found in [Genrich81]. We shall use duplication-free PrTN: Each time two tokens of the same value appear in a place, they merge into one token. Moreover we assume that a token is not destroyed when firing a transition. Thus we actually use conservative duplicate-free PrTN.

To construct a PrTN from a set of rules, we first transform the rules into a canonical form. In this notation, terms are taken out of literals and placed into conditions attached to each rule. Inside each predicate, terms are replaced by distinct variables associated with the predicate occurrence so that successive predicates in a rule do not share variables. Variables in a predicate may be grouped in vectors of variables as needed. Moreover, conditions are written in prenex form (all quantifiers are in front if there are any). Thus, all rules are of the form:

$$R(X) \leftarrow Q(P1(Y),P2(Z), \ldots, Pn(T), \Omega(X,Y, \ldots, T))$$

where $X, Y, Z, \ldots T$ are vectors of variables (tuple variables), Q is a set of universally quantified variables, and $\Omega(X, Y, \ldots, T)$ is a set of equations between the variables or their projections. To denote a domain variable of rank i in a vector X, we use the notation Xi, which is the projection of X over its ith component. Examples of rules written in canonical form are given in Fig. 10.12. They refer to the following relations:

PARENT(ascendant, descendant) abbreviated with predicate letter P.
ANCESTOR(ascendant, descendant) abbreviated with A.
CIRCUIT(Name, Wire#, Origin, Extremity, Impedance);
WIRE(Name, Wire#, Origin, Extremity, Impedance);

The PrTN representing a set of rules is defined as follows:

1. Each relation predicate P is represented by a place p.
2. Each rule R is represented by a transition r linked by input edges with all relation predicates appearing in the rule condition and by output edges with all relation predicates appearing in the action expression.
3. The sum of variables appearing in the predicate P of the condition of a rule R is used as a label of the edge linking the representing place p to the transition r.
4. The algebraic sum of variables appearing in the predicate P of the action expression of a rule R (the sum obtained by keeping the action signs, $+$ for insert and $-$ for delete) is used as labels of the edge linking the transition r to the representing place p.
5. The universal quantifiers Q and the condition Ω are distributed over the transitions according to the variables that label transition input edges.

Rules without conditions are not represented in the PrTN: they are facts and correspond to tokens in the PrTN as classical database tuples.

Definition of the grandfathers of brothers (function b):
$$GP(X) \leftarrow P(Y) \land P(Z) \land Y1 = b(X1) \land Y2 = Z1 \land X2 = Z2$$

Defintion of ancestors:
$$A(X) \leftarrow P(Y) \land X = Y;$$
$$A(X) \leftarrow A(Y) \land P(Z) \land X1 = Y1 \land X2 = Z2 \land Y2 = Z1.$$

Definition of wires:
$$WIRE(X) \leftarrow CIRCUIT(Y) \land X = Y;$$
$\neg WIRE(X), \neg WIRE(Y), WIRE(Z) \leftarrow WIRE(T) \land WIRE(U) \land T.origin =$
  $U.origin \land T.extremity = U.extremity \land T.wire\# \neq U.wire\# \land$
  $T.name = U.name \land X = T \land Y = U \land Z1 = T1 \land Z2 = T2 \land Z3 = T3$
  $\land Z4 = T4 \land Z5 = (T.impedance * U.impedance)/T.impedance +$
  $U.impedance);$
$\neg WIRE(X), \neg WIRE(Y), WIRE(Z) \leftarrow WIRE(T) \land WIRE(U) \land COUNT$
  $(<T>) = 1 \land COUNT(<U>) = 1 \land T.extremity = U.origin \land$
  $T.name = U.name \land X = T \land Y = U \land Z1 = T1 \land Z2 = T2 \land Z3 = T3$
  $\land Z4 = T4 \land Z5 = T.impedance + U.impedance;$

FIGURE 10.12 Examples of rules in canonical form

Figs. 10.13, 10.14, and 10.15 show the PrTN corresponding, respectively, to the grandfather, the ancestor, and the wire examples.

To show the dynamic power of the model, let us recall a few classical notions of Petri net theory. A *marking* is a distribution of tokens over the places of a PrTN. An *initial marking* consists of labeling a PrTN with a particular marking. We introduce the specific notion of *base marking,* an initial marking where tokens representing database tuples are distributed only in places corresponding to database relations. A *source marking* is a marking in which only source relations received tokens. A transition *t* is *enabled* whenever the three following conditions are satisfied:

1. Each input place *p* contains at least one token.
2. The tokens (tuples) occurring in the input places have values satisfying the transition condition according to the edge labels.
3. The transition firing should produce or delete tokens.

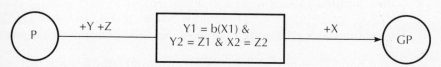

FIGURE 10.13 PrTN for grandfather of brothers

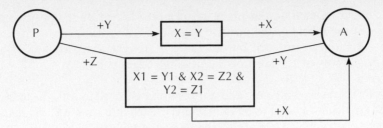

FIGURE 10.14 PrTN for ancestors

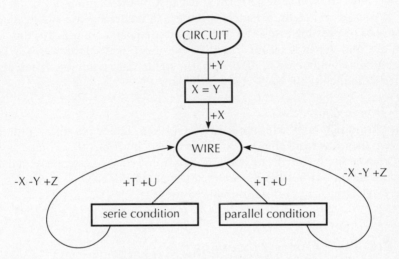

FIGURE 10.15 PrTN for wires

A *transition firing* produces tokens according to the labels of the output edges. Let us recall that we use duplication free and conservative PrTN; thus tokens are not destroyed in the input places, and existing tokens are not produced twice. Tokens are produced if the output edge of a firing transition is labeled by a positive variable. Negative variables correspond to deletions of tuples; a token generated by a firing transition with a negative sign entails a deletion of the similar token if it exists in the target place. Thus our slightly extended PrTN can model updates. It is important to notice that duplicate-free PrTN have the same properties as general PrTN [Giordana85]. Conservative PrTN also have similar properties to classical PrTN because a conservative PrTN may always be represented by an equivalent PrTN by adding edges carrying tokens back to the source. For simplicity, PrTN here means conservative duplicate-free PrTN.

Firing a transition produces several actions:

1. Remove from each input place p a number of tokens equal to the number of positive symbols labeling the edges (p, t).

2. Add to each output place p' tokens specified by the positive symbols of the labels of the positive edges (t,p').
3. Remove from each output place p' tokens specified by the negative symbols of the label of the negative edges (t,p').

Given a PrTN, a marking $M0$, and a transition t enabled in $M0$, the marking $M1$ obtained by firing t is said to be immediately reachable from $M0$. *Reachability* is defined as the transitive closure of the immediate reachability relation.

The activation of a PrTN corresponds to a forward execution of the corresponding rules. Inference is performed using forward chaining by firing transitions. When no transition is enabled, the PrTN has reached a stable state that corresponds to possible results for the derived predicates. In general, this state is not unique and depends on the order of transition firing. However, for DATALOG rules involving no negation or sets, the stable state is unique. It corresponds to the least model of the DATALOG program.

Comparison of Graph Models
All the previous models are intended to represent deductive query processing. However, they have differences, as summarized in Table 10.1. Some are top-down oriented (active predicate connection graphs, rule/goal graphs), and others are more general but bottom-up oriented (extended PrTNs). Most graph models can be extended to support additional features.

10.5 Recursive Query Processing

10.5.1 Problem of Recursive Rules

The problem of optimizing queries on recursively derived predicates, called *recursive relations,* has been studied for several years [Gallaire78, Minker82]. It is a difficult but important problem. Indeed, recursion is a basic construct in AI-oriented applications. A good introduction may be found in [Bancilhon86c].

> **Definition 10.21 Recursive relation**
> Relation R defined by a set of DATALOG rules including a derivation cycle of the form:
> $\{R \leftarrow \ldots R1 \ldots; R1 \leftarrow \ldots R2 \ldots; Rn \leftarrow \ldots R \ldots\}$ with $n \geq 1$.

The best-known example of a recursive rule is the definition of the ANCESTOR (ascendant,descendant) derived relation from the PARENT (parent,child) base relation. When abbreviating PARENT by PAR and ANCESTOR by ANC, the following rules define the ANCESTOR relation:

$$(\text{r1}) \ \text{ANC}(x,y) \leftarrow \text{PAR}(x,y)$$
$$(\text{r2}) \ \text{ANC}(x,y) \leftarrow \text{PAR}(x,z),\text{ANC}(z,y)$$

TABLE 10.1 Comparison of graph execution models

Graph feature	AND/OR tree	Active PCG	Rule/goal graph	Extended PrTN
Function	No	No	No	Yes
Negation	No	No	No	Yes
Update	No	No	No	Yes
Non-Horn condition	No	No	No	Yes
Bottom up	Yes	No	No	Yes
Top down	Yes	Yes	Yes	No
Recursion	No	Yes	Yes	Yes

Rule r2 is recursive. It is even linearly recursive because the recursive relation is defined as a function with only one occurrence of itself.

Definition 10.22 Linear recursive rule
Recursive rule in which the recursive predicate appears only once in the rule body.

It is possible to give a nonlinear definition of the ANCESTOR relation by replacing r2 by the following rule:

$$\text{ANC}(x,y) \leftarrow \text{ANC}(x,z),\text{ANC}(z,y).$$

This rule is quadratic as ANC appears twice in the rule body.

Another generic example is the SAME-GENERATION-COUSIN relation (abbreviated SG), which may be derived from the PARENT relation. There are several ways to derive SG from PARENT. First, we assume that all persons in the database are their own same-generation cousins; that gives the initialization rule (r1). In fact, the HUMAN relation (abbreviated HUM) can be derived from the PARENT relation, but we assume here that it is a base relation. Next, a person x is the same-generation cousin of a person y if two of their parents are same-generation cousins; that entails rule (r'2). Thus a possible set of rules to generate the SG relation is:

$$(\text{r1}) \quad \text{SG}(x,x) \leftarrow \text{HUM}(x)$$
$$(\text{r'2}) \quad \text{SG}(x,y) \leftarrow \text{PAR}(xp,x),\text{SG}(xp,yp),\text{PAR}(yp,y)$$

There are several other ways to define the same-generation cousins. First, since SG is a symmetrical relation ($\text{SG}(x,y) \leftrightarrow \text{SG}(y,x)$), we may interchange variables xp and yp in the body of rule (r'2). Thus, we obtain:

$$(\text{r3}) \quad \text{SG}(x,y) \leftarrow \text{PAR}(xp,x),\text{SG}(yp,xp),\text{PAR}(yp,y)$$

Rules r'2 and r3 are linear, although rule r3 is more complex than rule r'2.

It is also possible to generate the same-generation cousins in a nonlinear way. Starting from a person x, we can go up and down in the ancestor hierarchies through the same-generation cousins several times. The following rule results from going up and down twice (Fig. 10.16):

(r2) $SG(x,y) \leftarrow PAR(xp,x), SG(xp,z1p), PAR(z1p,z), PAR(z2p,z), SG(z2p,yp),$
$PAR(yp,y)$

Approximately it defines the same-generation cousins. In the remainder of this chapter, we shall use this definition of same-generation cousins. Thus the complete set of rules is:

(r1) $SG(x,x) \leftarrow HUM(x)$
(r2) $SG(x,y) \leftarrow PAR(xp,x), SG(xp,z1), PAR(z1,z), PAR(z2,z), SG(z2,yp),$
$PAR(yp,y)$

The purpose of this complex choice is to illustrate algorithms with nonlinear rules.

It is also possible to use functions in recursive rules. Two typical examples are a graph traversal with computation and the reverse of a list. Indeed functions are useful to manipulate recursive data structures. First, let us assume a relation describing a labeled graph as follows: GRAPH(SOURCE,DESTINATION,LABEL). The following rules build a deduced relation PATH with the same attributes that give all paths in the graph with a composed label as follows:

$$PATH(x,y,z) \leftarrow GRAPH(x,y,z)$$
$$PATH(x,y,f(z1,z2)) \leftarrow GRAPH(x,z,z1), PATH(z,y,z2)$$

For example, if $f(z1,z2) = z1 + z2$ and if labels represent distances, the previous rules compute all paths with associated lengths. Second, let us assume a LIST relation of a unique attribute whose domain is all possible lists of integers. For example, tuples in the list predicate may be: [] (the empty list), [1],[2],[1,2],[2,1]. We define the REVERSE derived predicate, which gives the inverse of a list. The given definition requires a concatenation function denoted | and a length function giving the length of a list denoted $1g$. The set of rules is the following:

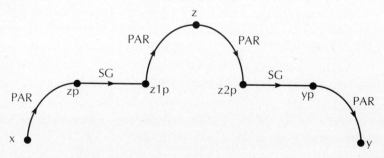

FIGURE 10.16 Going up and down in the ancestor hierarchies as in r2 rule's body

APPEND(X,[],X|[]) ← LIST(X)
APPEND(X,W|Y,W|Z) ← APPEND(X,Y,Z),LIST(W)
INVERSE([],[]) ←
INVERSE(W|X,Y) ← INVERSE(X,Z),APPEND(W,Z,Y),$1g(W) \leq 1$

Assuming that the concatenation function is defined as follows:

$$[i1,i2, \ldots , ik] \mid [i'1,i'2, \ldots , i'q] = [i1,i2, \ldots , ik,i'1,i'2, \ldots , i'q]$$

the APPEND predicate gives for any two lists X and Y, the result of their reverse concatenation Y|X. Thus the last rule states that if the inverse of X is Z and if W has no more than one element, then the inverse of W|X is Z|W. APPEND and INVERSE are two linearly recursive predicates.

The problem is the optimization of queries that use recursive predicates. Often such queries give values for certain variables of the recursive predicate. The problem is to find the corresponding values of the noninstantiated variables. In certain cases, all variables in the query may be given. The answer is then a Boolean one, specifying whether the query tuple belongs to the recursively defined predicate. A few examples of queries with the previous recursive predicate definitions are:

1. Who are the ancestors of John?
   ? ANC(x,John)
2. Is Peter an ancestor of John?
   ? ANC(Peter,John)
3. Who are the same-generation cousins of John?
   ? SG(John,x)
4. What are the length of all paths going from a to b?
   ? PATH(a,b,z)
5. What is the inverse of the list [1,2,3,4,5]?
   ? INVERSE([1,2,3,4,5] ,x)

In the following sections, we examine how to solve such queries. Although we try to present the main methods, our survey is far from complete. In particular, an interesting method derived from regular grammar theory may be found in [Chang81]; a method derived from automata theory is proposed in [Marque-Pucheu84], and another method derived from resolution is presented in [Henschen84].

10.5.2 Bottom-up Evaluation

Naive Generation
The bottom-up approach performs a simple forward chaining starting from the extensional database. *Naive generation* is a special case of the bottom-up approach.

Definition 10.23 Naive generation
Bottom-up evaluation technique computing a deduced relation by applying all rules to all produced tuples at each step of the inference process, up to saturation of the deduced relation.

Naive generation can be performed using relational algebra. The condition part of a rule is translated into a relational algebra expression. In general, an initialization rule generates a first value R_0 for the recursive predicate R. Then the recursive rule is translated in an iterative computation, as follows:

$R := R_0;$
while "R changes" **do**
    $R := R \cup E(R);$

where $E(R)$ is the relational expression derived from the rule body. The process stops when the application of E to R does not generate new tuples. Indeed we compute the least fixpoint of an equation $R = F(R)$ where $F(R) = R_0 \cup E(R)$, that is, the smallest value of R that does not change when transformed by F. It may be shown that this fixpoint exists [Aho79]. (For specialists of lattice theory, this holds because F is increasing and the relations of schema R form a lattice. Thus Tarski's theorem can be applied [Tarski55].) In the case of finite relations, it is obtained as $F^N(\emptyset)$ for a certain N, where F^N means N successive applications of F and $\emptyset$ is the empty relation. The proposed fixpoint computation is a way to compute the least model of the DATALOG program. Thus naive evaluation computes the program semantics.

Let us give an illustration of naive evaluation using the ancestor example. Rule r1 gives a first value to ANC, which is the PAR relation. Then rule r2 is translated in a loop of joins of PAR with ANC followed by a union of the results with ANC. Fig. 10.17 illustrates a naive computation of the ancestors of John.

In the case of same-generation cousins, the process is similar. Rule r1 allows the system to initialize the SG predicate. Then the iterative joins of PARENT, SG, PARENT, PARENT, SG, PARENT give new elements in SG.

Finally, note that naive evaluation may be not possible with functions. For instance, if one starts generation with the LIST example, the second rule never stops: It generates more and more lists by successive concatenation. Thus in the case of infinite domains, the naive bottom-up evaluation may not terminate.

A detailed study of the naive generation process [Bancilhon86a] shows two weaknesses of the method, in addition to the fact that termination is guaranteed only without function symbols:

1. At each iteration, redundant work is performed. As new results are added to the previous one, the relational operations are still applied to the previously processed tuples. Thus naive generation leads to redoing,

RULES
ANC (x, y) ⟵ PAR (x, y)
ANC (x, y) ⟵ PAR (x, z), ANC, (z,y)

NAIVE PROGRAM
ANC : = ∅;
while "ANC changes" do
ANC : = ANC UPAR ⋈ ANC;

DATABASE AND SUCCESSIVE COMPUTATIONS

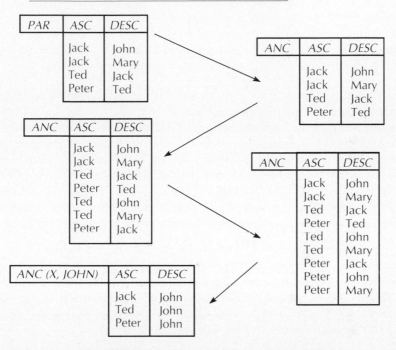

FIGURE 10.17 Naive evaluation of ANC(x,John)

at each recursion step, inferences performed at the previous step. For example, in Fig. 10.17 the join of tuple <Peter,Ted> with tuple <Ted,Jack> is done at each iteration step (at least three times).

2. Where constants appear in the query, useless work is performed, producing tuples not necessary to generate the query answer. These tuples are eliminated by the final select performed on the queried recursive predicate. For example, to compute the ancestors of John, the method computes the ancestor of everybody and then selects those of John.

To conclude, naive evaluation leads to iterative relational algebra programs to compute recursive query answers. Thus it can be applied to compile a query referencing a recursive predicate in a relational algebra program.

Seminaive Generation

To avoid performing redundant generation, it is possible to consider only new inferences at each iteration. Such inferences must instantiate variables in the rule body with at least one new tuple just generated during the previous iteration. Thus using new tuples at step $i - 1$, it is possible to compute new tuples at step i without redoing work already done at step $i - 1$. This technique is called *seminaive generation*.

> **Definition 10.24   Seminaive generation**
> Bottom-up evaluation technique computing a deduced relation by applying the rules only to new tuples produced at the previous step of the inference process, up to saturation of the deduced relation.

The idea of seminaive generation is differential in nature. Below, we develop this idea more formally, as done in [Bancilhon86a].

Let $F(R)$ be the relational algebra expression derived from the recursive rule body. At step i, we only have to compute the new tuples ΔR_i. To compute them, we need to perform new inferences, thus using the new tuples ΔR_{i-1} produced at iteration $(i-1)$ at least in one occurrence of R in $F(R)$. As $Ri + 1 = Ri \cup F(R_{i-1} \cup \Delta R_{i-1})$, we obtain $\Delta R_i = (Ri \cup F(R_{i-1} \cup \Delta R_{i-1})) - Ri$. In general, ΔR_i cannot be computed simply as a function of ΔR_{i-1}. However, in the case of linear rules, where the recursive predicate appears only once in the rule body, we have:

$$F(R_{i-1} \cup \Delta R_{i-1}) = F(R_{i-1}) \cup F(\Delta R_{i-1}) = R_i \cup F(\Delta R_{i-1}).$$

The new tuples to be added to Ri may then be computed with $F(\Delta R_{i-1})$ (which includes ΔR_i). In general the new tuples produced at step i can be generated as $\Delta R_i = dF(R_{i-1}, \Delta R_{i-1})$, where dF is in a sense a differential of F [Bancilhon86a]. For example, with a quadratic rule, such as the same-generation cousins, $dF(SG, \Delta SG)$ should include the following join expressions:

$$P \bowtie \Delta SG \bowtie P \bowtie P \bowtie SG \bowtie P$$
$$P \bowtie SG \bowtie P \bowtie P \bowtie \Delta SG \bowtie P$$
$$P \bowtie \Delta SG \bowtie P \bowtie P \bowtie \Delta SG \bowtie P.$$

Based on the above principles, the seminaive algorithm [Bancilhon86b, Bayer85] performs a differential computation of the recursive relation R as follows:

```
ΔR := R₀
R := ΔR;
while ΔR ≠ Ø do
begin
      ΔR = df(R,ΔR);
      ΔR = ΔR − R;
      R = R ∪ ΔR;
end;
```

Where the same tuples cannot be produced at each iteration, the difference is not necessary. This case requires acyclicity of the database and acyclicity of the rules [Gardarin86]. It holds for the computation of the ancestors of John as illustrated in Fig. 10.18.

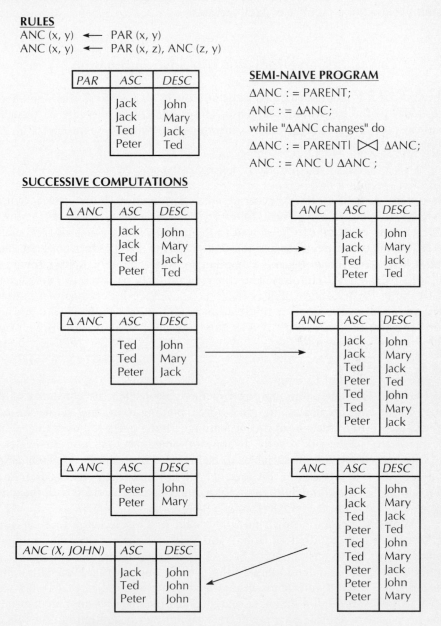

RULES
ANC (x, y) ⟵ PAR (x, y)
ANC (x, y) ⟵ PAR (x, z), ANC (z, y)

PAR	ASC	DESC
	Jack	John
	Jack	Mary
	Ted	Jack
	Peter	Ted

SEMI-NAIVE PROGRAM
ΔANC : = PARENT;
ANC : = ΔANC;
while "ΔANC changes" do
ΔANC : = PARENT| ⋈ ΔANC;
ANC : = ANC U ΔANC ;

SUCCESSIVE COMPUTATIONS

Δ ANC	ASC	DESC
	Jack	John
	Jack	Mary
	Ted	Jack
	Peter	Ted

ANC	ASC	DESC
	Jack	John
	Jack	Mary
	Ted	Jack
	Peter	Ted

Δ ANC	ASC	DESC
	Ted	John
	Ted	Mary
	Peter	Jack

ANC	ASC	DESC
	Jack	John
	Jack	Mary
	Ted	Jack
	Peter	Ted
	Ted	John
	Ted	Mary
	Peter	Jack

Δ ANC	ASC	DESC
	Peter	John
	Peter	Mary

ANC	ASC	DESC
	Jack	John
	Jack	Mary
	Ted	Jack
	Peter	Ted
	Ted	John
	Ted	Mary
	Peter	Jack
	Peter	John
	Peter	Mary

ANC (X, JOHN)	ASC	DESC
	Jack	John
	Ted	John
	Peter	John

FIGURE 10.18 Seminaive evaluation of ANC(x,John)

The seminaive algorithm may be implemented directly above a DBMS. Such an implementation would not be efficient because the algorithm performs a loop of joins, differences, and unions as many times as necessary for saturation. To improve performance, it is worth noticing that the relations involved in the loop remain the same (R, ΔR, relations of dF); good management of the main memory could avoid a large number of I/O operations.

10.5.3 Difficulties and Tools for Top-down Evaluation

The top-down evaluation method aims at moving backward the constants from the query to the extensional database. Unfortunately, in the case of recursive relations, the top-down approach as introduced so far may be unsuccessful. For example, with the rule:

$$\text{ANC}(x,y) \leftarrow \text{ANC}(x,z), \text{PAR}(z,y)$$

the query ? $\text{ANC}(\text{John},y)$ generates the instantiated body $\text{ANC}(\text{John},z)$, $\text{PAR}(z,y)$. Trying to solve $\text{ANC}(\text{John},z)$ yields the same subquery as the initial one. Thus no constant can be moved to the parent relation, and all facts of the PARENT relation are retrieved as relevant. Thus the method does not help. Note that it is not true for all queries. For example, with the query $\text{ANC}(z,\text{John})$, we obtain $\text{ANC}(x,z),\text{PAR}(z,\text{John})$. Thus the relevant facts for this query are all facts of the form $\text{PAR}(?,\text{John})$, that is $\sigma_{\text{DESC} = \text{``John"}}$ (PAR). Extensions of top-down derivation that avoid loops or full relation instantiations mix backward and forward chaining. First we need to understand how constants migrate through rules using top-down derivation.

Sideways Information Passing
To focus on relevant data, top-down methods propagate the constants of the query to the base predicates. In other words, bindings (variables set to constant values) passed to a rule's head by unification with the query are used to evaluate the predicates in the rule's body. It appears sometimes that base predicates in the rule body force certain variables to be bound. For example, with the simple nonrecursive rule $\text{GP}(x,y) \leftarrow \text{PAR}(x,z), \text{PAR}(z,y)$ and the query ? $\text{GP}(\text{John},y)$ which looks for the grandchildren of John, unifying the rule head with the query brings out $\text{GP}(\text{John},y) \leftarrow \text{PAR}(\text{John},z), \text{PAR}(z,y)$.

A sophisticated top-down method would first retrieve the facts of form $\text{PAR}(\text{John},?)$ (the children of John) and then use the results (the children's names) $c_1,c_2, \ldots$ to instantiate z in $\text{PAR}(z,y)$. Subqueries of form $\text{PAR}(c_i,y)$ would retrieve the grandchildren of John. Thus it appears that even with nonrecursive rules, when a variable is instantiated in a base predicate, it instantiates other variables through a database search. Then the newly instantiated variable may propagate to another base predicate, enabling new instantiation. The process of passing information from a predicate to another predicate is called *sideways information passing* [Ullman85].

> **Definition 10.25 Sideways information passing**
> Propagation of constants instantiating bound variables x of a predicate $P(\ldots x, \ldots, y, \ldots)$ to another predicate $Q(\ldots, y, \ldots)$ by performing a selection in P on x followed by a join with Q on y.

When a sideways information passing is performed, it appears sometimes that starting from a predicate name with variables bound in certain positions, we reach the same predicate name with variables bound in other positions. Thus it is necessary to distinguish which argument is bound and which is free in a predicate. This is the purpose of the notion of *adornment* [Ullman85]. An adornment for an n-ary predicate p is a string a of length n on the alphabet $\{b, f\}$, where b stands for bound and f stands for free. A fixed order of arguments is assumed in the predicate; thus if f (respectively b) stands in position k of the adornment, the place k of the predicate is filled up with a free variable (respectively a bound variable, such as a constant). For example, we may write $ANC^{bf}(John, x)$ as John is a constant and x a free variable.

To understand better how bindings can be propagated in a given rule, it has been proposed to use *sideways information passing graphs* [Beeri87]. A sideways information passing (sip) graph is a labeled graph that describes how the bound variables in the rule's head (variables that become constants after unification with the query marked with a b in the rule head adornment) are migrated into the rule's body. A sip graph represents a decision about the order in which the predicates of the rule's body will be evaluated and how constants will be passed from predicates to others [Beeri87]. There are several possible sip graphs for a given rule, depending on the rule head binding, the order of predicate evaluation, and the chosen propagations. A sip graph is built from the predicate occurrences appearing in the rule, simply called predicate (a predicate name is repeated in the graph as many times as it appears in the rule). A node of a sip graph is either a predicate or a group of predicates. An arc $N \rightarrow p$ links a group of predicates N to a single predicate p. An arc $N \rightarrow p$ is labeled by variables that must appear as arguments of the predicates in N and of the p predicate. To clarify the representation, we draw a sip graph directly on the rule's predicates. The predicates of the rule are written from left to right according to the chosen order for the body's predicates (the head is always the left-most predicate); the sip graph nodes are represented as bubbles. Two sip graphs are represented in Figs. 10.19 and 10.20 for the rules defining the ancestors and the same-generation cousins.

A sip graph is valid if there exists an ordering of the predicates such that the rule's head predicate precedes all predicates of the rule's body and, for any arc, any predicate of the source precedes the target predicate. The sip graphs of Figs. 10.19 and 10.20 are valid. Because we are interested only in recursive predicate evaluation using backward information passing, we shall consider only sip

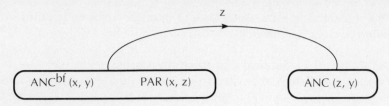

FIGURE 10.19 Sip graph for the rule $ANC^{bf}(x,y) \leftarrow PAR(x,z), ANC(z,y)$

graphs in which all arcs link a set of predicates including the rule's head to an occurrence of the recursive predicate. That is the case for the sip graphs of Figs. 10.19 and 10.20. It is possible, however, to add edges modeling the information passing between base predicates.

The meaning of a sip graph arc $N \rightarrow p$ is the following: Assuming that the join of all predicates in the source node N has been performed, it would be possible to propagate the values of the label variables to the target predicate p; these propagated values would bind the corresponding variables of the target predicate p. Where the source bubble (N) contains the rule's head predicate, an arc models the propagation of a query constant to a rule's body predicate (p), using backward chaining and semijoins. Such a propagation is called *sideways information passing*. A sip graph is valid if it defines a possible order of joins that performs successively all the sideways information passing portrayed on the graph, starting from the rule head with bound variables. Thus a valid sip graph defines a possible strategy to evaluate a rule when a given set of head arguments is bound to constants.

There exist several sip graphs for a given rule and a given query. A sip graph is increasing if it is valid and, for any arc $N \rightarrow p$, N contains all nodes that precede p in the validity order. The meaning of an increasing sip graph is that it

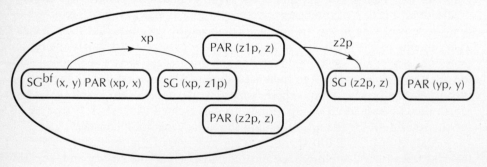

FIGURE 10.20 Sip graph for the rule
$SG^{bf}(x,y) \leftarrow PAR(xp,x), SG(xp,z1p), PAR(z1p,z), PAR(z2p,z), SG(z2p,yp), PAR(yp,y)$

models a rule evaluation strategy in which, starting from the rule head, more and more joins are performed to pass bindings. Finally, following [Beeri87], an increasing sip graph is total if all possible bindings are passed through the arcs — that is, if any arc $N \to p$ is labeled by the intersection of the variable sets appearing in N and in p, with obvious notations: label$(N \to p)$ = var(N) ∩ var(p). The sip graphs of Figs. 10.19 and 10.20 are total.

Adorned Rules
When a sip graph has been chosen for constant propagations from the head to the recursive predicates in the body, it is possible to rewrite the rule with adorned predicates. The adornments will clearly exhibit the chosen information passing strategy. Adornments are not written for nonrecursive predicates but could be.

> **Definition 10.26 Adorned rule**
> Rule rewritten with adorned predicates (predicates indexed by string of b and f marking bound and free arguments) according to a sip graph (and therefore a query).

With more details, being given a recursive rule, the rule head is rewritten accordingly to the unification performed with the query. The adornment is then propagated to the other recursive predicates following the chosen sip graph arcs. A target recursive predicate is adorned with b in the positions corresponding to variables labeling arcs coming in and f for the others. Adorned rules capture the selected information passing strategy for the recursive predicates. Also adornment allows rewriting algorithms to distinguish predicates with the same names but different instantiated variables.

To illustrate, we give below the adorned rules for the ancestors and the same-generation-cousins examples. These rules are adorned according to the total sip graph of Figs. 10.19 and 10.20.

$$\text{ANC}^{bf}(x,y) \leftarrow \text{PAR}(x,z), \text{ANC}^{bf}(z,y)$$
$$\text{SG}^{bf}(x,y) \leftarrow \text{PAR}(xp,x), \text{SG}^{bf}(xp,z1p), \text{PAR}(z1p,z),$$
$$\text{PAR}(z2p,z), \text{SG}^{bf}(z2p,yp), \text{PAR}(yp,y)$$

Because the adornments of recursive predicates are always the same, they may be implicit from the query but this is not the general case. For example, with the rule ANC$(x,y) \leftarrow$ PAR(x,z), ANC(y,z) and a sip graph similar to that of Fig. 10.19, the adorned rule will be:

$$\text{ANC}^{bf}(x,y) \leftarrow \text{PAR}(x,z), \text{ANC}^{fb}(y,z).$$

Here, adornment distinguishes between the two occurrences of the ANC predicate. In the following, we use adorned predicates to present optimization algorithms based on rule rewriting.

10.5.4 Interpreted Methods

The *interpreted methods* for recursive query processing are optimization methods applied at run time using both the rules and the data.

> **Definition 10.27 Interpreted methods**
> Methods for optimizing recursive query evaluation applied at run time using both the given rules and the data contained in the database.

Interpreted methods are extensions of top-down derivation. They evaluate efficiently and correctly recursive rules for focusing on relevant data. The key idea is to use the initialization rules and forward chaining when backward chaining is not directly possible with the recursive rules. Thus, they mix top-down and bottom-up approaches. We distinguish two methods, although they are very close. Both generate loops of queries to the DBMS. They memorize information to determine the termination condition.

Generation from Relevant Facts

This method was described at first in [Lozinskii85] and is called APEX. The method relies on relevant facts. It assumes pure DATALOG rules, without functions. In such a context, the tuples generated to answer a query are derived from values recorded somewhere in the database. Thus, if a constant a must appear in a predicate $R(x_1, x_2, \ldots, a, x_{q+1}, \ldots)$ to satisfy the query, the tuples of the answer must be generated by migrating a from database tuples to the answer. Therefore it is possible by studying the variable migrations to determine a set of database tuples that must participate in the inference process to generate a query answer.

The migrations of variables are studied using a rule system graph that represents the connections between rules. A system graph is a variation of a duplication-free PrTN as introduced, with specific notations. This graph allows the method to determine the migration paths of bound variables from the query to the base predicates. It is possible by migrating constants from the query to the base predicates to determine a first set of relevant facts for certain base predicates. Each base predicate may then be initialized with the determined relevant facts, and a forward-chaining process may start. This process generally leads to a first set of answers (possibly empty), but it is incomplete because the facts of the predicates are only generated by direct migrations of constants. To complete the method, a query/subquery approach is integrated in the generation process [Lozinskii85], which performs the sideways information passing.

The idea is to generate subqueries when a join has to be processed with a nonbase predicate in order to find new relevant tuples. More precisely, each time a join is required with a predicate in the forward-chaining process, subqueries are generated on this predicate to find possible joining tuples. The subqueries are generated using sideways information passing from the known tuples to be joined. The subqueries are solved using APEX, which is indeed recursive. The subqueries determine, via the rules, new relevant facts in the base predicates. These facts are used to generate new answers and new subqueries. APEX generates all answers derived from the database. APEX terminates when no new relevant facts are produced by the subqueries.

To illustrate APEX, we apply it to the ancestor example defined with the following rules:

$$(r1) \ ANC(x,y) \leftarrow PAR(x,y)$$
$$(r2) \ ANC(x,y) \leftarrow PAR(x,z), ANC(z,y)$$

The query is ? $ANC(John,y)$. Let us denote by $P.i$ the variable corresponding to place i of P. The migration set of ANC.1 (which is bound to John in the query) is {PAR.1}, both via rules r1 and r2. The first relevant facts are then of type $PAR(John,a_i)$ for $i \in [1,n]$. Rule r1 gives then a set of facts for ANC as follows:

$$PAR(John,a_i) \rightarrow ANC(John,a_i) \ for \ i \in [1,n].$$

One then tries to execute r2 using forward chaining with the relevant facts $PAR(John,ai)$, as follows:

$$PAR(John,a_i), \ ANC(a_i,y) \rightarrow ANC(John,y) \ for \ i \in [1,n]$$

to get new solutions. The join in the condition leads to new subqueries:

$$\{? \ ANC(a_i,y) \ for \ i \in [1,n]\}.$$

These subqueries yield new relevant facts, of type $PAR(ai,bj)$, which determine new answers through rule r1, then new subqueries through rule r2, and so on. The process stops when no new relevant facts are produced.

A different approach, proposed in [Kifer87], may be applied in the context of functions. The idea is to use the system graph to propagate a filter in the graph from a node representing the query answer. The filter may contain term profiles that allow it to support function symbols. The filter that represents a restriction criterion is moved up toward the base predicates in such a way that only relevant tuples will be processed later using forward chaining. Because the method does not incorporate a query/subquery approach, the filter cannot be moved up the graph when it references a term appearing in a join. Thus the method does not focus on relevant data in all cases. A similar method dealing in a different way with functions (functions are supposed to be interpreted and dominance relations between functions are assumed to be known) and supporting range queries has been proposed in the context of production rules modeled with PrTN [Gardarin85].

Query Subquery (QSQ)

With QSQ [Vieille86], as in APEX, the rules are used for generating new answers and deriving new subqueries. The search of relevant facts is performed using backward chaining. Predicates are explored in a backward direction, linearly from left to right and in-depth first search (when a deduced predicate is met, the rules defining it are explored before moving to the next predicate), as with classical PROLOG interpreters. When a recursive predicate is met, subqueries are generated using sideways information passing. Two versions of the method have been implemented; an iterative one manages a dynamic list of subqueries to process, and a recursive one recalls itself each time a new subquery is generated. The recursive method solves recursively the generated subqueries up to saturation; the iterative version memorizes the generated tuples and subqueries in main memory. Thus with the iterative version, subqueries bearing on the same predicates may be applied globally to the database. This limits the number of processed subqueries. For example, a set of subqueries of the form $\{?\ R(ai,y)$ for $i \in [1,n]\}$ is replaced by a unique subquery ? $R(a_1 \vee a_2 \vee \ldots \vee a_n,y)$. In other words, sideways information passing is performed in a set-oriented way and not one constant at a time. Also the termination condition is enriched. A subquery is executed only if it was not already processed. Thus the termination condition is twofold: the process stops if no new subquery is generated or no new relevant fact is produced.

These differences give a method that is more efficient than APEX in processing time but requires more memory size because relevant facts and subqueries are kept in main memory. The query-subquery method works correctly with cyclic data and terminates (for example, with a parent relation in which a person is his own ancestor). This is due to the fact that already processed subqueries are detected and not processed twice. This is not true with a straightforward implementation of APEX.

10.5.5 Compiled Methods

In opposition to interpreted methods, *compiled methods* are not dynamic; they elaborate database request programs independent of the database content.

> **Definition 10.28 Compiled methods**
> Methods for optimizing recursive query evaluation executed at compile time, without using the data, transforming the rules with the query in a program focusing on relevant data.

In general, for a given query and a given rule program, compiled methods generate optimized relational algebra programs, which are then executed. The program may be executed as many times as desired, without recompiling the query, which saves compilation time. Because compilation (or interpretation) algorithms are complex, the repetitive execution of a query will not pay for repetitive compilations. This leads us to think that compilation methods are generally superior to interpreted methods; however, it is difficult to compare compilation and interpretation methods without specific implementation measures.

The naive and seminaive methods are compiled methods. They translate a rule program into relational algebra expressions with loops executed up to recursive predicate saturation. The resulting programs have been given. The problem with compilation methods is to get efficient relational algebra programs. A well-known heuristic consists of applying restriction at first to focus on relevant data. Thus a compilation method should push selection before recursion — that is, perform selection operations before loops of joins. Optimizing after translating into relational algebra programs is not easy. It is better to rewrite rules in such a way that a naive or seminaive evaluation leads to relational algebra programs performing selection before recursion. There are two methods that rewrite rules to focus on relevant data.

Alexander Method

Given a query, the Alexander method [Rohmer86] rewrites each rule by decomposing each recursive predicate R into two predicates, a problem predicate PB_R and a solution predicate SOL_R. Thus, a recursive query ? $R(c,y)$, where c is a constant, is decomposed into two predicates PB_$R^{bf}(c)$ and SOL_$R^{bf}(x,y)$. The adornment of the predicates is used to memorize the constant position. Knowing the first instance of the problem predicate (c), the algorithm rewrites the rules in such a way that the instances of SOL_$R^{bf}(x,y)$ are generated in forward chaining from the c problem. Thus it can be expected that the forward-chaining process (seminaive generation applied to the rewritten rules) would perform only relevant inferences.

Let $B1,B2, \ldots , R,Q1,Q2, \ldots \rightarrow R(x,y)$ be a recursive rule in which $B1,B2, \ldots$ are base predicates, $Q1, Q2, \ldots$ being base or derived predicates. The rewriting of such a recursive rule in several rules with stronger conditions is performed as follows. First, the problem PB_$R^{bf}(c)$ is added to the rule condition $B1,B2, \ldots R,Q1,Q2, \ldots$; this is natural as the problem is a supplementary condition to generate solutions. The constant c is then propagated by performing sideways information passing successively in the rule body, in the order the predicates are written (from left to right), up to reach the recursive predicate R. Here the instantiated variable generates a new problem on R that must be solved to get the initial problem solutions. Thus R is once more decomposed into two predicates, PB_$R^{xx}(v1)$ and SOL_$R^{xx}(v1,v2)$. Therefore we now obtain two rules:

$$PB\_R^{bf}(c),B1,B2, \ldots \rightarrow PB\_R^{xx}(v1),CONT(v1, \ldots)$$
$$CONT(v1, \ldots),SOL\_R^{xx}(v1,v2),Q1,Q2, \ldots \rightarrow SOL\_R^{bf}(x,y)$$

the first generating new relevant problems, the second generating solutions. The continuation predicate $CONT(v1, \ldots)$ is necessary to save variable instances that appear in the first rule to bring them to the second. It memorizes the links between the two rules. Note that, when several CONT predicates are used, they have to be distinguished by a number (CONT1,CONT2, \ldots). In the case where $Q1,Q2, \ldots$ still contain the recursive predicate R, the sideways information passing must go on from the bound variable $v1$ or $v2$ (determined by the SOL_R

predicate adornment in the second rule) to the next occurrence of R. Then R is again split in two predicates RB_R and SOL_R. The decomposition of a rule into two rules is thus applied successively, up to the point where all recursive predicate occurrences are replaced by problem and solution predicates. Each time the recursive predicate is met, (the Gordian knot), it is cut in two parts: a problem predicate and a solution predicate. This justifies the name of the method, which, as Alexander, cuts the Gordian knot in two to undo it.

Globally the Alexander algorithm first rewrites a query ? $R(c,y)$ as a rule $PB\_R^{bf}(c), R(c,y) \to REP(y)$ which is added to the rule program. Then the problem $PB\_R^{bf}(x)$ is added to each rule's body whose rule's head unifies with the query, x being the variable substituted to c during the unification process. Next, all rules that include one or several occurrences of the recursive predicate R are transformed as indicated. Finally, the resulting rules are run using seminaive forward chaining. The method has been demonstrated to be correct (in the sense that the rewritten system is equivalent to the initial one plus the query) and to focus (more or less completely) on relevant data [Kerisit86]. Rewritten rule transformations are, however, necessary to avoid redundant work. Also to maximize focusing on relevant data, it is necessary to reorder the predicates in each rule according to a total sip graph.

Let us now give the rewritten systems for finding the ancestors and the same-generation cousins of John.

1. Linear definition of Ancestors with query $ANC(John,y)$:

    (r1) $PB\_ANC^{10}(x), PAR(x,y) \to SOL\_ANC^{10}(x,y)$
    (r2) $PB\_ANC^{10}(x), PAR(x,z) \to PB\_ANC^{10}(z), CONT(x,z)$
    $CONT(x,z), SOL\_ANC^{10}(z,y) \to SOL\_ANC^{10}(x,y)$
    (q) $PB\_ANC^{10}(John)$
    $SOL\_ANC^{10}(John,y) \to REP(y)$

2. Quadratic definition of same-generation-cousins with query $SG(John,y)$:

    (r1) $PB\_SG^{10}(x), HUM(x) \to SOL\_SG^{10}(x,x)$
    (r2) $PB\_SG^{10}(x), PAR(xp,x) \to PB\_SG^{10}(xp), CONT1(x,xp)$
    $CONT1(x,xp), SOL\_SG^{10}(xp,z1), PAR(z1,z), PAR(z2,z) \to$
    $PB\_SG^{10}(z2), CONT2(x,z2)$
    $CONT2(x,z2), SOL\_SG^{10}(z2,yp), PAR(yp,y) \to SOL\_SG^{10}(x,y)$
    (q) $PB\_SG^{10}(John)$
    $SOL\_SG^{10}(John,y) \to REP(y)$

Magic Sets and Extensions

The magic set method is based on the idea of a little genius who marks useful tuples of recursive predicates before applying a seminaive generation. Tuples of a recursive predicate R are marked using a special magic predicate denoted MAGIC_R. Thus inferences using bottom-up evaluation are applied only to relevant tuples marked with the magic predicate. The first version of magic sets [Bancilhon86b] was applicable to linear rules and a few other cases. A generalized version has been proposed under the name "generalized magic sets" [Beeri87]. We will describe this version.

The starting point is a program of adorned rules and a sip graph. The first intent is to construct a rule set that models the constant migrations according to the sip graph in such a way that it generates the magic marks (the tuples of the magic predicates). Thus for each recursive predicate R^{xx}, a magic predicate MAGIC_R^{xx} is generated. The variables of MAGIC_R^{xx} are the bound variables of R^{xx}, therefore the arity of MAGIC_R^{xx} is the number of b in the adornment xx. The first set of rules generates the magic predicate instances by passing all constants according to the sip graphs.

A second set of rules is necessary to generate the query answer. The seminaive generation process must be performed only for tuples marked by magic predicate values. Consequently the rules generating the answers are obtained by adding the correct magic predicates to the initial rule bodies. For example, a rule

$$B1, B2, \ldots, R^{bf}, Q1, Q2 \ldots \rightarrow R^{bf}(x,y)$$

where R is a recursive predicate, will be transformed in:

$$\text{MAGIC\_}R^{bf}(x), B1, B2, \ldots, R^{bf}, Q1, Q2 \ldots R^{bf}(x,y)$$

which means that the rule must be fired only for tuples of R^{bf} marked with magic predicate values.

The slightly more difficult problem to solve is the construction of the rules to generate the magic predicates. Magic predicates must mark useful tuples and, if possible, only useful tuples. A first constant is known for a magic predicate — the constant derived from the query. For example, with the query $R(\text{John},x)$, the generation process for the magic predicates will be initialized by MAGIC_$R^{bf}(\text{John})$. The generation of the other tuples of magic predicates is done by modeling with rules the sideways information passings given by the sip graphs. To focus as much as possible on relevant tuples, we shall use a total sip graph. Thus for each occurrence of a recursive predicate R^{xx} appearing in a rule body, a magic rule must be built to constrain the bound variables of R^{xx} as follows: The rule head is MAGIC_$R^{xx}(\ldots)$ and the rule body is composed of all predicates that precede R^{xx} in the total sip graph, recursive predicates being replaced by corresponding magic predicates. The variables are determined by the sip graph and by the bound positions of the adornment. A detailed explanation and a partial proof of the validity of the method may be found in [Beeri87].

The rewritten rules by generalized magic sets for the ancestors, same generation cousins, and reverse lists are:

1. Linear definition of Ancestors with query ANC(John,y):

(r1) $MAGIC\_ANC^{10}(x)$, $PAR(x,y)$ → $ANC^{10}(x,y)$

(r2) $MAGIC\_ANC^{10}(x)$, $PAR(x,z)$ → $MAGIC\_ANC^{10}(z)$
        $MAGIC\_ANC^{10}(x)$, $PAR(x,z)$, $ANC^{10}(z,y)$ → $ANC^{10}(x,y)$

(q) $MAGIC\_ANC^{10}(John)$

2. Quadratic definition of same-generation-cousins with query SG(John,y):

(r1) $MAGIC\_SG^{10}(x)$,$HUM(x)$ → $SG^{10}(x,x)$

(r2) $MAGIC\_SG^{10}(x)$,$PAR(xp,x)$ → $MAGIC\_SG^{10}(xp)$
        $MAGIC\_SG^{10}(x)$,$PAR(xp,x)$,$SG^{10}(xp,z1)$,$PAR(z1,z)$, $PAR(z2,z)$ →
                $MAGIC\_SG^{10}(z2)$
        $MAGIC\_SG^{10}(x)$,$PAR(xp,x)$,$SG^{10}(xp,z1)$,$PAR(z1,z)$,$PAR(z2,z)$,
                $SG^{10}(z2,yp)$,$PAR(yp,y)$ → $SG^{10}(x,y)$

(q) $MAGIC\_SG^{10}(John)$

3. List reverse with query REVERSE(list,y):

(r1) $MAGIC\_APPEND^{110}(X,[])$ → $APPEND^{110}(X,[],X|[])$

(r2) $MAGIC\_APPEND^{110}(X,W|Y)$,$LIST(W)$ → $MAGIC\_APPEND^{110}(X,Y)$
        $MAGIC\_APPEND^{110}(X,W|Y)$,$LIST(W)$,$APPEND^{110}(X,Y,Z)$ →
                $APPEND^{110}(X,W|Y,W|Z)$

(r3) $MAGIC\_REVERSE^{10}([])$ → $REVERSE^{10}([],[])$

(r4) $MAGIC\_REVERSE^{10}(W|X)$ → $MAGIC\_REVERSE^{10}(X)$
        $MAGIC\_REVERSE^{10}(W|X)$,$REVERSE^{10}(X,Z)$ →
                $MAGIC\_APPEND^{110}(W,Z)$
        $MAGIC\_REVERSE^{10}(W|X)$,$REVERSE^{10}(X,Z)$,$APPEND(W,Z,Y)$ →
                $REVERSE^{10}(W|X,Y)$

(q) $MAGIC\ REVERSE^{10}(list)$

There is a great similarity between generalized magic sets and the Alexander method. In the magic sets rewritten rules, the "problem" predicates of Alexander are renamed "magic" and the "solution" predicates keep their original name. Instead of using continuation predicates, generalized magic sets repeat the previous rule's condition. This is not optimal because it leads the system to reevaluate conditions during forward chaining. Thus a solution that memorizes intermediate predicates (the continuation predicates of Alexander) has been proposed under the name extended supplementary magic sets [Beeri87]. However, at least two differences appear between the Alexander method and extended supplementary magic sets:

1. The Alexander method propagates constants in the order of the rule predicates, while magic sets choose the best sip graph. This may require a reordering of the rules' body predicates in the case of the Alexander method.

2. The Alexander method first adds the answer definition (the REP predicate) to the rule program before transformation. This is necessary if one wants to get a correct answer without too many tuples in the case where too many magic constants are generated. To be correct, magic sets generally require one to run the query again on the generated result to eliminate nonrelevant tuples.

Magic Functions

In [Gardarin86], a new method based on a functional approach was introduced. Rules are rewritten as functional equations to compute a query answer. In [Gardarin87], which extends this functional approach, the method is called *magic functions*. The idea of this approach is that a relation instance defines derived functions; each function is a mapping from one set of values in one column to the corresponding set of values in another column. The merit of the functions is to move up constants as function arguments; that is why they are called magic functions. Rules are then rewritten using magic functions as a system of equations between functions. The equations are solved to get the query answer functional expression.

Let us give a view of the method using the following example, which defines the odd ancestors in a redundant manner.

$$\text{ANCESTOR}(x,y) \leftarrow \text{PARENT}(x,y)$$
$$\text{ANCESTOR}(x,z) \leftarrow \text{PARENT}(x,y),\text{ANCESTOR}(y,v),\text{ANCESTOR}(v,z)$$
$$\text{ANCESTOR}(x,z) \leftarrow \text{ANCESTOR}(x,y),\text{ANCESTOR}(y,v),\text{ANCESTOR}(v,z)$$

With the query ?Ancestor(a,z), the method leads to the fixpoint equation between the magic functions Ancestor(X) and Parent(X), which, respectively, maps a set of persons X to their ancestors and parents:

$$\text{Ancestor}(X) = \text{Parent}(X) + \text{Ancestor}(\text{Ancestor}(\text{Parent}(X))) + \text{Ancestor}(\text{Ancestor}(\text{Ancestor}(X)))$$

A way of using the fixpoint equation is to compute at compile time a symbolic solution to it and then to derive the relational algebra program from the symbolic form. This is possible when the generated language can be recognized and expressed in a polynomial form. In the example, by successive approximations (applying Tarski's theorem), one derives:

$$\text{Ancestor}(a) = \text{Parent}(a) + \text{Parent}^3(a) + \text{Parent}^5(a) + \ldots + \text{Parent}^{2n+1}(a)$$

for some n that gives the fixpoint. This formula yields a program to compute the polynomial. Indeed, the program computes the transitive closure of the grandparent relation starting from the parent of a.

The language generated by applying the successive approximation process to the fixpoint equation is not always recognizable. In such cases, the fixpoint equation is used only at run time. Each functional term of the solution is successively computed and applied to the data, if it has not already been, up to the point where no new data can be generated [Gardarin87].

With the odd ancestor example, the functional approach appears much simpler and more efficient than the magic set or Alexander methods. A strength of the method is its ability to discover redundant rules. Also it is well founded on rigorous mathematics. Unfortunately the algorithm (based on a graph analysis) to translate rules in functional equations given in [Gardarin86] applies only to rules composed with binary predicates. The translation algorithm has been extended to support nonbinary predicates and rules with function symbols in [Gardarin87]. The method consists of transforming the rules in binary rules using a sip graph; then each binary predicate $P(x,y)$ is replaced by a functional equation $p(x) = y$. Finally, the system of simultaneous equations is solved to express the query answer as a functional equation.

10.5.6 Optimization Methods for Strongly Linear Rules

Counting Methods
The counting method was proposed in [Sacca86c]. It can be applied to strongly linear rules of the form:

$$R(X, Y) \leftarrow B1(X, Y)$$
$$R(X, Y) \leftarrow B2(X, X1), R(X1, Y1), B3(Y1, Y)$$

where $B1$, $B2$, and $B3$ are base relations or nonrecursive predicates derived from base relations. $X, Y, X1, Y1$ represents variables or vectors of variables. This simple type of rule has a general solution of the form:

$$R = B1 \cup B2 \bullet B1 \bullet B3 \cup \ldots \cup B2^n \bullet B1 \bullet B3^n$$

where $\bullet$ is a join followed by a projection on correct attributes, and B^n represents n successive auto-joins of $B2$ followed by projections.

From a query $R(a, Y)$, the idea of counting is to rewrite the rules with counters that memorize the distance from a in number of inferences down through $B2$ and in number of inferences high through $B3$. The result should retain only tuples from $B3$ that correspond to the same number of inferences from a through $B2$, then from corresponding elements (via $B1$) through $B3$. The modified rule program is:

```
COUNT(0,a)
COUNT_B2(J,X),B2(X,X1) → COUNT_B2(J+1,X1)
COUNT_B2(J,X),B1(X,Y) → REVERSE_COUNT_B3(J,Y)
REVERSE_COUNT_B3(J,Y1),B3(Y1,Y) → REVERSE_COUNT_B3(J−1,Y)
REVERSE_COUNT_B3(0,Y) → R(Y)
```

This rule program counts from a while performing the transitive closure of $B2$: it keeps in COUNT_B2 the elements of the transitive closure with their distance from a. Then it performs a join with $B1$ and starts a reverse counting while computing the transitive closure of B3 from the retrieved elements in B3. When the reverse counters reach 0, a result tuple is generated in $R(Y)$. The method works for acyclic data. An extension is possible by checking the maximum value for the counters in the case of cyclic data, but this deteriorates the performance. This method is efficient and can be mixed with magic sets to get a magic counting method [Sacca86].

Graph Operators

Several graph traversal algorithms have been proposed to implement recursive queries in the case of strongly linear rules. Such operators require a special internal data structure based on graph or join indexes to be efficient. A survey and a new proposal may be found in [Gardarin-Pucheral87].

10.5.7 Comparison of Recursive Query Processing Methods

All the previous methods are intended to solve recursive queries. Their differences are summarized in Table 10.2. Most of them mix backward chaining (to

TABLE 10.2 Comparison of recursive query processing methods

	Feature					
Method	Type of chaining	Types of rule	Type of data	Compiled	Function	Redundancy elimination
Naive	Forward	All	All	Yes	Yes	No
Seminaive	Forward	All	All	Yes	Yes	No
PROLOG	Backward	Based	All	No	No	No
APEX	Backward forward	All	Acyclic	No	Yes	No
QSQ	Backward forward	All	All	No	No	No
Magic set	Backward forward	Linear	All	Yes	No	No
Extended magic set	Backward forward	All	All	Yes	Yes	No
Alexander	Backward forward	All	All	Yes	Yes	No
Magic function	Backward forward	All	All	Partly	Yes	Partly
Counting	Backward forward	Linear	All	Yes	Yes	No
Graph	Backward forward	Linear	All	Yes	Yes	No

move constants from the query to the base predicates) with forward chaining (to compute tuples). Some are interpreted, while others are compiled. Some apply to all rules, while others assume linear rules; even PROLOG-style evaluation requires that rule bodies start with nonrecursive predicates (denoted based in Table 10.2). Certain methods require the data to be acyclic. Not too many methods apply when functions are used and almost none eliminates redundant rules.

10.6 Deductive DBMS Architectures

We consider here the possible approaches to extend a classical relational DBMS toward a deductive one. Another possibility is to start with a logic programming language such as PROLOG and to extend it with a file system and then with DBMS functionalities. We shall not consider this class of approach, which entails the development of a new DBMS. Our classification is based on considerations given in [Jarke84] and [Bocca86].

10.6.1 Loose Coupling

A first approach, called *loose coupling,* consists of starting on the one hand with an existing relational DBMS and, on the other hand with an existing logic programming language (for example, a PROLOG interpreter or a DATALOG one); a call interface is then built to offer access facilities from the logic programming language to the DBMS.

> **Definition 10.29 Loose coupling**
> Architectural approach to building a deductive DBMS consisting of extending a logic programming language with special built-in predicates invoking a relational DBMS and returning new facts to the logic program.

The loose coupling approach is illustrated in Fig. 10.21.

With loose coupling, the user clearly sees two types of systems. He or she writes rule programs using the logic programming language (PROLOG) and invokes the DBMS using predefined predicates with a specific syntax, for example SQL. The result of a DBMS retrieval call is a set of tuples that are added as facts to the logic program; thus the program is modified during execution, at each DBMS call that produces a side effect (the insertion of new facts). It is also possible to update the database from the logic program using special predicates, such as INSERT, DELETE, or UPDATE with arguments that are constants or instantiated variables in the program context.

The systems obtained using loose coupling are far from satisfying the deductive DBMS objectives. Indeed certain required functions are not offered.

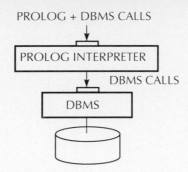

FIGURE 10.21 Loose coupling architecture

There exist two types of facts (the logic program facts and the database facts), rules are not integrated in a knowledge base, the query languages for base relations and deduced relations are different, and so on. Also the performances are generally poor. The optimization of the number and extent of DBMS requests and the optimization of the number of tuples used for the inference process are completely under the control of the rule programmer. However, loose coupling is a realistic approach, although its limitations are not well understood. Several prototypes and even commercial products have been built using a loose coupling approach.

10.6.2 Tight Coupling

A second approach, called *tight coupling,* consists of modifying or extending a rule interpreter to support references to database predicates in the rule conditions.

> **Definition 10.30 Tight coupling**
> Architectural approach to building a deductive DBMS consisting of coupling a rule interpreter on top of a relational DBMS such that any database relation can be used as a normal predefined predicate in a rule program.

This approach is illustrated in Fig. 10.22.

With tight coupling, the DBMS is made invisible to the user. Base predicates with their instances are included in the logic universe offered to the programmer. They are referenced in the logic program as classical relations, sometimes with a prefix (often edb_) specifying that they are predicates in the extensional database.

The rule interpreter is built as a layer on the DBMS. It retrieves facts in the database when needed in the inference process. For this purpose, queries to bring

DATALOG OR PROLOG

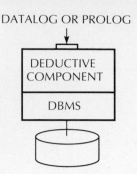

FIGURE 10.22 Tight coupling architecture

relevant facts in the program universe are given to the DBMS. These queries are optimized in number and result size. Two types of implementation of the query generation process are possible.

The first implementation is called *static tight coupling*. It proceeds using a precompiler. The precompiler performs a first evaluation of the logic program assuming that every database predicate is true. This evaluation allows the precompiler to generate queries that will, at execution time, instantiate all possibly relevant tuples from the database. As constants are passed along during the precompiler evaluation, queries benefit from a certain sideways information passing. Tuples that do not have the constant values in the correct position are not read in main memory. As a second more precise evaluation, the real execution is performed; this time, extensional predicates are instantiated in the rule interpreter environment by running the previously generated queries.

The second implementation is called *dynamic tight coupling*. This approach performs a unique evaluation. When a database predicate is invoked, a query is in principle issued to the DBMS to evaluate the predicate. Certain optimizations are possible in such a way that not all tuples of database predicates need be instantiated in main memory. Possible optimizations are to instantiate constants as much as possible to restrict the searched predicate tuples, avoid sending twice the same query, and delay certain query evaluations to pack them with others. Query subquery can be applied with dynamic tight coupling to evaluate recursive queries.

Along with tight coupling, it is possible to develop a rule management subsystem that stores rules in databases and retrieves them when required. Thus tight coupling presents the advantage of offering a homogeneous logic programming interface, which allows the user to define extensional and intensional predicates. These predicates and rules may be saved. Moreover efficient query optimization techniques may be developed. It is even possible to extend the rule interpreter with specific access methods to perform more efficiently certain inferences — for example, for recursive rules [Bocca86]. We then reach the limits of tight coupling and are close to integration.

10.6.3 Integration

The last approach is called *integration*. This time, the inference subsystem is completely integrated within the relational DBMS and works on the DBMS internal model and buffers. It works as an extension of the already existing inference facilities.

> **Definition 10.31: Integration**
> Architectural approach to building a deductive DBMS consisting of integrating inside a relational DBMS a rule definition language and an inference subsystem to answer queries and execute updates on deduced relations.

This approach is illustrated in Fig. 10.23.

Integration requires one to modify the source code of an existing DBMS or to redo the whole system. The DBMS is modified by including the management of a rule base, a deductive query interpreter (or compiler), and specific compilation techniques and operators to deal with recursive rules. In general, relational algebra is not enough and must be extended with functions [Zaniolo85] or fixpoint operators. Such an approach allows users to expect integrated interfaces

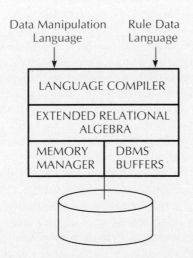

FIGURE 10.23 Example of an integrated architecture

(for example, a similar syntax for the rule and query languages) and good performance.

10.7 Conclusion

In this chapter, a synthesis of the research being done in deductive databases has been examined. Among the various approaches, we mainly focus on the integration of a logic programming language inside an extended relational DBMS. This approach is probably a long-term one, while coupling PROLOG with a relational DBMS is a short-term approach. Products are already sold as relational DBMS interfaces. They are a very first approach to knowledge base management.

Several desirable features for a rule language to declare knowledge around a relational database have been studied. Most of them were integrated to a logic programming language called DATALOG, with a fixpoint semantics. The main extensions of DATALOG, which seems to be necessary for rule programming, are the support of functions, negations, and sets. However, not much is known about implementing such extensions. The notion of stratification of a DATALOG program with negation and sets seems to be a dominant approach whose limits are not well understood.

Another type of rule language that could be more practical than DATALOG may be derived from production rules. Production rules are used in the most successful expert systems. Thus such languages could offer a powerful tool for deductive database applications. However, the integration of an inference component based on general production rules in a deductive DBMS leads to several difficult problems. Also the advantages of production-rule-based languages versus extended DATALOG have not been demonstrated.

The optimization of queries bearing on derived predicates is a complex problem. First, the optimization in presence of a large number of rules has not been well studied. Approaches using a graph-oriented representation of the rules have been the most investigated. However, performance has not been well estimated or measured. The use of metarules has also not been well investigated. Second, recursive query processing is a complex problem. Although several techniques have been proposed to optimize recursive rules, there has not been much implementation with actual applications. Also benchmarks have not even been defined. Moreover, several open questions remain to be solved.

One problem that is not well understood is the optimization of queries in the presence of functions. Although a few solutions have been proposed [Gardarin87, Kifer87], not many techniques have been specified to avoid infinite generation. Unification using interpreted functions also has to be explored. Moreover the relationship between complex data structures and functions is not clear. A second problem, which is even more difficult, is the simplification of rule systems. It may appear that rules are redundant or have common parts. It is then important to see this redundancy and to simplify the rule system. This is even more important if one uses a rewriting algorithm to optimize recursive rules, such as Alexander or magic sets. These algorithms generally generate complex rule systems that must be simplified before execution. Unfortunately the problem is complex and in theory undecidable.

Other important problems remain, such as checking rule consistency and handling metarules and integrity constraints between derived predicates. Also the compilation of a rule base probably has to be considered. We could envision that a kernel of representative queries be compiled in advance. The deductive DBMS would have to determine what can be used for new queries and what compiled results should be saved. This could greatly improve performance in avoiding re-compilation. Finally the most important issue is probably to build a realistic prototype working with one or more actual applications.

10.8 References and Bibliography

[Artificial Int.80] Artificial Intelligence, V13, North Holland, 1980.

[Abiteboul87a] Abiteboul S., Grumbach S., "Une Approche logique à la manipulation d'objets complexes," T.S.I., V6, N5, 1987.

[Abiteboul87b] Abiteboul S., Vianu V., "A Transaction Language Complete for Database Update and Specification," Proc. of ACM PODS, 1987.

[Aho79] Aho A. V., Ullman J. D., "Universality of Data Retrieval Languages," Conf. of POPL, San Antonio, Texas, 1979.

[Apt86] Apt C., Blair H., Walker A., "Towards a Theory of Declarative Knowledge," in *Foundations of Deductive Databases and Logic Programming*, Minker J. (ed.), Morgan Kaufmann, Los Altos, 1987.

[Bancilhon86a] Bancilhon F., "Naive Evaluation of Recursively Defined Relations," in *On Knowledge Base Management Systems*, Springer-Verlag, 1986.

[Bancilhon86b] Bancilhon F., Maier D., Sagiv Y., Ullman J. D., "Magic Sets and Other Strange Ways to Implement Logic Programs," 5th ACM Symposium on Principles of Database Systems, Cambridge, Massachusetts, 1986.

[Bancilhon86c] Bancilhon F., Ramakrishnan R., "An Amateur's Introduction to Recursive Query Processing Strategies," ACM SIGMOD'86, Washington, D.C., May 1986.

[Bayer85] Bayer R., "Query Evaluation and Recursion in Deductive Database Systems," Technical Report, Technische Universitaet, Munich, West Germany, January 1985.

[Beeri86] Beeri C. et al., "Sets and Negation in a Logical Database Language (LDL1)," Proc. of ACM PODS, 1987.

[Beeri87] Beeri C., Ramakrishnan R., "On the Power of Magic," ACM PODS, 1987.

[Bidoit86] Bidoit N., Hull R. "Positivism versus Minimalism," Proc. of ACM PODS, 1986.

[Bocca86] Bocca J., Decker H., Nicolas J. M., Vieille L., Wallace M., "Some Steps towards a DBMS Based KBMS," IFIP World Congress, 1986.

[Brownston85] Brownston L., Farrel R., Kant E., Martin N., *Programming Expert Systems in OPS5: An Introduction to Rule Based Programming*, Addison-Wesley, 1985.

[Buchanan84] Buchanan B., Shortliffe E., *Rule Based Expert Systems,* Addison-Wesley, 1984.

[Chandra80] Chandra K. A., Harel D., "Computable Queries for Relational Databases," Journal of Computer and Systems Science, 1980.

[Chandra82] Chandra K. A., Harel D., "Horn Clauses and the Fixpoint Query Hierarchy," Proc. 1st ACM Symposium on Principles of Database Systems, 1982.

[Chang78] Chang C. L., "Deduce 2: Further Investigations of Deduction in Relational Data Bases," in [Gallaire78].

[Chang81] Chang C. L., "On Evaluation of Queries Containing Derived Relation in a Relational Database," in [Gallaire81].

[Chang86] Chang C. L., Walker A., "PROSQL: A Prolog Programming Interface with SQL/DS," 1st Int. Workshop on Expert Database Systems, 1986.

[Clark78] Clark C., "Negation as Failure," in *Logic and Databases,* Gallaire and Minker, (eds.), Plenum Press, 1978.

[Clocksin81] Clocksin W. F., Mellish C. S., *Programming in Prolog,* Springer-Verlag, 1981.

[Coscia86] Coscia P., Franceschi P., Kouloumdjian J., Levi G., Moll G. H., Simonelli C., Sardu G., Torre L., "The Epsilon Knowledge Base Management System: Architecture and Data Base Access Optimization," in [ESPRIT86].

[Cuppens86] Cuppens F., Demolombe R., "A Prolog-Relational DBMS Interface Using Delayed Evaluation," in [ESPRIT86].

[Delobel86] Delobel C., "Bases de données et bases de connaissances: Une Approache systèmique à l'Aide d'une algèbre matricielle des relations," Journees Francophones, Grenoble, January 1986.

[Demolombe84] Demolombe R., "Syntactical Characterization of a Subset of Domain Independent Formulas," Internal Report, ONERA-CERT, Toulouse, 1984.

[Denoël86] Denoel E., Roelants D., Vauclair M., "Query Translation for Coupling Prolog with a Relational Data Base Management System," in [ESPRIT86].

[ESPRIT86] CEE, ESPRIT Project, *Integration of Logic Programming and Data Bases,* Proc. Venice Workshop, December, 1986.

[Findler79] Findler N. (ed.), *Associative Networks,* Academic Press, 1979.

[Gallaire78] Gallaire H., Minker J., *Logic and Databases,* Plenum Press, 1978.

[Gallaire81] Gallaire H., Minker J., Nicolas J. M., *Advances in Database Theory,* V1, Plenum Press, 1981.

[Gallaire84] Gallaire H., Minker J., Nicolas J. M., "Logic and Databases: A Deductive Approach," ACM Computing Surveys, V16, N2, June 1984.

[Gardarin84] Gardarin G., Gelenbe E. (eds.), *New Applications of Databases,* ICOD II Workshop, 1984, Academic Press, 1984.

[Gardarin85] Gardarin G., De Maindreville C., Simon E., "Extending a Relational DBMS towards a Rule Base System: A PrTN based Approach," CRETE WORKSHOP on AI and DB, June 1985.

[Gardarin86] Gardarin G., De Maindreville C., "Evaluation of Database Recursive Logic Programs as Recurrent Function Series," ACM SIGMOD'86, Washington, D.C., May 1986.

[Gardarin87] Gardarin G., "Magic Functions: A Technique for Optimization of Extended Datalog Recursive Programs," Very Large Data Bases, Brighton, England, September 1987.

[Gardarin-Pucheral87] Gardarin G., Pucheral P., "Optimization of Generalized Recursive Queries Using Graph Traversal," Internal report INRIA, 1987.

[Genrich78] Genrich H., Lautenbach K., "Facts in Places: Transition Nets," Lecture Notes in Computer Sciences, 64, Springer-Verlag, 1978.

[Genrich81] Genrich H., Lautenbach K., "System Modelling with High Level Petri Nets," Theoretical Computer Sciences, N13, 1981.

[Giordana85] Giordana A., Saitta L., "Modelling Production Rules by Means of Predicate Transition Networks," Information Sciences Journal, V35, N1, 1985.

[Guessarian87] Guessarian I., "Some Fixpoint Techniques in Algebraic Structures and Application to Computer Science," INRIA-MCC Workshop, 1987.

[Hayes-Roth85] Hayes-Roth F., "Rule Based Systems," Communications of the ACM, V28, N9, September 1985.

[Henschen-Naqvi84] Henschen L. J., Naqvi S. A., "On Compiling Queries in Recursive First-Order Databases," JACM, V31, N1, January 1984.

[Itoh86] Itoh H., "Research and Development on Knowledge Base Systems at ICOT," Proc. 12th Very Large Data Bases, Kyoto, Japan, August, 1985.

[Jarke83] Jarke M., Koch J., "Range Nesting: A Fast Method to Evaluate Quantified Queries," Proc. ACM SIGMOD Conf., 1983.

[Jarke84] Jarke M., Vassiliou Y., "Data Bases and Expert Systems: Opportunities and Architectures for Integration," in *New Applications of Data Bases,* G. Gardarin, E. Gelenbe (eds.), Academic Press, 1984.

[Jarke84b] Jarke M., Koch J., "Query Optimization in Database Systems," Computing surveys, V16, N2, June 1984.

[Kerisit86] Kerisit J. M., "Preuve de la méthode d'Alexandre par une approche algébrique," Bull. Internal Report, May 1986.

[Kiernan87] Kiernan G., Le Maoult R., Pasquer F., "Le Support de domaines complexes dans SABRINA: Une Approche par intégration d'un interpréteur LISP," Journées BD3, 1987.

[Kifer86] Kifer M., Lozinskii E., "Filtering Data Flow in Deductive Databases," ICDT Conf., Rome, September 1986.

[Kifer87] Lozinskii E., Kifer M., "Implementing Logic Programs as a Database System," Data Engineering Conference, Los Angeles, 1987.

[Kowalski75] Kowalski R., "A Proof Procedure Using Connection Graphs," Journal of the ACM, V22, N4, October 1975.

[Kuper86a] Kuper G., "Logic Programming with Sets," Proc. ACM PODS, 1987.

[Kuper86b] Kuper G., "LPS: A Logic Programming Language for Nested Relations," Unpublished manuscript, 1986.

[Lloyd87] Lloyd J., *Foundations of Logic Programming,* 2d ed., Springer-Verlag, 1987.

[Lozinskii85] Lozinskii E. L., "Evaluating Queries in Deductive Databases by Generating," IJCAI Proc., Los Angeles, August 1985.

[Lozinskii86] Lozinskii E. L., "A Problem-Oriented Inferential Database System," ACM TODS, V11, N3, September 1986.

[McKay81] McKay D., Shapiro S., "Using Active Connection Graphs for Reasoning with Recursive Rules," Proc. IJCAI, 1981.

[Maier85] Maier D., Warren D., "Computing with Logic: Logic Programming with Prolog," Unpublished memorandum, 1985.

[Maindreville86] De Maindreville C., Simon E., "Deciding Whether a Production Rule Program is Relational Computable," Internal Report INRIA, February 1987.

[Maindreville87] De Maindreville C., Simon E., "Query Processing Techniques for Production Rule Programs in a DBMS," Journées bases de données avancées, May 1987.

[Marque-Pucheu84] Marque-Pucheu G., Martin-Gallausiaux J., Jomier G., "Interfacing PROLOG and Relational DBMS," in *New Applications of Data Bases,* Academic Press, 1984.

[Merrett84] Merrett T. H., *Relational Information Systems,* Prentice-Hall, 1984, Chapter 5.

[Minker82] Minker J., Nicolas J. M., "On Recursive Axioms in Deductive Databases," Inf. Systems, V8, N1, January 1982.

[Naqvi86] Naqvi S., "A Logic for Negation in Database Systems," Workshop on Deductive Databases, University of Maryland, 1986.

[Nicolas83] Nicolas J. M., Yazdanian K., "An Outline of BDGEN: A Deductive DBMS," IFIP Congress 83, Paris, 1983.

[Nilsson80] Nilsson N., *Principles of Articial Intelligence,* Tioga Publication, 1980.

[Peterson81] Peterson J., *Petri Net Theory and the Modelling of Systems,* Prentice-Hall, 1981.

[Przymusinski86] Przymusinski T., "On the Semantics of Stratified Deductive Databases," Workshop on Deductive Databases, University of Maryland, 1986.

[Reiter78] Reiter R., "On Closed World Data Bases," in *Logic and Databases,* Gallaire and Minker (eds.), Plenum Press, 1978.

[Reiter84] Reiter R., "Towards a Logical Reconstruction of Relational Database Theory," in *On Conceptual Modelling,* Springer-Verlag, 1984.

[Rohmer85] Rohmer J., Lescoeur R., "La Methode d'Alexandre: Une Solution pour traiter les axiomes récursifs dans les bases de données déductives," Internal Report, Bull. Research Center, DRAL/IA/45.01, March 1985.

[Rohmer86] Rohmer J., Lescoeur R., Kerisit J. M., "The Alexander Method — A Technique for the Processing of Recursive Axioms in Deductive Databases," New Generation Computing, V4, 1986.

[Rosenkrantz80] Rosenkrantz D., Hunt H., "Processing Conjunctive Predicates and Queries," Proc. of 6th VLDB Int. Conf., Montreal, 1980.

[Rosenthal86] Rosenthal A., Heiler S., Dayal U., Manola F., "Traversal Recursion: A Practical Approach to Supporting Recursive Applications," ACM SIGMOD 1986 Proc., Washington, D.C., May 1986.

[Sacca86] Sacca D., Zaniolo C., "Magic Counting Methods," MCC Technical Report DB-401-86, December 1986.

[Sacca86b] Sacca D., Zaniolo C., "Implementing Recursive Logic Queries with Function Symbols," MCC Technical Report, 1986.

[Sacca86c] Sacca M., Zaniolo C., "On the Implementation of a Simple Class of Logic Queries for Databases," 5th ACM Symposium on Principles of Database Systems, Cambridge, Massachusetts, 1986.

[Sagiv87] Sagiv Y., "Optimizing Datalog Programs," 6th ACM Symposium on Principles of Database Systems, San Diego, March 1987.

[Shmueli86] Shmueli O., Tsur S., Beeri C., Naqvi S., Ramakrishnan R., "Sets and Negations in a Logic Database Language (LDL1)," MCC Technical Report DB-375-86, 1986.

[Stonebraker86] Stonebraker M., Rowe A. L., "The Postgres Papers," University of California, Berkeley, ERL M86/85, November 1986.

[Tarski55] Tarski A., "A Lattice Theoretical Fixpoint Theorem and Its Applications," Pacific Journal of Mathematics, N5, 1955, pp. 285–309.

[Ullman82] Ullman J. D., *Principles of Database Systems,* Computer Science Press, 1982.

[Ullman85] Ullman J. D., "Implementation of Logical Query Languages for Databases," ACM SIGMOD 1985, in ACM TODS, V10, N3, September 1986.

[Valduriez86] Valduriez P., Boral H., "Evaluation of Recursive Queries Using Join Indices," Proc. First Intl. Conference on Expert Database Systems, Charleston, 1986.

[Van Emden76] Van Emden M., Kowalski R., "The Semantics of Predicate Logic as a Programming Language," J. ACM V23, N4, October 1976.

[Van Gelder86] Van Gelder A., "A Message Passing Framework for Logical Query Evaluation," Proc. ACM SIGMOD Conf., Washington, D.C., May 1986.

[Vieille86] Vieille L., "Recursive Axioms in Deductive Databases: The Query Sub-query Approach," Proc. First Intl. Conference on Expert Database Systems, Charleston, 1986.

[Wong76] Wong E., Youssefi K., "Decomposition: A Strategy for Query Processing," ACM TODS, V1, N3, September 1976.

[Zaniolo85] Zaniolo C., "The Representations and Deductive Retrieval of Complex Objects," Proc. of 11th Int. Conf. VLDB, August 1985.

[Zaniolo86] Zaniolo C., "Safety and Compilation of Non Recursive Horn Clauses," MCC Tech. Report DB-088-85.

11

OBJECT ORIENTATION IN RELATIONAL DATABASE SYSTEMS

11.1 Introduction

Relational database technology has proved to be successful at supporting standard data processing (business) applications, such as accounting, inventory control, and payroll. This success is due to the mathematical simplicity of the relational model founded on set theory [Codd70]. However, there are now emerging nonstandard applications that require database management functions, such as knowledge bases, office automation, and computer-aided design (CAD). One common requirement of these applications is the efficient support of objects of rich type [Batory84] and of complex objects [Lorie83, Lum85]. This requirement is one salient feature of *object orientation* [Deppish86].

Although the relational model has powerful concepts such as set orientation, it is generally considered insufficient for supporting object orientation and other features (such as recursion). For instance, current relational systems must provide additional tools, such as a report generator, to display the data in a hierarchical fashion. Two different approaches have been proposed to solve this problem. The first is to replace the relational model with a data model with richer semantics. Over the last decade, a large number of new data models have been proposed. They include the entity-relationship model [Chen76] and semantic data models [Tsur84, King85]. Some are based on powerful paradigms such as logic- [Kuper85], functional- [Shipman81], or object-oriented [Maier86] data models.

These models, however, do not have the simplicity of the relational model, and research to define a universal data model for all types of applications is ongoing.

Another approach is to retain the relational model and extend it with simple and powerful constructs. One main extension is to relax the constraint that relations be in 1NF. The main advantage of that approach is simplicity and thus viability. However, this dichotomy is very simplistic since some proposed extensions of the relational model can be so significant that they lead to a totally different and complex model.

In this chapter, we concentrate on the second (more "relational") approach to support some aspects of object orientation. In Section 11.2, we introduce the performance problems posed by the management of potentially large atomic objects and complex objects to current RDBMSs. Two powerful solutions to these problems are the support of abstract data types (ADTs) and hierarchical objects, respectively. Section 11.3 describes the use of ADTs in a relational database system. Section 11.4 presents a general data model that extends the definition of relations to contain hierarchical objects and an associated algebra. This model is shown to subsume other data models. In Section 11.5, we discuss implementation techniques for complex objects. These techniques are critical for the efficient manipulation of objects and subobjects. In Section 11.6, we discuss the incorporation of object identity at the conceptual level to model graph structures. This important feature leads to a purely object-oriented data model but deviates significantly from the relational model.

11.2 Object Support in Current Relational Database Systems

In this section, we describe the way atomic objects and complex objects may be supported in current relational database systems. We also show that the current solution leads to both increased complexity of application programs and poor performance.

11.2.1 Support of Atomic Objects

An *atomic object* is a data unit of a particular type that provides an abstraction to higher system levels manipulating it; its internal structure is hidden from higher levels.

Definition 11.1 Atomic object
Unit of data treated atomically for higher levels of abstraction.

For example, a float number is an atomic object. An atomic object can be a very large object with its own structure. Examples of large atomic objects are documents, graphics, and images. Atomic objects must be manipulated through specific operations that understand their structure. Examples of such operations are the counting of the number of words in a document or the superimposition of two images. Although the definition of domain in the relational model is not constrained, standard RDBMSs typically provice a few built-in data types, such as integer, float, and string, which are sufficient for business applications. The way they can handle large atomic objects is by managing them as long string attributes. Thus the DBMS is used to store and retrieve the objects, but their interpretation (to apply specific operations) is done by general-purpose programs interfacing the DBMS via a preprocessor. The general-purpose programming language is used to supplement the DBMS with a much richer typing system. It follows that many primitive data processing functions are performed by the application programs rather than the DBMS. There are several problems with this approach. First, the code for interpreting the objects might be redundantly stored in many application programs. Second, there are strong data/program dependencies; changing the object format implies the modification of all application programs that interpret the object. Finally, and most important, this approach may be inefficient because the application program written in a general-purpose language has very little control over the operating system managing the objects. If the object is large, only segments of it will be kept in the program address space. Accessing other segments will generate page faults and possibly disk accesses.

One solution is to augment the relational database system with richer types. Thus the DBMS can interpret the structures of the atomic objects and use database techniques to manage them (indexing, buffering). However, a large number of primitive types is probably necessary to support various application areas. In the spectrum of all possible types, the extreme point is the union of all base types found in programming languages (array, matrix, list, bit map, and so on). This solution is clearly unrealistic. Instead of having a fixed set of data types, a better solution is to make the DBMS types extendable by the user so that specific and changing requirements can be rapidly accommodated. ADTs provide an adequate support for such extendability.

11.2.2 Complex Object Support

A complex object is an object whose attributes need not be atomic but may be objects themselves. The structure of a complex object is not flat as a relational tuple but is typically hierarchical. A *complex object* is defined as a root object and a hierarchy of subobjects. In this section, we use the following general definition of complex object (a more formal definition will be given in Section 11.4):

> **Definition 11.2 Complex object**
> Object having a hierarchical structure whose attributes can be atomic
> objects or objects themselves.

The nonatomic objects contained in an object are called subobjects or component objects. Complex terms (functors) present in logic programming [Zaniolo85], office automation objects [Adiba85, Banerjee87a], or CAD design objects [Batory85] are examples of complex objects. As an example, consider an office automation system where cabinets are simulated. A *cabinet* is a hierarchical object that contains a set of drawers, each drawer containing a set of folders and each folder containing a set of documents. These objects can be easily represented in the relational model by grouping the subobjects of the same type in a relation and linking the subobjects of different types in terms of matching join attributes. Four relations are thus necessary to model a set of cabinets

1. CABINET (CAB#, PROPERTIES, . . .)
2. DRAWER (DRW#, CAB#, PROPERTIES, . . .)
3. FOLDER (FDR#, DRW#, PROPERTIES, . . .)
4. DOCUMENT (DOC#, FDR#, DESCRIPTION, DATE, AUTHOR, . . .)

The main problem of this approach is low performance for retrieving entire complex objects. For example, the materialization of a particular cabinet will require three joins (a costly operation) of the above relations. The problem can be viewed as optimizing joins on foreign keys. For instance, the efficient retrieval of a cabinet and all its dependent drawers can be seen as optimizing the join between relations CABINET and DRAWER on foreign key CAB#. One way to achieve this optimization is to cluster the cabinet tuple and the matching drawer tuples together (in the same disk extent). Efficient manipulation of complex objects is difficult to achieve because there are generally multiple access patterns to the object and its subobjects. For example, if a complex object stores the drawers within their cabinet, one type of query may retrieve all information concerning the drawers of a particular cabinet, whereas another type of query may be interested in retrieving information pertinent to drawers independent of their cabinet (for example, the DRW# of all drawers created in May 1987). Since the objects can be clustered in only a single way (without replication), favoring some access patterns is generally done at the expense of others. Also supporting multiple access patterns leads to additional complexity of the storage structures and algorithms.

The extension of relational database systems to handle complex objects faces two issues. First, a complex object model must be defined as an extension of the relational model. The primary extension consists of relaxing the 1NF constraint and allowing attributes to be set valued or tuple valued. The specification of such a model includes a well-defined algebra to manipulate complex objects. Second, complex objects must be efficiently implemented to favor some predefined access patterns.

11.3 Support of Abstract Data Types

Current relational database systems fail to support atomic objects of various kinds as required by many emerging application areas. One main desirable extension is a rich typing capability. In this section, we present the use of abstract data types (ADTs) as a viable solution.

11.3.1 Abstract Data Types

ADTs [Guttag77] offer a powerful abstraction capability that has been extensively exploited in programming languages. An *ADT* is an object type that defines a domain of values and a set of operations applicable to those values.

> **Definition 11.3 Abstract data type (ADT)**
> Object type together with a collection of operations applicable to objects of that type.

Thus an ADT encapsulates the data type and its related operations so that implementation details are hidden from higher levels. An ADT capability provides program modularity since changing the ADT implementation does not affect the upper layers that manipulate it through abstract operations. In addition, an important feature of an ADT is the ability to extend the basic data types supplied by a programming language with user-defined data types. An example of an ADT is a matrix with operations invert, add, and multiply. The type matrix can use the base type integer and related arithmetic operations to define and manipulate the elements of the matrix.

ADTs have been considered a solution to the connection between programming languages and relational database systems. The expected goal of this approach is to augment the DBMS with the capability of defining and manipulating atomic objects of any type. The operations on objects of a new type are defined by user-supplied procedures written in a programming language. The data manipulation language must then be extended so that ADT operations can be combined with database access.

Various approaches to the integration of ADTs in a relational database context have been proposed [Batory84, Osborn86, Rowe79, Stonebraker83, Stonebraker84, Su83] with various degrees of functionality. The highest level of functionality can significantly reduce the need for programming language preprocessors. In the following sections, we distinguish these approaches according to three important dimensions: ADT granularity, implementation language for ADTs, and support of ADT hierarchies.

11.3.2 ADT Granularity

In a relational system, two different granules may be considered for using ADTs: relation or domain.

When a relation is considered an ADT [Rowe79, Schmidt77, Wasserman79], operations to manipulate a relation are ADT operations. Thus database operations are encapsulated in the ADTs and are no longer under the control of the DBMS, since relations are embedded in the ADT programming language. This approach provides a high level of abstraction and therefore increases data independence, data protection, and data integrity. For example, a WINE abstract data type with associated update operations new_wine and new_price and retrieval operations $_price and FF_price could be supported. The operation that inserts a new wine can perform many kinds of complex checking. Although this approach has obvious advantages, its main drawback is the lack of control of database operations by the DBMS at the expense of performance.

A more recent approach attempting to support possibly very large objects allows ADTs to be defined over domains [Osborn86, Stonebraker83, Stonebraker85]. With this approach, database operations, such as retrieval of a set of objects, are entirely controlled by the DBMS. When a new domain type is added, related operations on objects of that domain must be specified by the ADT implementer. In [Osborn86], three types of operations are isolated: primitive, aggregate, and transformation operations.

Primitive operations define the methods for inserting, updating, displaying, and querying values of the related domain. The querying of ADT objects uses predicates that take ADT values as arguments and return a value true/false.

Definition 11.4 Primitive operation on ADT domain
Operation that specifies a method for inserting, updating, displaying, or testing values of the ADT domain.

Among all possible operations, two operations are mandatory. An object value has two representations: an external representation for display on a terminal or a special device (for example, a videoscreen) and an internal representation for storage on secondary memory (for example, a magnetic or optical disk). Therefore an operation that converts a value from its external to internal representation (input mode) and the inverse operation that converts a value from its internal to external representation (output mode) must be specified. Let us consider the following relation:

WINE (W#, VINEYARD, VINTAGE, DATE_OF_BUY)

where W# is of type INTEGER, VINEYARD and VINTAGE of type STRING(15), and DATE_OF_BUY of abstract data type DATE. The insertion of a new wine can be expressed in SQL notation as:

INSERT INTO WINE (W#, VINEYARD, VINTAGE, DATE_OF_BUY)
VALUES 210, "Beaujolais-Village," 1982, "July 14, 1983."

The external representation of the date "July 14, 1983," is a string. An input operation for type DATE will convert the string into an object of type DATE that can therefore be interpreted by other operations. Note that the input operation is more involved for more complex ADTs that cannot be entered directly at the terminal, as in the case of image or long text.

Some other primitive operations, such as equality or less_than predicates, are normally needed for relational operations such as restriction and join; however, they are not compulsory for all date types. For instance, equality of two long documents does not make much sense to us. However, date equality or inequality seems useful, perhaps to retrieve all wines bought before a certain date,

SELECT W#
FROM WINE
WHERE DATE_OF_BUY < "August 1, 1983"

The less_than operator related to the ADT DATE is interpreted as a predicate with two arguments of type DATE. Other operators might be defined to test or update objects of type DATE. The following query retrieves all pairs of wines that have been bought at least within a 30-day period:

SELECT W1.W#, W2.W#
FROM WINE (W1), WINE (W2)
WHERE W1.DATE_OF_BUY < DAY_ADD(W2.DATE_OF_BUY, 30)

The operator DAY_ADD returns the date obtained by adding some number of days to an argument date. The example shows a combined use of two ADT operators (< and DAY_ADD).

Aggregate operations for ADTs are useful to compute a single ADT value from a set of values. Aggregates such as MIN and AVERAGE on built-in data types are generally provided by relational query languages such as SQL. Therefore it is desirable to apply aggregates to ADTs as well.

Definition 11.5 Aggregate operation for ADT
Aggregate operation that takes a set of values as input and returns a single ADT value.

In a relational language such as SQL, the input set of values is obtained from a relation. For example, the query that retrieves the most recently bought wine can be expressed as:

SELECT VINEYARD
FROM WINE
HAVING DATE_OF_BUY = MAX_DATE (DATE_OF_BUY)

The function MAX_DATE takes as input the set of all dates present in relation WINE and returns the latest one.

Transformations [Osborn86] are ADT operations more powerful than the previous one. They transform a relation into a result relation.

> **Definition 11.6: Transformation**
> Function mapping one relation into another.

A typical example of use of transformation is the conversion of a relation storing a document in some form (such as a set of components) into a relation storing the document in another form (such as a set of lines). Transformations can also be used to express complex queries on a relation. Let us assume that the quality of a wine can be derived by applying some complex rules to the attributes of a WINE tuple. One might wish to write a transformation that maps relation WINE into the following relation.

GOOD_WINE (VINEYARD, VINTAGE, QUALITY).

This example is interesting since the transformation may be expressed itself as a query in the relational language. However, for a very complex mapping, such as the previous conversion example, a general-purpose programming language is necessary.

11.3.3 ADT Implementation Language

In order to specify abstract data type operations, three different kinds of language may be considered: general-purpose programming language (such as Pascal), relational query language (such as SQL), or programming language with database access primitives (such as Pascal/R).

The use of a general programming language for ADTs entails all data accesses to be controlled by the DBMS. Furthermore an atomic object must be virtually in main memory for manipulation by the related ADT operations. Virtual memory management is necessary for large objects. Since the ADT language does not provide database access, only domain granularity can be supported. Thus relations cannot be considered ADTs. Although many different languages may be desirable for implementing ADTs (C, Pascal, PROLOG, LISP, and others), an important decision of the DBMS designer is whether the language should be compiled or interpreted. These two possibilities exhibit performance/ease-of-control trade-offs.

With the compilation approach, ADT operations are compiled into machine code. When necessary, an ADT operation is loaded and linked to the DBMS. Therefore one can view the DBMS and the set of all ADT operations as a single reentrant program executed by user processes. The value of this approach is that compiled ADT operations run efficiently. However, user-written operations can contain errors. If a run-time error occurs in an ADT operation, the process executing the DBMS code will crash without returning anything to the user but an error code from the operating system. If a set operation is performed on a relation, an error occurring with one tuple will crash the entire operation. One simple way to deal with this situation is to let the user hang himself by writing sloppy code. In other words, ADT operations should be extensively tested before their incorporation in the DBMS. Another, more involved, approach makes the process manager, usually provided by the operating system, part of the DBMS. Such a process manager would take specific action in case of process termination upon error in an ADT operation. An example of such action is the creation of a new process having the same context as the one terminated and then jumping to the instruction after the crashed ADT operation. Such a solution is hard to implement. Note that the literature on prototyped systems supporting ADTs is quite evasive about this issue.

With the interpretation approach, ADT operations are stored in source code. The DBMS is coupled with an interpreter for the ADT implementation language. When necessary, an ADT operation is loaded and given to the interpreter. Compared to the compilation approach, an interpreted operation runs less efficiently. The main advantage is that the DBMS has better control over errors in ADT code. An interpreter can detect run-time errors and return error messages to the DBMS without terminating the user process. Such a solution has been implemented in the SABRINA system using a LISP interpreter [Kiernan87].

The use of a data manipulation language (or query language for short) to implement ADTs has been proposed in [Stonebraker84] for the language QUEL. This approach is proposed for domain granularity. Thus an attribute of type query language can be valued by one or more commands in the query language. Although our presentation is based on the proposal by Stonebraker for QUEL, we will use SQL to express examples for uniformity with the previous chapters. Let us consider the following relations:

WINE (**W**#, VINEYARD, VINTAGE, DATE_OF_BUY, ON_HAND)
STOCK (**W**#, **STORE,** QTY)

Relation keys are **bold face** type. ON_HAND is of type SQL and holds a query whose execution gives information on the quantity of wines on hand. The insertion of a new wine can be expressed as

INSERT INTO WINE (W#, VINEYARD, VINTAGE, DATE_OF_BUY,
    ON_HAND)
        VALUES 210, ''Beaujolais-Village,'' 1982, ''July 14, 1983,''
            ''SELECT STORE, QTY
            FROM STOCK
            WHERE W#=210''

When executed, the query for ON_HAND will yield a relation with two attributes. To exploit such a capability, the query language must be extended in several ways. The major extension is to allow the ".'' operator to take a left operand of type query language and a right operand of type attribute name. Thus the ".'' operator can be used to refer to attributes generated by an attribute of type query language. For example, the following query refers to attributes of ON_HAND in the projection and selection clauses:

```
SELECT VINEYARD, VINTAGE, ON_HAND.STORE
FROM WINE
WHERE W# = 210
       AND ON_HAND.QTY > 500
```

Such a query expressed in pure SQL would require a join between relations WINE and STOCK. If several stores hold a quantity greater than 500 for a given wine, attributes VINEYARD and VINTAGE will have duplicate values. For instance, if stores 20 and 35 have wine 210 in quantity greater than 500, the result relation would be as follows:

Vineyard	Vintage	Store
Beaujolais-Village	1982	20
Beaujolais-Village	1982	35

Another extension to the query language is to allow the comparison of attributes of type query language. Since these attributes yield relations, operators that compare relations are needed. In [Stonebraker 84], several operators, such as relation equality ($==$) and relation inclusion ($<<$), are proposed. For example, the following query returns all pairs of wine numbers with identical on-hand information.

```
SELECT W1.W#, W2.W#
FROM WINE (W1), WINE (W2)
WHERE W1.ON_HAND == W2.ON_HAND
```

The use of a query language as data type is very powerful. In particular, hierarchical objects such as ON_HAND in relation WINE can be supported more explicitly; joins need not be specified.

The two approaches shown for implementing ADTs, general-purpose programming language, and query language exhibit respective advantages. In order to combine their capabilities, a third approach is to use a programming language with data access primitives included. Such an approach has been propounded in Pascal/R [Schmidt77] and POSTGRES [Stonebraker 86]. This approach can accommodate both relation and domain granularity, thereby providing a high level of abstraction. Pascal/R enriches the language Pascal with a data-type relation on which tuple-at-a-time operations are supplied. In POSTGRES, domains can be of type QUEL or of type PROCEDURE. The type procedure can be viewed as a generalization of the type query language. Attributes of type procedure are procedures written in a programming language with embedded data access statements. Procedures are executed with a specific command and parameter values. Compared to the previous approach, where the query language is a data type, the use of procedures avoids duplicating possibly large amounts of code.

In the example, the query defining attribute ON_HAND is duplicated for each different W#. If ON_HAND were of type procedure, a single parametrized query needs to be defined as a procedure

```
ON_HAND_PROC (WINE#)
        SELECT STORE, QTY
        FROM STOCK
        WHERE W# = WINE#
```

Thus the values of attribute ON_HAND of type procedure are all ON_HAND_PROC (WINE#). As shown in [Stonebraker86], the use of a programming language with data access commands for implementing ADTs allows the support of complex objects with shared subobjects.

11.3.4 Support of ADT Hierarchies

It is customary to organize abstract data types as hierarchies. The basis for the ADT hierarchy is the subtype relationship between types. Types $T_1, T_2, \ldots, T_n$ are subtypes of type T if they can be thought of as special cases of type T. Inversely the supertype T is a generalization of types $T_1, T_2, \ldots, T_n$ [Smith77]. The specialization provided by subtypes is called is_a relationship. For example, types text and images are subtypes of type long_string. All ADTs can be partially ordered based on the subtype relationship. Since subtypes can be defined over system-provided types, *ADT hierarchies* can be defined.

Definition 11.7 ADT hierarchy
Hierarchy of types based on the subtype relationship and rooted with a system-defined type

An example of an ADT hierarchy whose root is type long_string is given in Fig. 11.1. In this example, all ADTs are subtypes of long_string.

Each abstract data type contains a set of operators applicable to objects of that type. An important capability associated with the support of ADT hierarchies is *operator inheritance*.

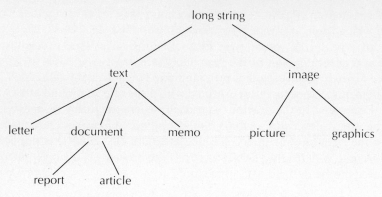

FIGURE 11.1 Example of ADT hierarchy

> **Definition 11.8 Operator inheritance**
> All operators related with a data type are inherited by all its subtypes
> either directly or transitively.

Let us assume that the operator search_string is defiend over the type text. By inheritance, search_string can be applied to objects of type letter, document, report, and so on. However, search_string is defined only for the type text.

Sometimes operators already existing in a type need to be redefined for some subtypes. In this case, operator inheritance is avoided. Rather operators redefined in a subtype overload the inherited operators. For example, if a print operator is defined for text and redefined for document (to cope with the document features), the print operator for document overloads the print operator for text. All subtypes of document inherit the print operator for document unless they are redefined.

The immediate advantages of supporting ADT hierarchies are increased modularity, functionality, and efficiency. Better modularity stems from the hierarchy of abstractions. Functionality is increased by operator inheritance and operator overloading since operators need not be redefined unless necessary. Efficiency of the DBMS is increased since redundancy of operator definitions is minimized.

11.4 Complex Object Model

The 1NF constraint of the relational model requires complex hierarchical objects to be normalized. By relaxing the 1NF constraint, complex objects may be supported more directly and hence more efficiently. The objective of a complex object model is to combine the respective advantages of the relational model and the hierarchical model [Tsichritzis76]. In particular, set operations should be applicable to hierarchically structured objects. Such a model can be used at a conceptual or internal level. When used at the internal level, the conceptual level can be based on the relational model and thus take advantage of relational database design technology (normalization). However, normal forms for complex objects can also be found. For example, [Ozsoyoglu85a, Ozsoyoglu87] describe a normal form for nested relations, relations whose attributes may be relations, based on multivalued dependencies. Such normal forms will help the design of conceptual schemas for complex objects. In this section, we present a general model that supports hierarchical objects [Bancilhon86]. This model subsumes many other complex object models that are more restrictive. Then we present an algebra for complex objects. This algebra is a simple extension of relational algebra.

11.4.1 Definition of Complex Objects

We now make the notion of a complex object more precise. A formal definition of the model and its powerful properties is given in [Bancilhon86]. Objects are defined recursively as follows:

1. Integers, floats, Booleans, and strings are objects called *atomic objects*. In addition, ADT objects are atomic objects.
2. If $O_1, O_2, \ldots, O_n$ are objects and $a_1, a_2, \ldots, a_n$ are distinct attribute names, then $[a_1:O_1, a_2:O_2, \ldots, a_n:O_n]$ is an object called a *tuple object*.
3. If $O_1, O_2, \ldots, O_n$ are objects, then $[O_1, O_2, \ldots, O_n]$ is an object called *set object*.

Tuples can have atomic, tuple, or set-valued attributes. The first option provides direct support for normalized relations. The second provides the ability to support hierarchical terms as in [Zaniolo85]. Finally, set-valued attributes allow nested relations as in [Bancilhon82, Ozsoyoglu87], or simple sets of atomic values as in [Ozsoyoglu85b]. The recursive definition of objects allows an unbounded degree of nesting. Examples of objects are:

an atom	10
a set	{1,2,3}
a tuple	[name:Smith, age:30]
a relation	{[name:Smith, age:30], [name:Doe, age:50]}
a hierarchical tuple [Zaniolo 85]	[name: [first:John, last:Doe], age:27]
a tuple with attributes being set of atoms [Ozsoyoglu 85b]	[name:Smith, children:{Jim, Ann}]
a tuple with nested relation [Bancilhon 82]	[wine#:210, on_hand:{[store:10, qty:250], [store:20, qty:500]}]

The definition of complex objects is quite general. For example, a set of integers is an object. In a database system, complex objects having the same schema need to be grouped into sets so that set operators may be efficiently applied to them. Typically the concept of relation must be extended to allow attributes to have complex objects as values.

> **Definition 11.9 Complex relation**
> Set of tuples whose attribute values are complex objects.

A database can thus be modeled as a list of complex relations. The rationale behind this approach is that an algebra for complex relations can be defined as an extension of relational algebra [Schek86, Zaniolo85].

The following example illustrates a wine database scheme composed of two complex relations: WINE and SALE. The database, called WINES, is itself modeled as a tuple object. For simplicity, we did not list the types of atoms.

```
WINES = [WINE: {[W#,
                ON_HAND: {[STORE, QTY]},
                VINEYARD,
                VINTAGE,
                PRICE: {[DATE, AMT]}]},
         SALE: {[DATE: [MONTH, YEAR],
                CITY,
                CUSTOMER: {[NAME,
                            WINE: {[W#, QTY]} ]} ]} ]
```

A graphical representation of this schema is given in Fig. 11.2, where * denotes a set, • denotes a tuple, and a leaf is an atom. A relational representation of this database would require six relations. Compared to the relational model, a complex object model essentially decreases the explicit use of joins. Fig. 11.3 illustrates an instance of object WINE using a graphical representation. The same object is described in tabular form as in [Schek86] in Fig. 11.4.

11.4.2 Algebra for Complex Relations

Since relational algebra is restricted to flat relations, it is not sufficient for manipulating complex relations. Therefore an algebra for complex relations is required. Such an algebra is useful as a target language for mapping queries of higher level and as a framework for query optimization where algebraic transformations can be used. Several algebras for complex objects have been formally proposed with various degrees of generality. [Zaniolo85] has introduced an extended relational algebra (ERA) for relations having nested tuple valued attributes. [Ozsoyoglu85b] proposed an algebra for summary tables — relations with attributes whose

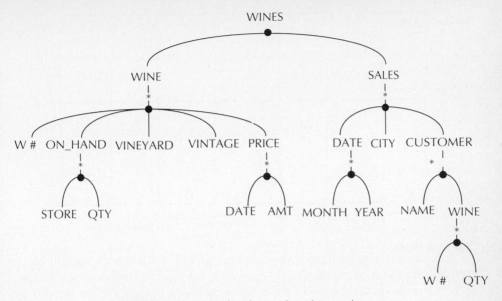

FIGURE 11.2 Example of complex object schema

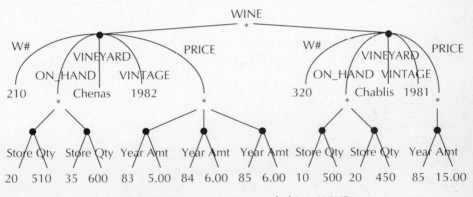

FIGURE 11.3 An instance of object WINE

values can be sets of atoms. [Abiteboul84] and [Schek86] have independently defined an algebra for non – first normal form (NFNF) relations — relations with relation valued attributes. [Fisher83] has proposed operations for one-level nested relations. More recently, FAD [Bancilhon87], a full data programming language including algebraic operators for complex objects, has been specified.

   In this section, we describe a simple algebra for complex relations. This algebra is general in the sense that it subsumes all of the mentioned algebras with

W#	ON_HAND		VINEYARD	VINTAGE	PRICE	
	STORE	QTY			YEAR	AMT
210	20 35	510 600	Chenas	1982	83 84 85	5.00 6.00 6.00
320	10 20	500 450	Chablis	1981	85	15.00

FIGURE 11.4 Tabular representation of object WINE

the exception of FAD (which supports more general objects with built-in identity). When operating on traditional relations, the algebra for complex relations reduces to relational algebra. This algebra contains the usual set union, set difference, and Cartesian product (applied to complex relations), plus complex restrict, complex project, and complex join operators. In addition, the algebra includes two restructuring operators, flatten and group.

Complex Restrict

The *complex restrict operator,* noted C-RESTRICT, can select on the basis of a complex condition whose predicates can apply to both objects and subobjects.

> **Definition 11.10 Complex restrict**
> Operation tha produces, from a complex relation, a relation, of same scheme, and whose tuples satisfy a complex condition.

Complex restrict is specified as C-RESTRICT (C-RELATION, C-CONDITION).

The complex condition is a Boolean expression, with operators AND, OR, and NOT, on predicates. We distinguish three kinds of predicates: simple, nested tuple, and nested set. Simple predicates are those used in relational algebra, for example, AGE > 25.

Nested tuple predicates apply to attributes of nested tuples. The "." operator is used to designate an attribute in a nested tuple. The "." operator takes a tuple-valued attribute as left operand and an attribute name as right operand. An example of nested tuple predicate is NAME.FIRST = "John."

Nested set predicates apply to attributes of tuples contained in nested sets, for example, attribute AMT in set PRICE nested in relation WINE (see Fig. 11.2). In order to designate any element in a nested set, we use the "*" operator. The "*" operator takes a set-valued attribute as left operand and an attribute name as right operand. An example of nested set predicate is: PRICE * AMT

< 5.00. A nested set predicate will entail keeping only the tuples satisfying the predicate.

We will now illustrate the use of complex restrict with some examples. The following restrict operator with nested tuple predicate returns all the sales of 1986 from the WINES database.

C-RESTRICT (SALE.DATE.YEAR = 1986)

Let us assume a complex relation PERSON of structure

PERSON: {[name, children: {first_name}]}

The following operation gives all persons who have a child named Ann:

C-RESTRICT (PERSON, "Ann" in children)

A possible result is

{[name: Smith, children: {Ann, Jim}]}

An example of restrict operator with nested set predicate can be expressed on the wine database to return the wines "Chenas" if they were ever priced less than $6.00.

C-RESTRICT (WINE, VINEYARD = "Chenas" AND PRICE * AMT < 6.00)

The result relation is given in tabular form in Fig. 11.5.

Complex Project
The complex project operator, noted C-PROJECT, projects a relation over attributes of objects and subobjects. However, C-PROJECT does not restructure the

| W# | ON_HAND | | VINEYARD | VINTAGE | PRICE | |
	STORE	QTY			YEAR	AMT
210	20 35	510 600	Chenas	1982	83	5.00

FIGURE 11.5 Result of complex restrict

operand relation. Therefore the result relation schema is a subtree of the operand relation schema. As in the traditional projection, duplicates produced in a set object or set subobject are eliminated.

Definition 11.11 Complex project
Operation that produces a complex relation from an input complex relation by keeping only the specified attributes and removing the duplicates in each set object.

Complex project is specified as C-PROJECT(C-RELATION,C-LIST) where C-LIST defines the list of attributes to keep. C-LIST is recursively defined as follows: C-LIST is a list of A_1, A_2, . . . , A_n where A_i is one of attribute_name, attribute_name : [C-LIST], and attribute_name : {[C-LIST]} where [ ] and { } designate a tuple or set structure, respectively.

We illustrate the application of C-PROJECT on the WINES database. First, we have the following equivalence:

C-PROJECT (SALE,DATE: [MONTH, YEAR]) ↔ C-PROJECT (SALE,DATE)

The operation

C-PROJECT (SALE, DATE:[YEAR], CITY)

returns a relation of structure {[DATE: [YEAR], CITY]}.

The following operation

C-PROJECT (WINE, ON_HAND, VINEYARD, PRICE:{[AMT]})

produces the result illustrated in Fig. 11.6.

ON_HAND		VINEYARD	PRICE
STORE	QTY		AMT
20 35	510 600	Chenas	5.00 6.00
10 20	500 450	Chablis	15.00

FIGURE 11.6 Result of complex project

Flatten

The new operator *flatten* transforms a complex relation into a 1NF relation. Only atomic valued attribute names appear in the result relation, that is, set-valued and tuple-valued attribute names disappear.

> **Definition 11.12 Flatten**
> Operator that normalizes (unnests) a complex relation.

For instance, the operation

FLATTEN (C-PROJECT (WINE, ON_HAND, VINEYARD))

produces the normalized relation of Fig. 11.7.

Group

The new operator *group* is the inverse of flatten. Thus it transforms a 1NF relation into a complex relation. The grouping is specified by the structure of the complex relation.

> **Definition 11.13 Group**
> Operator that groups the attributes of a 1NF relation according to a given hierarchical structure.

Group is specified as GROUP (RELATION, C-LIST) where C-LIST is similar to that of complex project. However, all attributes of the relation must appear in C-LIST. For example, let R be a relation defined as

R = FLATTEN (C-PROJECT (WINE, W#, ON_HAND))

The following operation groups the wine numbers and quantities by store:

GROUP (R, STORE, WINE: {[W#, QTY]})

The resulting complex relation is illustrated in Fig. 11.8. Note that attribute names for set- and tuple-valued attributes must be introduced.

STORE	QTY	VINEYARD
20	510	Chenas
35	600	Chenas

FIGURE 11.7 WINE relation after projection and flattening

STORE	WINE	
	W#	QTY
10	320	500
20	210	510
	320	450
35	210	600

FIGURE 11.8 Result of grouping

Complex Join

Similar to the traditional join, the *complex join operator,* denoted C-JOIN, can be defined as a complex restriction of the Cartesian product of two complex relations. However, it is desirable to have a specific join operator for performance reasons. Our definition of complex join imposes the constraint that the join condition applies on attributes of the same type at the first level of the complex relations. However, unlike the traditional join, join attributes need not be atoms but may be tuple valued or set valued.

> **Definition 11.14 Complex join**
> Operation combining two complex relations into a third one by concatenating each pair of tuples that satisfy a condition on the first-level attributes.

Complex join is specified as

C-JOIN (C-RELATION1, C-RELATION2, J-CONDITION)

The join condition is a Boolean expression, using AND, OR, and NOT, of predicates of the form $A1$ op $A2$, where $A1$ and $A2$ are attribute names of C-RELATION1 and C-RELATION2 respectively, and op is a comparison operator. Depending on the type of $A1$ and $A2$ (integer, string, tuple, set), many different comparison operators may be used. For instance, if $A1$ and $A2$ are set-valued attributes, the predicate $A1 \subset A2$ is valid.

The main limitation of complex join is that the attributes used in the condition must appear at the first level of the complex relation. For example, we cannot join directly relations WINE and SALE (see Fig. 11.2) on W# since W# in SALE is not at the first level. Thus relation SALE must first be restructured to be joinable with WINE. The join can therefore be expressed as

C-JOIN (WINE, FLATTEN(SALE), W# = W#)

This constraint on join attributes permits efficient implementation of the join operation [Bancilhon 82].

11.5 Implementation Techniques for Complex Objects

In this section, we present and compare two different implementation techniques for complex objects supported at a conceptual level. These techniques have been analyzed in detail in [Valduriez86b]. The first, *direct storage model,* maps the objects directly into a physical address space so that subobjects and objects are clustered together. The second, *normalized storage model,* has several variants. The idea is to decompose and store the atomic values of objects of the same type in flat files and to capture the connections between objects and subobjects in structures called join indexes.

For all techniques, we assume that each tuple is assigned a surrogate for tuple identity, called TID (tuple identifier). A TID is a value unique within a relation that is created by the system when a tuple is instantiated and which the system never modifies. TIDs permit efficient updates and reorganizations of files since references do not involve physical pointers. Most RDBMSs, including INGRES and System R, support the notion of tuple identifier.

11.5.1 Direct Storage Model

In the *direct storage model,* complex objects are stored directly as they are defined in the conceptual schema.

Definition 11.15 Direct storage model
Model in which a complex object is implemented and stored with its subobjects.

This is a natural way to store conceptual objects. For example, if the database is composed of set objects, the direct storage model will store each set object (which can be a nested set) in a separate file. Each record of a file represents a complex object. There are several solutions for clustering the attributes of a complex object, stemming from an ordering of the nested sets based on the hierarchy. A simple solution consistent with the hierarchical manipulation of objects is depth-first ordering.

The clustering of the records in a file can only be done based on attributes of the root objects. The file WINE can only be clustered on W#, VINEYARD, and/or VINTAGE, using a single attribute or multiattribute file structure. Therefore the access to objects based on attributes other than those of the root objects must be done with auxiliary structures or through sequential scans.

The primary advantage of this approach is that retrievals of entire complex objects are efficient. Compared to a mapping of a relational schema where each relation is stored in a file, this model avoids many joins. Another strong advantage of this model is that the compilation of queries that deal with conceptual complex objects is simplified because there is a one-to-one correspondence between conceptual object and internal object.

The main drawback of this approach is that retrievals of certain subobjects are inefficient because they are clustered according to a topological order. For example, the following query on the schema of Fig. 11.2 "retrieve all stores having a wine in qty > 500" will not be efficiently processed because the stores and quantities are clustered according to the wines (and not quantities). This is typically the main drawback of hierarchical systems.

11.5.2 Normalized Storage Model

In the *normalized storage model,* complex objects are not stored directly. Rather they are decomposed into sets of tuples of atomic values. Thus each set object corresponds to a normalized relation.

Definition 11.16   Normalized storage model
Model in which a complex object is decomposed into normalized (at least 1NF) relations.

For instance, the complex object WINE can be decomposed in three flat relations: WINE, ON_HAND, and PRICE. The TIDs of WINE, ON_HAND, and PRICE are denoted by W_TID, OH_TID, and P_TID, respectively. The connection between a tuple WINE and its subobjects is kept by adding the W_TID in the subobject relations. Fig. 11.9 illustrates the normalized schema for the complex relation WINE.

Several variants of the normalized storage model may be defined according to a vertical partitioning function. This function decomposes a relation in one or more files, where each file contains a certain number of attributes. The most frequently used variant groups all attributes of a relation in the same file. Another interesting variant stores all values of each attribute of a relation together on a separate file [Batory79, Copeland85], where each attribute value is associated with the TID of its tuple. A hybrid variant groups the attributes according to their affinities, such that attributes frequently used together are stored in the same file [Navathe84].

The different variants of the normalized storage model provide better performance of subobject retrievals. However, the composition of complex objects requires multiple joins, a costly operation. One way to support efficiently the

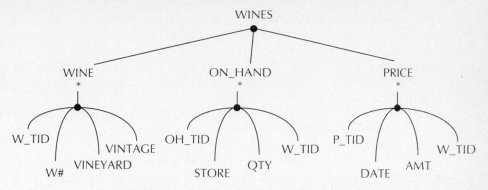

FIGURE 11.9 Normalized schema for WINE

retrieval of complex objects is to use join indexes that store in a uniform and compact way the complex object structures. Two versions of join indexes exist: a binary join index proposed in [Valduriez87] for simple objects and a more generalized version called hierarchical join index adapted to complex objects.

A *binary join index* (BJI), or simply join index, is an abstraction of the join of the two relations.

Definition 11.17 Join index of two relations
Set a pairs of TIDs, each from one relation, so that the corresponding tuples match the join predicate.

A join index is therefore implemented by a binary relation. For example, the connection between relations WINE and ON_HAND (Fig. 11.9) is given by storing explicitly the TID of WINE in ON_HAND. This connection can be stored explicitly in a join index (OH_TID, W_TID) as shown in Fig. 11.10.

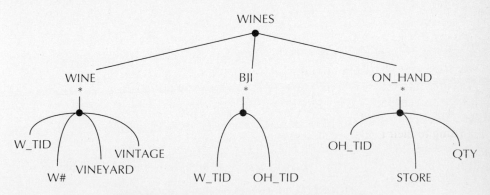

FIGURE 11.10 Example of binary join index (BJI)

Join indexes are very efficient for optimizing joins, mainly because a join index is separated from the base data and is so small that it can fit in main memory. They can be used systematically for capturing the joins materializing complex objects and for optimizing other kinds of joins. For example, the join between WINE and SALE on W# can be captured by a join index. In this latter case, a join index is an accelerator for joins.

When intended as an acceleration mechanism, join indexes should be used only for the most important joins. Join indexes are an attractive tool for optimizing both relational queries and recursive queries [Valduriez86a].

In order to support complex objects, the notion of join index can be extended to that of a more general structure, called *hierarchical join index* (HJI). A hierarchical join index can capture the structure of a complex object by using the TIDs of the connected relations that make up the whole object.

> **Definition 11.18 Hierarchical join index**
> Complex object where each tuple object is replaced by its TID and each set of atoms is ignored.

The purpose of a hierarchical join index is similar to the map for complex design objects [Lorie83]. Fig. 11.11 proposes two examples of hierarchical join indexes for two different complex objects.

Therefore rather than having several binary join indexes, a single and bigger hierarchical join index can be used. Like the direct storage model, a hierarchical join index can be clustered only on the root TID. When the root TID of a complex object is obtained, then the whole structure of the complex object is given directly. Hierarchical join indexes are better than binary join indexes for retrievals of entire objects. Therefore binary and hierarchical join indexes should be used in a complementary manner.

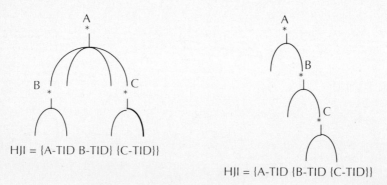

HJI = {A-TID B-TID} {C-TID}}

HJI = {A-TID {B-TID {C-TID}}

FIGURE 11.11 Hierarchical join indexes

11.5.3 Comparisons

A complex object storage model must be able to provide efficient support for a wide variety of query types. The difficulty lies in achieving two conflicting goals: efficient support for retrieving a single entire complex object and retrieving its components. The first goal leads to clustering of a full complex object in the same memory extent, while the second goal leads to clustering of the individual components.

These implementation techniques of complex objects have been analyzed in [Valduriez86]. The normalized storage model is superior when data are shared over multiple applications having different access patterns. The direct storage model is superior when a particular access pattern heavily dominates and that pattern consists of selecting a few objects, projecting on many attributes, and using the same attributes as the selection criteria in all requests. However, such applications currently exist in sufficient number to warrant the direct storage model.

Two open issues remain regarding the form of support of such applications. One is that applications such as CAD are usually supported by file systems that store each complex object as a long bit/byte string file with indexing by file name. This approach could be supported in the normalized storage model by representing the complex object as a single attribute whose value is a long string. A second issue is whether such applications will continue to have a single access pattern. Many long-term visionaries of CAD, for example, argue that eventually CAD data will be heavily shared by multiple applications, including several phases of design, as well as manufacturing, component and product inventories, sales, and business planning.

Therefore it is not clear that a single point along the spectrum of all variants of these techniques is best. An alternative is to provide support for the full spectrum, where the storage model can be any combination of these variants. The difficulty of this approach is to find a single query processing algorithm that generates correct query programs and is efficient for such a general storage model. In other words, the more general (and powerful) the storage model is, the more difficult the query processing is. An attempt to define such a query processing algorithm for complex objects is proposed in [Khoshafian87a, Khoshafian88].

11.6 Support of Object Identity

The use of identifiers for tuple objects, called TIDs, is essential for the efficient implementation of hierarchically structured objects. This use of object identifiers is generally limited to the internal level of the system; TIDs are not visible at the conceptual or external level. INGRES [Stonebraker76] is a notable exception since TIDs can be used to express semantic integrity constraints. Object-oriented programming languages such as Smalltalk-80 [Goldberg 83] support *object identity* as a fundamental notion [Khoshafian86].

> **Definition 11.19 Object identity**
> Property of an object that distinguises it from all other objects (of the real world), regardless of its content, location, or addressability.

In this section, we discuss the incorporation of object identity at the conceptual level of a database system. We first review the problems associated with the traditional support of identity in the relational model. We show that this important feature provides better object orientation. In particular, graph structures instead of trees can be strictly modeled. Therefore a combination of the respective advantages of the relational model and the network model [Taylor76] can be expected. However, the resulting model deviates significantly from the simplicity of the relational model.

11.6.1 Object Identity in the Relational Model

The primitive objects of the relational model are relations, tuples, and attributes. Relations are identified by an external name provided by the user. Attributes are traditionally identified by their values. Thus identity for relations and attributes is trivial. Tuple identity is more involved. The main solution, originated by [Codd70], is to use one or more attributes of a tuple as a key of the relation. A tuple key is unique for all tuples in the relation. This solution also applies to the complex object model introduced in Section 11.4, where only the first-level tuples need identification.

This approach poses some problems because the key attributes play a dual role of identity and descriptive data [Hall76]. The major problem for the user is that key attributes may not be manipulated like other attributes. In particular, a key attribute cannot be updated simply as any nonkey attribute. For example, a country name may be used as the key of a relation COUNTRIES. Country name may also be used as a foreign key in a relation CITIES to specify where the city is. However, after a revolution, for instance, a country name may be changed from Dahomey to Benin. All tuples for cities in Dahomey need to be changed accordingly. Another frequent problem is that attributes may not exist in a relation to provide identity for all tuples. For example, two different persons may have the same first and last names. Therefore artificial attributes such as person number must be introduced by the user for identity. Such artificial identifiers, such as social security number, are not easy to generate and may require additional information about the object. A solution to these problems is the built-in support of identity in the data model. [Cobb79] has argued for such a solution in the model RM/T and has proposed additional operators to deal with identity.

When an object is inserted in the database, it is automatically assigned a unique identifier that will never change.

11.6.2 Object Identity in the Complex Object Model

In this section, we incorporate object identity for the complex object model defined in Section 11.4 and discuss the consequences. The model with identity is inspired by FAD [Bancilhon87]. In that model, there are three types of objects: atomic, tuple, and set objects. Each object is assigned a unique identifier. It is customary to assume that the identifier of an atom is the atom's value. For example, integer 25 is unique in the system, but two persons may be 25 years old, in which case 25 will be replicated. Thus only tuple and set objects need be assigned an object identifier.

The definition of objects with built-in identity is derived from the definition in [Bancilhon87]. An object O is a couple (identifier, value) where (1) the identifier provides a unique and invariant reference to O and (2) the value of O is one of the following:

- An element of a system or user-defined domain of values, if type is atom.
- $[a_1:I_1, a_2:I_2, \ldots, a_n:I_n]$ where each a_i is a distinct attribute name and I_i is an identifier, if type is tuple.
- $\{I_1, I_2, \ldots, I_n\}$ where the I_is are distinct identifiers, if type is set.

This definition supports graph-structured objects. Any object can have multiple parents that refer to it by its identifier. Compared to the hierarchical model, shared objects are not replicated. Assuming that the database is a set of complex relations, two kinds of sharing may occur. The first one is sharing of subobjects within the same complex relation. As an example, let us consider relation WINE of Fig. 11.2. Let us assume that the PRICE for wines 210 and 300 should always be identical. This can be represented by having the set object PRICE of one wine, say 210, referred to by the other wine object. This sharing of subobjects is illustrated in Fig. 11.12, where we added identifiers for tuples (t_1 and t_2) and for sets (S_1) to the graphical representation introduced in Section 11.4.

The second kind of sharing is coreferencing of objects in a complex relation from another relation. This kind of sharing is visible at the schema level. For example, let us consider again the wine database of Fig. 11.2. The relationship between a sale and the wines sold is given by the attribute W# in relation SALE. Therefore to associate information of SALE and WINE, a join on W# is necessary. With object identity, the corresponding wines may be directly referenced from the sales as shown in Fig. 11.13 in which the schema of relations WINE and SALE of Fig. 11.2 has been simplified. Attribute W# in SALE has been replaced by an attribute WINE whose value is the identifier of the corresponding

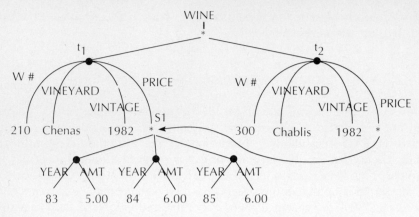

FIGURE 11.12 Objects with sharing of subobjects

wine. An advantage of such schema is that join queries can be replaced by path traversals [Maier86] using the "." operator. For instance, the query "names of customers having bought vineyards of 1982 in quantity > 100" and those vineyards could be expressed as:

```
SELECT NAME, WINE.VINEYARD
FROM SALE
WHERE QTY > 100
        AND WINE.VINTAGE = 1982
```

The incorporation of identity as an integral part of the complex object model requires extensions of the language for manipulating objects with identity and

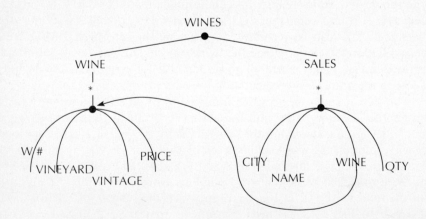

FIGURE 11.13 Complex object schema with sharing

additional implementation techniques to cope with shared objects. The main extension to the language is to provide several ways of testing the equality of two objects. In [Khoshafian86], three types of equality are proposed: identity equality, shallow equality, and deep equality.

Definition 11.20 Identity equality
Two objects with the same identifiers are identity equal.

In the example in Fig. 11.14, the objects $t_1.b$ and $t_3.b$ are identity equal because their identifier is t_2.

Definition 11.21 Shallow equality
Two objects with equal values are shallow equal.

This definition is not recursive (holds only for the first level of objects). For example (in Fig. 11.14), objects t_1 and t_3 are shallow equal but t_1 and t_4 are not (because the value of $t_1.b$, that is, t_2, is different from that of $t_4.b$, that is, t_5). Deep equality is meant to support recursive equality.

Definition 11.22 Deep equality
Two atomic objects with the same value are deep equal. Two set objects are deep equal if the elements in their value are pairwise deep equal. Two tuple objects are deep equal if the value they take on the same attributes are deep equal.

This definition is recursive and permits comparison of the corresponding subobjects of two objects. For example, t_1 and t_4 are deep equal but t_1 and t_3 are not.

Similar to equality, two kinds of copy operators, shallow copy and deep copy, can be added [Bancilhon87]. Shallow copy duplicates only the first level of the object, while deep copy duplicates the object with all its subobjects. Other operators, such as set operators, need to be defined to exploit object identity. For example, we can have two kinds of union operators: value based or identity based. A value-based union does the union of two sets based on the values of their elements. Identity-based union does the union of two sets based on the iden-

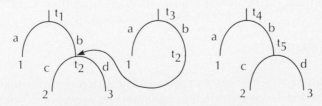

FIGURE 11.14 Objects with identity

tifiers of their elements. Several other operators for manipulating objects with identity are given in [Bancilhon87]. Their description is beyond the scope of this chapter. The resulting language, although very powerful, deviates significantly from relational languages that are traditionally value based and not identity based.

In addition to the operators that deal with object identity, implementation techniques are necessary to support object sharing. Such techniques were not needed for the object model described in Section 11.4 since only hierarchical (not shared) structures are supported. Object sharing at the conceptual level poses some difficult implementation issues.

One difficulty is the implementation of object identifiers. Tuple identifiers can be used as identifiers. They provide uniqueness for all tuples within a single relation and are independent of the location of the object. However, they do not provide global system uniqueness because they are unique only within a single relation. A better way to support identity is through surrogates [Hall76, Codd79, Meier83]. A surrogate is a system-generated, globally unique identifier that provides full data independence. The typical generation of surrogate involves a global counter or a combination of date and clock time.

Another difficulty is the mapping of conceptual shared objects to internal objects. There is no sharing at the internal level since object identity is mapped into surrogate values. Therefore graph structures must be mapped into trees. A shared object, such as set S_l in Fig. 11.12, can be stored in two ways. First, it can be stored separately from its parents as in the normalized storage model and the parents would store the surrogate of the object. Second, the shared object may be stored with one parent as in the direct storage model and the other parents would refer to it by a link. There are several ways to implement such a link. For efficient access to the shared object, the link can be the path from the root of the hierarchy to the object [Khoshafian87b]. For instance, if object S_1 of Fig. 11.12 is stored with object t_l, then the link to that object in t_2 can be WINE.t_1.S_1. One serious problem with this direct approach is that the object storing a shared subobject may be deleted. However, if the shared subobject has other parents, it cannot be deleted. A solution is to find another parent where the subobject can be stored. In order to make the operation efficient, additional index structures are required [Khoshafian 87b].

In summary, the built-in support of object identity in a conceptual model provides many advantages. It can lead to a purely object-oriented data model that deviates from the relational model. Its implementation is quite involved.

11.7 Conclusion

Relational database technology can be extended with object-oriented features. In this chapter,we have concentrated on an important aspect of object orientation:

the support of possibly large, rich atomic objects and the support of structurally complex objects. Traditional relational database systems are not able to support this aspect efficiently. The most promising solutions are the support of abstract data types (ADTs) and of complex objects by the RDBMS. For both solutions, there is an increasing degree of object orientation support depending on the level of functionality introduced.

ADTs provide the capability to extend the basic data types of the database system with user-defined data types and related operations. We have reported on approaches to the integration of ADTs in a relational context according to three important dimensions: ADT granularity (relation or domain), language to implement ADT operations (programming language, database language, or programming language with data access), and support of ADT hierarchies. The highest level of functionality and performance is obtained when ADTs are implemented in a programming language with data access on both relation and domain and when ADT hierarchies with operator inheritance and operator overloading are supported. The highest level of funtionality may well reduce the need for programming language preprocessors.

The motivation for the support of complex objects is to combine the respective advantages of relational, hierarchical, and network models. For instance, set operators should be applicable on complex hierarchies. The main extension to the relational model for supporting complex objects is to relax the 1NF constraint and allow set-valued or tuple-valued attributes. We have defined a model that supports complex, hierarchically structured objects. This model is a generalization of other complex object models. We have also proposed an algebra for this model. When operating on traditional relations, the algebra reduces to relational algebra.

Implementation techniques of complex objects are critical for the efficient manipulation of objects and subobjects. We have reviewed and compared two alternative techniques: the direct storage model and the normalized storage model. Each technique can be superior to the other under certain access patterns.

The built-in support of object identity in the conceptual object model provides additional functionality. Graph structures can be directly manipulated and most join operations replaced by simpler path traversals. This important feature can lead to a purely object-oriented data model. However, the resulting model deviates significantly from the relational model.

The support of atomic objects of rich type and of complex objects entails significant extensions to relational database systems. This additional capability is one important aspect of object orientation. However, there are other capabilities that are desirable for supporting new database applications. Examples of such capabilities are the support of dynamic schema evolution [Banerjee87b], of long-duration transactions for design applications [Bancilhon85], and of historical versions of data [Copeland82]. Active research is underway to address all of these problems.

11.8 References and Bibliography

[Abiteboul84] Abiteboul, S, Bidoit, N., "An Algebra for Non Normalized Relations," ACM Int. Symp. on PODS, March 1984.

[Adiba85] Adiba M., Nguyen G. T., "Handling Constraints and Meta-Data on a Generalized Data Management System," *Expert Database Systems,* L. Kerschberg (ed.), Benjamin-Cummings Publ. Co., 1985.

[Bancilhon82] Bancilhon F., Richard P., Scholl M., "On Line Processing of Compacted Relations," Int. Conf. on VLDB, Mexico, September 1982.

[Bancilhon85] Bancilhon F., Kim W., Korth H., "A Model for CAD Transactions," Int. Conf. on VLDB, Stockholm, August 1985.

[Bancilhon86] Bancilhon F., Khoshafian S., "A Calculus for Complex Objects," ACM Int. Symp. on PODS, Portland, Oregon, March 1986.

[Bancilhon87] Bancilhon F., Briggs T., Khoshafian S., Valduriez P., "FAD, a Powerful and Simple Database Language," Int. Conf. on VLDB, Brighton, England, September 1987.

[Banerjee87a] Banerjee J. et al., "Data Model Issues for Object Oriented Applications," ACM TODS, V5, N1, January 1987.

[Banerjee87b] Banerjee J., Kim W., Kim K.-J., Korth W. "Semantics and Implementation of Schema Evolution in Object-Oriented Databases," ACM SIGMOD Int. Conf., San Francisco, May 1987.

[Batory79] Batory D. S., "On Searching Transposed Files," ACM TODS, V4, N4, December 1979.

[Batory84] Batory D. S., Buchmann A. P., "Molecular Objects, Abstract Data Types, and Data Models: A Framework," Int. Conf. on VLDB, Singapore, August 1984.

[Batory85] Batory D. S., Kim W. "Modeling Concepts for VLSI CAD Objects," ACM TODS, V10, N3, September 1985.

[Chen76] Chen P. P., "The Entity-Relationship Model: Towards a Unified View of Data," ACM TODS, V1, N1, March 1976.

[CODD70] Codd E. F. "A Relational Model for Large Shared Data Banks," Comm. of ACM, V13, N6, June 1970.

[Codd79] Codd E. F., "Extending the Relational Model to Capture More Meaning," ACM TODS, V4, N4, December 1979.

[Copeland82] Copeland G., "What If Mass Storage Were Free," Computer, IEEE Computer Society, V15, N7, July 1982.

[Copeland85] Copeland G., Khoshafian S., "A Decomposition Storage Model," ACM-SIGMOD Int. Conf., Austin, Texas, May 1985.

[Deppisch86] Deppisch U., Paul H-B., Scheck H-J. "A Storage System for Complex Objects," Int. Workshop on OODBS, Pacific Grove, California, September 1986.

[Fisher83] Fisher P. C., Thomas S. J. "Operations for Non-First-Normal Form Relations," IEEE Computer Software and Applications Conf., New York, October 1983.

[Goldberg83] Goldberg A., Robson D., *Smalltalk-80: The Language System and Its Implementation,* Addison-Wesley, 1983.

[Guttag77] Guttag J., "Abstract Data Types and the Development of Data Structures," Comm. of ACM, V20, N6, June 1977.

[Hall76] Hall P. et al., "Relations and Entities," in *Modeling in DBMS,* Nijssen (ed.), North-Holland, 1976.

[Khoshafian86], Khoshafian S., Copeland G., "Object Identity," Int. Conf. on OOP-SLA, Portland, Oregon, September 1986.

[Khoshafian87a] Khoshafian S., Boral H., Copeland G., Valduriez P., "A Query Processing Strategy for the Decomposition Storage Model," Int. Conf. on Data Engineering, Los Angeles, February 1987.

[Khoshafian87b] Khoshafian S., Valduriez P., "Sharing Persistence and Object-Orientation: A Database Perspective," Int. Workshop on Database Programming Languages, Roscoff, France, September 1987.

[Khoshafian88] Khoshafian S., Valduriez P., Copeland G., "Parallel Query Processing of Complex Objects," Int. Conf. on Data Engineering, Los Angeles, February 1988.

[Kiernan87] Kiernan G., LeMaoult R., Pasquer F., "The Support of Complex Domains in a Relational DBMS Using a LISP Language Processor," Research Report, INRIA, France, 1987.

[King85] King R., McLeod D., "Semantic Database Models," in *Database Design,* S. B. Yao (ed.), Springer-Verlag, 1985.

[Kuper85] Kuper G. M., Vardi M. Y., "On the Expressive Power of the Logic Data Model," ACM SIGMOD Int. Conf., Austin, Texas, May 1985.

[Lorie83] Lorie R., Plouffe W., "Complex Objects and Their Use in Design Transactions," ACM SIGMOD Int. Conf., San Jose, California, May 1983.

[Lum85] Lum V. et al., "Design of an Integrated DBMS to Support Advanced Application," Int. Conf. on Foundations of Data Organization, Kyoto, May 1985.

[Maier86] Maier D., Stein J., Ottis A., Purdy A., "Development of an Object-Oriented DBMS," Int. Conf. on OOPSLA, Portland, Oregon, September 1986.

[Meier83] Meier A., Lorie R., "A Surrogate Concept for Engineering Databases," Int. Conf. on VLDB, Florence, Italy, October 1983.

[Navathe84] Navathe S., Ceri S., Wiederhold G., Jinglie D., "Vertical Partitioning Algorithms for Database Design," ACM TODS, V9, N4, December 1984.

[Osborn86] Osborn S. L., Heaven T. E., "The Design of a Relational Database System with Abstract Data Types for Domains," ACM TODS, V11, N3, September 1986.

[Ozsoyoglu85a] Ozsoyoglu Z. M., Yuan L-Y., "A Normal Form for Nested Relations," ACM Int. Symposium on PODS, Portland, Oregon, March 1985.

[Ozsoyoglu85b] Ozsoyoglu G., Ozsoyoglu Z. M., Mata F., "A Language and a Physical Organization Technique for Summary Tables," ACM SIGMOD Int. Conf., Austin, Texas, May 1985.

[Ozsoyoglu87] Ozsoyoglu Z. M., Yuan L-Y., "A New Normal Form for Nested Relations," ACM TODS, V12, N1, March 1987.

[Rowe79] Rowe L., Shoens K., "Data Abstraction, Views and Updates in RIGEL," ACM SIGMOD Int. Conf., Boston, June 1979.

[Schek86] Schek H-J., Scholl M. H., "The Relational Model with Relation-Valued Attributes," Information Systems, V11, N2, 1986.

[Shipman81] Shipman D., "The Functional Data Model and the Data Language DAPLEX," ACM TODS, V6, N1, 1981.

[Schmidt77] Schmidt J., "Some High Level Language Constructs for Data of Type Relation," ACM TODS, V2, N3, September 1977.

[Smith77] Smith J. M., Smith D. C. P., "Database Abstractions: Aggregation and Generalization," ACM TODS, V2, N2, June 1977.

[Stonebraker76] Stonebraker M., Wong E., Kreps P., Held G., "The Design and Implementation of INGRES," ACM TODS, V1, N3, September 1976.

[Stonebraker83] Stonebraker M., Rubenstein B., Guttman A., "Application of Abstract Data Types and Abstract Indices to CAD Databases," ACM SIGMOD Int. Conf., San Jose, California, May 1983.

[Stonebraker84] Stonebraker M., Anderson E., Hanson E., Rubenstein B., "QUEL as a Data Type," ACM SIGMOD Int. Conf., Boston, June 1984.

[Stonebraker86] Stonebraker M., Rowe L. A., "The Design of POSTGRES," ACM SIGMOD Int. Conf., Washington, D.C., May 1986.

[Su83] Su S. Y. W., " 'SAM': A Semantic Association Model for Corporate and Scientific Statistical Databases," Information Science, No. 29, 1983.

[Taylor76] Taylor R. W., Frank R. L., "CODASYL Data-Base Management Systems," ACM Computing Surveys, V8, N1, March 1976.

[Tsichritzis76] Tsichritzis D. C., Lochovsky F. H., "Hierarchical Data-Base Management: A Survey," ACM Computing Surveys, V8, N1, March 1976.

[Tsur84] Tsur S., Zaniolo C., "On the Implementation of GEM: Supporting a Semantic Data Model on a Relational Back-End," ACM SIGMOD Int. Conf., Boston, June 1984.

[Valduriez86a] Valduriez P., Boral H., "Evaluation of Recursive Queries Using Join Indices," Int. Conf. on Expert Database Systems, Charleston, South Carolina, April 1986.

[Valduriez86b] Valduriez P., Khoshafian S., Copeland G., "Implementation Techniques of Complex Objects," Int. Conf. on VLDB, Kyoto, August 1986.

[Valduriez87] Valduriez P., "Join Indices" ACM TODS, V12, N2, June 1987.

[Wasserman79] Wasserman A., "The Data Management Facilities of PLAIN," ACM SIGMOD Int. Conf., Boston, June 1979.

[Zaniolo85] Zaniolo C., "The Representation and Deductive Retrieval of Complex Objects," Int. Conf. on VLDB, Stockholm, August 1985.

12
DISTRIBUTED DATABASES

12.1 Introduction

Since the early 1960s, centralizing an organization's data in a large and expensive computer has been the single approach to data processing. Recent developments in the areas of database technology, computer networks, mini computers and microcomputers have made the distributed database approach a practical alternative. A *distributed database* is a collection of logically related data distributed across several machines interconnected by a computer network. An application program operating on a distributed database may access data stored at more than one machine.

A distributed database has four main advantages. First, each group (or person) having a computer has direct control over its local data, resulting in increased data integrity and more efficient data processing. Second, compared to the centralized approach in which the data must be transferred from each group to the central computer, the communication overhead is reduced. Third, the distributed approach is the natural solution to data processing in a geographically dispersed organization. Fourth, performance and reliability may be increased by exploiting the parallel processing and redundancy capabilities of multiple machines.

The need to integrate and share the data located and managed on different computers is the basis for a distributed database. Such data sharing requires the interconnection of the various computers through a local or general network and specific software support to manage and process distributed data. Such software must provide high independence from the distributed environment. Relational database technology has been successful at providing data independence, making transparent to the application programs any change in the physical or logical data structure. Therefore it has been the natural support to distributed data sharing. As a result, most relational database systems today offer solutions to share distributed data.

The implementation of a distributed database poses new and challenging problems that stem from the combination of database system and distributed computing technologies. These problems have been studied extensively and new principles and solutions have been produced, thereby making distributed databases an important area of computer science. A comprehensive treatment of distributed database technology was first given in [Ceri84], and a more recent one is available in [Ozsu89]. The objective of this chapter is to provide a brief introduction to distributed databases. Therefore we limit ourselves to the presentation of the functionalities, objectives, and technical issues of distributed databases. We also show how distributed database functions can be ideally organized in an architecture. Finally, we illustrate the application of distributed database technology in three relational database systems, each having a different objective.

Section 12.2 of this chapter introduces the different distributed database capabilities that can be provided by a database system. Section 12.3 presents the main objectives of distributed databases. In Section 12.4, we summarize the major technical issues that must be addressed to implement and manage distributed databases: data dictionary management, data definition, semantic data control, query processing, and data management. Most of these issues have been solved in the context of the relational model. Therefore we will continue to use the relational model terminology in this chapter. In Section 12.5, we present the architectures that can be devised for organizing the schemas and functions of distributed databases. Sections 12.6 – 12.8 illustrate a peculiar implementation of distributed databases in three different relational database systems: R*, INGRES/STAR, and the DBC/1012.

12.2 Distributed Database Capabilities

The distributed database capabilities offered by current database systems range from remote database access to heterogeneous distributed database. A more recent use of the distributed database approach is to distribute the data across the nodes of a multiprocessor computer so that performance and reliability are increased.

A *remote database* (Fig. 12.1) is a database located on a computer other than where the user (or application) is executing. In general, the user is aware of the remote database location, which must be specified to access the data. A data communication component is necessary for accessing the remote database.

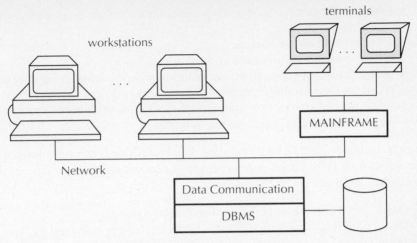

FIGURE 12.1 Remote database

> **Definition 12.1 Remote database**
> Database located on a computer other than where the user is executing and accessed by user-specified communication commands.

A local database may also reside on the computer where the user is running. The user can then download remote database data to the local database. Recent developments in microcomputer technology have favored the workstation/server organization, in which the remote database is managed on a mainframe server by a DBMS and private databases are managed on workstations by a microversion of the same DBMS. The interconnection server/workstation is typically handled by a local network. The remote database approach provides little functionality and thus does not face the problems of distributed databases.

A *distributed database* is a set of cooperating databases residing on different machines, called sites, interconnected by a computer network. A user at any site can access the data at any site.

> **Definition 12.2 Distributed database**
> Set of cooperating databases, each resident at a different site, that the user views and manipulates as a centralized database.

The main difference from a remote database is that the user is not aware of data distribution and perceives the distributed database as a nondistributed database. The management of a distributed database requires the following system components at each site: a data communication component, a local DBMS, and a distributed DBMS (DDBMS). The main functions of the DDBMS are:

1. Management of a global data dictionary to store information about distributed data.
2. Distributed data definition.
3. Distributed semantic data control.
4. Distributed query processing, including distributed query optimization and remote database access.
5. Distributed transaction management including distributed concurrency control, recovery, and commit protocol.

A distinguishing property of a distributed database is that it can be homogeneous or heterogeneous (Fig. 12.2). A *homogeneous distributed database* is one where all the local databases are managed by the same DBMS.

> **Definition 12.3 Homogeneous distributed database**
> Distributed database in which each local database is managed by the same DBMS.

This approach is the simplest one and provides incremental growth, making the addition of a new site in the network easy, and increased performance, by exploiting the parallel processing capability of multiple sites. A good example of homogeneous distributed database will be illustrated by the R* system.

A *heterogeneous distributed database* is one where the local databases need not be managed by the same DBMS.

> **Definition 12.4 Heterogeneous distributed database**
> Distributed database in which the local databases are managed by different DBMSs.

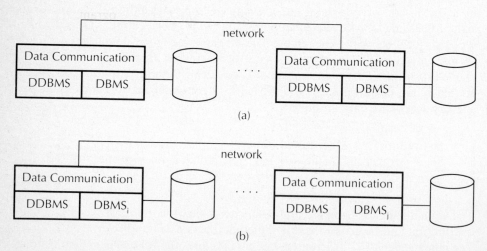

FIGURE 12.2 Distributed databases. (a) Homogeneous (same local DBMSs) and (b) heterogeneous (different local DBMSs)

For example, DBMSi can be a relational system while DBMSj can be a hierarchical system. This approach is by far more complex than the homogeneous one but enables the integration of existing independent databases without requiring the creation of a completely new distributed database. In addition to the main functions, the DDBMS must provide interfaces between the different DBMSs. The typical solution used by RDBMSs is to have gateways that convert the language and model of each different DBMS into the language and model of the RDBMS. An example of heterogeneous distributed database will be illustrated by the INGRES/STAR system.

The most recent use of the distributed database approach consists of distributing the data across the nodes of a shared-nothing multiprocessor computer [Stonebraker86a]. This approach can be viewed as a peculiar implementation of a homogeneous distributed database. It is based on the "divide and conquer" paradigm whereby the data are distributed (divide) so that performance is significantly increased by intensive parallel processing (conquer).

A typical shared-nothing multiprocessor database is illustrated in Fig. 12.3. The distributed architecture consists of two kinds of nodes. Disk nodes include a processor, a local main memory, and a disk unit on which resides a local database. Diskless nodes are generally used to interface with remote host computers or workstations. There is no sharing of main memory by the nodes — hence the term *share nothing*. The only shared resource is the network, with which the nodes can exchange messages. One similarity with the homogeneous distributed database approach is that the data are distributed across nodes managed by the same local system. Therefore the DDBMS component must implement solutions to global data dictionary, distributed data definition and control, distributed query processing, and distributed transaction management. However, the major difference with a homogeneous distributed database is that a node of the multiprocessor is not a site at which a user can run an application program. Applica-

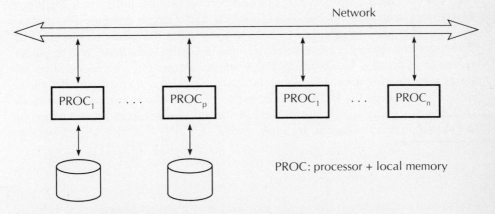

FIGURE 12.3 Shared-nothing multiprocessor database

tion programs run typically on a host computer or private workstation and interface the multiprocessor system through a specific network. Therefore the multiprocessor computer is seen as a black box, often called *database machine,* by the users.

> **Definition 12.5 Database machine**
> Combination of hardware and software specifically designed for efficient support of database management functions.

The fact that a database machine is a black box is often a reason for not including shared-nothing multiprocessor databases in the presentation of distributed database technology. However, given their growing importance, we will illustrate this kind of system by an introduction to the DBC/1012 database machine.

12.3 Objectives

A distributed database may provide various levels of transparency; however, each level of transparency participates to the same goal: making the use of the distributed database equivalent to that of a centralized database. All of the following objectives are rarely met by a single system. Rather, depending on the targeted applications, a DDBMS will meet only a subset of these objectives. For example, a homogeneous DDBMS will not provide DBMS transparency.

12.3.1 Site Autonomy

Site autonomy is an important objective that enables any operational site to control and process its local data independent of any other site. Therefore each site must store all data dictionary information necessary to be autonomous, without relying on a centralized global data dictionary and a global database administrator. The immediate advantage of site autonomy is that the administration of the distributed database need not be centralized. Each local database may be independently controlled by a local database administrator. Intersite cooperation requires coordination among the local database administrators using specific capabilities provided by the DDBMS. The support of site autonomy can range from no autonomy (centralized control) to full site autonomy (decentralized control). In practice, hybrid solutions are often used.

12.3.2 Location Transparency

Location transparency is the primary objective of distributed databases. It hides the fact that the data may not be stored at the user site. The database user does not need to know the data location. Therefore queries involving relations stored at different sites need not specify the relation locations. Location transparency provides physical independence from the distributed environment. The data location information is maintained in the data dictionary and used by the DDBMS to find the data. The main advantage is that the database may be physically reorganized by moving relations to different sites, without any impact on the application programs that access them.

12.3.3 Fragmentation Transparency

The simplest way to store a conceptual object (relation) in a distributed database is at a single site. However, for performance reasons, it is often desirable to divide a relation into smaller fragments, each stored at a different site. A fragment is generally defined by restriction (horizontal fragmentation) and/or projection (vertical fragmentation) and is therefore another relation. Thus fragmentation is particularly simple in the context of the relational model. Fragmentation enhances the performance of database queries by increasing the locality of reference. For example, consider an EMPLOYEE relation in a database distributed between New York and Paris. The optimal fragmentation is probably to store the American employee tuples in New York and the European employee tuples in Paris. The fragmentation definition is application dependent.

Fragmentation transparency makes fragmentation transparent to the user, who sees only nonfragmented relations. Fragmentation information is stored in the data dictionary and used by the DDBMS to automatically map queries on conceptual relations, called *global queries,* into queries on fragments, called *fragment queries.*

12.3.4 Replication Transparency

Data replication in some form is the single solution to reliability. In a distributed database, data replication can be used for reliability, availability, and performance. In general, the unit of fragmentation is the fragment, or the relation if fragmentation is not supported. A fragment is replicated when it is stored as two or more copies, each at a different site. The immediate advantage of replication is high availability. If a site fails, the fragment copy is still available at another site. Furthermore replication may enhance performance by increasing locality of reference. If communication is the dominating cost factor, replicating a fragment at the sites where it is frequently accessed will favor local accesses and avoid remote accesses. The main problem of replication is the complexity and overhead required to keep the copies identical. The update to one copy must be propagated to all its copies. Furthermore when a site recovers from a failure, all its replicated fragments must reach the same state as the other copies that might have been updated while the site was down. The trade-offs between retrieval and update performance make replication definition (which fragments should be replicated on how many copies?) a difficult problem, which is highly application dependent.

Replication transparency makes such replication invisible to the user, who sees only nonreplicated relations. Replication information, stored in the data dictionary, is used by the DDBMS for mapping global queries into fragment queries and to manage copy consistency for update queries and recovery after failure.

12.3.5 DBMS Transparency

DBMS transparency hides the fact that the local DBMSs may be different — it may have a different conceptual data model (relational, network, and so on) and a different language. DBMS transparency is the objective of heterogeneous distributed databases. It is probably the most difficult to achieve. As a consequence, there are very few marketed heterogeneous DDBMSs. The support of DBMS transparency requires a mechanism to translate the data model and language between local database systems. The usual solution consists of using a pivot data model and associated language and a translation mechanism from and to this pivot model for each different database system. For simplicity and efficiency, the relational model is generally chosen as the pivot model.

12.3.6 Expandability

Expandability provides smooth incremental growth of the system with minimal impact on the application programs. When site autonomy is fully supported, expandability is easy to achieve. Increasing capacity and processing needs may be fulfilled by adding one or more sites in the computer network.

12.3.7 Increased Performance

Increased performance is a more recent objective. This can be achieved in the context of a high-speed network by exploiting parallel processing. The goal is to provide throughput that is linear in the number of computers across which the data are fragmented. The main idea is that a powerful computer may be built out of several smaller and less powerful ones. This idea led to some parallel database machine designs [Stonebraker79]. Performance improvement is obtained by carefully fragmenting the data across many computers so that parallelism is maximized when processing a distributed query. The issue remains of placing the data so that most of the queries get processed in parallel.

12.4 Issues

The database system issues become much more complex in a distributed environment because of specific aspects of distributed databases.

First, relations of the same database may reside at more than one site. In addition, a conceptual object can be fragmented and/or replicated. Fragmentation and replication are necessary for performance and availability reasons. They have a strong impact on data dictionary management, data definition, semantic data control, and query processing.

Second, a user transaction that involves data resident at several sites can be executed as several subtransactions, each at a different site. Therefore each site has only partial information to decide whether to commit the subtransaction's updates. Transaction management — in particular, concurrency control and commit processing — must ensure synchronization among all participating sites.

Third, since data copies may continue to be updated at various sites while one site is down, the recovery of a failed site requires the cooperation of other sites in order to keep replicated copies identical.

Finally, the support of DBMS transparency adds another translation mechanism between the different models and languages. This translation mechanism must be combined with several other functions, such as data dictionary, data definition and control, and query processing.

12.4.1 Data Dictionary

The data dictionary includes information regarding data descriptions, data placement, and semantic data control. It can be itself managed as a distributed database. The data dictionary can be centralized in one site, fully replicated at each site, or itself fragmented. Its content can be stored differently according to the kind of information; some information might be fully replicated while others might be distributed. For example, information that is most useful at query compile time, like security control information, could be duplicated at each site. The implementation of the data dictionary depends on the degree of site autonomy that must be supported. For example, full site autonomy is incompatible with a centralized data dictionary.

12.4.2 Data Definition

Data definition in a distributed database is much more difficult than in a centralized database. Data definition includes the introduction of new database objects and their placement in the network. The way a new object is created depends on the degree of site autonomy and management of the data dictionary. With a centralized data dictionary, the data definition command involves only one site, the one that stores the data dictionary. With a fully replicated data dictionary, all sites of the network must be synchronized to perform the data definition operation. If the data dictionary is fragmented (for full site autonomy), data definition must be done on a site pair basis whereby two sites, the site at which the object is created and another site, cooperate to exchange data definition information. In this case, only the sites that are aware of the new object definition will be able to access it.

The actual placement of a new object in the distributed database has to deal with the issues of data fragmentation, replication, and location. Data placement is probably the most important and difficult aspect of distributed database design, for it affects the performance of database applications and the cost of data storage. The problem is simplified by the practical assumption that the database queries are small compared to the data accessed. Therefore data communication is minimized by always routing a query to the data and not the data to the query. Data placement must be done with the objective of minimizing a complex cost function involving retrieval and update performance, data availability, and data storage. This should lead to the optimal specification of fragments and their optimal number of copies. Since the problem is NP-hard, heuristic solutions are necessary.

12.4.3 Data Control

Semantic data control typically includes view management, security control, and semantic integrity control. The complexity added by the distributed environment concerns the control definition and enforcement. The problem of managing semantic data control rules is similar to the data definition problem.

In a distributed database, a view can be derived from fragmented relations stored at different sites. The mapping of a query expressed on views into a query expressed on conceptual relations can be done as in centralized systems by query modification. With this technique, the qualification defining the view is found in the data dictionary and merged with the query to provide a query on conceptual relations. Such a modified query can then be processed like any other user query. Views derived from fragmented relations may be costly to evaluate. An efficient solution is to avoid view derivation by maintaining actual versions of the views, called *snapshots* [Adiba81]. A snapshot represents a particular state of the database and is therefore static; it does not reflect updates to base relations. Snapshots must be periodically refreshed, which should be done when the system is idle. Furthermore snapshots derived by restriction-projection do not need entire recalculation but rather calculation of the differential data.

The additional problems of authorization control in a distributed environment stem from the fact that objects and subjects are distributed. These problems are: remote user authentication, management of distributed authorization rules, and handling of user groups. Remote user authentication is necessary since any site of a distributed database may accept queries initiated (and authorized) at remote sites. In order to prevent the remote access by unauthorized users (such as from a site that is not part of the distributed database), users must also be identified and authenticated at the accessed site. The simplest solution consists of replicating the information for authenticating users (user name and password) at all sites.

The main problem of semantic integrity control in a distributed environment is that the cost incurred in communication and local processing for enforcing distributed assertions can be prohibitive. The two main issues are the definition of distributed assertions and enforcement algorithms that minimize the cost of distributed integrity checking. Surprisingly, few solutions to distributed integrity control have been proposed. In [Simon86], we have shown that distributed integrity control can be completely achieved by extending a centralized method based on the compilation of semantic integrity assertions (see Chapter 6). The method is general since all types of assertions expressed in first-order predicate logic can be handled. It is compatible with fragment definition and minimizes intersite communication. Best performance of distributed integrity enforcement can be obtained if fragments are defined carefully. Therefore the specification of distributed integrity constraints is an important aspect of distributed database design.

12.4.4 Query Processing

Query processing maps a user query expressed on a distributed database into a sequence of operations on local databases. With the relational model, the user query is typically expressed in a high-level language (such as relational calculus) while the sequence of operations is expressed in some variation of relational algebra. This mapping is difficult because relations can be fragmented and/or replicated. Furthermore the number of strategies for executing a single query in a distributed database is far higher than in a centralized system. Therefore query optimization is more involved. Heuristics should be used to avoid the prohibitive cost of the exhaustive search approach.

The cost function to minimize is generally the total cost incurred in executing the query [Sacco82], which is the sum of all execution times at the various sites participating in the query. It can also be the response time of the query [Epstein78], in which case one tries to maximize the parallel execution of operations.

In a distributed database, the total cost to be minimized is the sum of IO, CPU, and communication costs. The communication cost is the time needed for exchanging data between sites participating in the execution of the query. This cost is incurred in processing the messages and in transmitting the data over the communication network. An important factor is the network topology. In a wide area network such as the Arpanet, the communication cost dominates the IO cost by more than one order of magnitude. In a local area network such as the Ethernet, the communication cost becomes comparable to the IO cost. Therefore query optimization for wide area networks can be simplified to the minimization of the communication cost. However, query optimization for local area networks needs to consider the general total cost function.

Two basic approaches to optimize distributed joins, the most difficult operation, have been devised. One optimizes the ordering of joins directly, while the other approach replaces joins by combination of semijoins. The semijoin operation has the important property of reducing the size of the operand relation. When the main cost component considered for query optimization is communication, semijoin is particularly useful for improving the processing of distributed join operations by reducing the size of data exchanged between sites. However, using semijoin may result in an increase in the number of messages and local processing time. The first distributed database systems such as SDD-1 [Bernstein81], which were designed for wide area networks, make extensive use of semijoins. The recent systems such as R* [Williams82] assume faster networks and do not employ semijoins. They perform joins directly since using joins leads to lower local processing costs than using semijoins. However, semijoins are still beneficial in the context of fast networks when they induce a strong reduction of the join operand [Valduriez82, Valduriez84]. Some recent query optimization algorithms aim at selecting an optimal combination of joins and semijoins.

12.4.5 Transaction Management

Transaction management in a distributed database is also much more difficult than in a centralized database. A transaction is typically executed as several subtransactions, each at a different site. In general, local information about each subtransaction is insufficient to decide whether local updates can be committed. Therefore global information must be managed at the expense of communication overhead. The distributed environment has an impact on all aspects of transaction management: concurrency control, reliability, and commit processing.

The solutions to concurrency control in distributed databases are based on the two main classes of approaches: timestamping and locking. Timestamping requires the initial ordering of the transactions based on global system time and the global synchronization of the transactions at commit time. This global synchronization is based on the maintenance of a global precedence graph, which incurs the main communication overhead. Locking requires the maintenance of a global waiting graph to detect the presence of global deadlocks, which also incurs the main communication overhead. Most commercial DDBMSs implement the locking approach.

Reliability and availability can be improved by a distributed database that supports replication. When a site becomes nonoperational after a site failure or communication link failure, the local databases at the operational sites remain accessible and can be updated. In addition, these local databases may store copies that are also resident at the failed site. The procedure to recover a failed site is therefore a distributed operation that must reconstitute the copies consistent and up-to-date from the remote sites. The problem becomes much harder when more than one site having the same copies has failed and recovered at different times.

Committing a transaction executed as multiple subtransaction is a distributed operation that requires the synchronization of all participating sites. The most popular mechanism to perform this operation atomically is the two-phase commit protocol.

12.5 Architectures

Similar to centralized databases, distributed databases may be implemented in many different ways depending on their objectives and design choices. However, for our purposes, it is useful to consider a reference architecture and a functional architecture for distributed databases.

The reference architecture is shown in Fig. 12.4. It provides an ideal organization of a distributed database that implements all possible levels of transparency. This architecture is given in terms of schema levels (boxes) and schema mappings (lines). Depending on which levels of transparency are supported, the architecture of a distributed database may include only a subset of these schema levels. Furthermore since the mapping from one schema level to another can have a high processing cost, some schema levels are often combined for performance reasons. The reference architecture is a simple extension of the three-level ANSI/SPARC architecture for centralized database systems. Therefore data independence is easily achieved. All the schema information is stored in the data dictionary.

The schema levels that describe the distributed database independent of any site are global. The global conceptual schema defines all the relations contained in the distributed database and provides physical data independence from the distributed environment. Logical data independence is achieved by the global external schemas, each supporting a different application class. The placement schema indicates the way the relations are placed in the network. Thus it contains all information regarding data fragmentation, replication, and location. The placement schema provides fragmentation, replication, and location transparency.

The schema levels that describe a local database are local. The local conceptual schema and the local internal schema are those of the ANSI/SPARC architecture. The local external schema has a different role. It maps the fragments described by the placement schema into the external objects of the local database. This mapping is dependent of the local DBMS. Therefore local external schemas

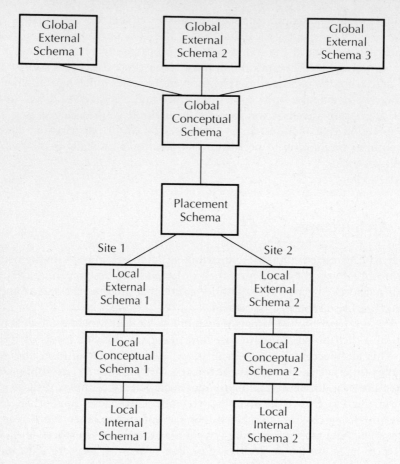

FIGURE 12.4 Reference architecture for distributed databases

provide DBMS transparency and are the basis for supporting heterogeneous environments.

A typical functional architecture for distributed databases is shown in Fig. 12.5. The functions can be grouped in two different components: the user component that handles interaction with the users and the data component that manages the data. A single user query involves the user component at the user site and the data components at one or more sites.

The user component consists of four modules. The user interface analyzes user queries and returns the results. Semantic data control performs view, authorization, and semantic integrity controls. Global query processing maps a query enriched with semantic data controls into a set of local queries, each for a different site. Transaction management coordinates the distributed execution of the

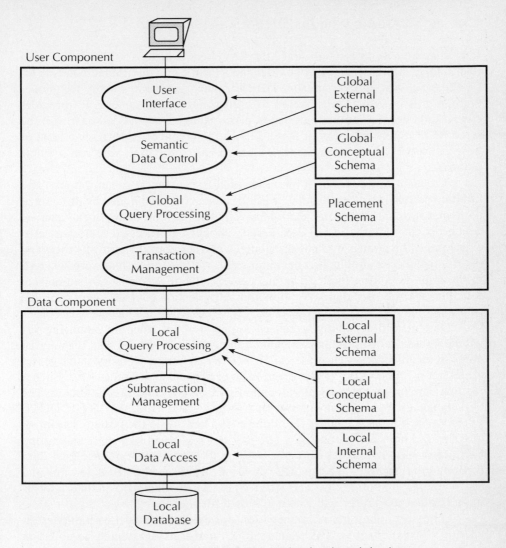

FIGURE 12.5 Functional architecture for distributed databases

query by communicating with the data components at which the local queries run.

The data component consists of three modules. Local query processing performs decomposition and optimization of a local query. Subtransaction management cooperates with the user components and other data components to synchronize the execution of the subtransactions of the same transaction. Local data access includes the remaining functions for database management (such as access methods and logging).

12.6 R*, a Homogeneous DDBMS

In this section, we briefly introduce the R* system, which exemplifies the way a relational database system can be extended to work in a distributed context. R* [Williams82] was an experimental DDBMS that incorporates many techniques of System R [Astrahan76] adapted to a distributed environment. R* provides cooperation between autonomous sites, each managing a local database with the same RDBMS (an extension of System R) and interconnected through a local or general network. This cooperation is transparent to the user, who sees a single database.

The main objectives of R* were location transparency, site autonomy, and minimal performance overhead. The performance overhead added by distributed data management functions should be minimal. In particular, local queries, which do not require remote data access, should be processed almost as efficiently as if the system was not distributed. Furthermore the cost of processing distributed queries should also be minimized. All these objectives were achieved in the implementation of R*. The main extensions of System R for supporting distribution concerned data definition and authorization control, query compilation and optimization, query execution, and transaction management.

Data definition and authorization control were extended for managing distributed objects and users. In particular, naming was modified so that the internal name of an object is system-wide unique and never changes. Internal name generation can be done at the object creation site independent of other sites. Such a naming convention provides both location transparency and site autonomy. The SQL language was supplemented with two new statements. An INTRODUCE DATABASE statement enables the addition of a new site in the system. The introduction of a new site is done on a site-pair basis whereby two sites, an existing one and the new one, mutually agree to share their data and exchange their data dictionary information. This avoids synchronizing all sites to add a new one and thus achieves site autonomy. The MIGRATE TABLE statement enables relocating a relation to another site where it is used the most.

Query compilation and optimization was extended to deal with queries involving distributed objects [Lohman85]. R* performs distributed compilation whereby a single site, called a *master site,* makes global decisions and other sites, called *apprentice sites,* subsequently make local decisions. The master site is the one where the query is issued; the apprentice sites are the remaining sites that store data involved in the query. The optimizer of the master site makes all intersite decisions, such as the selection of the sites and the method for transferring data, and generates a global access plan, which is then sent to all apprentice sites. The apprentice sites make the remaining local decisions (such as the ordering of joins at a site) and generate the local access plans. The objective function of R*'s optimizer is a general total cost function, including local processing (similar to System R function) and communications cost. The optimization algorithm is also based on the exhaustive search of the solution space. As in the centralized case, the optimizer must select the join ordering, the join algorithm (nested loop or merge join), and the access path for each relation. In addition, the optimizer must select the sites of join results and the method of transferring data between sites.

Query execution in R* may require the coordination of distributed processes when the query involves multiple sites. Similar to System R, R* uses the process model. A single R* process is initially allocated at the user site to interact with the user application program. This process is maintained until the application program terminates. Thus it may serve more than one transaction of the same user. Compared to the pure process model, which creates one process per transaction, R* reduces process creation overhead. When remote data access is required for that user, a dependent R* process is created at the remote site. Any dependent process may generate the creation of a dependent process at another site. Intersite communication is done between R* processes (under full control of R*).

Transaction management underwent significant changes to deal with distributed transactions. Concurrency control in R* is based on a locking algorithm, which supports both local and global deadlock detection. The atomicity of a transaction that runs on several sites is achieved through a two-step commit protocol.

The architecture of an R* site is illustrated in Fig. 12.6. R* is composed of

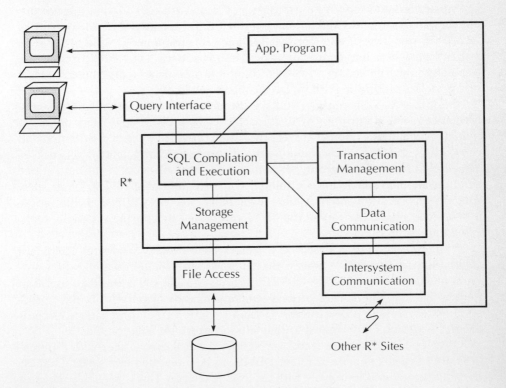

FIGURE 12.6 Architecture of R*

four components: RDS*, RSS*, TM*, and DC*. The RDS* (R* Relational Data System) extends the RDS of System R to support distributed database management. It performs SQL compilation, which includes parsing, data dictionary management, authorization control, and query optimization, and it controls the run-time execution of the compiled access plans. The RSS* (R* Relational Storage System) provides low-level support for file management and transaction management. The TM* (R* Transaction Manager) performs the various functions for controlling distributed transactions. It performs two-step commit coordination, deadlock detection, and recovery. The DC* (R* Data Communication component) provides message communication between an R* site and the other R* sites.

12.7 INGRES/STAR, a Heterogeneous DDBMS

INGRES/STAR, marketed by Relational Technology Inc., is the first commercial version of a DDBMS designed for heterogeneous environments. It provides transparent and simultaneous access from various DBMSs interconnected through a local or general network. INGRES/STAR achieves four primary objectives: location and replication transparency, performance, reliability, and open architecture framework.

Location and replication transparency allows the user to view a set of distributed and/or replicated relations as a single database. A global data dictionary records information about data location and replication and is used to translate a user transaction into transactions on local databases. Distributed transaction atomicity is guaranteed by a two-step commit protocol and a distributed concurrency control algorithm with global deadlock detection.

Similar to Distributed INGRES [Stonebraker77, Stonebraker86b], performance remains a primary goal. It is achieved by a distributed query optimization algorithm that exploits parallel processing, provided by data distribution and replication, and minimizes communication cost in case of a general network.

Reliability is enhanced by allowing data to be replicated. If the data at one site become unavailable after a failure, copies remain accessible at other sites. Therefore replication enhances data availability. Recovery after a media failure is fast since a database can be rapidly reconstructed by copying the useful replicated data from other sites.

Query execution is based on a master-slave process structure. There is a single "master INGRES" process that interacts with the user's application program at the user site. A slave INGRES process at each site stores data useful to the application. The master process sends commands directly to its slave processes. When a slave process needs to send a relation to another site, a receptor process is dynamically created at that site to receive the relation.

An open architecture framework allows heterogeneous sites with different operating systems and/or different DBMSs to be integrated in a single database that can be accessed uniformly with the SQL language. This is probably the most

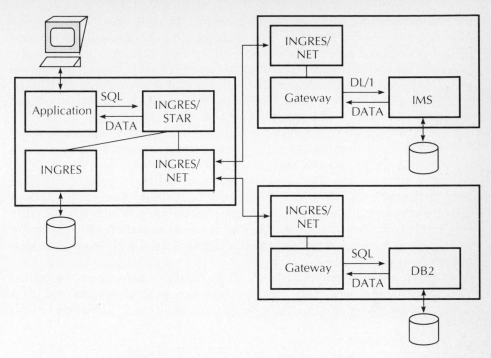

FIGURE 12.7 Architecture of INGRES/STAR

powerful aspect of INGRES/STAR. The architecture of INGRES/STAR has a number of properties. First, the local DBMSs need not be changed. Second, security and integrity are managed by the local DBMSs. Third, the distributed database is the union of the local databases. Fourth, several distributed databases can be defined on the same set of local databases. Multiple updates to a distributed database can be handled concurrently or differed.

The architecture of INGRES/STAR is shown in Fig. 12.7 for a heterogeneous environment. The pivot model is the relational data model, and the common interface between the various machines is the standard SQL. INGRES/STAR includes two main components: INGRES/NET and Gateways. INGRES/NET is a distributed communication system that allows different operating systems, such as UNIX and MVS, to exchange information. A Gateway is a specific interface that converts SQL into the language of a particular DBMS — for example, DL/1 for the IMS system.

12.8 DBC/1012, a Shared-Nothing Multiprocessor System

The DBC/1012 Database Computer, marketed by Teradata Corp. [Neches85, Teradata84], exemplifies the use of distributed database technology for improving performance and data reliability/availability. The DBC/1012 is an example of a shared-nothing multiprocessor database machine. The implementation consists of two types of processors built with off-the-shelf components, called interface processors (IFPs) and access module processors (AMPs), communicating via a fast interconnection network, called Ynet. Each component processor (IFP or AMP) runs a copy of the Teradata Operating System (TOS). An overview of the architecture of DBC/1012 is given in Fig. 12.8.

IFPs manage the communication with the host computers and perform the functions of query manager-optimizer. They control query execution by communicating with AMPs over the Ynet.

The Ynet is a network connecting IFPs and AMPs. To increase reliability and performance, the DBC/1012 employs two independent Ynet networks. Both Ynets interconnect all processors and operate concurrently. If one fails, the other continues to operate as a backup. The Ynet is not a classical bus. It has a binary tree topology, where each node of the tree contains active logic to perform sort-merge functions.

AMPs primarily perform the low-level database management functions. They also support important database functions such as logging and data reorganization.

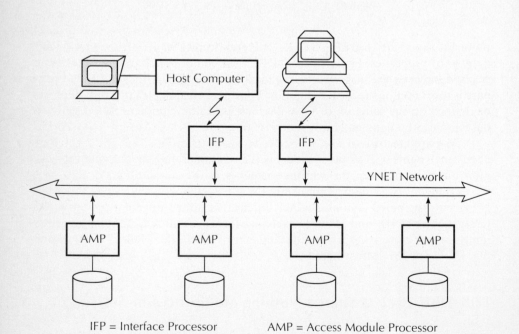

IFP = Interface Processor   AMP = Access Module Processor

FIGURE 12.8 Architecture of the DBC/1012

The DBC/1012 implements the relational model. Users access data managed by the DBC/1012 through host-resident software supplied by Teradata. The interface language of the DBC is DBC/SQL, an implementation of SQL. The data dictionary is replicated on each IFP. Query processing is implemented on IFPs by two modules: the DBC/SQL parser and the scheduler. The parser analyzes a DBC/SQL request and interprets it into an optimized sequence of lower-level operations corresponding to the request execution plan. The target language generated by the parser is probably close to relational algebra with synchronization commands. The DBC/SQL parser has access to the data dictionary to get information on relations, views, users, access rights, and so on. Execution plans may be cached in memory in case they are used again soon.

The scheduler controls and synchronizes the execution of the operations in the execution plan. Operations are sent over the Ynet to be executed by the appropriate AMPs. The control of execution of one request is thus centralized in one IFP. However, the data of each relation are horizontally fragmented over many AMPs by hashing on an attribute. Therefore the execution of a single operation like selection in one relation can be done in parallel by many AMPs, each performing a subset of the operation.

All the data controls are done partially by the AMPs. Because of horizontally fragmented placement of data, a centralized controller (the IFP's scheduler) is necessary. Each AMP runs a copy of a low-level database system on the Teradata Operating System (TOS). TOS provides services suitable for database management (such as buffer management). The high performance of the database functions is due to their implementation on many AMPs together with horizontal fragmentation. Furthermore a merge operation used frequently for producing sorted results is done by the Ynet when the data are transferred to the IFP (the initial sorts are done locally on each AMP; then the final merge is done). A hash-based join algorithm is supported. For increasing reliability, data replication is supported: the same tuples can be redundantly stored on two AMPs.

Concurrency control uses the two-phase locking algorithm. The locks can be acquired on variable size granules: database, relation, or tuple. Locks can be implicitly or explicitly acquired. Deadlocks are detected using a distributed graph checking algorithm because data are distributed. In case of deadlock, a victim transaction is chosen to be restarted.

In summary, the DBC/1012 is a powerful relational database machine, which employs intensive parallelism for increasing performance and reliability. The hardware architecture is modular and can accommodate up to 1024 processors. Such a large number of processors makes this approach somewhat different from traditional distributed databases implemented on many fewer sites. Performance measurements [Decker86] have shown that price and performance are superior to that of a conventional DBMS. The DBC/1012 achieves the same performance as a mainframe for approximately one-fourth of the cost. It shows linear capacity growth; the addition of components results in proportionally increasing performance.

12.9 Conclusion

Distributed database technology has become an important area of data processing. Distributed databases are inherently more complex than centralized databases. Therefore this chapter was limited to the introduction to the motivations,
functionalities, technical issues, and architectures of distributed databases. A
thorough treatment of the subject can be found in [Ozsu84].

The primary objective of a distributed database is to provide the user with
the illusion that the database is centralized. Such independence from the distributed environment requires various levels of transparency: fragmentation,
replication, and location transparency. Other important objectives include site
autonomy, expandability, high data availability, performance, and support of
heterogeneous environments. Distributed database systems today achieve only
some of these objectives.

The relational data model and associated languages have been the natural
support for distributed databases for two main reasons. First, distributed databases require various levels of data independence that can be built simply with
the relational model. For example, since a fragment of relation is itself a relation,
fragmentation is easier to handle. Second, relational languages are high level and
set oriented, which makes distributed query optimization possible. As a result,
the most successful distributed database systems today are relational.

We have illustrated the application of distributed database technology by
presenting three relational database systems: R*, a homogeneous distributed
database system; INGRES/STAR, the first marketed heterogeneous distributed
database system; and the DBC/1012, a multiprocessor database machine. The
DBC/1012 exemplifies the recent use of distributed database technology for improving performance and data reliability and availability through large-scale
parallelism.

12.9 References and Bibliography

[Adiba81] Adiba M., "Derived Relations: A Unified Mechanism for Views, Snapshots
and Distributed Data," Int. Conf. on VLDB, Cannes, France, September 1981.

[Astrahan76] Astrahan M. M. et al., "System R: A Relational Approach to Database
Management," ACM TODS, V1, N2, June 1976.

[Bernstein81] Bernstein P. A., Goodman N., Wong E., Reeve C. L., Rothnie J. B. Jr.,
"Query Processing in a System for Distributed Databases (SDD-1)," ACM TODS
V6, N4, December 1981.

[Ceri84] Ceri S., Pelagati G., *Distributed Databases: Principles and Systems,* McGraw-
Hill, 1984.

[Decker86] Decker J., "C31 Teradata Study," RADC – TR – 85 – 273, Rome Air Development Center, New York, March 1986.

[Epstein78] Epstein R., Stonebraker M., Wong E., "Query Processing in a Distributed
Data Base System," ACM SIGMOD Int. Conf., Austin, Texas, May 1987.

[Lohman85] Lohman G. et al., "Query Processing in R*," in *Query Processing in Database Systems,* Springer-Verlag, 1985.

[Neches85] Neches P. M., "The Anatomy of a Data Base Computer System," COMPCON Int. Conf., San Francisco, February 1985.

[Ozsu89] Ozsu T., Valduriez P., *Principles of Distributed Database Systems,* Prentice-Hall, 1989.

[Sacco82] Sacco M. S., Yao S. B., Query Optimization in Distributed Data Base Systems, in *Advances in Computers,* V21, Academic Press, 1982.

[Simon84] Simon E., Valduriez P., "Design and Implementation of an Extendable Integrity Subsystem," ACM SIGMOD Int. Conf., Boston, June 1984.

[Simon86] Simon E., Valduriez P., "Integrity Control in Distributed Database Systems," Hawaii Int. Conf. on System Sciences, Honolulu, January 1986.

[Stonebraker77] Stonebraker M., Neuhold E., "A Distributed Database Version of INGRES," 2d Berkeley Workshop on Distributed Data Management and Computer Networks, Lawrence Berkeley Laboratory, May 1977.

[Stonebraker79] Stonebraker M. "MUFFIN: A Distributed Database Machine," Conf. on Distributed Computing Systems, Huntsville, Alabama, October 1979.

[Stonebraker86a]. Stonebraker M., "The Case for Shared Nothing," Database Engineering, V9, N1, March 1986.

[Stonebraker86b] Stonebraker M. (Ed.), *The INGRES Papers,* Addison-Wesley, 1986.

[Teradata84] Teradata Corporation, "Database Computer System Concepts and Facilities," Document C02 – 0001 – 01, Teradata Corporation, Los Angeles, October 1984.

[Valduriez82] Valduriez P., "Semi-Join Algorithms for Distributed Database Machines," Int. Conf. on Distributed Databases, Berlin, September 1982.

[Valduriez84] Valduriez P., Gardarin D., "Join and Semi-Join Algorithms for a Multi-Processor Database Machine," ACM TODS, V9, N1, March 1984.

[Williams82] Williams R. et al., "R*: an Overview of the Architecture," 2d Int. Conf. on Databases, Jerusalem, June 1982.

AUTHOR INDEX

437

CONCEPT INDEX